DOCUMENTING
LATIN AMERICA
Gender, Race, and Empire

DOCUMENTING LATIN AMERICA

Gender, Race, and Empire

Volume 1

Edited by

ERIN E. O'CONNOR
Bridgewater State College

LEO J. GAROFALO
Connecticut College

Prentice Hall

Boston   Columbus   Indianapolis   New York   San Francisco   Upper Saddle River
Amsterdam   Cape Town   Dubai   London   Madrid   Milan   Munich   Paris   Montréal   Toronto
Delhi   Mexico City   São Paulo   Sydney   Hong Kong   Seoul   Singapore   Taipei   Tokyo

Editorial Director: Craig Campanella
Executive Editor: Jeff Lasser
Editorial Project Manager: Rob DeGeorge
Editorial Assistant: Amanda Dykestra
Senior Marketing Manager: Maureen E. Prado Roberts
Marketing Assistant: Marissa O'Brien
Senior Managing Editor: Ann Marie McCarthy
Project Manager: Debra Wechsler
Operations Specialist: Christina Amato
Cover Designer: Bruce Kenselaar

Manager, Visual Research: Beth Brenzel
Photo Researcher: Nancy Tobin
Manager, Cover Visual Research & Permissions: Karen Sanatar
Cover Photo: HIP/Scala/Art Resource, NY
Full-Service Project Management: Madhavi Prakashkumar
Composition: S4Carlisle Publishing Services

Text Font: Garamond 3

Credits and acknowledgments borrowed from other sources and reproduced, with permission, in this textbook appear on appropriate page within text.

Library of Congress Cataloging-in-Publication Data
Documenting Latin America / edited by Erin E. O'Connor, Leo J. Garofalo.
   p. cm.
  Includes bibliographical references.
  ISBN-13: 978-0-13-208508-3 (v. 1)
  ISBN-10: 0-13-208508-9 (v. 1)
  1. Latin America—History—To 1830—Sources. I. O'Connor, Erin. II. Garofalo, Leo.
  F1410.D63 2011
  980—dc22

                                                   2010017428

Prentice Hall
is an imprint of

www.pearsonhighered.com

ISBN 13: 978-0-13-208508-3
ISBN 10:   0-13-208508-9

Contents

Thematic Index

Citizenship and Liberation

- Afro-Latin Americans: Chapters 5, 7, 29, 30
- European *creoles* and colonists: Chapters 21, 25, 26, 27, 28, 29
- Indigenous people: Chapters 23, 25, 26, 27, 28
- Leaders: Chapters 25, 26, 27, 28, 29
- Women: Chapters 25, 27

Conquest and Empire Building

- Afro-Latin Americans: Chapters 3, 5, 6, 7
- Indigenous peoples: Chapters 1, 2, 4, 6
- Women: Chapters 2, 7, 16

Conversion and Religious Practice

- Afro-Latin Americans: Chapters 6, 7, 12, 14
- European *creoles* and colonists: Chapters 9, 10, 16
- Indigenous peoples: Chapters 6, 8, 18
- Missionaries and Church officials: Chapters 6, 8, 16, 18, 24
- Women: Chapters 9, 10, 14, 16, 18

Economy, Labor, and Markets

Chapters 3, 17, 21, 22

Gender and Colonial Life

- Afro-Latin American women: Chapters 11, 12, 14, 20, 29
- Female leaders: Chapters 2, 10, 14, 16, 19
- Female warriors: Chapters 16, 25, 27
- Honor and marriage: Chapters 9, 12, 13, 15, 20, 23
- Indigenous women: Chapters 2, 17, 18, 19, 20, 25
- Women's economic activity: Chapters 11, 12, 17, 18, 19

Institutions of Rule and Subjects' Actions

- Cabildo town councils: Chapters 21, 22, 25
- Indian communities: Chapters 1, 4, 8, 23, 25, 27, 28
- Indian leaders: Chapters 2, 4, 8, 19, 23, 25
- Petitioning the Crown: Chapters 7, 21, 23, 24, 25
- Courts and litigation: Chapters 4, 12, 13, 17, 18, 19
- Resisting taxation and abuse: Chapters 21, 24, 25, 26, 30

Slave-holding Society and Slavery

Chapters 6, 7, 11, 12, 14, 20, 29, 30

Warfare and State Power

Chapters 2, 5, 7, 25, 28

Preface

Although the numerous ways of analyzing the past are part of what make the study of history interesting, they also make it challenging to create texts and document collections that are both meaningful and accessible. Trying to cover everything can make it difficult for readers to keep track of a book's central purpose, whereas too narrow of a focus fails to provide a broader sense of the course of history. To avoid being either too general or too narrow, *Documenting Latin America* focuses on the central themes of race, gender, and politics and develops them deeply.

The majority of primary-source documents in these volumes have been translated and introduced by scholars who have used them in their research. A few of these sources are from works already published in Latin America, but most of them came from either state or religious archives, and none of the archival documents have ever appeared before in English. These archival sources are the heart of *Documenting Latin America*, uncovering many different ways that race, gender, and politics have intertwined over the course of centuries to make Latin America the complex and fascinating world region it is today. Some of the materials derived from scholarly research explore Latin American history, politics, and culture from the perspectives of less-powerful peoples, whereas others address the importance of race and gender from the viewpoints of political and intellectual elites. Additionally, the editors have identified and presented document excerpts that they

refer to as *classic* documents that have long been available in English. They have chosen these sources based on their importance to the themes of the volume, their accessibility, and their proven success in stimulating classroom discussion.

The chapters in *Documenting Latin America* offer a broad scope and solid coverage of Latin American history. In each volume, documents presented come from many different regions of Latin America, and they consider themes and challenges particular to different periods of time. However, the editors have not attempted to give equal coverage to all regions and problems in Latin American history. Instead, the editors selected documents either to complement others in the volumes or to offer unique perspectives on historical problems. Using these criteria allowed for the inclusion of documents from areas of Latin America that cannot be found in many, if any, other volumes available at the time of this publication. This unique blend of perspectives of history from both above and below, from understudied as well as often-studied regions, and from a combination of archival and classic sources allows readers to engage in a meaningful way with Latin America's past.

To aid readers in the task of interpreting original sources, these volumes are broken down into sections, each of which contains several chapters focused around a central theme or historical development. The introduction to each section defines any unusual or important terms, identifies key issues in a particular era, and relates terms and problems to the documentary history's broader focus on race, gender, and politics. Each chapter also begins with a short introduction that provides the reader with the context in which the document took place. The introduction is followed by a brief list of questions to consider when analyzing the document. The central feature of each chapter is a short document or set of documents. Most of the sources are excerpts from longer documents, but they provide readers with ample text and information to develop their own understanding of Latin American history. Using analytical guidelines from the questions, and context from the introduction, *in conjunction with* evidence from the document, helps readers to analyze the document and to form an argument about a given event or problem in Latin American history. Similarly, reviewing the introduction to the *section* in which a chapter appears can help to place an individual case within a wider historical moment or trend. The interplay between the details in the documents with the images and broader issues presented in various introductory materials gives the best picture of the dynamics of gender, race, and politics in Latin America.

Each chapter offers italicized terms, questions for further study, and an annotated list of suggested sources. Italicized terms, institutions, and names are defined in the text or footnotes; if they appear frequently in the volume, they are also listed in the glossary at the end of the book. In addition to facilitating reading comprehension, the glossary also provides information about how some of these terms had distinct meanings in different regions or time periods. The questions offered in each chapter not only help readers to make sense of the document at hand, but they also provide potential topics for papers, exams, and in-class discussions. In addition, the suggested sources section at the end of each chapter shows where one can find more secondary or scholarly sources, primary documents published in English, and visual and film materials. This section provides a brief description of each item listed, and it is particularly useful for readers who want to explore further the issues raised in the chapter for a research paper, class presentation, or other class activities. The editors and contributors of the volumes

have recommended a variety of materials, including in many cases Web sites, documentaries, feature films, and literature. Each chapter can therefore be used to obtain either a solid understanding of one case and a particular point or serve as a springboard for launching a larger project following a reader's personal interests.

Acknowledgments

This document history has been, from its inception, the epitome of collaborative work. We are tremendously grateful to everyone who made it possible for us to see our vision through to publication. First and foremost we thank our contributors, wonderful scholars all, who shared their expertise and time to create a unique and valuable resource. They responded with enthusiasm to our project and with good humor when we pressed them to meet deadlines or make changes. We also wish to thank the many fine individuals at Pearson who made it possible to complete this project. While working on the volumes, Erin benefitted greatly from a Bridgewater State College (BSC) Faculty and Librarian Research Grant (2009), which provided course release. Leo appreciates years of generous research support from Connecticut College's R.F. Johnson and Hodgkin Faculty Development Funds.

The following reviewers offered helpful insights and suggestions as the manuscript evolved: Jurgen Buchenau, University of North Carolina; Timothy Coates, The College of Charleston; Paula De Vos, San Diego State University; Kevin Gannon, Grand View College; Erick D. Langer, Georgetown University; Stephen E. Lewis, California State University, Chico; Nichole Sanders, Lynchburg College; Joan E. Supplee, Baylor University; Angela Vergara, California State University, Los Angeles; Rick Warner, Wabash College; and Gregory Weeks, University of North Carolina, Charlotte.

College students remain at the heart of this document history. Striving to make Latin American history come alive for our students led us to create these volumes. We especially thank the students—too many to name individually—who tested all or parts of these volumes in classes. Erin thanks her BSC classes on Colonial Latin America (2008, 2009), Modern Latin America (2008), and Gender, Race and Nation in Latin America (2009). Leo thanks his Connecticut College classes on Rebellion and Revolutions in Latin America (2008), Modern Latin America (2008 & 2010), Introduction to Latin American and Caribbean History (2008 & 2010), and Crossing the Ocean: Spain and the Americas (2009).

Finally, we must acknowledge our debts to our families and friends who sacrificed time with us so that we could work on this project, and who put up with hearing about it more than they probably wanted to. Friends, you know who you are. And to Eliana Iberico Garofalo, Natalia Garofalo-Iberico, Howard Brenner, Samuel Brenner, and (last but of course not least) Anya Brenner: You are, as you know, always and forever in our hearts.

Erin E. O'Connor, *Bridgewater State College*

Leo J. Garofalo, *Connecticut College*

Maps

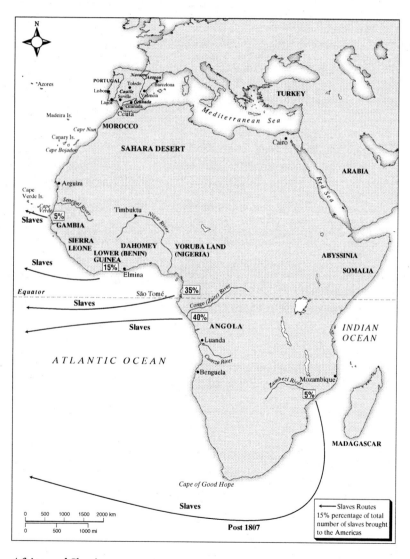

Africa and Iberia

Chichimecas

*Hernán Cortés
1519-1521*

Tenochtitlán

Arawaks

**SPANISH
CONQUESTS**

**AZTEC
EMPIRE** FORMER
MAYAN
EMPIRE

Caribs

Chibchas

Muras

•*Quito*

Shuar

Tapajós

*Francisco Pizarro
1532-1536*

Caiapós

Tobajaros

Pachacamac
•*Cuzco*

Tupi

Tupinambá

*Pedro
Álvares
Cabral
1500*

PACIFIC
OCEAN

Bororós

**INCA
EMPIRE**

Payaguás

**PORTUGUESE
CONQUESTS**

Guaraníes

Charrúas

Pampas

Mapuches

ATLANTIC
OCEAN

0   500   1000   1500   2000 km

0   500   1000 mi

Iberian Conquests and Indigenous Peoples

Source: Adapted from *Born in Blood and Fire: A Concise History of Latin America*, 2nd edition by John Charles Chasteen. Copyright © 2006, 2001 by W. W. Norton & Company, Inc. Used by permission of W. W. Norton & Company, Inc.

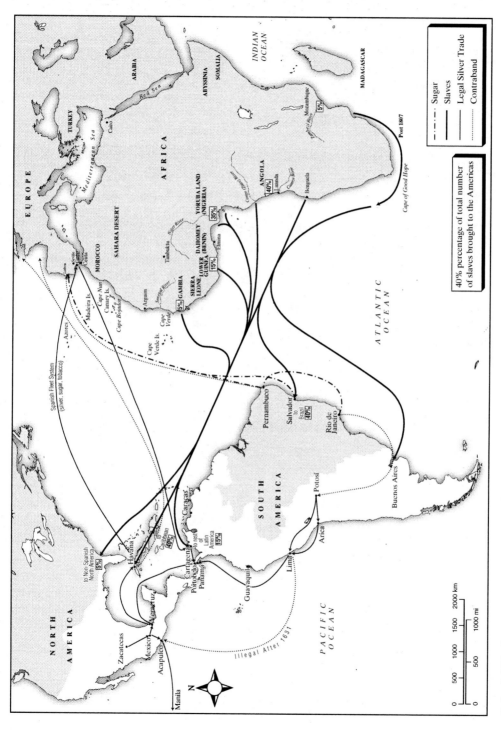

Colonial Trade

Source: Adapted from *Colonial Latin America*, 2nd ed. by Mark Burkholder and Lyman L. Johnson (1994): Volume 1 Map 3A. By Permission of Oxford University Press, Inc.

Colonial Latin American Viceroyalties

Source: Adapted from *Modern Latin America*, 6th ed. by Thomas E. Skidmore and Peter H. Smith (2005): Volume 1 Map 4A. By Permission of Oxford University Press, Inc.

Independence Struggles and New Nations, 1811–1839

Source: Adapted from *Born in Blood and Fire: A Concise History of Latin America*, 2nd edition by John Charles Chasteen. Copyright © 2006, 2001 by W. W. Norton & Company, Inc. Used by permission of W. W. Norton & Company, Inc.

Introduction

"Doing" Latin American History in the Era of Empires

There are many different ways of approaching and studying history. To make sense of the past, professional historians not only specialize in particular world regions, but they also focus on specific types of history—such as political, cultural, economic, military, or social history. Historians also differ in their specific focus within a field of study. For example, some political historians might examine history from the perspective of central government officials, whereas others explore how ordinary men and women experienced and influenced politics. Similarly, many economic historians trace how goods were produced and exchanged between different world regions, but there are numerous others who study labor relations. Social and cultural historians often look at history from the perspectives of less-powerful groups in past societies or at the interactions between powerful and less-powerful individuals and groups, and their work often overlaps at least as much with anthropology as it does with other fields of history.

Documenting Latin America focuses on the central themes of race, gender, and politics. These themes are especially important for understanding and evaluating the history of Latin America, where identities were forged out of the conflicts, negotiations, and intermixing of peoples from Europe, Africa, and the Americas. Over time, and due largely to unequal power relations that were central features of colonialism, racial ideologies developed to justify European domination over indigenous and African peoples. Gender, too, played a pivotal role in determining colonial experiences: Not only were women denied access to political (and often economic) power, but Spanish colonizers also used gender ideas to justify their dominance over non-European peoples. Race and gender inequalities continued to haunt Latin American nations in the aftermath of independence; in fact, one often finds greater constraints on indigenous peoples, Afro-Latin Americans, and women of all classes and races *after* independence than during the colonial period. By the mid-twentieth century, based largely on non-Europeans' and women's own initiatives, state officials began to offer some political rights and social reforms to previously marginalized groups. Today, women and non-Europeans still face serious challenges with sexism and racism, but they have also carved out important niches for themselves in Latin American national politics.

Documentary sources presenting gender, race, and politics, therefore, provide readers with the tools to develop a broad understanding of the course of Latin American social, cultural, and political history. However, the purpose of focusing on a particular theme or angle of history is not to ignore other avenues of exploration. Although historians specialize in particular fields of historical inquiry, every scholar must explain how her or his specialty relates to other fields in order to create a meaningful narrative about the past. The same occurs with chapters in this volume: The histories of race and gender explored in the ensuing chapters also draw on labor, biographical, economic, and military histories to offer a full and balanced picture of Latin America.

Powerful Terms, Terms of Power

Gender. Race. State. Empire. Nation. Subaltern. Elite. All of these are central concepts developed in *Documenting Latin America*. However, none of these terms are simple or static; instead, they are complex and change over time. Furthermore, scholars sometimes disagree on how to define terms and how they function in history. It is, therefore, important to discuss how the editors and contributors of these volumes define, approach, and engage with core terminology throughout the chapters of this collection of primary-source documents.

Politics, Power, and Belonging: States, Empires, and Nations

When one thinks of the state, it is typically state institutions, such as ministries of finance or Superior Courts, that come to mind, or perhaps the state officials who administer these organizations at the central, regional, and local levels. Members of a country, however, sense that the state is more than just institutions and administrators: Many U.S. citizens, for instance, take particular pride in living under a state that they believe advances the rule of law, equality before the law, justice, and freedom. All states are comprised of two components that operate simultaneously: The *state system* includes government infrastructure, the administrative hierarchy, and policies; equally important, the *state idea* indicates a set of ideologies aimed at legitimizing a given ruling regime.[1] To function, a state system requires a significant portion of the population to accept the state idea, and no state idea can succeed in the long term if a viable state system is lacking. This description of the state can help readers to understand two central features of Latin American politics since 1500 that are apparent in historical documents. First, the state is made up of a series of practices that institutionalize unequal power relations, whether between local versus central government officials, between state

authorities and the poor, or between men and women. Second, although the poor, non-Europeans, and women were excluded from government institutions throughout most of history, the existence of state ideas that required some degree of ideological acceptance gave less-powerful peoples opportunities to interact with, take advantage of, and even shape the state. Many of the chapters in these volumes reveal ways in which both the powerful and the humble played roles in the historical development of Latin American politics and states. Latin America also underwent a shift from *empires* in the pre-Hispanic and colonial periods to *nation states* following independence. As with the broader concept of the state, *empires* and *nation states* are terms that require explicit discussion and definition.

Latin America's colonial history encompasses a period when Portuguese and Spanish emperors ruled almost all of the Western hemisphere's territory, population, and wealth (mines, plantations, taxes, and tribute). Even before the arrival of Europeans, imperial rulers dominated the most densely populated regions of the Americas, with the *Aztecs* controlling the large urban centers of the Valley of Mexico and the Incas presiding over the peasant populations of the Andes. On the most basic level, the term *empire* describes the political organization of a collection of states and territories ruled by an emperor. Empires primarily fostered vertical links between subjects and the emperor, that is between the ruled and the ruler, rather than favoring horizontal ties that bring together regions, unite competing social sectors, or reconcile the elite groups dominant in each jurisdiction. In fact, a key strength of the Iberian empires was their ability to maintain a level of competition, antagonism, and even distrust among subjects. Competition and overlapping jurisdictions ensured that individual subjects and different sectors or institutions depended on the mediation and favor offered by the imperial administration and, ultimately, the king or queen.[2] The documents collected in Volume I of *Documenting Latin America* show how Spain and Portugal extended their imperial power

---

[1] Philip Abrams, "Notes on the Difficulty of Studying the State (1977)," *Journal of Historical Sociology* 1, no. 1 (March 1988): 58–89.

[2] Henry Kamen, *Empire: How Spain Became a World Power, 1492–1763* (New York: Harper Collins, 2003).

into the Americas and built institutions by combining European models with local indigenous customs and by drawing on the traditions established by Europeans, Africans, and missionary colonizers. Iberian imperial policies simultaneously favored and bolstered the dominance of wealthy European men while still providing the poor, non-Europeans, and women with some ways to protect and advance their interests. Particularly important to the state idea of the colonial period was the notion that the monarch was a compassionate, protective paternal figure who was concerned with the plight of all subjects living within the empire. If monarchies lost this legitimacy and subjects questioned their benevolence, European empires would lose much of their power and hold over Latin American populations.

Contradictory and coercive, the Iberian colonial states were also remarkably enduring. When they finally dissolved in the early nineteenth century, these massive European empires were replaced with (in most cases smaller) *nation states*. Benedict Anderson transformed the study of nations and nationalisms when he identified modern nations as *imagined communities*, a term still frequently used among scholars. Anderson asserted that all modern nations are communities because a critical mass of each nation's members not only identify themselves with a particular territory or government, but they also possess a strong sense of belonging together due to shared language, customs, and values. This community, however, is *imagined* rather than real because all national territories are too large for members to all know each other directly, and because class, race, and gender divisions preclude a natural sense of unity.[3] When scholars discuss *modern nation states* in any part of the world, they are referring to large (usually contiguous) territories governed by a central state, in which a significant or particularly powerful portion of the population is convinced that members of the territory form a single national community. The state system—clear leadership, laws, infrastructure, and monetary systems—is combined with the patriotic sentiment of the nation. In fact, nationalism often provided the state idea through which central government authorities sought to increase and legitimize their power.[4] Though nations are part of modern history—the earliest date back to the late eighteenth century—they often claim to be ancient and to build on a long-standing and natural cultural identity. Yet the question of national culture is problematic, because all nations are made up of people of many different customs, religions, and even languages. Therefore, one must always ask: Whose culture becomes the national culture? How and why are other cultures excluded, and with what implications for the marginalized groups? The answer to these questions is often the story of interethnic and gender domination. In Latin America, race and gender divisions threatened to undermine nationalistic claims by revealing the exclusive nature of the state and enduring hierarchical social practices, which did not allow women and non-whites full membership in the nation state. The struggle to overcome interethnic and gender divisions in Latin America has been a long process that remains incomplete.

Identity and Power: Gender and Race, Subaltern and Elite

Every individual in the modern world is shaped by his or her race, gender, and relative economic and social power. These forces are so prominent that they often seem natural or straightforward, but they are, in fact, quite complicated. Even some scholars, for example, associate gender only with women, and race exclusively with peoples of non-European heritage. However, men as well as women live gendered lives, and peoples of European descent are influenced by their racial identities—albeit not in the same ways as non-Europeans. Moreover, although one can find consistencies in race and gender ideologies over time, the meaning given to these identities is both culturally specific and historically dynamic. In short, race and gender are constructed identities rather than biological categories.

---

[3]Benedict Anderson, *Imagined Communities: Reflections on the Origins and Spread of Nationalism*, rev. ed. (New York: Verso, 1992 [1983]).

[4]For a good discussion of the state in the nation state, see E. J. Hobsbawm, *Nations and Nationalism since 1780: Programme, Myth, and Reality* (New York: Cambridge University Press, 1990).

Genetic studies make clear that biogenetically distinct races do not exist: Races are cultural inventions that respond to specific ideologies and historical circumstances (e.g., justifying conquest, coercing laborers, imposing religious conversion). In the most basic sense, race divides humans into distinct groups based on their supposed inherited physical and behavioral differences. Starting in the fifteenth century, Europeans and their American-born descendants developed a notion of race that reflected their attitudes and beliefs about the African, American, and Asian peoples they were encountering. Iberian colonizers typically believed that birth determined a person's physical and intellectual characteristics; they even thought temperament derived from race. However, to establish an individual's race, the state or those around an individual relied on cultural markers like religion, dress, occupation, place of birth, language, marriage partner, and the like.[5] Thus, race functioned more like what one might call ethnicity today. Consequently, by changing or manipulating the emphasis within a combination of these characteristics a person's race might change! By the time Latin American nations achieved independence, modern ideas about race as a biological category had begun to take shape, and peoples of European descent used these notions to identify some so-called races as inherently superior (European or "white") or inferior (indigenous, African, and Asian). Such assertions were problematic in Latin American nation states, however, as the supposedly inferior peoples were also purportedly fellow members in the imagined community of the nation; in some cases these groups even accounted for the majority of the nation's population. The historical figures and authorities presented in these volumes debated and deployed these markers of difference in a variety of ways, and one can trace how the significance of race developed over the course of time.

Gender functions similarly to race in the study of history, as it, too, is socially constructed and has been used to justify unequal power relations. Joan Scott developed a two-tiered definition of gender, which many historians continue to use as a foundation for gender analysis in the twenty-first century.[6] Scott asserts that on one level gender is "a constitutive element of social relationships based on perceived differences between the sexes." This suggests that gender informs both relations between the sexes and also how individuals and societies make sense of assumed sexual differences. Many times, the supposedly inherent differences between men and women were (and are) socially structured—in other words, girls were taught to behave one way, boys another. By the time individuals reach maturity, these behaviors seem natural and timeless rather than learned. Scott's definition of gender also has another important part to it. She argues that gender is "a primary field within which or by means of which power is articulated." Here, she means that gender ideologies (assumptions about male and female qualities, or parental versus childlike qualities) can be manipulated by individuals and groups either to express power or try to increase their power over others. Gender often functions this way in politics, and not only when women are involved. For example, when state officials use ideas about manliness to exclude certain adult men from political participation, they are using gender ideas to justify their actions. Gender, thus, encompasses ideas about how men and women are supposed to act, and it influences relationships, including political relationships, between individuals or groups.

Gender is, therefore, one of the essential building blocks of all societies and states, and understanding how gender functioned and changed over time is a crucial part of studying history. In Latin America, for example, colonial state officials identified indigenous peoples as *niños con barbas* (bearded children) who, although they might achieve physical maturity, were ostensibly perpetual children in other ways. This gendered racial notion justified the unequal power relations between colonizers and colonized peoples, although this state-sanctioned

---

[5]Magnus Mörner offers one of the fundamental discussions of race in the Americas. His work still represents an important point of departure for any study of ethnicity, class, and social identity construction in the Americas. Magnus Mörner, *Race Mixture in the History of Latin America* (Boston: Little, Brown, 1967).

[6]Joan Wallach Scott, "Gender: A Useful Category for Historical Analysis," in *Gender and the Politics of History* (New York: Columbia University Press, 1988), 28–50.

interethnic paternalism did not always work in practice as it was meant to in theory, as many chapters in Volume I show. Women continued to be excluded from politics after independence, but their marginalization held new meaning in the republican era. Denying women political rights helped to define the political nation as a male domain, and excluding women served to obfuscate class and race divisions between men in a given nation. Gender and race, therefore, upheld the politics of exclusion in Latin America just as they did in the United States and other parts of the world. And, just as in other societies, one can still find ways that these notions limit the rights and power of women and non-whites in contemporary Latin America.

Wealthy European men—the *elite*—benefited the most from gender and race ideologies, which helped them to rule over, exploit, and marginalize other groups. In many ways, *elite* is a clear-cut term that refers to those individuals or groups who dominate politics, the economy, and society. However, different kinds of elites existed, and it is important that one avoid the trap of thinking that elites were somehow uniform or homogenous. For example, members of the intellectual elite, whose ideas greatly influenced society and politics, were not necessarily the wealthiest men or those in political power. Different elite groups also competed with each other over economic and political power, and they often held divergent ideas about how society, the economy, and politics should be structured. Another potential division appeared between political and religious elites: In certain periods and locations, Church and state officials allied closely, whereas in other circumstances these two elite groups were at odds with each other. Even within the Church, deep divisions surfaced between the regular clergy (who belonged to religious orders) and lay clergy (who ministered to the members of a diocese); in many instances, these different Church officials fought bitterly over the jurisdiction of particular populations. Sometimes elite factions even made alliances (usually brief) with less-powerful peoples in order to beat a competing elite faction.

At the other end of identity and power politics, one finds *subaltern* peoples. Although a sophisticated field of subaltern studies exists, in these volumes the term *subaltern* refers simply to those groups that were outside of the dominant power structure.[7] Most obviously, subalterns included indigenous peoples, Afro-Latin Americans, and peoples of mixed racial descent. However, it also included poor people of European descent and women across class and race lines. It is important to note that some individuals could be considered subaltern in some circumstances but part of the dominant power structure in others. Context mattered. An elite woman of European descent was part of the dominant race and class when considering her social status and power over non-Europeans, yet, throughout most of Latin American history, such a woman was excluded from political power and had limited rights to make decisions about the property she owned. Another example would be a male *cacique* (local indigenous leader) during the colonial period: in his case, he would be part of the political structure, at least at the local level, from which the elite woman was excluded. He also enjoyed privileges, exercised power over indigenous commoners, and could participate in commerce. But he was still subaltern, because he was excluded from the higher ranks of political power, and there were ways that his status was lower than Spanish men of lesser wealth. In cases like these, whether an individual would be considered subaltern or part of the dominant group depended on the nature of one's historical inquiry. The topic being explored, the forms of sociopolitical power under scrutiny, and the broad questions one is trying to answer, for example, determine which groups should be included in the category of subaltern or elite with any given chapters of this documentary history. Furthermore, subaltern groups or individuals did not necessarily share the same problems or goals, and

---

[7]South Asian studies groups coined this phrase for history from below. See Gayatri Chakravorty Spivak, "Can the Subaltern Speak?" in *Marxism and the Interpretation of Culture,* ed. Cary Nelson and Lawrence Grossberg (Urbana: University of Illinois Press, 1988), 271–313. A variety of scholars apply subaltern studies to Latin America; see Ileana Rodríguez, ed., *The Latin American Subaltern Reader* (Durham, NC: Duke University Press, 2001). Historians debate how to take Latin America's subalterns into account; a good discussion of this is Eric Van Young, "The New Cultural History Comes to Old Mexico," *Hispanic American Historical Review* 79, no. 2 (1999): 211–247.

they sometimes clashed and competed with each other. In the short term, an individual might improve his or her life through such contests, but in the long term competition among subalterns usually served to keep wealthy European men in power.

All of these terms refer to fluid categories and processes in history. They are complex rather than simple and historically adaptable rather than unchanging. All of the terms also focus on individuals' and groups' relative positions with regard to *power*. Instead of thinking of power as absolute or as something that one *holds*, it is more useful—and more historically accurate—to think of power as something that one *exercises*. This distinction is important because it indicates that even though subalterns were (and are) excluded from most formal positions of power, they might still exercise power in significant ways, particularly in an informal or local-level capacity. Power exists in a continuum, with different individuals and groups enjoying different kinds and levels of authority. Chapters in *Documenting Latin America* reveal myriad ways that wealthy European men wielded tremendous power and manipulated gender and race ideas to maintain inequalities. At the same time, many chapters allow readers to explore the numerous and sometimes surprising ways that women and peoples of indigenous or African descent manipulated ideologies that were meant to subordinate them in order to advance their personal or collective interests. These tensions, contradictions, and negotiations over gender, race, and politics were driving forces that moved Latin American history forward; they continue to shape the region today.

Getting the Most Out of Primary-Source Documents

Working with primary sources makes history both exciting and daunting. In the chapters to follow, readers can dive into the archives of Latin America's past alongside the historians whose work it is to make sense of what are sometimes confusing or conflicting accounts. The primary sources in *Documenting Latin America* offer unparalleled perspectives on the views and lives of men and women who witnessed or created key moments in Latin American history; nothing gives readers a truer and more in-depth understanding of the past. Making history is really a process of giving meaning to the written and visual remains of the past. This book requires readers to evaluate the past and draw their own conclusions, maybe even to question or challenge the editors' or contributing scholars' views of the past.

Primary sources include almost any materials that capture the memories and thoughts of people who lived through particular events or periods in the past. In these two volumes on Latin American history, readers encounter transcriptions of ships' logs, legal codes, scholarly essays, lists of possessions from wills, testimonial life accounts, portraits, and interrogations from court cases. Each source holds within it useful insights and potential pitfalls; the trick is to extract those insights while avoiding many of the pitfalls. Historians typically employ an array of strategies to recognize what the content of these sources means. A basic strategy is to ask oneself: Who created this source, under what circumstances, for what audience, and with what objective in mind? It is also imperative to consider whose voice, or what combination of voices, one "hears" while reading a document or viewing an image. A written source, or even a visual one, may contain input from one or more creators, speaking for themselves or on behalf of others. It is critical to determine this voice and authorship as accurately as possible. These volumes also present readers with information about people marginalized within Latin American society, many of whom were illiterate. Their thoughts and actions may be hidden within the words, impressions, or descriptions expressed by others, providing readers only indirect access to the voices of the marginalized. This raises questions about an author's viewpoint that may be distorting any given document. Such distortions within a source do not mean that one must discount everything one reads; instead, the challenge is to figure out how an author's perspective affects what a reader gleans from a particular document. A good technique for doing this is to question: What other perspectives might there be on an issue or event being presented in this document? It is critical to read documents or images "against the grain" or "between the lines" to discern and analyze the author's perspective, or to learn something that the author might have been hiding or ignoring. Implementing these methods, as well as others learned in class or on one's own while working with the materials, enables readers to develop their own ways of engaging with Latin American history and sources.

Questions to Ask When Interrogating a Primary Source

1. What type of source is this?
2. What is known about who created it, when, and where?
3. Whom did the author consider the audience for this piece?
4. What views or perspectives were presented? Were other views silenced or challenged?
5. Is there evidence of distortion in the document? How might this be explained?
6. What can the source tell a reader about an event or period in history? What are the limits to what it can reveal?
7. How does this source fit into a bigger historical picture or period? Does it challenge a bigger picture or narrative in any way?

Volume 1: Empires and Their Subjects

Volume I of *Documenting Latin America* allows readers to explore how Latin American empires and societies appeared and changed from the European invasions of the fifteenth and sixteenth centuries to the independence period of the early nineteenth century. Conquests in the Americas, the enslavement of Africans, and colonization coincided with the period during which Western Europe emerged from the Middle Ages, experienced the Renaissance, and created the mechanisms and institutions of early modern states and empires.[8] In this period, European

monarchies created mechanisms like councils of state and *viceroys* to govern overseas territories; they established trade monopolies and fleets to engage in global trade; and they extended the reach of royal courts and the *inquisition* to regulate subjects' activities and thoughts. In short, they made modern states and empires possible.

Unprecedented European expansion and the globalization of trade and human movement created new ways of interacting and organizing life, often with a unique set of peoples. Monarchs, nobles, bureaucrats, priests, and commoners of Europe, Africa, and the Americas came together—often through violence, always through negotiation of some sort, and occasionally though cooperation—to form the impressive and wealthy Spanish and Portuguese Empires and their diverse and numerous subjects in the Americas. These new American empires grew out of European practices of conquest and governance combined with Amerindian traditions of empire building; both Europeans and Amerindians contributed notions of subjects' rights and obligations. For example, indigenous ideas of reciprocity between the rulers and the ruled melded with European beliefs of a monarch's paternalistic protection and lenience. In the Americas, Spain and Portugal created systems of royal courts that all residents could access and through which some received special protection and rights (e.g., communal lands).

Empires had existed in the Americas prior to the arrival of Europeans. In fact, the relatively young *Inca* and *Aztec* Empires had been extending imperial control over new regions, independent ethnic groups, and important resources right up to the invasion. The *Mayan* polities had declined some time earlier. But in all three cases, and in a few other similar regions, the existence of dense populations of sedentary agriculturalists ruled indirectly by ethnically dissimilar leaders paved the way for the Spanish to impose their domination and meld their practices and institutions with the earlier Amerindian ways. Amerindian history also mattered tremendously for Portugal's colony in Brazil. Along the coast, the Portuguese found that the semisedentary Tupi-Namba organized into tribal societies could be engaged in trade and later forced to work on early sugar mills. In every part of the Americas

---

[8] "Early modern" refers to the period between the Middle Ages and the French Revolution (1789).

that the Spanish and the Portuguese turned to, the diversity of Amerindian society shaped the fundamental nature of the colonies established there. Not only were colonies made possible and profitable by the indigenous inhabitants, the *Aztec* and *Inca* Empires could not have been defeated without the internal diversity and politics of indigenous societies that produced people willing to ally with outsiders to defeat overlords.

Christopher Columbus, and the conquering soldiers in Mexico, offer examples of the conquistador's mindset; they also reveal the central role that indigenous allies played in early European victories, setting in motion the arrival of more Europeans and guaranteeing that ethnic groups would not all experience colonialism in the same way. In addition, not all Europeans were white, and not all conquests were successful. Afro-Iberians working as sailors, soldiers, and traders help explain the early importance of the African Diaspora to Iberian colonialism. The black anti-conquistador represented another result of the Diaspora, and Church and state authorities found they needed to negotiate and compromise with those they could not fully conquer, contain, or convert. Fluidity and flexibility characterized conquest society in the sixteenth century.

Mexico and the Andes offered populous and well-organized societies and rich mineral deposits. Consequently, these regions became the core of Spain's American empire at least until the eighteenth-century rise in economic and demographic importance of plantation colonies in other parts of South America and the Caribbean. In Brazil, no silver or gold deposits motivated efforts to control the workforce to guarantee mining production, at least not until gold and diamonds were found in the late colonial period; however, despite high levels of indigenous mortality and escape, the colonists used indigenous labor in northwestern Brazil's cane fields and mills until they accumulated the resources to import Africans as enslaved laborers.

The *colonial economies* survived the disruptions of warfare and the ongoing toll that disease took on indigenous populations, and they became centered on mining and plantations. These colonial economies eventually created extensive networks of trade and commercial activity, reaching all levels of society and

almost every village and town. The creation of the capital to invest in commerce and the demand for laborers also promoted a spectacular expansion of the slave trade in African peoples, and this trade grew in size and importance with each century. The African Diaspora and the creation of new multiethnic societies and networks of administration and evangelization endowed the Americas with new kinds of people, new kinds of beliefs and religious practices, and many institutions and strategies of rule that bound the system together and gave mature Iberian colonialism the flexibility to last for centuries until Spain and Portugal lost their hold over the American territories in the nineteenth century.

Conquest and incorporation into imperial systems, thus, took place through interplay between European and indigenous actors. African peoples played a role, too, but they often faced the greatest challenges in shaping American societies. This volume offers various documents and voices that record the historical agency that people of all walks of life and ethnic backgrounds exercised in the world's first era of globalization. Often these groups and individuals became visible in the historical record only when imperial states took real form. This happened when people faced judges in court, listened to and discussed the meaning of sermons, denounced their neighbors to Church investigators, recorded marriage in a parish book, dictated a will, or engaged in any of the other hundreds of ways of taking official or legal action.

Within colonial societies in the Americas, no one group was homogeneous, including the Europeans. For example, regional loyalties, social status, ethnic allegiance, institutional infighting, competition, and greed divided people in the colonies. The multiple and competing interests helped ensure that the functioning of colonial governance and the lives of subjects within the empire were not solely top-down processes. *Documenting Latin America* collects the kinds of court cases, petitions to authorities, and claims to rights that make the reality of subjects' negotiations abundantly clear.

Economic and cultural activities also expose the fact that indigenous and African peoples, alongside elite and plebeian Europeans, generated the wealth and values that built and sustained European power during this era. Notaries' records, litigation over property, and regulations of local marketplaces show how real people experienced colonialism, survived, and adapted. They also wrote poems and created visual art addressing these themes, and those sources are included in this volume as well. The interconnected colonial economy and the multiethnic cities it spawned were built from both above and below with participation at many levels. In fact, market participation and the growth of cities and towns marched forward in tandem with the creation of new kinds of societies, religious beliefs, and people of mixed ethnic heritage. Diversity and contradiction became hallmarks of mature colonial society during the seventeenth and eighteenth centuries.

How Iberians governed amidst diversity and contradictions remains one of the key questions motivating scholarly investigation and debate. *Colonial hegemony* remains one of the best ways to understand how Iberian domination secured a measure of consent by those at the bottom and the middle. Spanish and Portuguese colonialism allowed opportunities for people of many different backgrounds to find ways of belonging to these empires, although never as equals to Europeans. In particular, the colonized embraced Catholicism and the advantages Catholic institutions offered; many cases included in the volume demonstrate how common Catholic participation became. The construction of these colonial cultural identities and religious allegiances also made rebellion rare. Much more common were various forms of adaptive resistance, which allowed individuals and colonized groups to accept some change and make concessions in order to resist total transformation or specific, hated colonial impositions. People either changed in order to remain who they were, or they created new blended beliefs or rituals that combined elements from more than one tradition.

These arrangements between rulers and the ruled also broke down when the levels of domination rose, the processes of mediating conflict faltered, or when significant crises weakened the state at the center. Each of these occurred in the eighteenth and early nineteenth centuries. Increasing in intensity and frequency from the late 1700s forward, these disruptions to the "way things worked" under Iberian colonialism led to changing forms of resistance, rebellion, and consciousness. Eventually, at different

points in time groups at all levels of colonial Spanish American society questioned colonial rule, and many fought to end it. They often clashed with each over the alternatives to European domination. Smashing Iberia's American empires and colonial hegemony did not easily lead to national unity.

Spanish and Portuguese imperial archives are replete with remains of the elaborate Iberian bureaucracy, and colonized people's active and sustained engagement with it. Similarly, the national, regional, and local archives are crowded with a multitude of documents and wonderful, heartbreaking, and simply confusing stories about Latin America's colonial past. Historians, other scholars, and activists all mine these repositories for a glimpse of the past. In *Documenting Latin America*, readers dive into these collections to learn more about imperial aspirations and the limits of colonial domination. This process of domination and co-option not only helped establish the norms of colonial rule into the seventeenth century and beyond, but it also gave indigenous people a place in the Church, Brazilian slaves a forum for leadership, and non-Europeans—often women—additional tools to promote and protect their interests. Indians and women were well aware of their subordinated status in colonial society, but life in cities and towns afforded them opportunities to secure niches in an expanding economic system and even to parlay their knowledge of selling or healing to earn a living. A few women—both indigenous and Iberian—flaunted the norms barring women from public discourse, soldiering, or exercising political office. Colonial society became rich in its complexity and in the ways people found identity as subjects within empires ruled from a remote imperial center.

The age of reform following the eighteenth-century ascension of the Bourbon Dynasty to the Spanish and Portuguese thrones ushered in an era of unprecedented change in imperial rule. This period also coincided with the emergence of European *creole* and nativist identities and rising peasant and indigenous descent and revolt. *Creole* elites often feared both the upward mobility of social sectors normally relegated to inferior positions and work within society and a loss of privileges due to reforms from European rulers. Clergy worried of the fraying bonds of rural populations' loyalties. Certainly

resistance to higher taxes and outright rural insurrections throughout the eighteenth century proved that
many of these concerns were well founded. In fact,
when full-scale revolts broke out and hardened into
independence movements from the 1780s into the
1820s, *creole* patriots, parish priests, and indigenous
officials—all supposedly beholden to the colonial
state—figured prominently among those fighting
hardest to tear down the imperial system. In both
Spanish America and Brazil, formal independence
did not guarantee equality and full citizenship for all:
Indians, women, and Afro-Latin Americans, in particular, still faced systematic exclusion. Latin America's
diverse, multiethnic societies, with both mechanisms
of inclusion and exclusion and negotiation and coercion, would continue and would continue to change
well into the modern era of the nineteenth and
twentieth centuries.

"Doing" Latin American History in the Era of Empires

There are many different ways of approaching and studying history. To make sense of the past, professional historians not only specialize in particular world regions, but they also focus on specific types of history—such as political, cultural, economic, military, or social history. Historians also differ in their specific focus within a field of study. For example, some political historians might examine history from the perspective of central government officials, whereas others explore how ordinary men and women experienced and influenced politics. Similarly, many economic historians trace how goods were produced and exchanged between different world regions, but there are numerous others who study labor relations. Social and cultural historians often look at history from the perspectives of less-powerful groups in past societies, or the interactions between powerful and less-powerful individuals and groups, and their work often overlaps at least as much with anthropology as it does with other fields of history.

Documenting Latin America focuses on the central themes of race, gender, and politics. These themes are especially important for understanding and evaluating the history of Latin America, where identities were forged out of the conflicts, negotiations, and intermixing of peoples from Europe, Africa, and the Americas. Over time, and due largely to unequal power relations that were central features of colonialism, racial ideologies developed to justify European domination over indigenous and African peoples. Gender, too, played a pivotal role in determining colonial experiences: Not only were women denied access to political (and often economic) power, but Spanish colonizers also used gender ideas to justify their dominance over non-European peoples. Race and gender inequalities continued to haunt Latin American nations in the aftermath of independence; in fact, one often finds greater constraints on indigenous peoples, Afro-Latin Americans, and women of all classes and races *after* independence than during the colonial period. By the mid-twentieth century, based largely on non-Europeans' and women's own initiatives, state officials began to offer some political rights and social reforms to previously marginalized groups. Today, women and non-Europeans still face serious challenges with sexism and racism, but they have also carved out important niches for themselves in Latin American national politics.

Documentary sources presenting gender, race, and politics, therefore, provide readers with the tools to develop a broad understanding of the course of Latin American social, cultural, and political history. However, the purpose of focusing on a particular theme or angle of history is not to ignore other avenues of exploration. Although historians specialize in particular fields of historical inquiry, every scholar must explain how her or his specialty relates to other fields in order to create a meaningful narrative about the past. The same occurs with chapters in this volume: The histories of race and gender explored in the ensuing chapters also draw on labor, biographical, economic, and military histories to offer a full and balanced picture of Latin America.

Powerful Terms, Terms of Power

Gender. Race. State. Empire. Nation. Subaltern. Elite. All of these are central concepts developed in *Documenting Latin America*. However, none of these terms are simple or static; instead, they are complex and change over time. Furthermore, scholars sometimes disagree on how to define terms and how they function in history. It is, therefore, important to discuss how the editors and contributors of these volumes define, approach, and engage with core terminology throughout the chapters of this collection of primary-source documents.

Politics, Power, and Belonging: States, Empires, and Nations

When one thinks of the state, it is typically state institutions, such as ministries of finance or Superior Courts that come to mind, or perhaps the state officials who administer these organizations at the central, regional, and local levels. Members of a country, however, sense that the state is more than just institutions and administrators: Many U.S. citizens, for instance, take particular pride in living under a state that they believe advances the rule of law, equality before the law, justice, and freedom. All states are comprised of two components that operate simultaneously: The *state system* includes government infrastructure, the administrative hierarchy, and policies; equally important, the *state idea* indicates a set of ideologies aimed at legitimizing a given ruling regime.[1] To function, a state system requires a significant portion of the population to accept the state idea, and no state idea can succeed long-term if a viable state system is lacking. This description of the state can help readers to understand two central features of Latin American politics since 1500 that are apparent in historical documents. First, the state is made up of a series of practices that institutionalize unequal power relations, whether between local versus central government officials, between state versus central government officials, between state

authorities and the poor, or between men and women. Second, although the poor, non-Europeans, and women were excluded from government institutions throughout most of history, the existence of state ideas that required some degree of ideological acceptance gave less-powerful peoples opportunities to interact with, take advantage of, and even shape the state. Many of the chapters in these volumes reveal ways in which both the powerful and the humble played roles in the historical development of Latin American politics and states. Latin America also underwent a shift from *empires* in the pre-Hispanic and colonial periods to *nation states* following independence. As with the broader concept of the state, *empires* and *nation states* are terms that require explicit discussion and definition.

Latin America's colonial history encompasses a period when Portuguese and Spanish emperors ruled almost all of the Western hemisphere's territory, population, and wealth (mines, plantations, taxes, and tribute). Even before the arrival of Europeans, imperial rulers dominated the most densely populated regions of the Americas, with the *Aztecs* controlling the large urban centers of the Valley of Mexico and the Incas presiding over the peasant populations of the Andes. On the most basic level, the term *empire* describes the political organization of a collection of states and territories ruled by an emperor. Empires primarily fostered vertical links between subjects and the emperor, that is between the ruled and the ruler, rather than favoring horizontal ties that bring together regions, unite competing social sectors, or reconcile the elite groups dominant in each jurisdiction. In fact, a key strength of the Iberian empires was their ability to maintain a level of competition, antagonism, and even distrust among subjects. Competition and overlapping jurisdictions ensured that individual subjects and different sectors or institutions depended on the mediation and favor offered by the imperial administration and, ultimately, the king or queen.[2] The documents collected in Volume I of *Documenting Latin America* show how Spain and Portugal extended their imperial power

---

[1] We have taken this definition from Philip Abrams, "Notes on the Difficulty of Studying the State (1977)," *Journal of Historical Sociology* 1, no. 1 (March 1988): 58–89.

[2] Henry Kamen, *Empire: How Spain Became a World Power, 1492–1763* (New York: Harper Collins, 2003).

into the Americas and built institutions by combining European models with local indigenous customs and by drawing on the traditions established by Europeans, Africans, and missionary colonizers. Iberian imperial policies simultaneously favored and bolstered the dominance of wealthy European men while still providing the poor, non-Europeans, and women with some ways to protect and advance their interests. Particularly important to the state idea of the colonial period was the notion that the monarch was a compassionate, protective paternal figure who was concerned with the plight of all subjects living within the empire. If monarchies lost this legitimacy and subjects questioned their benevolence, European empires would lose much of their power and hold over Latin American populations.

Contradictory and coercive, the Iberian colonial states were also remarkably enduring. When they finally dissolved in the early nineteenth century, these massive European empires were replaced with (in most cases smaller) *nation states*. Benedict Anderson transformed the study of nations and nationalisms when he identified modern nations as *imagined communities*, a term still frequently used among scholars. Anderson asserted that all modern nations are communities because a critical mass of each nation's members not only identify themselves with a particular territory or government, but they also possess a strong sense of belonging together due to shared language, customs, and values. This community, however, is *imagined* rather than real because all national territories are too large for members to all know each other directly, and because class, race, and gender divisions preclude a natural sense of unity.[3] When scholars discuss *modern nation states* in any part of the world, they are referring to large (usually contiguous) territories governed by a central state, in which a significant or particularly powerful portion of the population is convinced that members of the territory form a single national community. The state system—clear leadership, laws, infrastructure, and monetary systems—is combined with the patriotic sentiment of the nation. In fact, nationalism often provided the state idea through which central government authorities sought to increase and legitimize their power.[4] Though nations are part of modern history—the earliest date back to the late eighteenth century—they often claim to be ancient and to build on a long-standing and natural cultural identity. Yet the question of national culture is problematic, because all nations are made up of people of many different customs, religions, and even languages. Therefore, one must always ask: Whose culture becomes the national culture? How and why are other cultures excluded, and with what implications for the marginalized groups? The answer to these questions is often the story of interethnic and gender domination. In Latin America, race and gender divisions threatened to undermine nationalistic claims by revealing the exclusive nature of the state and enduring hierarchical social practices, which did not allow women and non-whites full membership in the nation state. The struggle to overcome interethnic and gender divisions in Latin America has been a long process that remains incomplete.

Identity and Power: Gender and Race, Subaltern and Elite

Every individual in the modern world is shaped by his or her race, gender, and relative economic and social power. These forces are so prominent that they often seem natural or straightforward, but they are, in fact, quite complicated. Even some scholars, for example, associate gender only with women, and race exclusively with peoples of non-European heritage. However, men as well as women live gendered lives, and peoples of European descent are influenced by their racial identities—albeit not in the same ways as non-Europeans. Moreover, although one can find consistencies in race and gender ideologies over time, the meaning given to these identities is both culturally specific and historically dynamic. In short, race and gender are constructed identities rather than biological categories.

---

[3] Benedict Anderson, *Imagined Communities: Reflections on the Origins and Spread of Nationalism*, rev. ed. (New York: Verso, 1992 [1983]).

[4] For a good discussion of the state in the nation state, see E. J. Hobsbawm, *Nations and Nationalism since 1780: Programme, Myth, and Reality* (New York: Cambridge University Press, 1990).

Genetic studies make clear that biogenetically distinct races do not exist: Races are cultural inventions that respond to specific ideologies and historical circumstances (e.g., justifying conquest, coercing laborers, imposing religious conversion). In the most basic sense, race divides humans into distinct groups based on their supposed inherited physical and behavioral differences. Starting in the fifteenth century, Europeans and their American-born descendants developed a notion of race that reflected their attitudes and beliefs about the African, American, and Asian peoples they were encountering. Iberian colonizers typically believed that birth determined a person's physical and intellectual characteristics; they even thought temperament derived from race. However, to establish an individual's race, the state or those around an individual relied on cultural markers like religion, dress, occupation, place of birth, language, marriage partner, and the like.[5] Thus, race functioned more like what one might call ethnicity today. Consequently, by changing or manipulating the emphasis within a combination of these characteristics a person's race might change! By the time Latin American nations achieved independence, modern ideas about race as a biological category had begun to take shape, and peoples of European descent used these notions to identify some so-called races as inherently superior (European or "white") or inferior (indigenous, African, and Asian). Such assertions were problematic in Latin American nation-states, however, as the supposedly inferior peoples were also purportedly fellow members in the imagined community of the nation; in some cases these groups even accounted for the majority of the nation's population. The historical figures and authorities presented in these volumes debated and deployed these markers of difference in a variety of ways, and one can trace how the significance of race developed over the course of time.

Gender functions similarly to race in the study of history, as it, too, is socially constructed and has been used to justify unequal power relations. Joan Scott developed a two-tiered definition of gender, which many historians continue to use as a foundation for gender analysis in the twenty-first century.[6] Scott asserted that on one level gender is "a constitutive element of social relationships based on perceived differences between the sexes." This suggests that gender informs both relations between the sexes and also how individuals and societies make sense of assumed sexual differences. Many times, the supposedly inherent differences between men and women were (and are) socially structured—in other words, girls were taught to behave one way, boys another. By the time individuals reach maturity, these behaviors seem natural and timeless rather than learned. Scott's definition of gender also has another, important, part to it. She argues that gender is "a primary field within which or by means of which power is articulated." Here, she means that gender ideologies (assumptions about male and female qualities, or parental versus childlike qualities) can be manipulated by individuals and groups either to express power or try to increase their power over others. Gender often functions this way in politics, and not only when women are involved. For example, when state officials use ideas about manliness to exclude certain adult men from political participation, they are using gender ideas to justify their actions. Gender, thus, encompasses ideas about how men and women are supposed to act, and it influences relationships, including political relationships, between individuals or groups.

Gender is, therefore, one of the essential building blocks of all societies and states, and understanding how gender functioned and changed over time is a crucial part of studying history. In Latin America, for example, colonial state officials identified indigenous peoples as *niños con barbas* (bearded children) who, although they might achieve physical maturity, were ostensibly perpetual children in other ways. This gendered racial notion justified the unequal power relations between colonizers and colonized peoples, although this state-sanctioned

---

[5] Magnus Mörner offers one of the fundamental discussions of race in the Americas. His work still represents an important point of departure for any study of ethnicity, class, and social identity construction in the Americas. Magnus Mörner, *Race Mixture in the History of Latin America* (Boston: Little, Brown, 1967).

[6] Joan Wallach Scott, "Gender: A Useful Category for Historical Analysis," in *Gender and the Politics of History* (New York: Columbia University Press, 1988), 28–50.

interethnic paternalism did not always work in practice as it was meant to in theory, as many chapters in Volume I show. Women continued to be excluded from politics after independence, but their marginalization held new meaning in the republican era. Denying women political rights helped to define the political nation as a male domain, and excluding women served to obfuscate class and race divisions between men in a given nation. Gender and race, therefore, upheld the politics of exclusion in Latin America just as they did in the United States and other parts of the world. And, just as in other societies, one can still find ways that these notions limit the rights and power of women and non-whites in contemporary Latin America.

Wealthy European men—the *elite*—benefited the most from gender and race ideologies, which helped them to rule over, exploit, and marginalize other groups. In many ways, *elite* is a clear-cut term that refers to those individuals or groups who dominate politics, the economy, and society. However, different kinds of elites existed, and it is important that one avoid the trap of thinking that elites were somehow uniform or homogenous. For example, members of the intellectual elite, whose ideas greatly influenced society and politics, were not necessarily the wealthiest men or those in political power. Different elite groups also competed with each other over economic and political power, and they often held divergent ideas about how society, the economy, and politics should be structured. Another potential division appeared between political and religious elites: In certain periods and locations, Church and state officials allied closely, whereas in other circumstances these two elite groups were at odds with each other. Even within the Church, deep divisions surfaced between the regular clergy (who belonged to religious orders) and lay clergy (who ministered to the members of a diocese); in many instances, these different Church officials fought bitterly over the jurisdiction of particular populations. Sometimes elite factions even made alliances (usually brief) with less-powerful peoples in order to beat a competing elite faction.

At the other end of identity and power politics, one finds *subaltern* peoples. Although a sophisticated field of subaltern studies exists, in these volumes the term *subaltern* refers simply to those groups that were outside of the dominant power structure.[7] Most obviously, subalterns included indigenous peoples, Afro-Latin Americans, and peoples of mixed racial descent. However, it also included poor people of European descent and women across class and race lines. It is important to note that some individuals could be considered subaltern in some circumstances but part of the dominant power structure in others. Context mattered. An elite woman of European descent was part of the dominant race and class when considering her social status and power over non-Europeans, yet, throughout most of Latin American history, such a woman was excluded from political power and had limited rights to make decisions about the property she owned. Another example would be a male *cacique* (local indigenous leader) during the colonial period: in his case, he would be part of the political structure, at least at the local level, from which the elite woman was excluded. He also enjoyed privileges, exercised power over indigenous commoners, and could participate in commerce. But he was still subaltern, because he was excluded from the higher ranks of political power, and there were ways that his status was lower than Spanish men of lesser wealth. In cases like these, whether an individual would be considered subaltern or part of the dominant group depended on the nature of one's historical inquiry. The topic being explored, the forms of sociopolitical power under scrutiny, and the broad questions one is trying to answer, for example, determine which groups should be included in the category of subaltern or elite with any given chapters of this documentary history. Furthermore, subaltern groups or individuals did not necessarily share the same problems or goals, and

---

[7] South Asian studies groups coined this phrase for history from below. See Gayatri Chakravorty Spivak, "Can the Subaltern Speak?" in *Marxism and the Interpretation of Culture,* ed. Cary Nelson and Lawrence Grossberg (Urbana: University of Illinois Press, 1988), 271–313. A variety of scholars apply subaltern studies to Latin America; see Ileana Rodríguez, ed., *The Latin American Subaltern Reader* (Durham, NC: Duke University Press, 2001). Historians debate how to take Latin America's subalterns into account; a good discussion of this is Eric Van Young, "The New Cultural History Comes to Old Mexico," *Hispanic American Historical Review* 79, no. 2 (1999): 211–247.

they sometimes clashed and competed with each other. In the short-term, an individual might improve his or her life through such contests, but in the long-term intrasubaltern competition usually served to keep wealthy European men in power.

All of these terms refer to fluid categories and processes in history. They are complex rather than simple and historically adaptable rather than unchanging. All of the terms also focus on individuals' and groups' relative positions with regard to *power*. Instead of thinking of power as absolute or as something that one *holds*, it is more useful—and more historically accurate—to think of power as something that one *exercises*. This distinction is important because it indicates that even though subalterns were (and are) excluded from most formal positions of power, they might still exercise power in significant ways, particularly in an informal or local-level capacity. Power exists in a continuum, with different individuals and groups enjoying different kinds and levels of authority. Chapters in *Documenting Latin America* reveal myriad ways that wealthy European men wielded tremendous power and manipulated gender and race ideas to maintain inequalities. At the same time, many chapters allow readers to explore the numerous and sometimes surprising ways that women and peoples of indigenous or African descent manipulated ideologies that were meant to subordinate them in order to advance their personal or collective interests. These tensions, contradictions, and negotiations over gender, race, and politics were driving forces that moved Latin American history forward; they continue to shape the region today.

Getting the Most Out of Primary-Source Documents

Working with primary sources makes history both exciting and daunting. In the chapters to follow, readers will dive into the archives of Latin America's past alongside the historians whose work it is to make sense of what are sometimes confusing or conflicting accounts. The primary sources in *Documenting Latin America* offer unparalleled perspectives on the views and lives of real men and women who witnessed or created key moments in Latin American history; nothing will give readers a truer and more in-depth understanding of the past. Making history is, really, a process of giving meaning to the written and visual remains of the past. This book requires readers to evaluate the past and draw their own conclusions, maybe even to question or challenge the editors' or contributing scholars' views of the past!

Primary sources include almost any materials that capture the memories and thoughts of people who lived through particular events or periods in the past. In these two volumes on Latin American history, readers will encounter transcriptions of ships' logs, legal codes, scholarly essays, lists of possessions from wills, testimonial life accounts, portraits, and interrogations from court cases. Each source holds within it useful insights and potential pitfalls; the trick is to extract those insights while avoiding many of the pitfalls. Historians typically employ an array of strategies to recognize what the content of these sources means. A basic strategy is to ask oneself: Who created this source, under what circumstances, for what audience, and with what objective in mind? It is also imperative to consider whose voice, or what combination of voices, one "hears" while reading a document or viewing an image. A written source, or even a visual one, may contain input from one or more creators, speaking for themselves or on behalf of others. It is critical to determine this voice and authorship as accurately as possible. These volumes also present readers with information about people marginalized within Latin American society, many of whom were illiterate. Their thoughts and actions may be hidden within the words, impressions, or descriptions expressed by others, providing readers only indirect access to the voices of the marginalized. This raises questions about an author's viewpoint that may be distorting any given document. Such distortions within a source do not mean that one must discount everything one reads; instead, the challenge is to figure out how an author's perspective affects what a reader gleans from a particular document. A good technique for doing this is to question: What other perspectives might there be on an issue or event being presented in this document? It is critical to read documents or images "against the grain" or "between the lines" to discern and analyze the author's perspective, or to learn something that the author might have been hiding or ignoring. Implementing these methods, as well as others learned in class or on one's own while working with the materials, will enable readers to develop their own ways of engaging with Latin American history and sources.

Questions to Ask When Interrogating a Primary Source

1. What type of source is this?
2. What is known about who created it, when, and where?
3. Whom did the author consider the audience for this piece?
4. What views or perspectives were presented? Were other views silenced or challenged?
5. Is there evidence of distortion in the document? How might this be explained?
6. What can the source tell a reader about an event or period in history? What are the limits to what it can reveal?
7. How does this source fit into a bigger historical picture or period? Does it challenge a bigger picture or narrative in any way?

Volume 1: Empires and Their Subjects

Volume I of *Documenting Latin America* allows readers to explore how Latin American empires and societies appeared and changed from the European invasions of the fifteenth and sixteenth centuries to the independence period of the early nineteenth century. Conquests in the Americas, the enslavement of Africans, and colonization coincided with the period during which Western Europe emerged from the Middle Ages, experienced the Renaissance, and created the mechanisms and institutions of early modern states and empire.[8] In this period, European

monarchies created mechanisms like councils of state and *viceroys* to govern overseas territories; they established trade monopolies and fleets to engage in global trade; and they extended the reach of royal courts and the inquisition to regulate subjects' activities and thoughts. In short, they made modern states and empires possible.

Unprecedented European expansion and the globalization of trade and human movement created new ways of interacting and organizing life, often with a unique set of peoples. Monarchs, nobles, bureaucrats, priests, and commoners of Europe, Africa, and the Americas came together—often through violence, always through negotiation of some sort, and occasionally though cooperation—to form the impressive and wealthy Spanish and Portuguese Empires and their diverse and numerous subjects in the Americas. These new American empires grew out of European practices of conquest and governance combined with Amerindian traditions of empire building; both contributed notions of subjects' rights and obligations. For example, indigenous ideas of reciprocity between the rulers and the ruled melded with European beliefs of a monarch's paternalistic protection and lenience. In the Americas, Spain and Portugal created systems of royal courts that all residents could access and through which some received special protection and rights (e.g., communal lands).

Empires had existed in the Americas prior to the arrival of Europeans. In fact, the relatively young *Inca* and *Aztec* Empires had been extending imperial control over new regions, independent ethnic groups, and important resources right up to the invasion. The *Mayan* polities had declined some time earlier. But in all three cases, and in a few other similar regions, the existence of dense populations of sedentary agriculturalists ruled indirectly by ethnically dissimilarly leaders paved the way for the Spanish to impose their domination and meld their practices and institutions with the earlier Amerindian ways. Amerindian history also mattered tremendously for Portugal's colony in Brazil. Along the coast, the Portuguese found that the semisedentary Tupi-Namba organized into tribal societies could be engaged in trade and later forced to work on early sugar mills. In every part of the Americas

---

[8] "Early modern" refers to the period between the Middle Ages and the French Revolution (1789).

that the Spanish and the Portuguese turned to, the diversity of Amerindian society shaped the fundamental nature of the colonies established there. Not only were colonies made possible and profitable by the indigenous inhabitants, the *Aztec* and *Inca* Empires could not have been defeated without the internal diversity and politics of indigenous societies that produced people willing to ally with outsiders to defeat overlords.

Christopher Columbus, and the conquering soldiers in Mexico, offer examples of the conquistador's mindset; they also reveal the central role that indigenous allies played in early European victories, setting in motion the arrival of more Europeans and guaranteeing that ethnic groups would not all experience colonialism in the same way. In addition, not all Europeans were white, and not all conquests were successful. Afro-Iberians working as sailors, soldiers, and traders help explain the early importance of the African Diaspora to Iberian colonialism. The black anti-conquistador represented another result of the Diaspora, and Church and state authorities found they needed to negotiate and compromise with those they could not fully conquer, contain, or convert. Fluidity and flexibility characterized conquest society in the sixteenth century.

Mexico and the Andes offered populous and well-organized societies and rich mineral deposits. Consequently, these regions became the core of Spain's American empire at least until the eighteenth-century rise in economic and demographic importance of plantation colonies in other parts of South America and the Caribbean. In Brazil, no silver or gold deposits motivated efforts to control the workforce to guarantee mining production, at least not until gold and diamonds were found in the late colonial period; however, despite high levels of indigenous mortality and escape, the colonists used indigenous labor in northwestern Brazil's cane fields and mills until they accumulated the resources to import Africans as enslaved laborers.

The *colonial economies* survived the disruptions of warfare and the ongoing toll that disease took on indigenous populations, and they became centered on mining and plantations. These colonial economies eventually created extensive networks of trade and commercial activity, reaching all levels of society and

almost every village and town. The creation of the capital to invest in commerce and the demand for laborers also promoted a spectacular expansion of the slave trade in African peoples, and this trade grew in size and importance with each century. The African Diaspora and the creation of new multiethnic societies and networks of administration and evangelization endowed the Americas with new kinds of people, new kinds of beliefs and religious practices, and many institutions and strategies of rule that bound the system together and gave mature Iberian colonialism the flexibility to last for centuries until Spain and Portugal lost their hold over the American territories in the nineteenth century.

Conquest and incorporation into imperial systems, thus, took place through interplay between European and indigenous actors. African peoples played a role, too, but often faced the greatest challenges in shaping American societies. This volume offers various documents and voices that record the historical agency that people of all walks of life and ethnic backgrounds exercised in the world's first era of globalization. Often these groups and individuals became visible in the historical record only when imperial states took real form. This happened when people faced judges in court, listened to and discussed the meaning of sermons, denounced their neighbors to Church investigators, recorded marriage in a parish book, or engaged in any of the other hundreds of ways of taking official or legal action.

Within colonial societies in the Americas, no one group was homogeneous, including the Europeans. For example, regional loyalties, social status, ethnic allegiance, institutional in-fighting, competition, and greed divided people in the colonies. The multiple and competing interests helped ensure that the functioning of colonial governance and the lives of subjects within the empire was not solely a top-down process. *Documenting Latin America* collects the kinds of court cases, petitions to authorities, and claims to rights that make the reality of subjects' negotiations abundantly clear.

Economic and cultural activities also expose the fact that indigenous and African peoples, alongside elite and plebeian Europeans, generated the wealth and values that built and sustained European power during this era. Notaries' records, litigation over property, and regulations of local marketplaces show how real people experienced colonialism, survived, and adapted. They also wrote poems and drew pictures about these themes, and those sources are included in this volume as well. The interconnected colonial economy and the multiethnic cities it spawned were built from both above and below with participation at many levels. In fact, market participation and the growth of cities and towns marched forward in tandem with the creation of new kinds of societies, religious beliefs, and people of mixed ethnic heritage. Diversity and contradiction became hallmarks of mature colonial society during the seventeenth and eighteenth centuries.

How Iberians governed amidst diversity and contradictions remains one of the key questions motivating scholarly investigation and debate. *Colonial hegemony* remains one of the best ways to understand how Iberian domination secured a measure of consent by those at the bottom and the middle. Spanish and Portuguese colonialism allowed opportunities for people of many different backgrounds to find ways of belonging to these empires, although never as equals to Europeans. In particular, the colonized embraced Catholicism and the advantages Catholic institutions offered; many cases included in the volume demonstrate how common Catholic participation became. The construction of these colonial cultural identities and religious allegiances also made rebellion rare. Much more common were various forms of adaptive resistance, which allowed individuals and colonized groups to accept some change and make concessions in order to resist total transformation or specific, hated colonial impositions. People changed in order to remain who they were. Or they created new blended beliefs or rituals that combined elements from more than one tradition.

These arrangements between rulers and the ruled could also break down when the levels of domination rise, the processes of mediating conflict falter, or significant crises weakened the state at the center. Each of these occurred in the eighteenth and early nineteenth centuries. Increasing in intensity and frequency from the late 1700s forward, these disruptions to the "way things worked" under Iberian colonialism led to changing forms of resistance, rebellion, and consciousness. Eventually, at one point

or another, groups at all levels of colonial Spanish American society questioned colonial rule, and many fought to end it; they often clashed with each over the alternatives to European domination. Smashing Iberia's American empires and colonial hegemony did not lead easily to national unity.

Spanish and Portuguese imperial archives are replete with remains of the elaborate Iberian bureaucracy, and colonized people's active and sustained engagement with it. Similarly, the national, regional, and local archives are crowded with a multitude of documents and wonderful, heartbreaking, and simply confusing stories about Latin America's colonial past. Historians, other scholars, and activists all mine these repositories for a glimpse of the past. In *Documenting Latin America*, readers dive into these collections to learn more about imperial aspirations and the limits of colonial domination. This process of domination and co-optation not only helped establish the norms of colonial rule into the seventeenth century and beyond, but it also gave indigenous people a place in the Church, Brazilian slaves a forum for leadership, and non-Europeans—often women—additional tools to promote and protect their interests. Indians and women were well aware of their subordinated status in colonial society, but life in cities and towns afforded them opportunities to secure niches in an expanding economic system and even to parley their knowledge of selling or healing to earn a living. A few women—both indigenous and Iberian—flaunted the norms barring women from public discourse, soldiering, or exercising political office. Colonial society became rich in its complexity and in the ways people found identity as subjects within empires ruled from a remote imperial center.

The age of reform following the eighteenth-century ascension of the Bourbon Dynasty to the Spanish and Portuguese thrones ushered in an era of unprecedented change in imperial rule. This period also coincided with the emergence of European *creole* and nativist identities and rising peasant and indigenous descent and revolt. *Creole* elites often feared both the upward mobility of social sectors normally relegated to inferior positions and work within society and a loss of privileges due to reforms from European rulers. Clergy worried of the fraying bonds of rural populations' loyalties. Certainly resistance to higher taxes and outright rural insurrections throughout the eighteenth century proved many of these concerns well founded. In fact, when full-scale revolts broke out and hardened into independence movements from the 1780s into the 1820s, *creole* patriots, parish priests, and indigenous officials—all supposedly beholden to the colonial state—figured prominently among those fighting hardest to tear the imperial system down. In both Spanish America and Brazil, formal independence did not guarantee equality and full citizenship for all: Indians, women, and Afro-Latin Americans, in particular, still faced systematic exclusion. Latin America's diverse, multiethnic societies with both mechanisms of inclusion and exclusion and negotiation and coercion would continue and would continue to change on into the modern era of the nineteenth and twentieth centuries.

Section I

Imperial Aspirations and the Limits of Colonial Domination

Transatlantic colonization in the Americas followed Iberians' long history of warfare and trading and territorial claims in Europe and Africa. Europeans' efforts to circumvent Muslim-dominated routes and establish direct access to the trading centers of the Indian Ocean world helped spark and propel early European expansion and set colonial domination and imperialism in motion.[1] From approximately 1400 forward in Portugal and 1500 in Spain, Christian monarchies gained territorial and political control and sought wealth and power overseas.

Before the overseas expansion began, the Christians fought intermittent wars against the Moors from North Africa, who had conquered virtually all of Iberia between 711 and 718 and after hundreds of years had become Europeans, too. This *Reconquest*, as it came to be known, began far in the north in 718, often as battles among nobles over serfs, and eventually hardened during 750 years of warfare into a bitter intolerance by Christians of other religions. For centuries, Christians, Jews, and Muslims coexisted successfully in many parts of the peninsula. They lived with certain restrictions and tensions in the same medieval cities and under the same rulers whether Catholic or Muslim. This *"convivencia"* eventually eroded slowly into distrust,

hatred, and pogroms. As the conflict evolved into a clash between two sides (Christian and Muslim), each side developed strategies and institutions to help seize and hold territory and the people living there. As religious militancy and zeal increasingly formed the rationale and motivation for the wars, the advancing Christians became steadily more intolerant of the other religions on the peninsula, including Judaism. By the 1200s, the Moors were expelled from Portugal and confined to the Emirate of Granada in what became Spain under the Catholic monarchs Ferdinand and Isabel.

The centuries of wars that Christian Iberians fought to win territory by driving out Muslim rulers gave Spain and Portugal's overseas expansion the character and justification of crusades, wars to spread the faith and defeat nonbelievers. This sense of a Christian mission helped Iberian monarchs begin to build dynastic states and claim that their diverse subjects—speaking different tongues and equally loyal to regional interests—shared a common Christian bond and obligations to the crusading Crown. In particular, 1492 closed the last chapter of the medieval Christian *Reconquest* of Iberia, and 1492 proved a decisive year for the religious unification of Spain. From this year forward, all Spanish subjects would be Christians. Isabel and Ferdinand had already established the Spanish Inquisition in 1478 to seek out and punish Jewish converts to Christianity (*conversos*) who failed to remain true to their new faith. In 1492 after 10 years of fighting to seize

---

[1] For a general history comparing Spanish empire building with the British in North America, see John H. Elliot, *Empires of the Atlantic World: Britain and Spain in America, 1492–1830* (New Haven, CT: Yale University Press, 2006).

1

control of Granada, the victorious monarchs forced all remaining Jews to convert or face expulsion and permanent exile.[2] Despite assurances to the contrary given in order to obtain the surrender of Granada, Muslim subjects soon faced the same forced conversions, becoming *moriscos*. Many *moriscos* were expelled to North Africa a century later in 1609–1613. Militant Christianity and intolerance of difference came to characterize Iberian unification and subsequent expansion into the Atlantic and the Americas.

In these efforts to spread the faith and Spanish and Portuguese power, service to the monarchy and God could be combined with seeking personal fortune and the enrichment of the state. In fact, the Iberian monarchies depended heavily on the private organization, command, and financing of most of the fifteenth- and sixteenth-century expeditions of exploration, trade, and territorial conquest. The monarchs granted permission to specific commanders and financers to seek lands or trade in the Crown's name in exchange for a portion of the profits (the royal fifth) and allegiance of both the conquerors and those they conquered. This partnership between individuals and the state, often with papal sanction in hopes of spreading the faith, helped fuel the Spanish and Portuguese conquests of the Atlantic Islands[3] and the establishment and rapid growth of the Atlantic trade in enslaved Africans.[4] It also drove colonization of the Americas. Christopher Columbus came to the Americas four times under such an agreement. He first sought trade items and routes to Asia, but later he also labored to colonize and mine gold. In each case, he worked equally for the greater glory of God, the Spanish monarchs he served, and his family name and fortune. The accounts by Columbus and the other Spanish conquerors, called conquistadors, quoted in this section reflect these goals and the struggle to balance these motives

with the realities they encountered and the alliances they made in order to succeed.

A strong sense of purpose and justification motivated the Spanish and Portuguese, but they also relied heavily on the aid and participation of both Native American and African peoples to build European empires in the Americas. Columbus, and every Spaniard and Portuguese who followed him, sought allies and laborers among the Native Peoples. Colonial success depended on the extent that Native Peoples could be persuaded or forced to fight against Amerindian rulers, farm the lands, and mine for silver and gold. In the first stage of Spanish expansion, Columbus depended on the native population in the Caribbean; without indigenous laborers the farms and mines could not be worked, and without an indigenous population on the land there was nothing with which to reward loyal followers. In the subsequent stage of Spanish expansion onto the mainland, indigenous peoples played an even larger role. Indigenous allies, prisoners, and slaves made possible the stunning defeats of the *Aztecs* by Hernán Cortés (1519–1521) and the *Incas* by Francisco Pizarro (1531–1534). Once the fighting was over, colonists and the Crown alike depended on the productivity of indigenous society to build the cities, feed the colonists, and pay tribute. Native Peoples also sustained the missionaries who evangelized them and kept the mines running. In Brazil, the Portuguese first depended on the Tupi-Guaraní people to trade dyewood (Brazilwood) and other items, and they later needed indigenous laborers to start working the first sugar plantations until enough capital could be accumulated to import expensive enslaved African workers. For the first 200 years, Spanish and Portuguese empires in much of the Americas depended in one way or another on the numbers and productivity of Native Peoples.

Africans came to play an equally central role in the drama of conquest and colonization in the Americas because they had already been incorporated into the Atlantic system of trade and labor.[5] Well before Columbus embarked for the Americas,

---

[2]Portugal followed suit with forced conversions and expulsions of Jews in 1497.
[3]Azores, Madeira, Canaries, Cape Verde, and São Tomé.
[4]Beginning with sales in 1441, the Portuguese pioneered the slave trade.

[5]For an overview, see Herbert S. Klein, *The Atlantic Slave Trade* (New York: Cambridge University Press, 1999).

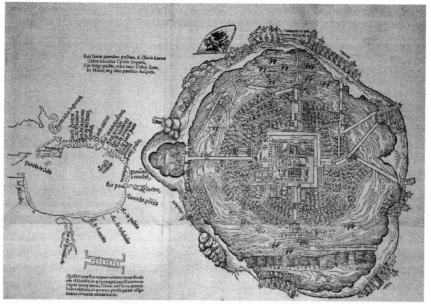

Source: Hernán Cortés, Praeclara Ferdina[n]di Cortesii de noua mars oceani. . . . (Nuremberg: Peypus, 1524). Facsimile. Rosenwald Collection, Rare Book and Special Collections Division, Library of Congress (60.02.00).

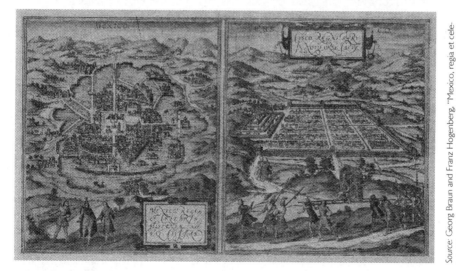

Source: Georg Braun and Franz Hogenberg, "Mexico, regia et celebris Hispaniae novae civitas" and "Cusco, regni Peru in novo orbe caput," in Civitates Orbis Terrarum (Cologne: T. Graminaeus, 1572), Jay I. Kislak Collection, Rare Book and Special Collections Division, Library of Congress (5).

This 1524 book published in Nuremberg contains the Hapsburg monarchy's coat of arms, a map of the *Aztec* capital, and the second and third letters sent by the Spanish conquistador Cortés to the Emperor Charles V. The letters provided Europeans with early accounts of Mexican peoples and culture. The map shows the Gulf Coast of Mexico, and the city plan shows a large and complex city, including a temple precinct and causeways to the mainland. What does the map tell viewers about the society Cortés conquered in 1519–1521? This first map and the plan draw on both European and indigenous sources. How does this representation of *Tenochtilán* contrast with the second set of images (from 1572) showing *Tenochtilán* and the South American *Inca* capital *Cuzco* side by side and drawing solely on European sources? What do all three images taken together tell viewers about the interests of the Spanish empire builders?

the Portuguese and then the Spanish launched expeditions into northern and western Africa. Gold and ivory initially attracted raiders and traders who established ports and trading enclaves on the islands in the Atlantic and along the coasts and rivers. However, people soon became the most valuable "commodity." Iberians enslaved African people and sent them to European cities and to labor on the Mediterranean-style sugar plantations being established on the Atlantic Island colonies like the Canaries, Cape Verde, and São Tomé. Two important results of the early slave trade should be noted. First, in the Atlantic world and in the Americas, the stigma of slavery was attached to Africans. Second, the Iberian trade in slaves taken in Africa as captives, or purchased from African slave traders or rulers, not only became the first step and a testing ground in Iberian expansion overseas, but also profoundly shaped the American experience. From the very beginning, Africans provided both empires with intermediaries, sailors, conquistadors, servants, artisans, and plantation laborers. Of course, Africans served their own interests by carving out spaces for life within colonial society or engaging in anticolonial resistance on the poorly controlled frontiers. In order to marshal this African labor and quell resistance, Europeans exported Iberian institutions and practices and developed new ones.

At first, practices and institutions fostered conquest and holding conquered lands; nevertheless, gradually, the goals shifted to favor royal control and the Church. To encourage conquistadors to invest their money and lives in finding and subjugating populous indigenous societies, victors were entrusted with the native populations of specific towns or attached to specific ethnic chiefs (called *caciques* or *kurakas*). These *encomiendas* allowed the *encomenderos*, who held them to collect tribute and labor services from Native Peoples in exchange for Christianizing them and caring for their well being. *Encomiendas* proved tremendously profitable in places where the indigenous population suffered lower mortality from the "Old World." Several factors came together to bring about the end of the *encomienda* system: Indigenous peoples opposed the exploitation of *encomenderos*, the

Crown feared *encomenderos*' power and autonomy, and missionaries desired better access to the people they aimed to convert. *The New Laws* of 1542 limited the *encomienda* system severely, and it was eliminated within a generation or two from most places.

Instead of a society dominated by *encomenderos*, the Spanish Crown favored direct royal control and laws to incorporate Europeans, Native Peoples, and Africans into a colonial economy and a Christian society. The Crown established *cabildos* (town councils) to govern the cities that colonists lived in and the towns to which the Indians belonged. *Corregidores* (rural magistrates) supervised the collection of tribute from Indians and their service in forced labor drafts. To govern all groups and to represent the king, the Crown appointed *viceroys* in Mexico City (1535) and Lima in Peru (1544). A judicial bureaucracy centered on the *audiencias* (royal high courts) located throughout Mexico and Peru managed disputes within this system and reached all the way back to the Crown's Council of the Indies established in 1524 to draft laws and hear appeals. The Church, too, expanded its roles as it ministered to a growing colonist and mixed-race population, mainly in cities. Church officials created a system of parish priests throughout the indigenous towns and neighborhoods, and they sent missionaries to convert Native Peoples in more remote regions. Crown and Church officials found that to govern was to mediate among the various levels of administration and the factions within American society. This rule, through negotiation and the need to incorporate Europeans, Africans, and Native Peoples, allowed individuals from these groups to find ways to articulate their interests within royal and Church institutions. The flexibility required by colonial society influenced the operation of the Iberian empires.

The lives of colonial subjects and their direct experience of empire help people today recognize the centrality of indigenous peoples, Africans, and their American-born descendants in the history of Latin America. The term "conquest" typically makes one think of conquerors defeating the *Aztec* and *Inca* empires, whereas "empire building" conjures up images of bureaucrats and missionaries ruling over Native Peoples and slaves. Although it is true that a small number of European men gained the most from building colonial empires, the document excerpts in this section reveal how peoples from many different backgrounds participated in the process of making colonial Latin America. Documents in which Columbus and Bernal Díaz describe their relations with indigenous peoples show that a complex web of enmity and alliances with indigenous peoples made European conquest possible. Indigenous and Afro-Latin American identities and experiences in the early colonial period were likewise much more complex than readers today usually assume. Garofalo's archival documents explore how Africans living and working in Diaspora on both sides of the Atlantic played key roles in forging empires and founding multiethnic societies. Matthew offers documents that allow readers to explore why a *Maya* from Guatemala tried to "pass" as a *Tlaxcalan* Indian in the late sixteenth century, building an identity on claims of military service to the Spanish during the campaigns of conquest that fanned out from central Mexico. Spanish and Portuguese empire building continued into the seventeenth century and often took place at the margins of colonial centers. Reports on the famous Brazilian *quilombo* of Palmares illustrate the power of *maroon* societies (runaway communities) to set limits on the reach of European empires. The primary-source documents at the heart of all these chapters relate a variety of personal experiences of conquest, colonization, and empire building in colonial Latin America and help readers to think beyond stereotyped interpretations of colonization.

Chapter 1

Christopher Columbus Evaluates Indigenous Societies

Leo J. Garofalo, Connecticut College

C hristopher Columbus recorded his first impressions of the Americas and the Amerindians he encountered in the Caribbean, creating some of the first and most influential accounts of the Americas. His letters and reports directed to the monarchs sponsoring his missions and other highly placed nobles and clergymen began to form Europeans' image of the "New World." The documents excerpted here show Columbus evaluating indigenous society and proposing various ways that Europeans could interact with the people he met during his first voyage (1492–1493).[6] The

---

[6]Columbus launched three other voyages in 1493–1496, 1498–1500, and 1502–1504.

Spanish monarchy authorized and partially financed Columbus's explorations. In return, Columbus promised to reach Asia and give Spanish merchants and royal power an opportunity to circumvent the Ottoman-controlled Mediterranean trade routes and the Portuguese maritime routes advancing south along western Africa and around the Cape of Good Hope at the southern extremity of Africa.[7] Not surprisingly, in his report to the Spanish Queen Isabel and King Ferdinand, Columbus discussed the opportunities for trade, the search for valuable exports, the potential for Christianizing local people, ethnic divisions, and slavery. Thus, Columbus sought both to describe the potential of the lands and people before him and to continue his search for a way west. In short, Columbus shaped his report to respond to the expectations of the Crown. These accounts of the first voyage come to readers today further mediated by Bartolomé de Las Casas. This Dominican friar, later famous for his denunciation of Spanish abuses during the conquest (see Chapter 6), made the only surviving copies of the digest of Columbus's log and perhaps incorporated additional information from a second account also penned by Columbus.

An Italian sea captain from Genoa (1451–1506), Columbus had courted royal backers for a westward voyage to Asia (the East Indies) since 1483. Relying on Marco Polo's map and miscalculations, Columbus underestimated the world's circumference and concluded that Japan could be reached by sailing 2,500 miles west of the Portuguese Azores in the Atlantic. Doubting these estimates and unwilling to grant the mariner such a large share of the potential profits (the Spanish Crown allowed him 10 percent of the profits), the Portuguese rejected Columbus's request for underwriters. In 1488, the Portuguese navigator Bartolomeu Dias sailed around Africa, establishing a Portuguese route to Asia's trade in spices and other luxuries and consolidating Portugal's hold on the trade in slaves from western and central Africa. Eager to catch up, the Spanish proved more willing to invest in Columbus's improbable venture. Even if he fell short of Asia and only secured claims to more islands in the Atlantic, Columbus would advance the Spanish sphere of control further to

the west. Newly united by the dynastic marriage between Queen Isabel of Castile and King Ferdinand of Aragon (1469) and fresh from the victorious conclusion to the campaign to drive Islamic rulers off the Iberian Peninsula (January 1492), the Spanish monarchs met Columbus in the newly conquered city of Granada. By April, they agreed to back his plan to sail west and claim for Spain territories and trade routes to Asia. The monarchs promised him various rewards, including the governorship of his discoveries and the title of Admiral of the Oceans. The chance to outmaneuver Mediterranean enemies and Iberian competitors for trade appealed to the Spanish Monarchs because it offered the chance to expand royal power, carry to new realms their crusade to promote Christianity, and find the resources needed to finance a more powerful state and fight against non-Christian empires. At first, Columbus's arrival fell well short of fulfilling these goals.

Columbus reached the Bahamas first and other Caribbean islands later and, eventually, the shores of Central America and northern South America. The people he encountered were not Japanese and Chinese; instead, he met and began to kidnap Amerindians. When Columbus arrived, many ethnic groups inhabited the Caribbean, and later researchers came to label them as *Arawaks* because of similarities with the Indians in northeastern South America.[8] The rapid destruction of these societies in the two decades after 1492 left little information about how Caribbean peoples understood their identities and occupied this broad region. What is known from the surviving documents is that the people who lived in the Bahamas called themselves Lucayo. Puerto Rico's inhabitants called themselves Borinquen. On the large islands like Hispaniola (modern Haiti and the Dominican Republic), Puerto Rico, and Jamaica, the original population reached into the hundreds of thousands. Perhaps a million people lived in all these Greater Antilles. They lived in permanent villages in thatch and wood houses with roofs that were conical or rectangular in shape, and arranged in irregular fashion around a central space where the ethnic chief or *cacique's* house was

[7]Rounding the Cape allowed the Portuguese to enter the Indian Ocean and trade with Asia.

[8]Some ethnographers divide them into Taínos/Gautiao, Caribs/Caribe, and Guanahatabeys/Ciboney and assign them geographical locations; Taínos in the Greater Antilles, Caribs in the Lesser Antilles, and Guanahatabeys/Ciboney in westernmost Cuba.

located. *Caciques* organized daily activities, rituals, and the storage of food and surplus goods for future use. Islanders cultivated cassava and tobacco for ceremonial use when rolled into large cigars and smoked through the nostrils. On some islands, a hundred people lived in each village. On others, villages might hold 1,000 to 2,000 residents. Likewise, some *caciques* only controlled their local villages, whereas in other regions they owed allegiance to other *caciques* and might even have belonged to regional chiefdoms.

Beginning with Columbus, historians treat early reports of cannibalism with suspicion. This label had fateful historical consequences throughout Spanish and Portuguese America. The charge of cannibalism among Amerindians allowed the Iberian colonial regimes to distinguish "good" Amerindian populations from "bad" ones, targeting the latter for punitive violence, even enslavement and extermination. This process of categorizing facilitated and attempted to justify to other Europeans Iberian acts of conquest and colonization. Columbus and the chroniclers and missionaries who followed him promoted a dualistic ethnic typology of "Arawaks" and "Caribs" and spread its use across the Caribbean. They described Caribs as fierce and cannibalistic. They often used this label for any group selected for enslavement or particularly resistant to evangelization. Queen Isabel's Royal Decree in 1503 legalized the plunder, enslaving, and sale only of "Carib" populations. When combined with European diseases, warfare among Spanish factions, and the exploitation of local populations to mine for gold, the practices of enslavement and raiding

Printed in Basel in 1494 and describing encounters with Amerindians, this edition of Christopher Columbus's letters to King Ferdinand and Queen Isabel of Spain was illustrated by five woodcuts. This account's seventeen editions made Columbus famous. In the part of the Caribbean described in the letters, Columbus met the *Taíno* people. He described them as "naked as the day they were born." The *Taíno* possessed complex religious, political, and social hierarchies and skills as farmers and navigators; nevertheless, their portrayals in text and image reflected little of this reality. This first illustration was probably imaginary and adapted from drawings of Mediterranean places (for instance, oared galleys were not used on Columbus's voyages). What could European readers learn from these accounts and their illustrations? What could they not discover about the Americas in them?

Source: Christopher Columbus (1451–1506), *De Insulis nuper in Mari Indico repertis in Carolus Verardus: Historia Baetica* (Basel: I.B. [Johann Bergman de Olpe], 1494). Jay I. Kislak Collection, Rare Book and Special Collections Division, Library of Congress (48.01.02).

devastated first the Native Peoples of the Greater Antilles and then the Lesser Antilles. Between 1492 and 1514, the population dropped from a million or more to approximately 30,000 (and to only a handful of people by the mid-1500s). Amerindian labor for Hispaniola and Cuba's sugar growing and placer mining was replaced by enslaved people brought from West Africa. Disease and the actions of the first Spanish colonizers in the Caribbean caused this acute labor shortage and a crisis in indigenous society just as the Spanish kingdom was attempting to become an empire and learn to govern new territories.

The Caribbean's native populations were the first to experience European methods of invasion and colonization and suffer the ecological and demographic consequences. Beginning in 1494, Columbus made Hispaniola the focus of conquest. Following Iberian practice and the model of subjugating the Canary Islanders, Columbus and subsequent explorers and conquerors assigned the native population under specific *caciques* to individual colonizers as a reward for service during the conquest. However, Columbus proved a poor administrator of colonizing efforts. The Spanish fought fiercely among themselves and so abused and decimated the local indigenous populations that the Crown stripped Columbus of his governorship and sent him back to Spain in chains and disgrace in 1499. Consequently, his family lost most of its privileges and grants. The Crown eventually created the administrative unit of the *Audiencia*[9] of

---

[9]Royal high court.

Santo Domingo to govern the Caribbean Islands and the littoral region of South America occupied by Spain. Colonizing efforts shifted to exploring and conquering the mainlands. Columbus's accounts, thus, initiated the process of building Spain's overseas claims in the Americas. The Caribbean became a testing ground for imperial strategies. These original voyages and the attempts to establish a Spanish presence in Hispaniola helped the Spanish Empire shape its view of Native Peoples in the Americas, adapt Iberian institutions to American realities, and determine how to extract benefits from these new claims.

Questions to Consider:

1. How did Columbus describe the Caribbean's potential and suggest ways to incorporate these new lands and peoples into European imperial and commercial systems?
2. What clues can you find in the letter to suggest what the Native Peoples that Columbus encountered might have thought of the Spanish?
3. What did Columbus write about religion and beliefs? How did Columbus try to take advantage of the Spanish monarchs' crusading spirit?
4. How did Columbus determine whether some people were more "civilized" than others? Might this letter tell readers today more about Europeans than about indigenous peoples?

Christopher Columbus's Account of His First Voyage, October 11, 1492 to January 2, 1493[10]

Thursday, 11 October. . . . They reached a small island of the Lucayos, called in the Indian language Guananhani.[11] Immediately some naked people appeared and the Admiral [Columbus] went ashore

---

[10]*Source:* Christopher Columbus, *The Four Voyages,* ed. and trans. J. M. Cohen (New York: Penguin Books, 1969), 53, 55–59, 60–67.
[11]Watling Island in the Bahamas, Columbus's first landfall. From here, he continued through the Bahamas to Cuba and the Island of Hispaniola (Haiti and the Dominican Republic today).

in the armed boat, as did Martin Alonso Pinzón and his brother Vicente Yanez, captain of the *Niña*.[12] The Admiral raised the royal standard and the captains carried two banners with the green cross which were flown by the Admiral on all his ships. On each side of the cross was a crown surmounting the letters F and Y (for Ferdinand and Isabel). On landing they

---

[12]Columbus set out in three ships: the *Niña, Pinta,* and *Santa Maria.*

saw very green trees and much water and fruit of various kinds. The Admiral called the two captains and the others who had landed and Rodrigo Escobedo, recorder of the whole fleet, and Rodrigo Sanchez de Segovia, and demanded that they should bear faithful witness that he took possession of the island—which he did—for his sovereigns and masters the King and Queen. He further made the required declarations, which are recorded at greater length in the evidence there set down in writing. Soon many of the people of the island came up to them. What follows are the Admiral's actual words in his account of his first voyage and the discovery of these Indies.[13]

'In order to win their friendship, since I knew they were a people to be converted and won to our holy faith by love and friendship rather than by force, I gave some of them red caps and glass beads which they hung round their necks, also many other trifles. These things pleased them greatly and they became marvelously friendly to us. They afterwards swam out to the ship's boats in which we were sitting, bringing us parrots and balls of cotton thread and spears and many other things, which they exchanged with us for such objects as glass beads, hawks and bells. In fact, they very willingly traded everything they had. But they seemed to me a people very short of everything. They all go naked as their mothers bore them, including the women, although I saw only one very young girl.

'All the men I saw were young. I did not see one over the age of thirty. They were well built with fine bodies and handsome faces. Their hair is coarse, almost like that of a horse's tail and short; they wear it down over their eyebrows except for a few strands at the back, which they wear long and never cut. They are the color of the Canary Islanders (neither black nor white). Some of them paint themselves black, others white or any color they can find. Some paint their faces, some their whole bodies, some only the eyes, some only the nose. They do not carry arms or know them. For when I showed them swords, they took them by the edge and cut themselves out of ignorance. They have no iron. Their spears are made of cane. Some instead of an iron tip have a fish's tooth

and others have points of different kinds. They are fairly tall on the whole, with fine limbs and good proportions. I saw some who had wound scars on their bodies and I asked them by signs how they got these and they indicated to me that people came from other islands nearby who tried to capture them and they defended themselves. I suppose and still suppose that they come from the mainland to capture them for slaves. They should be good servants and very intelligent, for I have observed that they soon repeat anything that is said to them, and I believe that they would easily be made Christians, for they appear to me to have no religion. God willing, when I make my departure I will bring half a dozen of them back to their Majesties, so that they can learn to speak. I saw no animals of any kind on this island except parrots.' These are the Admiral's own words.

Saturday, 13 October.[14] At daybreak many of these men came to the shore—all young, as I have said, and all of a good height—a very fine people. Their hair is not curly but straight and as coarse as horse hair. All have very broad brows and heads, broader than those of any people I have seen before. Their eyes are very fine and not small. They are not at all black, but the color of Canary Islanders, as could be expected, since this is in the same latitude as the Island of Hierro in the Canaries. They have very straight legs and no bellies, but well-formed bodies. They came to the ship in boats which were made from tree-trunks, like a long boat cut out of a single log. They are marvelously carved in the native style and they are so big that forty or forty-five men came in them. There are others smaller, so small that some carried only a single man. They row them with a paddle like a baker's shovel and they go wonderfully fast. If one capsizes they all start swimming and right it. They bale it out with gourds which they carry with them. They brought balls of cotton thread and parrots and spears and other things which it would be tedious to mention, and exchange them for anything that was given them. I watched carefully to discover whether they had gold and saw that some of them carried a small piece hanging from

---

[13]The Americas. This reference suggests here that Las Casas quoted these passages from Columbus's own writings.

[14]Las Casas consulted and incorporated two now lost sets of writings by Columbus. This accounts for the repetitions in the description of the island.

a hole pierced in the nose. I was able to understand from their signs that to the south, either inland or along the coast, there was a king who had large vessels made of it and possessed a great deal. I tried hard to make them go there but saw in the end that they had no intention of doing so. I decided to remain till the afternoon of the next day and then to sail south-west, for according to the signs which many of them made there was land to the south, south-west and north-west. They all indicated that men from the northwest often came to attack them. So I resolved to go southwest to seek the gold and precious stones.

This island is fairly large and very flat. It has green trees and much water. It has a very large lake in the middle and no mountains and all is delightfully green. The people are very gentle and anxious to have the things we bring. Thinking that nothing will be given them, however, unless they give something in exchange, and having nothing to give, they take anything they can, jump into the water and swim away. But they will give all that they do possess for anything that is given to them, exchanging things even for bits of broken crockery or broken glass cups. I saw one give sixteen balls of cotton for a [small copper coin], and in these balls there was more than an *aroba* [25 pounds] of cotton thread.

I should like to forbid this and let no one take any cotton except at my command; then if there were any quantity I would order it all to be taken for your Majesties. It grows here on this island, but owing to shortage of time I can give no exact account of it. And here too the gold is found that they wear hanging from their noses. But in order not to waste time I wish to go and see if I can strike the island of Chipangu [Japan].

Now when night fell they all went ashore in their boats.

Sunday, 14 October. At dawn I order the ship's boat and the boats of the caravels [ships] to be made ready, and coasted the island in a northeasterly direction in order to see other and eastward part and to look for villages. I saw two or three, whose people all came down to the beach calling to us and offering thanks to God. Some brought us water, others various sorts of food, and others, when they saw that I did not intend to land, jumped into the sea and swam out. We understood them to be asking us if we came from the

sky. One old man got into the boat, and all the others, men and women alike, shouted, 'Come and see the men who have come from the skies; and bring them food and drink.' Many men and women came, each bringing something and offering thanks to God; they threw themselves on the ground and raised their hands to the sky and then called out to us, asking us to land. But I was afraid to do so, seeing a great reef of rocks which encircled the whole island. Inside there is deep water which give sufficient anchorage for all the ships in Christendom. But the entrance is very narrow. It is true that there are some shoals within this reef, but the sea is as still as well water.

I went to view all this morning, in order to give an account to your Majesties and to decide where a fort could be built. I saw a piece of land which is much like an island, though it is not one, on which there were six huts. It could be made into an island in two days, though I see no necessity to do so since these people are very unskilled in arms, as your Majesties will discover from seven whom I caused to be taken and brought aboard so that they may learn our language and return. However, should your Highness command it all the inhabitants could be taken away to Castile or held as slaves on the island, for with fifty men we could subjugate them all and make them do whatever we wish. Moreover, near the small island I have described there are groves of the loveliest trees I have seen, all green with leaves like our trees in Castile in April and May, and much water.

I examined the whole of that anchorage and then returned to the ship and set sail. I saw so many islands that I could not make up my mind which to visit first. The men I had taken told me by signs that there were so many that it was impossible to count them. They mentioned more than a hundred by name. In the end I looked for the largest and decided to go to that one, which I am doing. It is about five leagues from the island of San Salvador, and the rest are rather more or rather less. All are very flat, without mountains and very fertile. All are populated and make war with one another, although the people are very simple and do not look savage.

Monday, 15 October. I stood off that night, fearing to approach land before morning because I did not know if the coast was free from shoals. At daybreak I hoisted sail. As the island was more than five leagues away—indeed more like seven—and the tide was against me, it was midday when reached this island. I found that the coast which faces San Salvador runs north and south for some five leagues, and the other coast which I followed runs east and west for more than ten leagues.[15] And as from this island I saw another larger one to the west, I hoisted sail to run all that day till night, since I should otherwise not have been able to reach its western point. I named this island Santa María de la Concepción. And it was almost sunset when I reached this point. I wished to learn whether there was gold there, because the men I had taken aboard at the island at San Salvador told me that here they wore very large gold bracelets round their legs and arms. I thought that this tale was probably a lie told in the hope of getting away. Generally it was my wish to pass no island without taking possession of it. Though having annexed one it might be said that we had annexed all. I anchored and stayed there until today, Tuesday, when at daybreak I approached the shore with the armed boats and landed.

There were many people all naked and like those of San Salvador. They let us go about the island and gave us all that we asked for. But as the wind was blowing from the southeast I did not wish to delay and went back to the ship. A large canoe happening to lie alongside the *Niña*, a little before midnight one of the men from San Salvador who was in the caravel jumped overboard and went off in it. A few minutes later another threw himself overboard also and swam after the canoe, which went so fast that no boat could overtake it, for it had a considerable start.

So they came to land and left the canoe. Several members of my crew went ashore after them and they ran off like frightened hens. We took the canoe they had abandoned aboard the caravel *Niña*; it was approached by another small canoe with a man who had come to barter a ball of cotton. Since he would not board the caravel some sailors jumped down and seized him. Having seen all this from the forecastle where I was standing, I sent for him and gave him a red cap and some green glass beads which I put in his arms and two hawk's bells which I put in his ears. I

told the sailors to give him back his canoe which they had taken on to the ship's boat, and sent him ashore. I then raised sail for the other large island which I saw to the west and ordered that the second canoe which the *Niña* was towing be set adrift. Shortly afterwards I saw the man to whom I had given these gifts come ashore.

I had not taken the ball of cotton from him, although he wished to give it to me. The people gathered around him and he appeared astonished. It seemed to him that we were good people and that the man who escaped in the canoe must have wronged us or we should not have carried him off.

It was to create this impression that I had him set free and gave him presents. I was anxious that they should think well of us so that they may not be unfriendly when your Majesties send a second expedition here. All I gave him was worth more than four *maravedis*.[16]

So I set sail for the other island about ten o'clock with a southeast wind which veered southerly. It is very large and, according to the signs made by the men we had brought from San Salvador, contains much gold, which they wear as bracelets on their arms and legs and in their ears and noses and round their necks. This other island was about nine leagues west of Santa María, and thus part of its coasts apparently runs from northwest to south-east, for upwards of twenty-eight leagues.

Like San Salvador and Santa María it is very flat with no mountains. All the beaches are free from rocks, although all have submerged reefs near shore, for which reason it is necessary to look carefully before anchoring and not to anchor too near land. The water, however, is always very clear and you can see the bottom. A couple of Lombard shots off land the water is so deep around all these that it cannot be sounded. They are all very green and fertile and subject to gentle breezes. They contain many things of which I do not know because I did not care to land and explore them, being anxious to find gold; and since these islands show signs of containing it—for the natives wear it round their arms and legs, and it is certainly gold, because I showed them some pieces

---

[15]Columbus exaggerated many of these estimates.

[16]Worth only a small amount of money.

which I have—I cannot fail, with God's help, to find out where it comes from.

When I was in mid-channel, between Santa María and this other island which I have named Fernandina [Long Island], I found a man alone in a canoe crossing from one to the other. He was carrying a lump of their bread, about the size of a fist, and a gourd of water and a bit of red earth which had been powdered and then kneaded; also some dried leaves which they must have valued very high since they gave me a present of them. He also carried a native basket containing some glass beads and two *blancas* [coins], by which I knew that he had come from San Salvador to Santa María and was now on his way to Fernandina. He came alongside and I let him come aboard as he asked. I had his canoe hauled aboard also and all that he carried kept safe. I ordered that he should be given bread and honey and something to drink. I shall carry him to Fernandina and restore all his possessions to him so that he may give a good account of us. Then when, God willing, your Highnesses send others here, we shall be favorably received and the natives may give us of all they possess.

Tuesday, 16 October. Having left the islands of Santa María de la Concepción at about midday for Fernandina, which appeared very large in the west, I sailed for the rest of the day in a calm and could not reach it in time to anchor for the water was not clear enough for me to see bottom and one has to take great care not to lose the anchors. So I lay off all that night and in the morning saw a village off which I anchored. This was the native village of the man I had found on the previous day with his canoe in mid-channel. He had given such a good account of us that canoes swarmed round the ship all that night. They brought us water and something of all they had. I ordered presents to be given to all of them, that is to say, strings of ten or a dozen small glass beads and some brass clappers of a kind that are worth a maravedi each in Castile and leather tags, all of which they value very highly, and when they came aboard I had them given molasses to eat. And afterwards at nine in the morning I sent a ship's boat ashore for water and they most gladly showed our men where it could be found and they themselves carried the full casks back to the boat. They were delighted to give us pleasure.

This island is very large and I decided to sail round it because as I understand, in it or near it, there is a goldfield. The island is eight leagues west of Santa María and from the cape where I touched, the coast runs north-north-west and south-south-east; I saw quite twenty leagues of it and it still continued. As I write this I have set sail with a south wind intending to push on round the island until I come to Samoet, which is the island or city where the gold is, for all who have come aboard the ship have said so. Both the people of San Salvador and Santa María told us so.

The people here are like the people of those islands; both in language and customs, though here they seem to me rather more civilized, more tractable and more intelligent, for I see they are better able to bargain for the cotton and other trifles which they have brought to the ship than were the other peoples. And I saw on this island cotton cloths made like shawls. The people are more friendly and the women wear a small piece of cloth in front which just hides their private parts.

This island is very green, flat and fertile and I have no doubt that they sow and reap Indian corn and other crops throughout the year. . . .

They have no religion and I think that they would be very quickly Christianized, for they have a very ready understanding. . . .

Wednesday, 17 October. At midday I set sail from the village off which I had anchored and where I had landed and taken water to make a circuit of this island of Fernandina. The wind was southwest and south. It was my intention to follow the coast of this island from where I was to the southeast, since it runs as a whole from north-north-west to south-south-east. I wanted to take my course to the south-south-east, because all the Indians whom I have aboard and others from whom I inquired tell me that southwards from here lies the island they call Samoet, where the gold is. Martin Alonso Pinzón, captain of the *Pinta*, in which I had placed three of these Indians, came to me and said that one of them had very explicitly given him to understand that the island could be rounded more quickly in a north-north-westerly direction.

I saw that the wind would not help me on the course I wished to steer and that it favored the other course, so I steered north-north-west, and when I was about two leagues from the island's cape [Long Island] I saw a marvelous harbor with an entrance, or rather two entrances, since there is an islet in the middle. Both entrances are very narrow, but it would have been large enough to provide anchorage for a hundred ships if it had been deep and free of rocks and the entrance channels had been deep also. I thought fit to examine it closely and take soundings; therefore I anchored outside and went in with all the ships' boats and we found that it was shallow. When I first saw it I thought it was the mouth of a river, so I had ordered casks to be brought to take water. On land I saw eight or ten men who quickly came up to us and pointed to a nearby village, where I sent my men for water, which they took, some going armed and others carrying the casks. As the village was some distance away I had to remain there for two hours.

During that time I walked among the trees, which were the loveliest sight I had yet seen. They were green as those of Andalusia in the month of May. But all these trees are as different from ours as day from night and so are the fruit and plants and stones, and everything else. It is true that some trees were of species that can be found in Castile, yet there was a great difference; but there are many other varieties which no one could say are like those of Castile or could compare with them. The people were all of the same kind as those already described; their condition was the same; they were naked and of the same height. They gave whatever they possessed for whatever we gave them and here I saw some ships' boys exchanging small bits of broken crockery or glass for spears.

The men who had gone for water told me that they had entered their houses and that they were very clean and well swept and that their blankets are like cotton nets. These houses are like large tents. They are high and have good chimneys. But of all the villages I saw none consisted of more than a dozen or fifteen houses. Here they found that married women wear cotton drawers, but girls do not, until they reach the age of eighteen. Here there were mastiffs and small dogs and here they met one

man who wore in his nose a piece of gold about half the size of a *castellano*[17] on which they saw letters. I was angry with them because they had not bargained for it and given as much as they were asked, so that we could examine it and see where the coin came from. They answered that they did not dare to bargain for it.

After taking the water I returned to the ship, raised sail and followed a north-westerly course along the shore to the point where the coast turns east-west. Later all the Indians insisted that this island was smaller than Samoet and that it would be better to turn back in order to reach that island sooner. Then the wind fell and began to blow west-north-west, which was unfavorable to the course we had been following. I therefore turned back and sailed all that night in an east-south-easterly direction, sometimes due east and sometimes southeast in order to keep clear of land, because the clouds were very thick and the weather very heavy. The wind was slight and I could not make land to anchor. In the night heavy rain fell from after midnight almost till daybreak and it is still cloudy with more rain to come.

We are now at the southeastern tip of the island, where I hope to anchor until the weather clears, and I can see the other islands to which I am going. It has rained practically every day since I have been in these Indies. Your highnesses must believe me that these islands are the most fertile, and temperate and flat and good in the whole world.

Suggested Sources:

William D. Phillips and Carla Rahn Phillips, *The Worlds of Christopher Columbus* (New York: Cambridge University Press, 1992), places Columbus in his time. Alfred W. Crosby outlines the ecological transformations caused by pathogens, European livestock, and American food crops in *Columbian Exchange: Biological and Cultural Consequences of 1492* (Westport, CT: Greenwood, 1972). Neil L. Whitehead writes about Native Peoples in the Caribbean and their

---

[17]A small coin.

reaction to Spanish colonization. See Neil L. Whitehead, "The Crises and Transformations of Invaded Societies: The Caribbean (1492–1580)," in *The Cambridge History of the Native Peoples of the Americas*, ed. Frank Salomon and Stuart B. Schwartz (Cambridge: Cambridge University Press, 1999), vol. 3, part 1, 864–903.

Sources written in the period also provide valuable insights. Ramón Pané compiled the earliest ethnographic account of Caribbean peoples' lives and religion in *An Account of the Antiquities of the Indians: Chronicles of the New World Encounter* (Durham, NC: Duke University Press, 1999). Additional letters and other documents related to Columbus are collected in Geoffrey Symcox and Blair Sullivan, *Christopher Columbus and the Enterprise of the Indies: A Brief History with Documents* (Boston: Bedford/St. Martin's, 2005). Alvaro Nuñez Cabeza de Vaca recorded his shipwreck in Florida and his travels among indigenous groups until reaching northern Mexico in *The Narrative of Alvar Nuñez Cabeza de Vaca*, trans. Fanny Bandelier (Barre, MA: The Imprint Society, 1972). For a film re-creation, see *Cabeza de Vaca*, dir. Nicolás Echevarria (Mexico/Spain: Producciones Iguana and Instituto Mexicano de Cinematografía, 1993). The fictional film *Jerico* follows a Spanish missionary in this early period as he abandons a raiding party and joins a tribe. See *Jerico*, dir. Luis Alberto Lamata (Venezuela: Bolivar Films, 1988).

Chapter 2

Politics, Gender, and the Conquest of Mexico

Leo J. Garofalo, Connecticut College

In sixteenth-century Mexico, everyone closely involved with the conquest knew that, along with the conquistador Hernán Cortés, the indigenous woman *doña* Marina played one of the most important roles in ending *Aztec* domination. Paradoxically she is absent from almost all accounts of the conquest, appearing in less than six pages total. The most Cortés said of her was to describe her as ". . . the interpreter . . ., Marina, who traveled always in my company after she had been given me as a present with twenty other women."[1] Yet, the image of her translating or mediating between the Spanish and their indigenous allies and foes appears repeatedly in both Mesoamerican and European illustrations of the

---

[1] Hernán Cortés, *Letters from Mexico*, trans. and ed. Anthony Pagdon (New Haven, CT: Yale University Press, 1986), 376.

conquest of New Spain. In short, *doña* Marina was central to the *Aztec* defeat, yet we know so little about her. The mystery shrouding *doña* Marina is heightened by the complex situation in which she found herself—as conquistador, concubine, and slave! The selection in this chapter helps reveal who *doña* Marina was and how she shaped the dramatic defeat of the *Aztec* overlords. In that drama, she became a principal protagonist alongside commanders like Hernán Cortés, numerous Indian allies, and common Spanish soldiers like Bernal Díaz, who wrote this alternative account of the conquest.

The invasion and defeat of the *Aztec* Empire in 1519–1521 initiated a shift in the Spanish conquest and colonization away from the Caribbean to the American mainlands and brought many millions of Native Peoples under the control of the Spanish king, Charles V, and his successors. The mainland invasions constituted a major shift toward huge royal profits from colonial tribute and mining, the imposition of European rule over large and sophisticated indigenous societies, and the transformation of many imported Hispanic ways and institutions. This new phase of Spanish colonialism began in Mexico with *doña* Marina and Cortés.

After sailing from Cuba in command of an *entrada* (raiding, exploring, and conquering mission), the conquistador Hernán Cortés finally landed his force near present-day Veracruz in Mexico and formed his first alliances with local non-*Aztec* populations against the *Aztec* Empire. The Caribbean islands that Cortés left behind in 1519 served as the springboard for launching the various campaigns that constituted the Spanish invasion and conquest of North and South America (Florida, Mexico, Panama, Venezuela and Colombia, and Peru). Spaniards from the islands hoped to find the wealth and success that had eluded colonizers in the Greater Antilles starting with Columbus. They sought large indigenous labor forces and productive gold and silver mines. The Spanish conquistadores who later followed Cortés's lead came to realize that successful colonization lay in permanent settlement in Central and South America; and they could only live as nobles if they defeated and then preserved and learned to exploit large, wealthy, sedentary, agricultural societies.

As Cortés and his raiders became aware of the *Aztec* Empire's existence, they realized that it held the riches and highly organized populace that they sought. They also learned that ethnic divisions within the empire constituted a key vulnerability. In the late 1420s, the Mexica people of the *Aztec* city-state *Tenochtitlán*-Tlateloco formed the Triple Alliance with two other Nahua-speaking city-states, and *Aztec* expansion began, conquering and incorporating other non-*Aztec* ethnic groups in Mexico's central highlands and beyond. The *Aztecs* demanded annual tribute and trade, but they allowed local rulers and deities to remain in place, preferring to rule indirectly. They placed garrisons in only the most rebellious of provinces.[2] When the Spanish arrived, the *Aztec* Empire was actively engaged in incorporating new territories and stamping out stubborn resistance in enclaves.[3] Thus, the multiethnic nature of the *Aztec* Empire and its recent expansion presented Cortés, and whomever could help him negotiate, an opportunity to forge political alliances against *Aztec* power. The Spanish found whole regions of non-Mexica ethnic groups committed to rolling back imperial *Aztec* expansion. Chapter 4 describes how indigenous groups and individuals allied with the Spanish carried the resulting privileges with them to other parts of Mesoamerica and claimed them throughout the colonial period.

The Spanish raiders understood and embraced the Mesoamerican political practices of gaining power and dominance in a region by combining diplomatic negotiation and intrigue with fierce fighting. Cortés inserted his small band of fighters into Mesoamerican politics and actively engaged local leaders by drawing on compatible Spanish and indigenous gender ideologies that established hierarchies of male power. For instance, the invaders understood and embraced the exchange of gifts and tribute that

---

[2]The Mendoza Codex contains *Aztec* Emperor Montezuma's detailed tribute rolls. Frances F. Berdan and Patricia Rieff Anawalt, eds., *The Codex Mendoza* (Berkeley: University of California Press, 1992.), vols. 1–4.

[3]The *Aztec* Empire offers an illuminating parallel with the youthful *Inca* Empire, which began its expansion in the 1440s by also stitching together many different ethnic groups and ruling them indirectly.

accompanied these negotiations and capitulations, including receiving and exploiting servants and enslaved men and women, who labored as cooks, porters, concubines, interpreters, guides, and even fighters. The most famous of the female slaves was Marina/Malintzin/Malinche, who rose to prominence as Cortés's capable translator and concubine. With Cortés, she bore a *mestizo* son, Martín, and later a daughter with the Spanish husband, Juan Jaramillo, Cortés assigned her. She outlived the conquest and established a noble and wealthy line of descendents independent of Cortés and his Spanish family.

Doña Marina's actions and her historical role in the Spanish victory outlived the conquest and continue to inspire debate. The honorific title *doña* in Spanish marked her elite status and association with

Doña Marina translates and mediates between *Aztec* emissaries and the Spanish conquistador Hernán Cortés and his army. Who is shown as present at these important diplomatic moments? How is *doña* Marina portrayed?

Source: Archivo General de la Nación, Mexico.

Cortés and eventual ownership of wealthy *encomiendas*. Malintzin was the *Nahuatl* version of her Spanish name, *doña* Marina. The Spanish corruption of Malintzin, La Malinche, eventually became a way to lament and denigrate her historical role as "a sell out to foreigners." Born into a household of Nahua nobles in a transitional zone between the *Nahuatl* speakers of central Mexico and the *Maya* speakers of the Yucatán, *doña* Marina apparently knew both *Maya* and *Nahuatl*, particularly the courtly speech required of diplomatic work. By working with Jerónimo de Aguilar, a Spaniard marooned for many years among the *Maya* on the Yucatán, *doña* Marina could help the Spanish communicate with any group that had *Nahuatl* speakers. After exploring and raiding along the coasts of the Yucatán and Tabasco to the south, Cortés arrived and landed in the rich Totonacapan agricultural territory in central Veracruz. With a capital at Cempoala, the Totonacs dominated this territory, but they had recently been brought under *Aztec* subjugation. It was here that *doña* Marina's interpreting and even diplomatic skills became fully evident, and the Spanish relied heavily on her as they pushed inland all the way to the *Aztec's* island capital.

Bernal Díaz, who chronicled his adventures with Cortés many decades later, provides us with our most lengthy description of *doña* Marina. Díaz attempted to set straight the record of the conquest of Mexico. With some justification, Díaz felt that Cortés and his official chronicler purposefully excluded *doña* Marina and the Spaniards' indigenous allies from the account. Furthermore, the old conquistador argued that Cortés and the chroniclers minimized the contributions and sacrifices of many other soldiers like himself in order to keep the best *encomiendas* and other rewards for Cortés's inner circle of allies and kinsmen. Long after the conquest and even today, *doña* Marina is often characterized as "La Malinche," the woman traitor who made possible the defeat of a great American empire by European outsiders and who bore the *mestizo* son of Cortés.[4] As readers follow the beginning of the Spaniards' inland

---

[4]*Source:* Frances Karttunen, "Rethinking Malinche," in *Indian Women of Early Mexico,* ed. Susan Schroeder, Stephine Wood, and Robert Hascket (Norman: University of Oklahoma Press, 1997), 299.

trek to the *Aztec* capital *Tenochtitlán*, judge what roles each of these people played in the surprising conquest of the spectacularly wealthy *Aztec* civilization. This account also reminds historians that individuals and individual campaigns built the Iberian empires by carving out space within an already diverse and populous indigenous world. Individuals like *doña* Marina bridged language and cultural gaps to put *Aztec* empire builders in direct contact—and conflict—with Spanish empire builders, initiating a new chapter in Latin American and world history.

Questions to Consider:

1. What parts of the story appear most reliable? What parts seem distorted by the conquistador Díaz, or simply recounted to conform to a preconceived model or storyline known to his intended Spanish audience?

2. What model of conquest was provided by the *Aztec's* defeat? What strategy developed to confront a more powerful imperial adversary? How and why was gender a crucial part of that strategy?

3. What does the account reveal about politics—struggles over power and leadership? Who held authority in both Spanish and indigenous societies? How did they exercise that power?

4. What does Díaz tell readers about the label of treachery associated with *doña* Marina? What choices faced *doña* Marina? How would readers today characterize her life and actions?

5. Why is she remembered so critically?

A Conquistador Recounts the Beginning of the Campaign to Defeat the Aztec Empire, 1519–1521[5]

Doña Marina's Story

Before speaking of the great Montezuma, and of the famous city of Mexico and the Mexicans, I should like to give an account of *Doña* Marina, who had been a great lady and a *cacique* over towns and vassals since her childhood.

Her father and mother were lords and *caciques* of a town called Paynala, which had other towns subject to it, and lay about twenty-four miles from the town of Coatzacoalcos. Her father died while she was still very young, and her mother married another *cacique*, a young man, to whom she bore a son. The mother and father seemed to have been very fond of this son, for they agreed that he should succeed to the caciqueship when they were dead. To avoid any impediment, they gave *Doña* Marina to some Indians from Xicalango, and this they did by night in order to be unobserved. They then spread the report that the child had died; and as the daughter of one of their Indian slaves happened to die at this time, they gave it out that this was their daughter the heiress.

The Indians of Xicalango gave the child to the people of Tabasco, and the Tabascans gave her to Cortés. I myself knew her mother and her half-brother, who was then a man and ruled the town jointly with his mother, since the old lady's second husband had died. After they became Christians, the mother was called Marta and the son Lázaro. All this I know very well, because in the year 1523, after the conquest of Mexico and the other provinces and at the time of Cristobal de Olid's revolt in Honduras, I passed through the place with Cortés, and the majority of the inhabitants accompanied him also. As *Doña* Marina had proved such an excellent person, and a good interpreter in all the wars of New Spain, Tlaxcala, and Mexico—as I shall relate hereafter—Cortés always took her with him. During the expedition she married a gentleman called Juan Jaramillo at the town of Orizaba. *Doña* Marina was a person of great importance, and was obeyed without question by all the Indians of New Spain. And while Cortés was in the town of Coatzacoalcos, he

[5]*Source:* Bernal Díaz del Castillo, *The Conquest of New Spain*, trans. J. M. Cohen (New York: Penguin Books, 1963), 85–87, 88–89, 98–99, 107–109, 110–112.

summoned all the *caciques* of the province in order to address them on the subject of our holy religion, and the good way in which they had been treated; and *Doña* Marina's mother and her half-brother Lazaro were among those who came. *Doña* Marina had told me some time before that she belonged to this province, and that she was the mistress of vassals, and both Cortés and the interpreter Aguilar knew it well. Thus it was that mother, son, and daughter came together, and it was easy enough to see from the strong resemblance between them that *Doña* Marina and the old lady were related. Both she and her son were very much afraid of *Doña* Marina; they feared that she had sent for them to put them to death, and they wept.

When *Doña* Marina saw her mother and half-brother in tears she comforted them, saying that they need have no fear. She told her mother that when they had handed her over to the men from Xicalango, they had not known what they were doing. She pardoned the old woman, and gave them many golden jewels and some clothes. Then she sent them back to their town, saying that God had been very gracious to her in freeing her from the worship of idols and making her a Christian, and giving her a son by her lord and master Cortés, also in marrying her to such a gentleman as her husband Juan Jaramillo. Even if they were to make her mistress of all the provinces of New Spain, she said, she would refuse the honor, for she would rather serve her husband and Cortés than anything else in the world. What I have related I know for certain and swear to. The whole story seems very much like that of Joseph and his brethren in Egypt, when the Egyptians came into his power over the wheat.[6]

To return to my subject, *Doña* Marina knew the language of Coatzacoalcos, which is that of Mexico, and she knew the Tabascan language also. This language is common to Tabasco and Yucatan, and Jeronimo de Aguilar spoke it also. These two understood one another well, and Aguilar translated into Castilian for Cortés.

This was the great beginning of our conquests, and thus, praise be to God, all things prospered with us. I have made a point of telling this story, because without *Doña* Marina we could not have understood the language of New Spain and Mexico. . . .

A Pause on the Coast

On Holy Thursday 1519 we arrived with all the fleet at the port of San Juan de Ulua. Knowing the place well from his previous visit under Juan de Grijalva, the pilot Alaminos at once ordered the vessels to anchor where they would be safe from the northerly gales. The royal standards and pennants were raised on the flagship, and within half an hour of our anchoring two large canoes or pirogues came out to us full of Mexican Indians. Seeing the large ship with its standards flying, they knew that it was there they must go to speak with the Captain. So they made straight for the flagship, went aboard and asked who was the *tatuan*, which in their language means the master. *Doña* Marina, who understood them, pointed him out; and the Indians paid Cortés great marks of respect in their fashion. They said that their lord, a servant of the great **Montezuma**, had sent them to find out what kind of men we were and what we were seeking, also to say that if we required anything for ourselves or our ships, we were to tell them and they would supply it.

Cortés thanked them through our interpreters, and ordered that they should be given food wine, and some blue beads. After they had drunk the wine he told them that he had come to visit and trade with them, and that they should think of our coming to their country as fortunate rather than troublesome. The messengers went ashore very contented, and next day, which was Good Friday, we disembarked with our horses and guns on some sand hills, which were quite high. For there was no level land, nothing but sand dunes; and the artilleryman Mesa placed his guns on them in what seemed to him the best positions. Then we set up an altar, at which mass was said at once, and built huts and shelters for Cortés and his captains. Our three hundred soldiers then brought wood, and we made huts for ourselves. We put the horses where they would be safe, and in this way we spent Good Friday.

---

[6]Biblical reference to the generosity that the enslaved Joseph showed his former persecutors when during a famine they turned to him for food.

On Saturday, which was Easter Eve, many Indians arrived who had been sent by a *cacique* called Pitalpitoque, whom we afterwards named Ovandillo and who was one of *Montezuma*'s governors.[7] They brought axes, and dressed wood for Cortés's hut and the others near it, which they covered with large cloths on account of the sun. For since it was Lent, the heat was very great. They brought fowls and maize-cakes and plums, which were then in season, and also, I think, some gold jewels; all of which they presented to Cortés saying that next day a governor would come and bring more provisions. Cortés thanked them warmly, and ordered that they should be given certain things in exchange, with which they went away well pleased.

Next day, Easter Sunday, the governor of whom they had spoken arrived. His name was Tendile, a man of affairs, and he brought with him Pitalpitoque, who was also an important person among them. They were followed by many Indians with presents of fowls and vegetables, whom Tendile commanded to stand a little aside on a hillock, while according to their custom he bowed humbly three times, first to Cortés and then to all the other soldiers standing nearby. . . .

[*Cortés and his band expected an attack when they awoke one morning to discover that the people and ambassadors Montezuma had sent to care for them had withdrawn at night.*]

When we heard the news we thought they meant war, and put ourselves very much on the alert. One day, as I and another soldier were posted on some sand dunes keeping a lookout, we saw five Indians coming along the beach, and so as to raise no alarm in the camp over so slight a matter allowed them to approach. They came up to us with smiles on their faces, paid us the usual respects, and asked us by signs to take them to the camp. I told my companion to stay on guard, and said I would go with them, for my feet were not as heavy as they are now that I am old. And when we came to Cortés they bowed low to him and said: 'Lope luzio, lope luzio,' which in their Totonac language means 'Prince and great lord.' The men had great holes in their lower lips, in which some carried stone disks spotted with blue, and others thin sheets of gold. They also had great holes in their ears, in which they had inserted disks of stone or gold; and they were very different in their dress and speech from the Mexicans who had been staying with us. Our interpreters did not understand these words 'Lope luzio;' and *Doña* Marina inquired in Mexican if there were no Nahuatlatos—that is to say interpreters of the Mexican language—among them. Two of the five answered yes, that they understood it, and bade us welcome, saying that their chief had sent them to inquire who we were, and tell us that he would be glad to be of service to such valiant men. For it appears that they knew about our deeds at Tabasco and Champoton [Spanish military victories in skirmishes]. They added that they would have come to see us before, but for their fear of the people of Culua who had been with us,[8] but that they knew these men had run off home three days before. As this conversation went on, Cortés learned that *Montezuma* had opponents and enemies, which greatly delighted him. After flattering these five messengers, Cortés dismissed them with presents, and a message to their *cacique* that he would very soon pay him a visit. From this time on we called these Indians the lope luzios. . . .

The Stay at Cempoala

. . . Our mounted scouts came to a great square with courtyards where they had prepared our lodgings, which appeared to have been lime-coated and burnished during the last few days. The Indians are so skillful at these arts that one of the horsemen took the shining whiteness for silver, and came galloping back to tell Cortés that our quarters had silver walls. *Doña* Marina and Aguilar said that it must be plaster, and we laughed at his excitement. Indeed we reminded him ever afterwards that anything white looked to him like silver. But enough of this. When we came to the buildings, this fat *cacique* came out to receive us in the courtyard. He was so fat that I must call him the fat *cacique*. He made a deep bow to

---

[7]Pitalpitoque was also the ambassador sent to meet the 1518 exploring and trading expedition commanded by Juan de Grijalva on behalf of Cuba's governor.

[8]The porters and other indigenous workers from an *Aztec* subject town assigned to support the Spanish and now ordered to abandon them.

Cortés and perfumed him [with incense] as is their custom, and Cortés embraced him. After leading us into our fine, large quarters, which held us all, they gave us food and brought us some baskets of plums, which were very plentiful at that season, also some of their maize-cakes. As we were hungry, and had not seen so much food for a long time, we called the town Villa Viciosa.[9] Others named it Seville.

Cortés gave orders that none of the soldiers should leave the square or annoy the inhabitants; and when the fat *cacique* learned that we had finished eating, he sent to tell Cortés that he wished to pay him a visit. He came with a great number of Indian dignitaries, all wearing large gold lip-rings and rich cloaks. Cortés also left his quarters to receive him, and greeted him with a great show of affection and flattery. Then the fat *cacique* ordered a present be brought of golden jewelry and cloth; and although it was small and of not great value, he said to Cortés: 'Lope luzio lope luzio! Please accept this; if I had more I would give it to you.' I have already explained that in the Totonac language lope luzio means lord of great lords.

Cortés replied through our interpreters that he would repay this gift in services, and if the *cacique* would tell him what he wanted it should be done for him, since we were the vassals of the Emperor Charles, a very great prince who ruled over many kingdoms and countries and had sent us to redress grievances, to punish evildoers, and to command that human sacrifices should cease. And he explained many things concerning our holy religion. On hearing this, the fat *cacique* heaved a deep sigh and broke into bitter complaints against the great *Montezuma* and his governors, saying that the Mexican prince had recently brought him into subjection, had taken away all his golden jewelry, and so grievously oppressed him and his people that they could do nothing except obey him, since he was lord over many cities and countries, and ruler over countless vassals and armies of warriors.

As Cortés knew that he could not then attend to their complaint, he answered that he would see their wrongs set right, but that he was now on the way to visit his acales—which is the Indian word for ships—and to take up residence in the town of Quiahuitzlan, and that as soon as he was settled there he would give the matter greater consideration. To this the fat *cacique* replied that he was quite satisfied.

Next morning we left Cempoala, and over four hundred Indian porters, here called *tamemes*, were awaiting our orders. Each can carry fifty pounds on his back and march fifteen miles with it. We rejoiced at the sight of so many porters, since hitherto those of us who had not brought servants from Cuba had had to carry our knapsacks on our backs. And only six or seven Cubans [enslaved Native People from Cuba] had come with the fleet, not the great number that Gomara states. *Doña* Marina and Aguilar told us that in time of peace the chiefs in these parts are compelled to provide tamemes to carry baggage as a matter of course, and from this time on, wherever we went we asked for Indians to carry our loads.

. . . When [the fat *cacique*] arrived he joined the *cacique* and the principal men of that town in their complaints against *Montezuma*. In speaking of his great strength, they gave vent to such tears and sighs that Cortés and the rest of us were moved to pity. Before describing the way they had been brought to subjection, they told us that every year many of their sons and daughters were demanded of them for sacrifices, and others for service in the houses and plantations of their conquerors. And they made other complaints; so many that I no longer remember them. They said that if their wives and daughters were handsome, *Montezuma*'s tax-gathers took them away and raped them, and that they did this in all thirty villages in which the Totonac language was spoken. . . .

While these conversations were going on five Indians came in great haste from the town to tell the *caciques* who were talking to Cortés that five of *Montezuma*'s Mexican tax-gathers had just arrived. The *caciques* turned pale at the news. Trembling with fear, they left Cortés and went off to receive the Mexicans. Very quickly they decorated a room with flowers, cooked them some food, and made them quantities of chocolate, which is the best of their drinks.

When the five Mexicans entered the town, they came to the square where the *caciques*' houses and our quarters were, and passed us by with cocksure pride, speaking not a word to Cortés or anyone else they saw. They wore richly embroidered cloaks and loincloths—for they wore loincloths at that time—and

---

[9]Town of abundance.

shining hair that was gathered up and seemed tied to their heads. Each one was smelling the roses he carried, and each had a crooked staff in his hand. Their Indian servants carried fly-whisks, and they were accompanied by the *caciques* of the other Totonac towns, who did not leave them until they had shown them to their lodgings and given them a meal.

As soon as they had dined, the tax-gathers sent for the fat *cacique* and the other chiefs and scolded them for having entertained us in their villages, since now they would have to meet and deal with us, which would not please their lord *Montezuma*. For without his permission and instructions they should neither have received us or given us golden jewels. They continued to reproach the fat *cacique* and his nobles for their actions, and ordered them to provide twenty Indians, male and female, as a peace offering to their gods for the wrong that had been done.

At this point Cortés asked our interpreters why the arrival of these Indians had so agitated the *caciques*, and who they were; and *doña* Marina, who understood perfectly, explained what was happening. As soon as Cortés understood what the *caciques* were saying, he reminded them that, as he had already explained, our lord the King had sent him to chastise evildoers and prevent sacrifices and robbery. He ordered them therefore to arrest the tax-gatherers for having made such a demand, and to hold them prisoners until their lord *Montezuma* was informed of the reason: namely that they had come to rob the Totonacs, to enslave their wives and children, and to do other violence.

When the *caciques* heard this they were appalled at his daring. To order them to manhandle *Montezuma*'s messengers! They were far too frightened. They dared not do it. But Cortés insisted that they must arrest them at once; and they obeyed him. They secured them with long poles and collars, as is their custom, so that they could not escape, and they beat one of them who refused to be bound. Furthermore, Cortés ordered all the *caciques* cease paying tribute and obedience to *Montezuma*, and to proclaim their refusal in all the towns of their friends and allies, also to announce that if tax-gatherers came to any other towns he must be informed, and would send for them. So the news spread throughout the province. For the fat *cacique* immediately sent messengers to proclaim it, and the chiefs who had

accompanied the tax-gatherers scattered immediately after the arrest, each to his town, to convey the order and give an account of what had happened. . . .

After these events the *caciques* of this village and of Cempoala, and all the Totonac dignitaries who had assembled, asked Cortés what was to be done, for all the forces of Mexico and of the great *Montezuma* would descend upon them, and they could not possibly escape death and destruction.

Cortés replied with an almost cheerful smile that he and his brothers who were with him would defend them and kill anyone who tried to harm them; and the *caciques* and their villagers one and all promised to stand by us, to obey any orders we might give them, and to join their forces with ours against *Montezuma* and all his allies. Then in the presence of Diego de Godoy the Notary they took the oath of obedience to his Majesty, and sent messengers to all the other towns in the province to relate what had happened. As they now paid no more tribute and the tax-gathers had disappeared, they could not contain their delight at having thrown off the tyranny of the Mexicans.

Suggested Sources:

In addition to the chapter by Frances Karttunen mentioned in the footnotes, more can be learned about Indian women's experience of the conquest and early colonial rule in Camilla Townsend's *Malintzin's Choices: An Indian Woman in the Conquest of Mexico* (Albuquerque: University of New Mexico Press, 2006); and Susan Schroeder, Stephanie Wood, and Robert Haskett, eds., *Indian Women of Early Mexico* (Norman: University of Oklahoma Press, 1997). As a bridge between two hostile societies, Marina/Malintzin/Malinche continues to stir passions in both Mexico and the United States. The film *Indigenous Always* follows this controversy. See *Indigenous Always: The Legend of la Malinche and the Conquest of Mexico,* dir. Dean Banda (Shorewood, WI: Wisconsin Public Television and Bandana Productions, 2000 [60 min.]). Inga Clendinnen reconstructs the specific roles of men and women in Aztec society in *Aztecs: An Interpretation* (Cambridge: Cambridge University Press, 1995). Karen Vieira Powers examines pre-Hispanic gender roles, colonial sexuality, and women's labor under Spanish rule in *Women in the Crucible of Conquest: The Gendered Genesis of Spanish American Society, 1500–1600* (Albuquerque: University of New Mexico Press, 2005).

Sixteenth-century fray Bernardino de Sahagún's and his Nahua colleagues included *Doña* Marina in the frontispiece and in six other illustrations when they wrote about the Spanish conquest. See Bernardino de Sahagún, *Florentine Codex: History of the Things of New Spain*, vols. 1–12, trans. and ed. Arthur J. O. Anderson and Charles E. Dibble (Salt Lake City: University of Utah Press, 1950–1982). Conquistadors like Cortés and Díaz wrote influential accounts of the conquest. See Hernán Cortés, *Letters from Mexico*, trans. and ed. Anthony Pagdon (New Haven, CT: Yale University Press, 1986); and

Bernal Díaz del Castillo, *The Conquest of New Spain*, trans. J. M. Cohen (New York: Penguin Books, 1963). Díaz challenged the official Spanish account written by Francisco López de Gómara (1511–1564) in *Cortés: The Life of the Conqueror by His Secretary*, trans. and ed. Lesley Byrd Simpson (Berkeley: University of California Press, 1964). For a compilation of indigenous elites' view of the Spanish invasion, see *The Broken Spears: The Aztec Account of the Conquest of Mexico*, trans. and ed. Miguel Leon-Portilla (Boston: Beacon Press, 1966). The Mexican feature film *La Otra Conquista* tells this same story featuring a noble Aztec scribe and a *doña*-Marina-like Aztec noble woman. See *La Otra Conquista* [The Other Conquest], dir. Salvador Carrasco (Mexico, 1998 [105 min.]).

Chapter 3

Afro-Iberian Sailors, Soldiers, Traders, and Thieves on the Spanish Main

Leo J. Garofalo, Connecticut College

The African Diaspora—the movement of Africans to the Americas—involved much more than bringing slaves to labor on plantations of the New World. The African experience in Spanish and Portuguese America was quite varied even though a majority labored in plantation colonies and came directly from Africa through the horrendous Middle Passage or descended from those who did. The diversity within the Diaspora appears in the jobs filled in the Spanish Caribbean and circum-Caribbean (called the Spanish Main) by Africans from Europe. These Afro-Iberians arrived both as slaves and as free men and women. This Afro-Iberian experience included sailors, soldiers, traders, and thieves, among others.

On both sides of the Atlantic, Africans shaped exploration and invasion, alongside Europeans and indigenous people. Long before Columbus crossed the Atlantic, Portuguese traders brought slaves and slave-produced sugar to Europe, introducing a western and central African population into Iberian cities from 1441 forward. Cities like Seville and Lisbon became Europe's largest slave markets, and they later equipped, manned, and loaded and unloaded ships sailing between Europe and the Americas. In the Americas, Africans and European-born Africans (Afro-Iberians) played a role in every part of the European enterprise—from the voyages and wars of conquest to the building of cities and markets and, eventually, to the American struggles to end colonial rule in the eighteenth and nineteenth centuries.

The initial search for trade goods like gold and ivory and sea routes to Asia ignited a European interest in island colonies and mainland enclaves along Africa's coasts. By the mid-1400s, Portuguese traders brought African people from south of the Sahara Desert to Portugal for sale as slaves, giving the Portuguese Crown a one-fifth cut of the profits (the royal fifth became customary among both the Portuguese and the Spanish). From Portugal, slave traders transported African slaves to Spain, where slave markets already existed for the buying and selling of Muslim, *morisco* (Christianized Iberian Muslims), and Slavic slaves. In Iberia, African slaves and their free descendants found places in every part of Iberian economic activity, working as servants, as market sellers, as farmers, in artisans' shops, and as the sailors and soldiers that allowed Spain and Portugal to dominate world trade for two centuries. In Portugal and Castile's coastal cities, Africans and Afro-Iberians sometimes comprised as much as 10 percent of the population.

The selections in this chapter highlight the centrality yet precariousness of Afro-Iberians' participation in Iberia's expansion. Of course, one will never

Spanish accounts of the conquests made many individuals and groups invisible. Indigenous warriors and *Doña Marina* are absent. Cortés leads the way. Not far behind is a black man without armor, carrying a spear and leading a horse. Was the black man a slave (a servant and somebody's property) or a black conquistador (making the mission possible and deserving reward)? How does he compare to the rest of the Spanish party? Why might have the friar Diego Durán included this black man or boy in his *History of the Indians* from which the illustration is taken?

Source: Meeting of Cortez and Montezuma. Miniature from the "History of the Indians" by Diego Durán, fol. 208v. 1579. Biblioteca Nacional, Madrid. Bridgeman-Giraudon / Art Resource, NY.

know about the lives and experiences of most African people crossing back and forth on the Atlantic; however, by piecing together the many small fragments that remain, historians can find and record individual lives. This reconstruction often depends on using infuriatingly short references from the very administrative documents—bureaucratic paperwork—that the Spanish used to try and regulate the movement of people and govern their actions. The official goal was not to leave a record of African endeavor, but historians can begin to understand the broader spectrum of those endeavors by looking at royal orders, lists of crews, court cases, and petitions involving property and travel.

This chapter includes different kinds of documents: a royal order, an inspection of a ship's crew, a will, and a criminal case containing various kinds of testimony. The first document is a 1539 royal order sent to the master pilots responsible for testing and licensing other pilots. Although Afro-Iberian and even African American pilots, quartermasters, and other officers could be found on Spanish and

Portuguese ships, Africans were more liberally represented among the sailors, *grumetes* (lower-ranked sailors), and cabin boys below them. The second document, therefore, moves down the chain of command aboard a vessel to a royal official's list of the sailors of all ranks he found onboard a ship anchored in Seville's river port during a 1632 inspection. The description of the crew and their identifying physical characteristics he compiled offer some of the very few—although limited and repetitive—records of actual sailors and soldiers aboard these vessels. For imperial bureaucrats in an era before photography, these descriptions served the purpose of legally establishing identity to help control the flow of people from the Americas and to prevent the transport of slaves to the Americas without paying royal taxes. In addition, blacks had to prove their freedom with letters of *manumission* and witnesses when embarking on any journey. The third document, a 1610 will dictated in Havana, reveals a black sailor's origins in Europe and his connections to the Church, his artisan-class neighborhood, and his family. Not all of a sailor's life was spent at sea; the long stints in harbor in the Americas, in Iberia, or in Africa could represent a financial hardship and an opportunity to engage in petty commerce for crews. Cartagena de Indias (the Colombian port city) was a major destination for transatlantic fleets and slave shipments. In 1608, a group of Afro-Iberian sailors in Cartagena was charged with stealing, or was the group simply participating in the small-scale buying and selling typical of sailors when in port?

Each of these individuals and their stories help illustrate the diversity of people, and the motives, that built the transatlantic links and networks that made seaborne empires possible. Commerce depended on shipping and defending those ships and the ports against pirates and privateers, especially against the British and Dutch. Without sailors and soldiers, Spain and Portugal could never have conquered, held, and colonized distant lands in the Americas, Africa, and Asia. How an empire became a reality and operated at the point where boots and feet hit the decks of ships and goods changed hands in the marketplaces appears in these sources.

Questions to Consider:

1. What were the Crown's interests in the Americas and in Afro-Iberians? What roles did Afro-Iberians play in the colonial project?
2. Explain the attitudes toward Afro-Iberians shown by people exercising different kinds of authority in these documents.
3. Which documents most directly capture Afro-Iberians' own voices? What do readers learn from an indirect source or one that distorts the subject? Identify different levels of status among Afro-Iberians and other Africans.
4. How do different sources reconstruct an individual's life and tell readers about the nature of race in the colonial system? Compare to Chapters 4, 10, and 12, for example.

An Afro-Iberian Pilot Allowed to Sail[1]

November 8, 1539. Royal Order to Sebastian Caboto, Pilot Major, to examine as a pilot Jorge Hernández, *vecino* of Seville, even though he is of dark color [*loro*].

He has proved he was a free man and a son of free people, married, and has in this city [Seville] a wife and children. And he has always lived in this same city and always honestly. And he has served us for thirteen years in the navigation of the Indies. He has done this with much diligence and he has worked to understand and know the navigation of the Indies and he has understood and known it very well and he has had and has experience and ability sufficient to be a pilot.[2] And although he has asked

---

[1]*Source:* Royal order to allow Diego Hernández to be examined as a pilot. See Archivo General de Indias [AGI], Indiferente, 2054, N127, 8-XI-1539, fols. 34v–35r.

[2]Punctuation is added to make the transcription and translation to English more readable.

you and requested that you examine him in the profession of being a pilot you have not wanted to do it. Without having any other fault save his color and even if this was a fault it does not affect his abilities and capacity, his life and habits make him exemplary as I state in this order, and in an inquiry my Council of the Indies made of this person. I order you to examine him in the profession of pilot following the regulations made by me as is customary and in view of the other pilots, and finding him competent give him the title of the said profession so that he can use it as my royal grant allows. When the case was seen by those of my Council it was agreed that my royal order should be proclaimed aloud and I agreed therefore I order you

to do it. And being the said Jorge Hernández free and married, together with the other people with whom you regularly gather to carry out these examinations, examine him in the profession of pilot even though he is of *loro* color. Having examined him and with your approval we order our officials in the *Casa de la Contratación* of the Indies[3] to allow him to use and exercise the profession of pilot without placing any impediment. Dated in the Town of Madrid November 8, 1539, I the King.

---

[3]Established in 1503, the House of Trade in Seville held the Spanish customs house and the royal officials charged with overseeing travel and trade with the Americas.

Black Sailors in Transatlantic Crews[4]

Francisco Trebiño, master, vecino of Seville in the neighborhood of San Estevan, vessel San Bartolome y Nuestra Señora de la Encarnación, in the River of Seville bound for Angola and its conquests and then to New Spain [Vera Cruz] or Tierra Firme [Cartagena]. Agent is Antonio Rodriguez Sierra and the monopoly holders are Melchor Fernandez Angel and Cristobal Mendez de Sosa.[5] Permission for 130 slaves.

River of the City of Seville, December 5, 1632.

- Captain, Juan Nuñez de Andrada, boat's owner, native of Lisbon [Portugal].
- Master, Francisco Trebiño, native of Ponte Vedra, son of Albares, [physical description], 27 years old.
- Notary, Francisco Pacheco, native of Lisbon, son of the same, 24 years old, [physical description].
- Pilot, Francisco Riberos, examined by the Portuguese King, native Villa de Conde, son of Amador, [physical description], 40 years old.

- Quartermaster, Salvador de Saa, native of La Palma [Canaries Islands], son of Sebastian, [physical description], 34 years old.
- Guard, Felipe del Valle, native of Seville, son of Juan, medium build, brown, large eyes and wide nose, 25 years old.
- Dispenser, Gonçalo de Hernandes, native of Villa Nueva, son of Sebastian, brown, eyebrows joined and large nose, 22 years old.
- Constable and second to pilot, Amaro Martin, native of the Island La Palma, son of Baltasar, tall, brown, black haired, a sign of a wound [physical description continues], 30 years old.
- Sailor and gunner, Juan Fernandes, native of La Palma, son of Antonio, medium build, smallpox scars, brown, [illegible word] hair, confirmed that he is free and gives witnesses attesting to this in writing.
- Sailor and gunner, Juan de Bergara, Native Fuente Ravia, son of the same, [physical description], 28 years old.
- Sailor and gunner, Manuel Martin, native Lagos, son of Domingo, [physical description], 25 years old.
- Sailor, Manuel Fernandes, native of Albor [Portugal], son of Pedro Yañes, [physical description], 25 years old.

---

[4]*Source:* The registration of the ships and crews bound for the West African coasts to buy or capture people to take as slaves to ports in Spanish America. See AGI, Contratación, 2890, R2, "Registro de esclavos," Sevilla, 5-XII-1632, fols. 45r–48r.

[5]The merchants who held the monopoly rights granted by the Spanish Crown to import and sell a specified number of slaves.

- Sailor, Juan de Santiago, native of Ayamonte, son of Juan Gonzales, [physical description], 28 years old.
- Sailor, Manuel Rorigues, native of Madiera Islands, son of Antonio, tall and thin, brown, small face, 25 years old.
- Sailor, Bartolome Martin, native of Santa Maria, son of Bartolome, [physical description], 28 years old.
- Sailor and carpenter, Pablo Fernandez, native of the Tercera, son of Gaspar, of light black color [*negro claro*], wide nose, large forehead, sound body, 29 years old. He showed his *carta de libertad* [letter proving free status].
- Sailor, Manuel Dias, native of Oporto, son of Antonio, [physical description], 20 years old.
- Sailor, Juan de Salzedo, native of San Lucar de Barrameda, son of Bernavel, light brown, sound body, thin face, large mouth, 34 years old. Confirmed that he is free.
- Sailor, Juan Rodrigues, native of Lisbon, son of Bartolome, medium build, blond, [physical description], 21 years old.
- Grumete, Sebastian Goncales, native of Ponte Vedra in Galicia, son of the same, [physical description], 19 years old.
- Grumete, Francisco Duarte, native Villa Nueva, son of Antonio, brown, frizzy hair, medium build, small face, 20 years old, confirmed that he is free with papers of written testimony.
- Grumete, Gaspar Antonio, native of Conde, son of Antonio Perez Lanzarote, [physical description], 20 years old.
- Grumete, Sebastian de Alanis, native of Villa Nueva, son of Juan, thin facial features, brown, of medium build, birthmark, hair hanging over his forehead, 19 years old. States that he is free.
- Grumete, Francisco Albares, native of Oporto, son of Antonio, [physical description], 18 years old.
- Grumete, Francisco, *negro*, he is the slave of the Captain Juan Nuñes, medium build, beginnings of a beard, 26 years old. The Captain is obligated to return him to Spain and present him in the *Casa de la Contratación* or pay the penalty of 100,000 *maravedis* for Our Majesty's Court and the value of the slave. . . . Signed Antonio de Medina [notary] and Juan Nuñez.
- Cabin Boy, Antonio Francisco, native of Garachico, son of the same, [physical description], 13 years old.
- Cabin boy Juan Rodrigues, native of Lisbon, son of the same, [physical description], 14 years old.
- Cabin boy, Julian Moreno, *negro* slave, of the Captain Juan Nuñez, round faced, well toasted in color, 10 years old. [signed an obligation to return him to Spain].

A Free Mulato Soldier's Will[6]

Last will and testament of Luis Pinelo. Havana. August 1, 1610. I Luis Pinelo, free *mulato*, unmarried, son of Bernabe Sanchez and Isavel Perez, deceased, *vecinos* of Seville. I am a soldier in the Company of Don Gaspar Çapata [Zapata] under the command of General Don Juan de la Cueva y Mendoza. At present I am in this Hospital of San Felipe and Santiago of the City of San Cristobal of Havana being ill with the

illness that God our Lord sent me. . . . I want to be buried in this Hospital with two sung masses.

- I give the accustomed alms. [I want] four masses said for the souls of my parents in Seville in the Cathedral, two in the Chapel of Our Lady of the Kings and two others in the Chapel of Our Lady of the Ancients. To be said by Jusefe de Rivera, chaplain of the galleon San Pablo of the Royal Armada, who is here present with me.
- A mass prayed to Souls in Purgatory to be said by the same cleric in the same cathedral in the Chapel of the Souls and for that I give the customary alms.

[6]*Source:* Court documents from 1610, including a will and witness testimony, housed in the Archivo General de las Indias in Seville, Spain, under the title of "Autos sobre los bienes de Luis Pinelo, mulato libre, soldado," Sevilla, 1610, AGI, Contratación, 296A, N3, R3 & R4, fols. 1–20v.

- For my soul twenty masses in Seville that my executors will attend and for that the customary alms.
- Alms for this Hospital, 6 *pesos* worth 8 *reales* each, for all the good and charity done in it to cure me.
- I owe no one.
- 183 *pesos* of mine, in possession of Bartolome Calsada, gunner on the flagship commanded by General Don Juan de la Cueva, that I gave him for safekeeping in the City of Portobelo [Panama].
- I am owed by Tomas de [illegible], gunner of the ship Santa Marta, 5 *pesos* that I lent to him as a favor in Cartagena de Indias [Colombia].
- I am owed by Marcos de Caravajal, a soldier of the ship Santa Marta, 2 *pesos*. He owed me three and he paid me one.
- [I leave behind] A sister of the same father and mother and who is called María de Ribera, free, in Seville in the house of Doña María de Pinelo who lives in Seville in the San Pedro neighborhood in the Square of Santa Catalina beside Santa Ines. She is unmarried and twenty-two years old.
- I collected the money for the wine from my rations and the quartermaster owes me nothing.
- My executors: Blas de Santa Cruz, aide of the Armada of Tierra Firme, the priest Jusepe de Rivera, chaplain who is here present, and Matheo Natera, solicitor for the Customs House and *vecino* in Seville.
- I want my sister to be the heir of my property to help her marry.

[*Signatures of the witnesses named above.*] [*The packet of documents ends with a list of belongings sold at auction on August 18, 1610, and a note that on November 29, 1610, Pinelo's sister in Seville requested the inheritance according to his will and was given an order for the galleon's quartermaster to pay her the remaining 158 pesos.*]

Supplementing Sailors' Wages with Petty Trade and Thievery[7]

Charges by Captain Pedro de Murguía against Francisco Machorro, *mulato*, sailor, Juan Moreno, cabin boy, and Diego, slave, *negro*, grumete, for stealing from his storehouse jugs of wine and oil. Seville, 1609.[8]

Beginning of the case. Cartagena, June 25, 1608. Due to the absence of the [Armada's commanding] General Juan de Salas y Valdes, the Capitan Bernardo de Mata [presides].[9] Yesterday night at around 10:00 in two storehouses belonging to Capitan Pedro de Murguía, owner of the fleet's flagship, Francisco Machorro, *mulato*, sailor of the said ship with the keys that the Capitan had in his power and that Juan Moreno had been persuaded to steal and with another *negro* [Machorro] opened the two storehouses and took out many of the jugs. [The bailiff] went from his lodgings with a lit torch to the storehouse that was in the house of Luis Gomez Barreto and encountering a *negro* carrying a jug asked him where he had taken them. The *negro* took him to the house of Manuel Perez, shopkeeper, who lives besides the Royal Customs House and in whose house they found seven jugs of wine and seven jugs of oil that the *negro* pointed out as the ones he had brought there with three local Indians following the orders given by Francisco the *mulato* overseer from the fleet's flagship. Then he went back to the warehouse with the *negro* and found beside it another jug of wine and oil and the said overseer with them. He had him arrested and placed in the city jail. He

---

[7] *Source:* Legal proceedings carried out in Cartagena's port before the accused men's commanding officers in the Spanish fleet. See AGI, Contratación 772, N13, "Autos del Capitán Pedro de Murguía contra Francisco Machorro, mulato, marinero, Juan Moreno, paje, y Diego, negro, grumete," Cartagena/Seville, 1609, fols. 1r–110r.

[8] Appealed to Seville.

[9] The Captain General of the Armada and Fleet, Estevan de Salas y Valdes, sailed on to Panama, leaving behind several ships and crews for repairs or because of insufficient crew. Left in charge by the fleet commander, Captain Bernardo de Mata investigated and prosecuted this case.

confiscated a box at the shopkeeper's said to be of Francisco the overseer, and [he] went to the house of Alonso Suarez, sailor from the fleet, where Francisco Machorro, *mulato*, lodges and arrested him and sent him to the jail.[10] . . .

Cartagena. June 25, 1608. Francisco Machorro, jailed, declares that they brought me to this jail saying that a servant of Capitan Pedro de Murguía had taken some jugs. . . . I am not guilty in any way because I did not do that, I did not know about it, I do not understand it except that in the past I lent money to buy certain things and not being careful and knowing about the case. I saw that the said Juan Moreno, Capitan Pedro de Murguía's servant, brought some jugs with some *negros* and he said to me that the quartermaster had let him have them for 200 *reales* saying they belonged to the soldiers who owed him money and thus I am not guilty. I ask to be released. He signs his name.

Cartagena. June 25, 1608. Declaration of Juan Moreno, cabin boy, servant of Capitan Pedro de Murguia. Said his name is Juan Moreno, and he is cabin boy to Capitan Pedro de Murguía, native of Seville. Thirteen years old. Asked if it is true that Capitan Pedro de Murguía had two storehouses in the city with jugs of wine and oil, one in the house of Luis Gomez Barreto city treasurer on the Street of the Ladies. Another in the house of Martin Vellido de Calatrava [and] that the jugs belong to the Capitan. He said he saw the storehouses filled with the wine and oil. He knew about the keys the Capitan kept in his room. He said the overseer and *mulato* sailor Francisco told him to take the keys when the Capitan was sleeping and not vigilant so that they could open the storehouses and take the wine and oil to sell. And a number of times he was persuaded by the *mulato* to take the keys and take out items. He took 150 jugs of wine and 100 jugs of oil to the houses of some shopkeepers and other people in order to sell them and particularly last night he and the *mulato* had taken the keys gone to the storehouses, opened them and took out 8 jugs of wine and 8 jugs of oil. They took seven of each to the

house of Manuel Perez, shopkeeper, with some *negros* to carry them. He said he was persuaded by Diego, *negro*, who came [to Cartagena] as a grumete on the same ship . . . and Diego offered to give Juan his part. He was given 10 *reales* once as his part after the sale of one batch of stolen jugs. He was never given more. Last night he was persuaded by the *mulato* Francisco Machorro to carry out the theft. He took the keys to the lodgings of Francisco Machorro which is under the arches near the port where Alonso Suarez stores a quantity of empty jugs and other things. He took out 8 jugs of each with the *mulato* and some *negros*. The bailiff found seven of each of them in the shop of Manuel Perez and came looking and found one more of each in the street. Cannot sign his name.

Declaration of Diego, *negro*, grumete on the flagship. He knows all the parties involved. He knew of the two storehouses because he helped put jugs of wine and oil in them. He knew of the keys in the Capitan's room. He answers that what happened was that Juan Moreno the cabin boy said that he wanted to open the storehouses to take wine and oil. . . . And they took 8 jugs of each the first time and this defendant took them to the house of a free *moreno* [*moreno horro*] who lives near the Nunnery that he believes is free. . . . Another time they took out 12 jugs, and took 6 to the free *moreno* and 6 to the house of a shopkeeper who lives on a corner beside the Cathedral. . . . The third time he went with Juan Moreno to remove 4 jugs of wine and 6 of oil. Juan Moreno ordered him to give a jug of oil to the *moreno* at the storehouse to keep him quiet. And another of wine to those who helped them carry the jugs. They took them to the house of the said shopkeeper and he bought them for $3\frac{1}{2}$ *pesos* each for the wine and 2 *pesos* for each jug of oil. He claimed to have given Juan Moreno 10 *pesos* once and another 10 *pesos* on another occasion. He only knows the *negros* that helped by sight not by name. Declares that he saw Machoro *mulato* talk with Juan Moreno frequently about keys and storehouses. Could not sign his name. 22 or 23 years old.[11] . . .

---

[10]The box contained men's clothing for Machorro's use and women's clothing, needles, and thread for sale.

[11]Three witnesses identify Diego and Francisco Machorro. The shopkeeper, Suarez, is arrested.

[*The declarations of three jailed shopkeepers are omitted. They came from Spain like the defendants who they knew and regularly traded with. Next, the three defendants are called forward and questioned.*]

Confession and protectorship of minor of Francisco Machorro.[12] Cartagena. June 27, 1608. Francisco Macharro. 22 years old. Native of Cadiz in the Kingdom of Castile. [Machorro] knows Juan Moreno the cabin boy . . . and Diego *negro* because he came in the same ship together. Asked about the storehouses. . . . He answers that he knows nothing about what is asked him in the question. Asked about the keys to the storehouses. He answers that he knows nothing about what is asked him in the question. Asked about the theft. He answers that he denies that he persuaded Juan Moreno the cabin boy to take the keys for the storehouses. And that night at the hour of praying the Ave Maria [Juan Moreno] arrived at the inn of Alonso Suarez where Francisco Machorro was lodged, Juan Moreno arrived and told him that he had some jugs of wine and oil and that he should take it to some shopkeeper known to this defendant and that he should store them so that another day he could sell them and from the earnings he would pay $9\frac{1}{2}$ *pesos* to Francisco. [Machorro] went with Juan and was given 8 jugs each of wine and oil that some *negros* took out of a house. And Francisco and the six *negros* and 2 local Indians carried them, and one *negro* remained behind in the street with two jugs one of wine and one of oil. The other fourteen jugs continued on with him. He went to Manuel Perez's house and asked him to keep them and that the owner would come in the morning. He returned for the other two jugs to bring them to the shop when the bailiff came upon them. He denies having sold the jugs to the shopkeeper or having done anything else wrong. He does not know the names of the *negros* and Indians. He denies the robbery of the storehouses eight days ago with Diego *negro*.[13] . . .

Confession of Juan Moreno.[14] Cartagena, June 28, 1608. Declares that he is a native of Seville. He has served as cabin boy in the ship commanded by Vincente de Urresti, a ship in the fleet under the command of Salas y Valdes, and he has served as cabin boy to Capitan Pedro de Murguía. He is 13 or 14 years old. [*He reaffirmed what he said in his declaration before Capitan Bernardo de Mata on June 25, 1608.*]

Confession of Diego *negro*. Cartagena, June 28, 1608. Declares his name is Diego de la Candelaria and that he is a *criollo* of the Canaries and that he is a slave of Graviel de Leon, *vecino* of Seville and that he came as a grumete in the flagship of the fleet. He does not know his age. Appears to be 24. He ratifies what he declared on June 25, 1608.

[*Each sailor presented his defense: The reality that* "there is no grumete or cabin boy sailing to the Indies who does not bring to sell something of his own that his mother or relatives in Spain give them or that they have traded for in other voyages that they have made." *Capitan Pedro de Murguía refuted the defense arguments. On July 12, Francisco Machorro's goods and clothing were sold at auction for 50 pesos 6 reales. Character witnesses were called.*]

Cartagena, July 8, 1608. Testimony of Anton Martin, 26 years old, a corporal of the soldiers protecting the galleon that just arrived from Margarita. He has known Juan for four years in the city of Seville where he met him in his parents' house and he does not know Capitan Pedro de Murguía. He knows him for a boy of 13 years. He has known him since he was 9 years old in Seville. He knows him to be a simple boy with very little inclination for this sort of thing [theft]. In all the time that he has known him he has never seen, heard, or learned that he committed any crime or acted badly. He saw him before in his parents' house inclined towards virtue and good customs because his parents are honorable people and good Christians and they do not give bad examples only good ones to their son and for this reason this witness cannot be persuaded that Juan Moreno could have done such a thing. Cannot sign his name. . . .

---

[12]Francisco Machorro is less than 25 years old; therefore, the court named Francisco Gomez as a protector of minors to defend him.

[13]Francisco Machorro testified that another Diego *negro* of the *Jolofo* caste and a slave belonging to Juan de Caravajal helped carry the jugs.

[14]A protector of minors and defender was also named for Juan Moreno and Diego, the black slave who arrived as a *grumete* with the fleet.

Cartagena, July 8, 1608. Testimony of Alonso Suarez, sailor on the warship named San Juan Baptista that provided defense to the fleet that came this year commanded by the General Juan de Salas de Valdes, 25 years old. He has known Francisco for 12 years in Cadiz and in New Spain and Cartagena and he knows the Capitan Pedro de Murguía. He said that the boy Juan came twice at the hour of the prayers looking for Francisco. When asked what for he said for an outfit of clothes he was going to give him. Juan's age is as the question says. . . . It is known that sailors, grumetes, and cabin boys buy and sell to sustain themselves, it is very common and well known. He knows Francisco Machorro to be an honorable man and that never before has there been any proceeding against him for any infraction. For being a youth, friend of virtue and keeping good company [Machorro] achieved his freedom thanks to a gentleman who was a duke and gave him the ducats with which he bought his freedom. And being a trustworthy man the gentleman wanted to take him to Italy and many honorable and important people have wanted to have him in their houses to entrust him with their property, but Francisco declined because he wanted to earn his own subsistence through his work and industriousness. . . . Signs his name.

Cartagena, July 8, 1608. Testimony of Capitan Sebastian Sanchez, resident of Cartagena, captain of the vessel named the Criolla that came with the fleet, more or less forty years old. He knows Francisco for 12 years in Cartagena and Cadiz where he was the slave of Don Juan Francisco, a gentlemen of that city. He knows Diego who came to Cartagena in the flagship. He does not know the others. . . . He said that for fear being whipped or mistreated slaves will perjure themselves. It is true that many of the sailors, grumetes, and cabin boys who come to the Indies in the fleet bring merchandise and wine and other things that they sell in the ports and that their parents and relatives give them or that they acquire. He has always considered Francisco both in the power of Don Juan Francisco his master and after as a free person to be faithful and of good behavior and a friend of being truthful. For being this way this witness and other people gave him clothing to sell and he gave good account of the sales without seeing, hearing, or knowing anything to the contrary. Signed his name. . . .

[*On July 23, 1608, Capitan Bernardo de Mata declared the three guilty. He exiled the cabin boy, Juan Moreno, from Cartagena and a 60-mile radius for two years. Diego de la Candelaria was removed from prison, bound, and taken to the plaza at the city docks and given 200 lashes. A week later, he was sold for 240 pesos (108 for court costs, and 132 for Capitan Pedro de Murguía). In February 1609, Seville's royal court revoked the order to torture Francisco Machorro, and Capitan Pedro Murguía's lawyer in Seville dropped the charges against Francisco de Machorro. In March, he was released to 2 years of exile.*]

Suggested Sources:

Seville became a racially diverse crossroads for the Mediterranean. See Ruth Pike, "Sevillian Society in the Sixteenth Century: Slaves and Freedmen," *Hispanic American Historical Review* 47 (1967): 346. Afro-Iberian soldiers joined the wars to establish Spanish rule in the Americas. See Matthew Restall, "Black Conquistadors: Armed Africans in Early Spanish America," *The Americas* 57, no. 2 (October 2000): 171–205. A few black conquistadors received royal rewards for their service in the conquest. See Peter Gerhard, "A Black Conquistador in Mexico," *Hispanic American Historical Review* 58, no. 3 (August 1968): 451–459. Sailors and many other men and women of African heritage came to the Americas outside the holds of slave ships sailing directly from Africa. See Leo J. Garofalo, "The Shape of a Diaspora: The Movement of Afro-Iberians to and from Colonial Spanish America," in *Africans to Colonial Spanish America*, ed. Sherwin Bryant, Ben Vinson, III, and Rachel Sarah O'Toole (Champaign: University of Illinois Press, forthcoming). Without sailors, the Spanish and Portuguese overseas empires could not have been built. See Pablo E. Pérez-Mallaína, *Spain's Men of the Sea: Daily Life on the Indies Fleets in the Sixteenth Century*, trans. Carla Rahn Phillips (Baltimore: The John Hopkins University Press, 2005). Africans and Europeans shaped many key aspects of the Atlantic worlds that defined Europe and Africa from the 1400s to the 1800s. See James H. Sweet, *Recreating Africa: Culture, Kinship, and Religion in the African-Portuguese World, 1441–1770* (Chapel Hill: University of North Carolina Press, 2003); David Northrup, *Africa's Discovery of Europe: 1450–1850* (Oxford: Oxford University Press, 2002); and John K. Thornton, *Africa and Africans in the Making of the Atlantic World, 1400–1800* (New York: Cambridge University Press, 1998).

Finding the voices of Afro-Iberians for the period before 1800 is not an easy task. A place to begin examining some of these in English and their original languages is *Afro-Latino Voices: Narratives from the Early Modern Ibero-Atlantic World, 1550–1808*, ed. Kathryn Joy McKnight and Leo J. Garofalo (Cambridge: Hackett, 2009).

Chapter 4

A Case of Contested Identity: Domingo Pérez, Indigenous Immigrant in Ciudad Real, Chiapas

Laura Matthew, Marquette University

Chiapas
in Audiencia
of Guatemala

The conquest in 1521 of the *Aztec* capital, *Tenochtitlán*, is a dramatic story by any account. In school textbooks, novels, films, and even history books, the exploits of Hernán Cortés and his small band of Spanish conquistadors often stand in for the European conquest of the Americas more generally. Fundamental to the European narrative of conquest is the conviction that a mere handful of

Spaniards managed, through wit, courage, luck (or divine intervention), and cultural and technological superiority to defeat great empires like the *Incas* and *Aztecs* and subjugate millions of people to colonial rule. This version of events, however, leaves out those who planned, coordinated, and fought the majority of conquest battles: indigenous people themselves.

Why would indigenous peoples ally themselves with foreign invaders? The answer is, almost always, to gain advantage over their neighbors and achieve glory for their own people. The Spanish offered new weapons like steel swords, fresh ideas of military strategy, and powerful new gods. Their arrival posed an irresistible opportunity for some, especially those chafing under *Inca* or *Aztec* hegemony. In the Andes, the Cañaris of northern Ecuador and Chachapoyas of southern Peru had been attempting to free themselves from *Inca* rule for nearly half a century when the Spanish arrived. Tlaxcala, the only **altepetl** (city-state) in central Mexico still independent of *Tenochtitlán* in 1519, also recognized the usefulness of these lost wanderers from across the sea. The *Tlaxcalteca* lords' decision to befriend the newcomers rather than kill them began a process of alliance building that culminated 2 years later, when *Tenochtitlán* fell to hundreds of thousands of Mesoamerican warriors—not only *Tlaxcalteca*—rebelling against their former imperial masters.

In the wake of *Tenochtitlán's* defeat, the nobility of central Mexico (including the recently defeated but still powerful rulers of *Tenochtitlán* themselves) formed new alliances with each other and with the Spanish. Meanwhile, leaders from the furthest outposts of the former *Aztec* Empire and beyond sent emissaries pledging their support to whoever filled the power vacuum in central Mexico in return for assistance against their own regional rivals. The first conquest expeditions emanating from central Mexico, under combined Nahua[1] and Spanish leadership, were initiated almost immediately. Later

expeditions into Central America, as far south as Colombia and Peru and back north into the Yucatán Peninsula, relied utterly on both indigenous allies and indigenous slaves.

This document records a dispute between indigenous conquistadors from 1587 in Chiapas, a primarily *Maya* area that is today a state in southern Mexico, but during colonial times was administered by the *Audiencia* of Guatemala. A father and son, Domingo Pérez and Pedro Gómez, lived in the *Tlaxcalteca* barrio of the small city, Ciudad Real de Chiapa, which was founded by Spanish conquistadors. They claimed exemption from tribute payments because, they said, Domingo Pérez was a *Tlaxcalteca* conquistador who fought alongside the Spanish. The indigenous councilmen of the *Tlaxcalteca* and *Mexicano*[2] barrios of Ciudad Real disagreed. They insisted that Domingo Pérez was actually a K'iche' slave from Guatemala who had been brought to Chiapas by his master, the Spaniard Alonso de Aguilar.

All of the Mesoamericans involved in this dispute were immigrants who came to Chiapas because of the conquest wars. In Chiapas, these began in 1524, when a group of *Tlaxcalteca* and Cholulteca captains led the Spaniard Pedro de Alvarado along Chiapas's cacao-rich Pacific coast en route to Guatemala. Reinforcements joined along the way, following the typical pattern of alliance-building and military campaigns that predominated in Mesoamerica before the arrival of Europeans. Several Mexica leaders of former *Aztec* strongholds in southern Mesoamerica contributed supplies and warriors. In 1527, two rival Spaniards, Pedro Portocarrero and Diego Mazariegos, entered Chiapas from Guatemala and Oaxaca, respectively, each with hundreds of indigenous allies from the outside and hundreds more *Maya* recruited locally. Portocarrero and his conquistadors were largely responsible for the initial military subjugation of the Chiapaneca, the most powerful regional highland group. Both Portocarrero

---

[1]"Nahua" is a modern scholarly term referring to the *Nahuatl*-speaking people of central Mexico. Although Nahua peoples shared a degree of common culture, language, and history, they did not view themselves as a single group. Ethnicity in central Mexico, as in many other parts of Mesoamerica, was narrowly defined by genealogical, political, and geographical affiliations.

[2]The Tlaxcalteca were often singled out as an exceptionally loyal group of Nahua allies. "Mexicanos" sometimes referred specifically to the *Mexica* of Tenochtitlán, but more commonly referred to any group of central Mexican Nahuatl speakers besides the Tlaxcalteca, much as modern scholars use the term "Nahuas."

and Mazariegos founded Spanish towns, the first step toward legal claim of territory under Spanish law. But politically, Mazariegos and his faction (which included the alleged owner of Domingo Pérez) were victorious. By May 1528, Portocarrero's town had been ordered dissolved. Its residents were moved to Mazariegos's Villa Real, later to become Ciudad Real de Chiapa (modern-day San Cristobal de Las Casas), the administrative center of the region under colonial rule where much of the testimony in this document was recorded.

Both Spaniards' most prominent indigenous allies were Nahuas from central Mexico. Several Nahua captains who came with Mazariegos appear as witnesses in this case. Juan de Luna is listed as a councilman of the Mexicano barrio litigating against Domingo Pérez and Pedro Gómez. Juan Bautista, who vouched for Domingo Pérez, served for many years as the tribute collector for the Spanish in the Llanos de Chiapa, a post modeled on the Mexica imperial tribute collectors (*calpixque*), but this time assigned to a *Tlaxcalteca*. But both Portocarrero and Mazariegos also brought Guatemalan *Maya* with them, especially K'iche', who had been defeated in 1524 by Pedro de Alvarado's army and subsequently served in campaigns against the Kaqchikel, Tzutuhil, Pipil, and other Central American groups. In and around Ciudad Real, some of the K'iche' and Nahua allies settled as colonists in their own ethnically defined barrios. This is another conquest-era pattern that follows pre-Hispanic precedents, especially under *Aztec* imperialism. In the largest colonial-era Nahua colony in Central America outside Santiago de Guatemala, eight barrios named after *altepetl* in central Mexico survived into the nineteenth century. The K'iche' barrio outside Ciudad Real, called Cuxtitali, remains a distinct neighborhood of San Cristobal de Las Casas to this day. Where one was born or lived was a potential marker of social identity—hence the importance attributed to Domingo Pérez's residence and Pedro Gómez's birth in the *Tlaxcalteca* barrio of Ciudad Real.

Of course, the reality was never so neatly defined. The sixteenth century saw tremendous movement of indigenous Mesoamericans far from the places and people that helped define who they were. Some of this population movement was voluntary. Young men marched off to war and adventure. Women and children followed as cooks, porters, and colonists. Merchants and muleteers seeking opportunity left behind families for years at a time and created new ones along their commercial routes. Other population movement was forced by circumstance (disease and the physical destruction of towns) or violence (*encomienda* labor, war captives, or slave raiding). Native slave labor was legal and considered a legitimate booty of conquest until 1542, when the Spanish Crown outlawed it. Both Spaniards and Nahuas in Chiapas and elsewhere were at pains to distinguish clearly between themselves as original conquistadors and the defeated peoples as conquered subjects and slaves—perhaps especially in Central America, where slave raiding, coerced labor, and forced migration were widespread. This distinction between Indian conquistador and Indian slave lies at the heart of Domingo Pérez and Pedro Gómez's case.

Readers may wish to know the outcome of this dispute. As is often the case, the document does not provide a complete answer. In the weeks following the testimony recorded here, a series of witnesses testified on behalf of the councilmen of the *Tlaxcalteca* and Mexicano barrios. These included Alonso Martin, an indigenous immigrant living in Ciudad Real, who came to Chiapas from the K'iche' *Maya* barrio of Utatlan in the city of Santiago de Guatemala. Martin claimed to have known both Domingo Pérez and Pérez's parents and grandparents, whom he said were natives of Guatemala and not of Tlaxcala. He also claimed that Domingo Pérez was indeed Alonso de Aguilar's slave, but a very high-ranking one who acted as Aguilar's overseer. The councilmen also brought in an indigenous barber and surgeon, who testified that the marks on Domingo Pérez's cheeks were indeed the brands commonly used for slaves.

Despite this damaging testimony, Spanish authorities in Ciudad Real ruled in favor of Domingo Pérez and Pedro Gómez. The higher court in Santiago de Guatemala, however, accepted an appeal by the councilmen of the *Tlaxcalteca* and Mexicano barrios. Perhaps Pedro Gómez anticipated this development, for when officials came to notify him of the continuation of the case at his home in Chiapas, his *mestizo* wife reported that he had gone to Santiago de Guatemala. Soon afterward, Gómez appeared before royal court officials in Guatemala to present his defense anew. This is the last, unfinished record we have of the case, bringing to an end what is known of this particular piece of litigation and reminding historians that the Spanish Empire was not won and held by Europeans alone. The invaders stumbled into a complex web of ethnic alliances and enmities. Their success as conquerors and colonial rulers depended on their ability to operate in this indigenous world and meld its logics with their own.

Questions to Consider:

1. Who were the witnesses? Did it matter whether they were Spaniards or Mesoamericans? Did they give different kinds of testimony?
2. How were the terms *Indian, conquistador,* and *slave* used? Did you encounter unusual or unexpected terms?
3. Why did the councilmen bring this case forward? Why did they expose Domingo Pérez and Pedro Gómez as K'iche'?
4. How did the Spanish react?

The Prosecutor Doubts the Claims by Pedro Gómez, Son of an Indian Conquistador[3]

Very illustrious lord, I Pedro Gómez, Indian resident of the barrio of the *Tlaxcaltecas* of this city [of Ciudad Real de Chiapas], appear before your lordship in the manner in which I am entitled and say that I have received the tribute given to your majesty, because my father Domingo Pérez, *Tlaxcalteca,* was one of those who are and were loyal in their service, aiding in the pacifications of Mexico and Michoacan and all of New Spain, Guatemala, and all of this province. And because the said Domingo Pérez my father came with Alonso de Aguilar, one of the conquistadors, to these parts, serving him and helping him in the said pacifications, and was an auxiliary (*mancebo*)[4] like the other conquistadors, for all these reasons the honorable Cristobal de Axcueta, judge for your majesty and inspector who came from this province, reserved him as a conquistador from the status of tributary and also his children, of which I am one. And neither my father nor I would be in

this city if we had gone to the city of Guatemala to carry the royal tribute.[5]

And afterwards, Agustin de Hinojosa, the judge who arrived to count the towns belonging to the royal crown, reserved me from tribute, for which . . . I make this demonstration and *probanza*[6] of my father. And although the probanza showed that he was a conquistador and *Tlaxcalteca,* it becomes necessary to show how my father served your majesty after this land was settled. A few years later he went with the captain Francisco Xilala in the pacification of Tanochel and all its province, and afterwards there was a rebellion and he returned to serve your majesty with the captain Pedro de Solorzano in the pacifications of Pochutla and Tila and many other towns. And he also went to the pacification of Pochutla with the lord judge Pedro Ramirez de Quiñones, and also

[3]*Source:* "El fiscal contra Pedro Gómez. hijo de indio conquistador," Archivo General de Centroamérica (Guatemala City), legajo 2799, expediente 40482.
[4]*Mancebo* can mean either "young man" or "apprentice."

[5]Had Domingo Pérez been a K'iche' from the barrio of Utatlan in Santiago de Guatemala, as his adversaries claimed, he would have come to Santiago from the highlands of Guatemala as a war captive required to pay tribute to a Spanish *encomendero* and/or the Spanish Crown.
[6]A *probanza de méritos y servicios* was a document detailing a conquistador's lineage and services to the Crown and requesting proper compensation. Native Mesoamerican conquistadors also created *probanzas,* both individually and collectively.

with the lord bishop *don* Fray Tomas Casillas, and here the natives of that place fought very fiercely and many Spaniards and Indians died.

And being very old, he returned to go with the captain Juan de Morales Villavecencio, and although in the rear for being an auxiliary, he would not have served in the wars except to serve your majesty in this and in others with the captains that I have mentioned, so that he and I as his son would be reserved from tribute, and even more so because he is from Tlaxcala and your majesty has made us free and exempt from tribute.

And thus the magistrates [*alcaldes*] of my barrio have seen that the old ones have died, and have entered charges contradicting my liberty and that of my father, for the passions they have against me. I refer to persons such as Anton Pérez and Grabiel Ximenez and some others, and *regidores* persuaded by these same *alcaldes*, because they are troublemakers and friends of sedition [*inquietos, bulliciosos amigos de revolver*]. For the *probanza* of my father shows the maliciousness of their testimony to the Real Audiencia,[7] and the head Spanish magistrate [*alcalde mayor*] failed to understand what they asked for in their blind passion, saying that my father was a slave of Alonso de Aguilar and that he was not a *Tlaxcalteca*. This is contradictory, for which the said Grabiel Ximenez deserves punishment for what he has falsely put forth, because in the probanza that my father made one of the witnesses is Grabiel Ximenez and there he declares that he [Domingo Pérez] is a conquistador as he is from Tlaxcala. And for the passions that he has regarding me, he now says that what he said is not true.

And thus everything that these men say and have informed you of is not true, because my father never was taken for nor was a slave. And if Alonso de Aguilar put some mark on him it was because all of the conquistadors in that time branded the slaves that they called *naborías*[8] in order to keep them from

fleeing, especially Alonso de Aguilar who was a very cruel man who branded all his Indians for their work gangs, including the Indians who gave tribute from their *encomiendas* and not because they were slaves, nor was my father who could not be one because he was a native of Tlaxcala, as I have said. Therefore:

I beg your highness for that which has been said and alleged that you pronounce me free from tribute, because your majesty has exempted me from tribute through this royal provision and the probanza of my father which shows him to be a conquistador, and for that which I have alleged, that my father served with the captains after the pacification of this land and recognized me as his son. . . . And I ask for justice . . . Pedro Gómez.

In Ciudad Real de Chiapa on the fourteenth day of the month of April, 1587, this petition is read before the very illustrious *señor licenciado*[9] Rodrigo de Moscoso, from the council of your majesty and your judge in the Real *Audiencia* of Guatemala and visiting judge general of these provinces.

On the fifteenth day of the same month and year, Tomás Lopez, magistrate of the barrio of the *Tlaxcaltecas*, and Gregorio Castellano and Francisco Lopez, councilmen, were notified of these proceedings and it was declared in *Nahuatl* by Gaspar de Solorzano, the witness being the said Gaspar de Solorzano. Blas Hidalgo.

In Ciudad Real of Chiapa on the sixteenth day of April, 1587, Grabiel Dominguez defender of the natives was notified of what has been said in person, by me the said notary, witnesses Gaspar de Solorzano. Blas Hidalgo.[10]

This is a true and faithful copy taken from a letter authorized by a royal provision of your majesty

---

[7]A royal judicial court for a province, in this case the Audiencia de Guatemala.

[8]*Naborías* were Indians separated by force or choice from their hometowns, where tributary counts were made. Naborías provided cheap labor. After the abolition of Indian slavery in 1542, they often avoided paying tribute based on population counts in their hometowns.

[9]A lawyer or university-educated person.

[10]Indian towns under colonial rule adapted the Spanish *cabildo* (town council) to their own forms of local government, which included town subdivisions like *barrios* that often represented particular lineages or ethnic affiliations (in this case, the barrio of the Tlaxcaltecas). Indian representatives (like the magistrate and councilmen here) presented cases to Spanish authorities when disputes could not be resolved internally. In the Spanish justice system, Indians were assigned "defenders" to assist them in their dealings with the court. Depending on availability, interpreters, notaries, and witnesses were most likely to be Spanish, especially in Spanish-American towns like Ciudad Real or Santiago.

sent from the Real Audiencia that resides in the city of Santiago de Guatemala, and signed by the señores, President, and judges, and signed by his secretary and registered and sealed with the royal seal, as follows:

Don Felipe by the grace of God king of Castile and Leon and Aragon . . . Insofar as in our *Audiencia* and royal office (*chancellería*) which is in the city of Santiago de Guatemala in the presence of our president and judges, Pedro Gómez and Catalina his wife, natives of the *parcialidad*[11] of the *Tlaxcaltecas* of the valley of this Ciudad Real de Chiapa, appeared and by petition made known to us that it has been one year since Agustin de Hinojosa, our assigned judge who went for the counting and census of the Indians of the said province . . . had reserved them from tribute, taking note that the licenciado Azcueta our judge and inspector of the said province had reserved them in accordance with the order that I present. And he asked that we present our letter and royal provision so that the order would be kept and fulfilled by our justices, as follows:

I, the captain Agustin de Hinojosa Villavicencio, assigned judge for your majesty for the count and census of the Indians that pay tribute to your majesty in this province de Chiapa, declare that during the count that was made in the Valley and parcialidad of the *Tlaxcaltecas*, Pedro Gómez appeared and by his petition said that in the census done by the licenciado Axcueta judge of your majesty he had been reserved from tribute as it says in the clause of the said census, in which it was originally written . . .

Pedro Gómez and Catalina his wife do not pay tribute because they are children of the said Domingo Pérez conquistador, for which reason and in observance of this I command the magistrates and councilmen of the said barrio who are now and were, from now and in the future, to neither ask nor charge the said Pedro Gómez for any tribute whatsoever, and to fulfill the tenor of the said clause under pain of punishment. And they will pay that which is asked of them, dated in the city of Chiapa on the fifth day of the month of January 1582, Agustin de Hinojosa by order of the señor judge Hernan Pérez, notary of your majesty.

Petition of the probanza. In the Ciudad Real de Chiapa on the sixth day of April 1584, before the illustrious señor Pedro de Heredia magistrate (*alcalde ordinario*) for your majesty in this city and its jurisdiction, was presented with the petition and interrogation questions in the following tenor:

Illustrious Señor, I Domingo Pérez, resident of the barrio of the *Tlaxcaltecas* of the valley of this city, do say that in my favor the señor licenciado Cristobal de Axcueta, judge who had been of the Real *Audiencia* of Guatemala and inspector of this said city and its province, reserved me from tribute because I am one of the first conquistadors that came to discover this province. And I found myself in the service of the conquistadors in all of the conquest and I stayed as a resident in the said barrio. And because of my merits I and my children were reserved from tribute, as has been said and confirmed in the order that I have presented in the Real *Audiencia* of Guatemala. And it shows and gives information of how I served your majesty in the pacification of these provinces and the province of Tlaxcala and of New Spain, where I am a native. And because Tlaxcala received the Marques del Valle[12] in peace and in the name of your majesty who came to the discovery and conquest of New Spain, your majesty has reserved them from tribute.

And I now have need in protection of my privileges to provide information in eternal memory of what has been said. I ask for mercy and beg that you order witnesses presented by me to be received and examined by the tenor of this interrogation that I now present, and for which I beg justice. Domingo Pérez.

And the witnesses presented by Domingo Pérez, Indian resident of the barrio of the *Tlaxcaltecas* of the valley of this Ciudad Real de Chiapa, will be examined according to the following questions:

First, if they know Domingo Pérez and Pedro Gómez his legitimate son born out of legitimate matrimony, say what they know.

Second, if they know that Domingo Pérez is a native of the people and city of Tlaxcala of New Spain,

---

[11]A *parcialidad* can be either synonymous with or a subsection of a barrio.

[12]Hernán Cortés.

and if they know that the city of Tlaxcala and its residents are free from tribute by the mercy of your majesty, say what they know.

Third, if they know that the city of Tlaxcala is free of tribute for having been loyal servants of your majesty and the crown of Castile, and they received Hernando Cortes in peace when he came to the conquest of the said New Spain and helped in that conquest . . . and placed themselves under the dominion of your majesty. And thus the residents of the province of Tlaxcala were divided amongst the captains that left on the conquests of the province of Guatemala and this province and other parts, say what they know.

Fourth, if they know that Domingo Pérez is one of those who left in support of the conquistadores who came in company of Don Pedro de Alvarado to the conquest of Guatemala, and from there came to this city and province with the conquistadors who came to the pacification of it and served in the conquest well and loyally, and is known and taken as a conquistador, say what they know.

Fifth, if they know and understand that because Domingo Pérez was one of these conquistadors, the señor licenciado Axcueta visitador who was of this city and province reserved him from tribute, declaring him such a conquistador so that neither he nor his children would pay tribute, and this grant he gave him for being as is said a conquistador, say what they know.

Sixth, if they know that for being such a conquistador and resident of the ciudad of Tlaxcala, he deserves to have your majesty confirm the grant that the said señor licenciado Axcueta gave him and his children, and in granting him this favor your majesty's conscience will be relieved, as a very Christian prince always grants mercy to those who serve him, say what they know.

Seventh, if they know that all of this is publicly and commonly known.

And later in the said Ciudad Real de Chiapa on the said day, month, and year before the said señor magistrate Pedro de Heredia and before me the notary, Domingo Pérez . . . presented as witness Garci Sanchez de Pinos, resident of this Ciudad Real de Chiapa, who was received and sworn in the name of God our Lord and Saint Mary his mother and by a sign of the cross that he made with the fingers of his right hand, by which he promised to speak the truth of what he knows, and was questioned according to the tenor of the interrogation, and he said the following:

1. To the first question he said that he has known Domingo Pérez, Indian and resident of the *Tlaxcaltecas* of the valley of this city, and Pedro Gómez his legitimate son, for more than 30 years in these parts, and this he says. . . . As to the general questions of the law, he is more than 50 years old and there is nothing in the questions of the general law that impedes his testimony.

2. To the second question he said that he had heard it said to Alonso de Aguilar, resident of this city now dead and conquistador of these parts, that Domingo Pérez, Indian, is a native of the city of Tlaxcala of New Spain, that he had brought him from there and this is how he knows it. And he had also heard it said as public and common knowledge. And he had also heard from many persons that the city of Tlaxcala and residents and natives of it are free and exempt from tribute by grace of your majesty for having served your majesty very well.

3. To the third question he said that he agrees with what the question says before this one, and has heard it publicly and commonly said that the natives of the city of Tlaxcala have been loyal servants of your majesty, and when Hernando Cortés came to this land which was when he came to the conquest of the said New Spain, the residents and natives of the city of Tlaxcala received them in peace. And these natives helped in all of the conquest of New Spain, until the land was pacified and placed under the dominion of your majesty. And the pacification of New Spain being completed, the natives of the city of Tlaxcala were divided between the captains that passed on to the province of Guatemala and to this province of Chiapa and to other parts. . . . And this is what he had heard said by Alonso de Aguilar many times, that the said Domingo Pérez, Indian,

had come with him from the city of Tlaxcala with other Indians, and had served him very well in these parts, and this is his answer.

4. To the fourth question he said that he saw Domingo Pérez, Indian, in the conquest of Lacandon and Pochutlan and Topiltepeque with his arms, and that he went to help the Spanish conquistadors who went on these conquests by order of the general Pedro Ramirez. And there he saw him serving and assisting very well in everything he was ordered to do with other *Tlaxcalteca* and Mexicano[13] Indians. And therefore this witness takes Domingo Pérez as a conquistador because he has heard the old conquistadors of this land say so, and it is said he served well and loyally in the said conquest, and this is publicly and commonly known.

5. To the fifth question, he has heard it said in this city that since Domingo Pérez is a conquistador, the señor licenciado Cristobal de Axcueta judge of the Real *Audiencia* of Guatemala and inspector of this province reserved and freed him from tribute, so that neither he nor his children would pay tribute.

6. To the sixth question he said that since Domingo Pérez is a resident and native of the said city of Tlaxcala, he deserves for your majesty to apply to him and approve the grant that the said señor licenciado Axcueta gave to him and his children, and that complying with the said grant it should be understood that this fulfills the obligations of the royal conscience.

7. To the last question, he says that what he has said is the truth . . .

And later in the same Ciudad Real de Chiapa on the seventh day of April, 1584, before the said señor magistrate, the said Domingo Pérez Indian for the said probanza presented as witness Juan Bautista, Indian resident of the barrio of the *Tlaxcaltecas* of the valley of this city of the royal Crown, and

through the interpretation of me the said scribe, the said señor magistrate received his oath by God our Lord . . .

1. To the first question he said that he has known Domingo Pérez, Indian and resident of the barrio of the *Tlaxcaltecas* of the valley of this city, and his son Pedro Gómez and his legitimate wife the Indian Beatriz, and he has known Domingo Pérez for 60 years in these parts, and Pedro Gómez since he was born. And of the general questions he said that he is 85 yrs old, and that Domingo Pérez is a friend of this witness but this will not stop him from telling the truth.

2. To the second question he said that he knows Domingo Pérez to be from the city of Tlaxcala in New Spain, because he has always heard this said by him and by other Indians living in this city. And he presently lives in the valley, and since he is from Tlaxcala, he knows that your majesty granted the *Tlaxcaltecas* the grace of not paying tribute.

3. To the third question he said what is said in the question, that the city of Tlaxcala and its people are free and exempt from tribute to any person, for having loyally served your majesty. And when Hernando Cortés entered into this war and lands and the said city, the *Tlaxcaltecas* and this witness received him in peace.

4. To the fourth question he said that he knows that Domingo Pérez, Indian, has been and lived in this city for some fifty years, and this witness saw Domingo Pérez in the conquest and pacification of . . . Pochutla and Topiltepeque with the captain Francisco Gil. And this witness saw that he served in these campaigns and provinces with his weapons, and always fulfilled what he was asked to do as a good soldier, and thus he is known and taken as a conquistador, and this is what he knows of the question.

5. To the fifth question he said that he understands Domingo Pérez, native of the city of Tlaxcala of New Spain, to be more than 70 years old, and as a conquistador your majesty was compelled to grant him the mercy of liberties from tribute, and this was confirmed in the

---

[13]The *Tlaxcalteca* were often singled out as an exceptionally loyal group of Nahua allies. "Mexicanos" referred to central Mexican *Nahuatl* speakers other than the *Tlaxcalteca*.

conscience of the señor licenciado Axcueta, *oidor* [*audiencia* judge] and *visitador* [carries out *visitas*] of these provinces, who reserved him and his children from tribute.

To the last question he said that everything he has said is publicly and commonly known.[14]

Reply. Grabiel Dominguez, defender of the Indians of this province, in name of the magistrates and councilmen of the *Tlaxcaltecas* and Mexicanos of the valley of this city in the case that they have brought against Pedro Gómez, Indian, concerning his claim to be reserved from tribute saying that he is the son of a conquistador and a *Tlaxcalteca*. I say that a copy was provided me of the petition presented by Pedro Gómez, and of the probanza that Domingo Pérez his father made, and other collections were presented. Despite the cases and reasons given and alleged, he should be declared a tributary because it is the truth that Domingo Pérez, father of the said Pedro Gómez, is not a native of the city of Tlaxcala of New Spain, neither were his parents, but rather he was born in the province of Guatemala where they were natives. And this is how the witnesses testify in his probanza, because . . . Grabiel Ximenez the aforementioned Indian witness says that he [Domingo Pérez] is a native of Tlaxcala because he is an Indian who was born and raised in the barrio of the Mexicanos of this city, and thus he is affectionately called this and it should not be given any credit because it is only a saying. And Gómez de Villafuerte and Garci Sanchez, witnesses in the probanza, do not declare nor did they know before that Domingo Pérez is a native of Tlaxcala, only that they met him in service of Alonso de Aguilar whom they heard say that he had brought him from the province of Guatemala, which is in effect true. And he told them he had been a conquistador of these provinces and of the pueblos of Pochutla, Topiltepeque, and Lacandon and other parts, and that for this reason he was declared a conquistador and was reserved from tribute payment. I say that if Domingo Pérez came to this province and town as

they say when it was conquered and pacified, it was in service of the said Alonso de Aguilar his master as a slave, which he was, and thus the said Alonso de Aguilar in those times marked and branded all of the slaves and Indians in his service on the left side of their face. For which reason and many others which we will allege and prove our case.

I ask and request that your highness . . . declare that Domingo Pérez is not *Tlaxcalteca* but rather was an Indian slave, and that Pedro Gómez should pay your majesty in tribute what all the tributaries of the said towns and barrios pay, as well as the costs of the proceedings that I protest, and I ask for justice etc. Grabiel Dominguez.

In Ciudad Real de Chiapa on the seventeenth day of April, 1587, this petition was read before the licenciado Rodrigo de Moscoso of the council of your majesty and your judge in the Real *Audiencia* of Guatemala and visiting chief judge of these provinces.

The said señor judge commanded that the process go forward and that this case be received within six days, considering as well the past proceedings and conclusions. Blas Hidalgo.

Suggested Sources:

Recent studies and new documentary collections of the conquest period abound. The conquest of Tenochtitlán is the most comprehensively covered. Stuart Schwartz's *Victors and Vanquished: Spanish and Nahua Views of the Conquest of Mexico* (Boston: Bedford/St. Martins, 2000) combines excerpts from Hernán Cortés and Bernal Díaz del Castillo with different indigenous-authored texts, some lamenting the violence, others rejoicing in their victory alongside the Europeans. James Lockhart's *We People Here: Nahuatl Accounts of the Conquest of Mexico* (Berkeley: University of California Press, 1993) presents remembrances of the conquest period written in Nahuatl. Charles Gibson's *Tlaxcala in the Sixteenth Century* (Stanford, CA: Stanford University Press, 1967) remains the standard work on the Tlaxcalteca's early alliance with the Spanish. In the Andes, Carolyn

---

[14] The sixth question is omitted in the document.

Dean explores the alliance of the Cañari and Chachapoya with the Spanish in *Inka Bodies and the Body of Christ* (Durham, NC: Duke University Press, 1999); Nicole Delia Legnani, *Titu Cusi: A Sixteenth-Century Account of the Conquest* (Cambridge, MA: DRCLAS/Harvard University Press, 2005) focuses on the view of the defeated yet loyal Inca Titu Cusi; whereas Kris Lane explores many different kinds of alliances in *Quito, 1599* (Albuquerque: University of New Mexico Press, 2002). Gonzalo Jiménez de Quesada's expedition to the interior of Colombia, discussed by J. Michael Francis in *Invading Colombia*, is an example of an invasion enabled by indigenous (and African) slaves and allies. J. Michael Francis, *Invading Colombia: Spanish Accounts of the Gonzalo Jimenez de Quesada Expedition of Conquest* (University Park, PA: Penn State University Press, 2008). Returning to Mesoamerica, Laura Matthew and Michel Oudijk's *Indian Conquistadors: Indigenous Allies in the Conquest of Mesoamerica* (Norman: University of Oklahoma Press, 2007) looks at less famous conquests, including paintings of the conquest from a native perspective. Some of the primary sources used in these studies appear in Matthew Restall and Florine Asselbergs' collection *Invading Guatemala: Spanish, Nahua, and Maya Accounts of the Conquest Wars* (University Park, PA: Penn State University Press, 2007). Indigenous allies remember their roles in Lisa Sousa and Kevin Terraciano, "The Original Conquest of Oaxaca: Nahua and Mixtec Accounts of the Spanish Conquest," in *Ethnohistory* 50, no. 2 (2003): 349–400; and Stephanie Wood's *Transcending Conquest: Nahua Views of the Conquest of Mexico* (Norman: University of Oklahoma Press, 2003). Finally, Matthew Restall's *Seven Myths of the Spanish Conquest* (Cambridge: Cambridge University Press, 2003) challenges the totalizing effect of European narratives of the conquest.

Chapter 5

Runaways Establish Maroon Communities in the Hinterland of Brazil

Leo J. Garofalo, Connecticut College

PERNAMBUCO

Palmares
in Captaincy of
Pernambuco

*ATLANTIC
OCEAN*

One of the most significant fugitive slave communities in the Americas flourished for a century in the forested interior of Brazil's colonial state of *Pernambuco* (today part of Alagoas). A confederation of eleven widespread towns, Palmares harbored perhaps as many as 20,000 to 50,000 people. They called the main fortified town Macaco. Palmares represented runaway slaves' success at forming a *maroon* state of politically integrated communities containing Africans of various ethnic groups, *creoles* born into slavery, and native Tupians (Tupinambá) and their native-African children.[1] Throughout the seventeenth century until its final destruction in 1695, Palmares, and other *maroon* communities or *quilombos* like it, threatened the valuable sugar plantation economy hugging Brazil's northeastern coast and a labor system based on African slave labor.[2] Brazil's Palmares and the runaway communities called *palenques* or *cumbes* in Spanish America showed how tenuous colonial officials' hold over people and territory could be and the surprising existence of alternatives to European-dominated colonial societies in the Americas.

Despite the odds and the multiple military campaigns launched by the Portuguese and Dutch against it, Palmares flourished in a colony shaped by an export economy and slave labor. Brazil boomed when the economy shifted from trade in dyewood, parrots, and animal skins to plantation agriculture. By 1600, sugar plantations displaced simply trading with the Tupinambá people of the coast. Brazil's plantation owners copied the Mediterranean practice of using slave labor to grow sugar. The Tupinambá first fell victim to this labor regime; however, once plantation owners accumulated enough capital, they preferred to buy African slaves as a long-term labor solution. Africans proved more accustomed to this kind of agricultural work and less likely to escape or die of disease. Slaves from Africa were in abundant supply because of Brazil's relative proximity to Africa and the fact that the Portuguese dominated the slave trade in the 1500s and 1600s.[3] Sugar accounted for as much as 90 to 95 percent of Brazil's export earnings between 1600 and 1650.[4] Brazil's sugar economy became so profitable that the Dutch, eager to control directly this wealth, captured and occupied northeastern Brazil from 1630 to 1654. Despite the united power of slaveholders and the great fortunes that motivated them, resistance to the

brutality and degradation of slavery could be fierce and occasionally successful.

The impact of sugar reached far beyond awakening the greed of landowners and the Dutch. The dominance of sugar production also encouraged people to supply locally grown food, livestock, and tools needed by these operations. The overwhelming power of planters and their merchant allies made even more remarkable the ability of slaves to escape this servitude and fight it in a collective fashion.

Although most *maroon* communities remained much smaller than Palmares, all of them challenged the established order that made the plantation world the center of Brazil's colonial society. This was a world dominated by the landowner and his big house and the slave quarters and the artisan, food producers, and merchants who supplied them. Runaways encouraged other slaves to flee, sometimes raided and kidnapped new members for their villages, and almost always engaged in some sort of trade or other economic interaction with colonial societies outside of the officially regulated and taxed channels. Much as they may have liked to forget these troublesome and ubiquitous runaways, Spanish and Portuguese authorities could not ignore *maroons* and their influence beyond the hidden, but never completely autonomous, communities. *Maroons* offered opportunities for trade outside of the plantation-dominated system, and they offered other runaways inspiration and sometimes a refuge.

Many fascinating questions arise about how Palmares functioned as a multiethnic society and a state. Among the most important are, to what extent does Palmares represent an example of "Afro-native cooperation" as historians Stuart B. Schwartz and Hal Langfur term it?[5] And was Palmares a pseudo-African state organized with African traditions of kingship, religion, slavery, and division of labor? Certainly the runaways integrated many indigenous people and their farming and building techniques

---

[1]The Tupians or Tupinambá were the main indigenous cultural group the Portuguese encountered in coastal Brazil.
[2]Before 1700, *macombo* most often appears as the word for a community of escaped slaves. After 1700, *quilombo* becomes more common.
[3]Stuart B. Schwartz, "Indian Labor and New World Plantations: European Demands and Indian Responses in Northeastern Brazil," *The American Historical Review* 80, no. 1 (February 1978): 43–79.
[4]Thomas E. Skidmore also offers a history of Brazil from the arrival of the Portuguese to the late twentieth century in *Brazil: Five Centuries of Change* (New York: Oxford University Press, 1999).

[5]Stuart B. Schwartz and Hal Langfur, "Tapanhuns, Negros da Terra, and Curibocas: Common Cause and Confrontation between Blacks and Natives in Colonial Brazil," in *Beyond Black and Red: African-Native Relations in Colonial Latin America*, ed. Matthew Restall (Albuquerque: University of New Mexico Press, 2005), 101.

Like the runaways in Portuguese Brazil, *maroons* in Mexico, Panama, Jamaica, Suriname, and Spanish South America created communities and defended them. This picture shows a *maroon* defender in Suriname fighting Dutch planters and European mercenaries. Violence often alternated with negotiations and long periods of hostile coexistence. How does the European artist choose to portray this *maroon* man from the 1770s? How does this compare with the *maroon* leaders in the portrait in Chapter 7? What message did the artist hope to convey to viewers in his day?

Source: Getty Images Inc. - Hulton Archive Photos.

into their communities. Tupians and their children, many with both indigenous and African heritage, figure among the prisoners captured in the military raids made against the *maroon* state and later sold as slaves. In addition to indigenous people and Brazilian-born blacks, Palmares was home to many people from different African regions and speaking different languages. Leaders claiming noble ancestry, military expertise, or religious and ritual knowledge forged a loose unity among these groups and integrated them into life in Palmares's farming villages. A supreme leader or king seemed to exercise some degree of authority over those directly in charge of each village or cluster of villages. Trade with backwoods farmers and cattle ranchers and raiding the more distant plantations supplemented Palmares's subsistence economy. Most *quilombos* in Brazil and elsewhere in the Americas existed not in total isolation from the rest of colonial society, but instead in close contact and often complete reliance on colonial society for trade and for the very people who replenished the runaway population.

For almost a hundred years, this constant and often violent interaction with Brazil's plantation society terrified colonizers. An outsider hostile to *maroons'* quest for independence and cultural autonomy penned this chapter's anonymous description of the next-to-last, late seventeenth-century campaign against Palmares. To a large extent, the author sought to celebrate the exploits of the governor and the military commander sent into the forests to attack the *maroons* and force them to negotiate. The campaign forced the leader of Palmares, Gangasuma, to enter into an agreement with the Portuguese. Gangasuma's successor, his son Zumba or Zumbi, later repudiated the agreement, initiating another cycle of raiding and war. Because Palmares blocked westward expansion, subsequent governors would again raise colonial forces to attack the *maroon* state. The colonial state's military victory followed upon the successful recruitment and incorporation into this effort of large numbers of Paulista *bandeirantes* (armed bands of Portuguese creoles and mixed indigenous-European individuals, usually from São Paulo, who pushed west to look for precious metals and capture Indians slaves). Palmares only ceased to exist as an independent political entity and population center after the destruction of its last fortified village following a 44-day siege. Although Palmares finally fell and no other *maroon* settlement rivaled its size and military strength in South America, slave revolts and runaway communities continued to appear across the continent, particularly in Brazil's plantation regions, until slavery's final abolition in 1888, well after independence from Portugal. Palmares and its last king,

Zumbi, continue to inspire Afro-Brazilian pride and serve as potent symbols of resistance to European domination and exploitation even today.[6]

Questions to Consider:

I. What did you learn of life in *quilombos* and how they were established and maintained? In what ways was Palmares linked to the rest of Brazil?

---

[6]The 1984 Brazilian film *Quilombo* celebrates Palmares.

2. How would you describe *quilombo* leadership? What kinds of authorities were mentioned, and on what did their power seem to be based?
3. What language and rhetoric did both sides use to describe each other and to negotiate with one another? To rally their forces? To acknowledge another's power? How was this language charged with references to gender, particularly paternalism?
4. Why do you think a peace accord was reached? Can you identify the different parties involved and what might have motivated each one?

Seventeenth-Century *Quilombo* of Palmares: A Chronicle of War and Peace in Brazil[7]

In a palm forest sixteen leagues [approximately 48 miles][8] northeast of Porto Calvo existed the *mocambo* of the Zambi (a general or god of arms in their language), and five leagues farther north that of Acainene (this was the name of the king's mother, who lived in this fortified mocambo about twenty-five leagues northeast of Porto Calvo, and which they call the Acainene Compound, since it is was fortified by a wall of earth and sticks).

To the east of these was the mocambo of the Wild Canes [Tabocas], and northeast of this one that of Bambiabonga. Eight leagues north of Bambiabonga was the compound called Sucupira; six leagues northward from this Royal Compound of the Macao [monkey], and five leagues to the west of this the mocambo of Osenga. Nine leagues northwest of the town of Serinhaem was the compound of Amaro, and twenty-five leagues northwest of Alagôas the palm forest of Andolaquituxe, the Zambi's brother.

---

[7]*Source:* Anonymous account written in the 1600s taken from the original manuscript in the Biblioeca Pública in Evora, Portugal, translated and published as the "Seventeenth-Century Quilombo of Palmares: A Chronicle of War and Peace" in Robert Edgar Conrad, *Children of God's Fire: A Documentary History of Black Slavery in Brazil* (Princeton, NJ: Princeton University Press, 1983), 369–377.
[8]A league is about 3 miles.

Among all these places, which were the largest and best fortified, there were others of less importance and with fewer people. It is widely believed that when blacks were first brought into the captaincies of Brazil they began to live in these Palmares, and it is certain that during the period of Dutch rule their numbers greatly increased.

They called their king Gangasuma (a hybrid term meaning "great lord" composed of the Angolan or Bunda word "ganga" and the Tupí Indian word "assú"). This king lived in a royal city which they called Macao. This was the main city among the other towns or mocambos, and it was completely surrounded by a wall of earth and sticks.

The second city was that known as Sucupira (later the camp of Good Jesus and the Cross founded by Fernão Carrilho). Here lived the Gangasona, the king's brother. Like the latter, all the cities were under the command of rulers and powerful chiefs, who lived in them and governed them.

Sucupira, the war command center where the confederation's defense forces and sentinels were trained, was also fortified, but with stone and wood. Nearly a league in length, it contained within its boundaries three lofty mountains and a river called Cachhingi, meaning "an abundance of water."

Before the restoration of *Pernambuco* from Dutch rule, twenty-five probing expeditions were sent into the area, suffering great losses but failing to uncover the secrets of those brave people. . . . The first was that of Captain Braz da Rocha Cardoso with six hundred men. Little was accomplished by this expedition because of the difficulties of the terrain, the roughness of the trails, and the impossibility of transporting equipment over unknown country. . . .

. . . Recovering the captaincy from Dutch rule with the surrender of Recife in January, 1654, [the governor] immediately undertook a campaign against Palmares, since for him these internal enemies were just as harmful and more barbaric and dreadful than the former. . . .

From March, 1657, to January, 1674, the date that Captain D. Pedro de Almeida assumed the governorship of the captaincy, it was for no lack of effort that victory was not achieved, . . .

The inhabitants of Alagôas, Porto Calvo, and Penedo were constantly under attack, and their houses and plantations robbed by the blacks of Palmares. The blacks killed their cattle and carried away their slaves to enlarge their *quilombos* and increase the number of their defenders, forcing the inhabitants and natives of those towns to engage in fighting at a distance of forty leagues or more, at great cost to their plantations and risk to their own lives, without which the blacks would have become masters of the captaincy because their huge and ever-increasing numbers.

This was the situation in January, 1674, when D. Pedro de Almeida took possession of the captaincy and at once attempted to pursue the conquest. . . . He prudently made all the necessary preparations for the first undertaking, assigning the expedition to Major Manoel Lopes Galvão. . . .

By September 23, 1675, Major Manoel Lopes was in Porto Calvo with 280 men, including whites, *mestizos*, and Indians, to attempt the action, and on November 21, after two months of preparation, they entered the wilderness where their labors and dangers were enormous and constant.

On January 22, 1676, they reached a well-garrisoned and populous city of more than two thousand houses, and after more than two hours of bitter fighting, with bravery displayed on both sides, our men set fire to some houses, which, being of wood and straw, quickly burned, turning the place into an inferno. The great fear which then possessed the blacks forced them to flee, and regrettably they abandoned the city. The next day, gathered at another place and with terror still reigning among them, they were again attacked, suffering considerable losses. . . . Many were killed or wounded in those two encounters, the others seeking refuge in the forests.

The nearby towns and villages immediately experienced the effects of these great victories; the terrible lesson forced many of the *quilombolas* to go in search of their old masters, since they no longer felt safe in that wilderness. . . .

D. Pedro de Almeida, satisfied with the results obtained, and wishing to take advantage of the experience acquired and the demoralization in which Major Manoel Lopes had left them, decided to commit new forces to the enterprise. To accomplish this he sent an invitation to Commander Fernão Carrilho, who was then in Sergipe and had become famous for the work he had accomplished in destroying the mocambos of the blacks and the villages of the Tapuia Indians who infested the backlands of *Bahia*. Accepting the honorable invitation, the latter left for Pernambuco with some of his relatives and dependents. . . .

Without delay Fernão Carrilho left for Porto Calvo where he was expected by the people who had assembled from the other parishes, which, according to orders, should have been 400 men; but only 185 were there, including whites, *mestizos*, and Indians of the people of Camarão [Indian commander in the war against the Dutch]. . . .

Commander Fernão Carrilho then spoke to the troops, telling them the following: "that number neither added to nor reduced the courage of valiant men; that only bravery itself made a soldier determined; that, while the multitude of the enemy was large, it was a multitude of slaves whom nature had created more to obey than to resist; that the blacks fought as fugitives, and they were hunting them down as lords and masters; that their honor was endangered by the disobedience of the black slaves; their plantations insecure because of their robberies; their lives placed in great jeopardy by their impudence; that no one among them fought for another man's property, and all defended their own; it being a great disgrace for every Pernambucan to be whipped by those whom they had themselves so many times whipped;. . . that if they destroyed Palmares they would have land for their farms, blacks for their service, and honor and esteem for themselves; and that, if he had taken this great task upon his shoulders, not being a resident of those captaincies, it was for the service of His Highness alone, and for the sake of obedience to the governor, D. Pedro de Almeida. . . ."

. . . Carrilho entered the forest in search of the Acainene Compound, a fortified mocambo 25 leagues northwest of Porto Calvo, where the king's mother lived, for whom the mocambo had been named. So impressed were the men by the magic words of Carrilho that each one thought of himself as invincible.

As soon as the blacks knew of their presence, they quickly abandoned the city, still in the state of terror inspired by Major Manoel Lopes. On October 4 our men attacked the fugitives with such force that they killed many and captured nine, but the king's mother was not found among them either dead or alive.

Not only did they gain advantages from the enemy's losses of a strong city and a large number if men; this victory also served to furnish our side with guides and information. From the prisoners it was learned that the king, Gangasuma, with his brother, Gangasona, and all the other rulers and main chiefs were at the compound called Sucupira, which was then serving as a stronghold where the king waited to engage us in battle. This mocambo was 45 leagues from Porto Calvo.

It appeared to Carrilho that to establish his camp under the best conditions it would be desirable to capture a more centralized position, and so Sucupira became his objective. . . . After a great expenditure of effort, our men found the mocambo, and when they spotted it from a distance they moved silently and with great caution to avoid being discovered. Eighty men then went out again to explore the site and to verify the existence of a stockade, and they returned with news that the terrorized blacks had set fire to the city, which even in ashes revealed its greatness. When Gangasuma had received the news carried by the fugitives from Cainene that Fernñao Carrilho was about to pursue them there, he

found it preferable to sacrifice the city to fire rather than to place his own people in danger.

As soon as this occurred . . . our men took possession of the site, and there Carrilho established his camp, giving it the name "Good Jesus and the Cross," fortifying it in the best possible way with batteries of cannon. [*After some successes on part of the fugitives, the reinforced expedition achieved another important victory, killing and capturing many blacks, including the field commander, General Gangamuiza, whom they executed along with other male prisoners.*] The King, who had also been present at the beginning of the battle, had fled with the few people he could rescue from the carnage. . . .

News of such a fortunate and magnificent action brought elation to the camp. Wisely taking advantage of this and prudently ignoring the deed practiced against the prisoners in order to keep the unanimous support of his men, Commander Carrilho sent . . . fifty fresh soldiers in pursuit of the King and the other fugitives.

After 22 days of hard campaigning in that wilderness, on November 11 they received news that the King, Gangasuma, was with Amaro in his mocambo nine leagues northwest of Serinhaem. This same Amaro, celebrated for his bravery, impudence, and insulting behavior, was also greatly feared by our men, and he made himself known by his incursions into the surrounding towns. He lived separated from the others as an independent ruler. His mocambo, which was known by his name, was fortified by high, thick palisades extending the length of a league and containing more than a thousand inhabited houses.

In this mocambo the fugitive king believed himself to be safe, but even there he could not escape the vigilance and tenacity of our men who were ambitious for glory and motivated by their comrades' example. Divided into two groups, they marched with the intention of besieging the site by closing up the single entrance to the mocambo. Fortunately or unfortunately, however, before the entrance area could be occupied, the blacks, aware of our men's intentions, began to evacuate the compound, but not before our men attacked. Many of them were killed and wounded on the ground, and 47 were captured, among them were two free black women and a little *mulato* girl, the daughter of a noble resident of Serinhaem who had been seized at that place. Also captured were Anajuba, two of the King's children named Zambi and Jacainêne, the former a man and the other a woman, and others numbering about twenty, among them children and grandchildren of the King. Among the dead were Tucúlo, a son of the King, Pacasâ and Baûbi, powerful chiefs among them. So greatly frightened was the King that he fled from our furious attack, and so badly disorganized that he left behind a gilded pistol and a sword, and he was reported wounded. . . .

This great event brought total disorganization to the blacks, who had lost any hope that they could remain any longer in those places, since they had lost their principal leaders, including the most capable and feared among them, and found themselves weakened and surrounded on all sides. . . .

[The Governor D. Pedro] therefore devised a plan to summon them to him and to offer them peace as a way to achieve complete pacification.

. . . The governor selected a young ensign who was accustomed to those marches and completely familiar with those backlands to search for the leaders and tell them that Commander Carrilho was prepared to return and destroy what was left and would not leave a single enemy alive; that if they wanted to live in peace with whites he would promise them, in name of the King, total peace and good treatment, and he would grant them a specified place for their dwellings and land for their gardens; and their women, children, and grandchildren who were prisoners and slaves would be returned to them, and they would remain in their positions of leadership. The one whom they referred to as King would remain commander of all those who had been born in Palmares, and these would be granted the privileges pertaining to the vassals of the King of Portugal, to come under the protection of our arms, and to serve our colors, when conditions might require this, all those who were born in freedom to remain exempt from slavery. . . .

King Gangasuma, having been informed of this or having judged by his own experience that he could no longer resist, or fearing further setbacks, or for other reasons which we cannot determine, accepted D. Pedro's offer; and . . . the ensign who had undertaken the assignment entered the plaza accompanied by two of the King's sons and ten more of the most important blacks of those *quilombos*, who had come, in conformity with the offer made to them, to prostrate themselves at the feet of D. Pedro. They had been sent by King Gangasuma to render vassalage in his name, to ask for peace and friendship, and to tell him that only he had been able to achieve what so many other governors and so many principal chiefs had attempted and never achieved; their conquest; that they would submit to him and subject themselves to his rule; that they did not desire any more war, and were only trying to save the lives of those who remained; that they were without cities, without sources of food, and, worse yet, without their wives and children. . . .

They wanted commerce and trade with the Portuguese residents, and aspired to be vassals of the king and to serve him in every way which he required, asking only freedom for those born in Palmares, promising that they would return all those who had fled from our towns and plantations, that they would themselves abandon Palmares and go to live in a place designated for their gardens and dwelling places. . . .

The governor then wished to have them baptized so that they might begin to enjoy the benefits of peace under divine influence; and since the blacks themselves wished to receive baptism, it was wisely decided to take advantage of this opportune occasion so that they might pledge themselves with utmost seriousness to the purpose for which they had come. A solemn mass was sung, and the vicar of the parish church rose to the pulpit and gave deserved thanks to God, repeated praise to St. Anthony, and to the governors the compliments they had earned. . . .

. . . Governor Ayres de Sousa convoked a council of all the leading men to decide how they might best guarantee the peace. . . . They agreed to make peace with the King of Palmares, acknowledging his obedience; that they [the blacks] be granted the site where they would choose to settle, a place suitable for their dwellings and their farms; that they must begin to live there within three months; that those born in Palmares would be free; that they were to return all the runaways who had come from our populated places; that they would have commerce and friendly trade with the whites; that they would acquire the privileges of the

King's vassals; that they would remain obedient to the orders of the government; that their King would continue as commander of all his people; and that the wives of the King and all the other rulers would be returned to them. There being some doubt among the members of the council that King Gangasuma would have sufficient power to dominate another rebellious runaway who lived at a distance from his mocambos, his son responded that the King would be able to manage all of them, and if some of them were insubordinate and insolent and resisted their subjugation, he would conquer them, and he would provide guides to our forces so that they might be overcome. And he immediately indicated the place which they regarded as most suitable for their settlement, which was an extensive forest situated in the headwaters of the Rivers Serinhaem and Formoso, which they called "Cacaú," where there was no lack of palm trees to provide them with food. With these matters clarified, the peace was agreed upon, the desired site was granted, and the council ended its meeting. And Governor Ayres de Sousa ordered that everything be recorded, so that the blacks could take with them in writing what the council had decided, and thus they were sent away in the company of a regimental major.

Suggested Sources:

Throughout the Americas, people fled from slavery, but only in few places did maroon communities form or survive. See Richard Price, *Maroon Societies: Rebel Slave Communities in the Americas* (Baltimore: Johns Hopkins University Press, 1973). Jamaica's maroons achieved victories. Refer to Mavis C. Campbell, *The Maroons of Jamaica, 1655–1796: A History of Resistance, Collaboration & Betrayal* (South Hadley, MA: Bergin & Garvey, 1988). Runaways and maroons often depended on good relations with indigenous populations. See Matthew Restall, ed., *Beyond Black and Red: African-Native Relations in Colonial Latin America* (Albuquerque: University of New Mexico Press, 2005). Stuart B. Schwartz covers the development of the slave system, regional variations, and how it generated slave resistance and negotiation in *Slaves, Peasants, and Rebels: Reconsidering Brazilian Slavery* (Urbana: University of Illinois Press, 1992). Plantation colonies grew by closely linking sugar and slavery. See Stuart B. Schwartz, ed., *Tropical Babylons: Sugar and the Making of the Atlantic World, 1450–1680* (Chapel Hill: University of North Carolina Press, 2004).

Slaves and maroons rarely found opportunities to record their own experiences. In one exceptional set of documents, slaves explain how they revolted, killed their overseer, and then negotiated a return to slavery. See Stuart B. Schwartz, "Resistance and Accommodation in Eighteenth-Century Brazil: The Slaves' View of Slavery," *The Hispanic American Historical Review* 57, no. 1 (February 1977): 69–81. More often maroons and slaves find their history recorded by others. See Robert Edgar Conrad, *Children of God's Fire: A Documentary History of Black Slavery in Brazil* (Princeton, NJ: Princeton University Press, 1983). *Quilombo*, directed by Carlos Diegues (Brazil, 1984), draws on the historical record and Afro-Brazilian culture today to tell the history of Palmares. Documentaries from surviving maroon communities in different parts of Latin America are beginning to appear to tell the history and current struggles of their communities. See *Quilombo Country: Afrobrazilian Villages in the 21st Century*, dir. Leonard Abrams (New York: Quilombo Films, 2006); and *Garifuna Journey*, dir. Andrea E. Leland and Kathy L. Berger (New York: New Day Films, 1998).

Section II

Church, Society, and Colonial Rule

Even though the spread of Christianity promoted imperialism and colonization, a surprising number of non-Europeans and women won spaces within the Church to worship and to build social status. When Iberian imperialism and evangelization sought to make all peoples Christians, they effectively made all Native Peoples in the Americas and Africans eligible for incorporation into the Church. Once converted, membership offered a modicum of protection from abuse, and many colonized people employed Christianity to protect further their interests under imperial rule. They used religious practice to express their spirituality and to claim higher status. The incorporation of colonized people and even slaves into the Church corresponded with an era of popular participation and enthusiasm for religious expression and with an era of Church attempts to reform and channel this exuberant religious expression. Religion both made people into colonial subjects and provided the colonized and enslaved with opportunities to express themselves and act within colonial society.

Native Peoples and Africans and their descendents joined *confraternities* (religious brotherhoods) in particular. In doing so, they either followed or created ethnic lines by allowing only people from a particular ethnic group to join or requiring those joining to embrace a dominant ethnic identity. Alternately, they might require acceptance of a general legal marker—like "Indian"—that could permit even broader membership. Other *confraternities* emphasized affiliations linked to occupations, home communities, or to a mixed group of devotees to a particular saint or miraculous image. In other words, some *confraternities* allowed only *Angolan* slaves, others allowed any "African" person, and still others embraced any tailor of whatever ethnicity or legal category living in a particular city. Both men and women could join *confraternities* and many did, together or separately. Some rural indigenous communities found that *confraternities* afforded protection for communal property; the protective oversight of the Church allowed these villagers to endow their towns' religious brotherhoods with the herds and lands they hoped to defend from colonists' encroachments and officials' extortions. *Confraternity* membership and other examples of official and unofficial religious practice marked gender, ethnicity, occupation, and neighborhood. Making these distinctions and their various combinations real in people's lives helped establish people's place within colonial society. Thus, religious practice within and alongside the Church both allowed individual and collective agency but also reinforced the distinctions and hierarchies of race and gender.

Certainly, these efforts assumed a basic hierarchy in which new converts to Christianity from Africa and America occupied a position inferior to European and American-born European Christians. Only people of entirely European descent, for instance, could be ordained as priests. The initial missionary optimism about rapid conversion gave way to a more pessimistic view of Native Peoples' ability to master and remain faithful to Christianity. Full conversion might take several generations. Church officials described religious paternalism and domination of European over non-European as parallel to the controlling guidance and power that men were supposed to exercise over women and children. Furthermore, many confraternities formally, or in practice, excluded those not able to claim the legal status of Spanish or Portuguese. Women in particular suffered a demotion in religious participation under Catholicism. In Mesoamerican and Andean societies, women had exercised public roles as ritual specialists, mastering and passing on religious and ceremonial knowledge. These formal and public roles were attacked and eliminated or driven underground by Catholic priests and their supporters. Women's claims to Christian ritual and religious participation—as nuns, mystics, and lay religious holy women—would remain widespread but tenuous for the rest of the colonial era. Officials viewed female religious expression and authority with suspicion and hostility. In fact, parish priests, confessors, and the Inquisition's investigators closely regulated female religious expression.[1] In other words, even though they were not alone or even unchallenged in their religious influence and power, European and **creole** men exercised dominant roles within the American Church and the American experiences of Catholicism.

Church and state were tightly intertwined in colonial Latin America with the purpose of maintaining a sociopolitical hierarchy that benefited a small group of wealthy European men and furthered the goals of an imperial monarchy. The Church reinforced the social hierarchies and legal inequalities that advantaged Europeans over Africans and Amerindians and men over women. The Church also served the Iberian monarchies

from the beginning as a formal partner in conquest and colonization. A 1455 papal bull allowed the Portuguese to enslave Africans in order to bring non-Christians to Christianity, and another in 1493 gave the Spanish the right to conquer and convert the Americas. In short, Spanish and Portuguese conquests overseas found justification in Christian evangelization, and religious practices and patriarchy supported the exploitation and subjugation of the many by the few.

Although Eurocentric and dedicated to evangelization, the Church was not monolithic, and it harbored some who advocated for an alternative. European missionaries jostled with conquistadors and Crown officials to offer a colonial paradigm based on evangelization and creating a more perfect Christian society. In a practical sense, the desire to establish a Christian utopia meant that the conquistadors could not operate completely without restraint because they competed with the priests for control over the indigenous population, and religious officials competed with each other over jurisdiction and power over indigenous peoples. Perhaps, most importantly, the overlapping jurisdictions and clashing paradigms meant that the Crown would be called on to intervene to mediate in local disputes and to distribute power in colonial society right from the beginning. One immediate result was that some priests criticized European policies toward Indians, even though they maintained contradictory stances toward African peoples. These priests influenced Crown policies, such as Queen Isabel's decree banning wholesale Indian slavery (1500), the Laws of Burgos (1512) to stop early violence toward Indians, and the New Laws (1542) meant to end private control over forced Indian labor and other abuses. Many missionaries sought to curb the mistreatment of Indians and Africans. This advocacy limited the conquistadors' progress toward establishing a feudal society with conquistador families at the top, and the Church critique influenced Crown officials' efforts to establish royal authority over broad new populations of free subjects and taxpayers in the colonies. The missionaries' efforts placed the subject peoples of the Americas and religious

---

[1]The *Inquisition* punished violations of Church dogma among non-Indians. Tribunals were first established in Lima (1570), Mexico City (1571), and Brazil (1590s).

culture at the center of the Iberian imperial projects and colonial life.

The Church brought indigenous people into colonial society early and offered them and Africans multiple ways to belong and express religious sensibilities. The initial missionary enthusiasm drove forward a push for rapid evangelization, including mass baptisms and the training of indigenous elites as translators and neophytes. These efforts led to the establishment of schools for the sons of indigenous nobility or local leaders and to a widespread *syncretism* in many places that combined Christianity with elements of pre-Hispanic beliefs and practices and with elements of African religion. The engagement between colonizers and the colonized came at a propitious moment when *confraternities*, popular saints, religious processions, and many other manifestations of religious identity and commitment abounded throughout the Catholic world. Local and popular traditions overlapped with official institutions and universal practices. Indeed, the exercise of power within religion and religious culture was multifocal and multidirectional, meaning that religious activities took place at many levels within a Church that stretched from Rome, across Catholic Europe, and into the multiethnic cities and predominantly indigenous countryside in the Americas.[2] "Multidirectional" means that ideas about how to understand spirituality and engage in rituals and ceremonies both originated in official acts and teachings and filtered up through society and into the Church's understanding of how faith operated and mattered at the individual and communal levels. The official Church had grown very wealthy and powerful by the end of the seventeenth century. The power of the archbishop rivaled that of the *viceroy*, and the Church became the institution to which colonial entrepreneurs turned for credit. Some scholars argue that a Hispanic Catholicism eventually grew out of this dynamic mix of competing

agendas and influences and eventually allowed the accumulation of local and popular custom and community-centered devotions to be made into doctrine.

Religious practice and figures within the Church both promoted and limited colonialism by

An Indian chronicler of Native Andean history and life under Spanish rule, Felipe Guaman Poma de Ayala, sought to describe with text and drawings for the Spanish king the proper and improper behaviors he observed. In a chapter dedicated to hereditary Andean nobles, he depicted exemplary Christians: a local Andean lord seated on a traditional ceremonial seat reading to his wife. In the drawings, what marks Christian behavior? How do the drawings also represent other hierarchies of rank or status? What role does clothing play in communicating meaning in these visual sources?

Source: The Royal Library/Drawing 289. Exemplary Christians. 761 [775]. Buen Cristiano Principal.

---

[2]Catholicism even adapted to society, or attempted to change it, in some parts of Asia such as Japan, the Philippines, and India.

raising powerful voices of critique and offering opportunities for incorporation and influence to Native People, Africans, and women. The excerpts from the writings of the principled *Dominican* friar Bartolomé de Las Casas highlight the debates missionaries sparked over the abuses perpetuated against Indians and Africans. Las Casas helps illustrate how even the imposition of Catholicism could force the imperial system to recognize the humanity and cultures of non-Europeans. The period letter that Beatty-Medina contextualizes illustrates the ability of *maroons* to limit the reach of European empires and find Churchmen to act as emissaries and intermediaries in these negotiations. To further their agendas, Church and state sought out ethnic chiefs—*caciques* and *kurakas*—particularly for the evangelization of indigenous populations. The cases of the Virgin of Guadalupe and a convert's troubling dreams show how missionaries and Christian Indians grappled with blending beliefs from two traditions. Continuing the focus on subordination and incorporation, McLeod provides sources regarding the role of ethnicity and gender in founding religious brotherhoods. Finally, Melvin's sources on race and hierarchy in devotional life show, however, that subordinates' manipulations of religious devotion were often highly charged and contested by authorities. These primary sources and the many stories they contain will leave readers with a deeper understanding of the many meanings, experiences, and uses of Catholicism in Latin American history.

Chapter 6

European Priests Discuss Ruling Indigenous and African Peoples

Leo J. Garofalo, *Connecticut College*

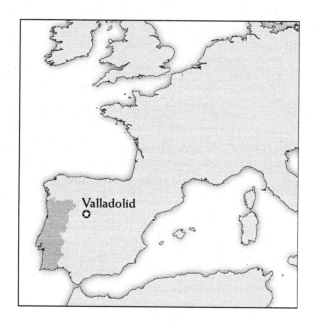

Valladolid

Sixteenth-century critics of the Spanish Conquest heralded Bartolomé de Las Casas as the "Protector of the Indians," and he is still a hero today for members of the Church who challenge injustice and the status quo.[3] Judging by his beginnings in southern Spain and his early actions in the Caribbean, Las Casas (1484–1566) seemed unlikely to become a hero for defenders of the poor and downtrodden. Las Casas grew up in Seville, Europe's second-largest slave market after Portugal's Lisbon

---

[3]Gustavo Gutiérrez, *Las Casas: In the Search of the Poor of Jesus Christ*, trans. Robert R. Barr (Maryknoll, NY: Orbis Books, 1992).

and an important gateway city, connecting Spain to Africa and the lucrative Portuguese slave trade as well as to the Americas. Although he saw African, *morisco*, and Moorish slaves from northern Africa, decades passed before Las Casas spoke out against African slavery and Europeans' justifications of the trade in African peoples. Las Casas also came of age in a time when Columbus's territorial claims brought millions more people under the sway of Spanish monarchy and the Catholic Church. However, the Crown and the Church could only claim the populous new lands in the Americas, and a victory for Christianity, if they succeeded in exerting control over America's diverse societies.

In 1502, at age 18, Las Casas became a part of Spanish conquest and its colonizing mission when he followed his father's lead and sailed to Hispaniola (his father had joined Columbus in 1493 and returned to Spain in 1498). In Hispaniola, Las Casas received in *encomienda* (trust) Native People organized by hometowns to work his lands and placer gold mines and to pay him tribute in goods. A year later, he joined the violent conquest of Cuba with the same goal: securing Indian labor. Again he received Indians in *encomienda* from Cuba's royal governor, and again he put them to work, farming and washing for gold. In return for free Indian labor, the Crown required that *encomenderos* such as Las Casas Christianize the Indians entrusted to them, maintain the peace, and collect the royal tribute due the Crown. The *encomienda* originated as a mechanism for securing territory and pacifying populations captured during the Christian **Reconquest** of the Iberian Peninsula that ended in 1492; however, in the Caribbean, the early *encomienda* system failed to protect, or even preserve for future exploitation and evangelization, the islands' indigenous populations.

The brutality of Cuba's occupation, combined with *Dominican* sermons decrying the destruction of Native Peoples, profoundly transformed Las Casas's view of the conquest and indigenous society. In 1510, Las Casas and other *encomenderos* began to hear fiery sermons in Hispaniola's churches denouncing the abuse of Indians. *Dominican* preachers refused to confess colonists who held Indians. Pondering the mistreatment he had witnessed, and castigated by the preachers' words, Las

Casas found his mission in life and became the first priest ordained in the Americas in 1510. In 1514, Las Casas concluded that the exploitation of Indians produced ill-gotten goods and everything done to the Indians was unjust and tyrannical. He traveled to Spain in 1515 to lobby King Ferdinand on behalf of the Indians and joined the *Dominican* order in 1522. Las Casas quickly became the most influential advocate for Indians' rights to govern themselves, to live free of exploitation, and to come to Christianity of their own free will and in peace.

Las Casas called for nothing less than a complete overhaul of Spain's colonial efforts in the Americas, and the Crown listened. He questioned the very right of Spain to conquer and rule the New World. The Crown wanted to resolve the question about the legitimacy of its conquest in order to fend off competing European claims and to reassert its status as a champion for the spread of Catholicism. Furthermore, Las Casas's attack on the *encomienda* system dominated by conquistadors helped the Crown limit the conquistadors' power and autonomy in the distant New World.[4] Las Casas gained access to King Ferdinand, and after him the Regent Cardinal Cisneros, who adopted one of his recommendations: He appointed three friars to administer the colonies from 1517 to 1520. However, these men failed to abolish the *encomienda*, judging Indians incapable of self-rule, and they recommended that African slaves be imported to relieve the pressure on Indian laborers. Charles V (or Charles I), the first ruler from the new Hapsburg dynasty, sympathized with Las Casas's view of Indians as rational, free, and capable of virtuous government, but the discovery and conquest of the *Aztecs* in 1519–1521 ensured that the Spanish could not abandon the New World or give up the *encomienda* as a reward and incentive for conquistadors. Already named "Protector of the Indians," Las Casas joined a *Dominican* mission for peaceful conversion in Guatemala in the 1530s.

---

[4]Las Casas's tracts enumerating Spanish atrocities against Indians gave fodder to Europeans elaborating an anti-Hispanic Black Legend. See Charles Gibson, *Black Legend: Anti-Spanish Attitudes in the Old World and the New* (New York: Knopf, 1971).

Back in Spain recruiting missionaries, he published the *Very Brief Account of the Destruction of the Indies*[5] and in general contributed to the 1542 *New Laws* abolishing the *encomienda* and asserting greater Crown oversight over colonists, Indians, and slaves. Las Casas returned to the Americas as Bishop of Chiapas in southern Mexico (1544–1550), but once again the implementation of the reforms proved difficult because of the resistance of colonists.

Las Casas returned to Spain in 1546 to complain of the lack of full implementation of the *New Laws*. From 1550 until his death in 1566, he remained in Spain as an advocate with influence at

Stories of Native Peoples killing themselves and their children to escape Spanish cruelties shocked Girolamo Benzoni (b. 1519). Like Bartolomé de Las Casas, he took up his pen in their defense, publishing in 1565 an account of travels through South and Central America, denouncing the mistreatment of the native population and the importation of African slaves. What acts does Benzoni's woodcut illustration document? How might the image speak differently than the text to people of his time? What does the woodcut not teach viewers?

Source: Girolamo Benzoni Girolamo Benzoni (b. 1519). *La historia del mondo nuovo di M. Girolamo Benzoni Milanese* [*The history of the New World of Mr. Girolamo Benzoni of Milan*]. [Venice: F. Rampazetto, 1565.] Rare Book and Special Collections Division, Library of Congress (68).

court. The first excerpt outlined the debate between conquest critics and advocates. Las Casas summarized and then refuted the arguments supporting the Spanish conquest and enslavement of Indians. This controversy attracted the king's attention. Suspending all conquests until their legitimacy could be established, King Charles V and the *Council of the Indies* called Las Casas before a panel in 1550 to argue publicly that conversion without force and entrusted entirely to missionaries should be Spain's only purpose in the New World.[6] Opposing him was the humanist writer Juan Ginés de Sepúlveda (1490–1573). To justify conquest by war, Sepúlveda relied on the Greek philosopher Aristotle and the Christian theologian Thomas Aquinas. Sepúlveda took Aristotle's idea that natural slaves existed and that they should be ruled by their more capable betters (as parents rule children, and men rule women). Sepúlveda also borrowed Aquinas's idea that certain conditions (e.g., tyranny or violation of natural law) justified war. The debate proved inconclusive; although Las Casas won more support because conquest without force became the official imperial policy, the reality in the Americas was often quite different for Native Peoples.

Las Casas is often blamed for encouraging the importation of enslaved Africans. How justified is this claim? Readers can judge by examining Las Casas's evolving position on African slavery through a series of excerpts from reports sent to royal authorities between 1516 and 1543. Each is a lengthy list of recommendations, including permissions for other colonists to import slaves. After a visit to Lisbon, Las Casas took a new position on slavery in 1552. He denounced the cruelty to African slaves and rejected as a lie the European justification that slavery brought Africans to Christianity and saved them from conversion to Islam. Before that, what exactly did he think about African slavery?

[5]Bartolomé de Las Casas, *A Short Account of the Destruction of the Indies*, ed. and trans. Nigel Griffin (New York: Penguin Books, 1992).

[6]The Jesuit António de Vieira (1608–1697) defended the Indians in Portuguese America. See Thomas M. Cohen, *The Fire of Tongues: António Vieira and the Missionary Church in Brazil and Portugal* (Stanford, CA: Stanford University Press, 1998).

Questions to Consider:

1. What arguments supported a "just war" against Native Peoples in the Americas? What evidence proved that some people were "natural slaves?" How did Las Casas refute these ideas?

2. What role did Las Casas suggest for the Spanish in the Americas?
3. What was his vision for African slaves? How did it change over time? How did this compare to his writings about Indians?

Las Casas's Views on Indigenous Slavery. Defense of the Indians, by the Most Reverend Fray Bartolomé de Las Casas

To King Philip II of Spain, 1550[7]

It is right that matters which concern the safety and peace of the great empire placed in your keeping by the divine goodness be reported to you, for you rule Spain and that marvelous New World in the name of the great Charles [V], your father, and you strive for immortal glory, not just with the imperial power but especially with the generous spirit and with the wisdom implanted in you by Christ. Therefore I have thought it advisable to bring to the attention of Your Highness that there has come into my hands a certain brief synopsis in Spanish of a work that Ginés de Sepúlveda is reported to have written in Latin. In it he gives four reasons, each of which, in his opinion, proves beyond reputation that war against the Indians is justified, provided that it be waged properly and the laws of war be observed, just as, up to the present, the kings of Spain have commanded that it be waged and carried out.

. . . First, I shall refute Sepúlveda's opinion that war against the Indians is justified because they are barbarous, uncivilized, unteachable, and lacking civil government.

Second, I shall show that, to the most definite ruin of his own soul, Sepúlveda is wrong when he teaches that war against the Indians is justified as punishment for their crimes against the natural law, especially the crimes of idolatry and human sacrifice.

Third, we shall attack his third argument, on the basis of which Sepúlveda teaches that war can be

waged unconditionally and indiscriminately against those people in order to free the innocent.

Fourth, I shall discuss how foreign to the teaching of the gospel and Christian mercy is his fourth proposition, maintaining that war against the Indians is justified as a means of extending the boundaries of the Christian religion and of opening the way for those who proclaim and preach the gospel.

When I have finished, the truth of this case and the magnitude of the crime committed by those who have maltreated the Indians by robberies, massacres, and other incredible misfortunes of war, and continue to do so, will be clear; and at the same time how groundless are the arguments of a man who is wrong both in law and in fact, by what design he was led to write that dangerous book, in what way he has distorted the teachings of philosophers and theologians, falsified the words of Sacred Scripture, of divine and human laws, and how no less destructively he has quoted statements of Pope Alexander VI to favor the success of his wicked cause. Finally, the true title by which the Kings of Spain hold their true rule over the New World will be shown. . . .

In Defense of the Indians

Chapter Four

. . . The distinction the Philosopher [Aristotle] makes between the two . . . kinds of barbarian is evident. For those he deals with in the first book of the *Politics*, and whom we have just discussed, are barbarians without qualification, in the proper and strict sense of the word, that is, dull witted

[7]*Source:* Bartolomé de Las Casas, "Preface to the Defense" and "Chapter Four," in *In Defense of the Indians*, trans. and ed. Stafford Poole (DeKalb: Northern Illinois University Press, 1992), 17, 21–22, 41–49.

and lacking in the reasoning powers necessary for self-government. They are without laws, without king, etc. For this reason they are by nature unfitted for rule.

However, he admits, and proves, that the barbarians he deals with in the third book of the same work have a lawful, just, and natural government. Even though they lack the art and use of writing, they are not wanting in the capacity and skill to rule and govern themselves, both publicly and privately. Thus they have kingdoms, communities, and cities that they govern wisely according to their laws and customs. Thus their government is legitimate and natural, even though it has some resemblance to tyranny. From these statements we have no choice but to conclude that the rulers of such nations enjoy the use of reason and that their people and the inhabitants of their provinces do not lack peace and justice. Otherwise they could not be established or preserved as political entities for long. This is made clear by the Philosopher and Augustine. Therefore not all barbarians are irrational or natural slaves or unfit for government. Some barbarians, then, in accord with justice and nature, have kingdoms, royal dignities, jurisdiction, and good laws, and there is among them lawful government.

Now if we shall have shown that among our Indians of the western and southern shores (granting that we call them barbarians and that they are barbarians) there are important kingdoms. Large numbers of people who live settled lives in a society, great cities, kings, judges and laws, persons who engage in commerce, buying and selling, lending, and the other contracts of the law of nations, will it not stand proved that the Reverend Doctor Sepúlveda has spoken wrongly and viciously against peoples like these, either out of malice or ignorance of Aristotle's teaching, and, therefore, has falsely and perhaps irreparably slandered them before the entire world? From the fact that the Indians are barbarians it does not necessarily follow that they are incapable of government and have to be ruled by others, except to be taught about the Catholic faith and to be admitted to the holy sacraments. They are not ignorant, inhuman, or bestial. Rather, long before they had heard the word Spaniard they had properly organized states, wisely ordered by excellent laws, religion, and custom. They cultivated friendship and, bound together

in common fellowship, lived in populous cities in which they wisely administered the affairs of both peace and war justly and equitably, truly governed by laws that at very many points surpass ours, and could have won the admiration of the sages of Athens, as I will show in the second part of this *Defense*.

Now if they are to be subjected by war because they are ignorant of polished literature, let Sepúlveda hear Trogus Pompey:[8]

Nor could the Spaniards submit to the yoke of a conquered province until Caesar Augustus, after he had conquered the world, turned his victorious armies against them and organized that barbaric and wild people as a province, once he had led them by law to a more civilized way of life.

Now see how he called the Spanish people barbaric and wild. I would like to hear Sepúlveda, in his cleverness, answer this question: Does he think that the war of the Romans against the Spanish was justified in order to free them from barbarism?[9] And this question also: Did the Spanish wage an unjust war when they vigorously defended themselves against them?

Next, I call the Spaniards who plunder that unhappy people torturers. Do you think that the Romans, once they had subjugated the wild and barbaric peoples of Spain, could with secure right divide all of you among themselves, handing over so many head of both males and females as allotments to individuals? And do you then conclude that the Romans could have stripped your rulers of their authority and consigned all of you, after you had been deprived of your liberty, to wretched labors, especially in searching for gold and silver lodes and mining and refining the metals? And if the Romans finally did that, as is evident from Diodorus,[10] [would you not judge] that you also have the right to defend your freedom, indeed your very life, by war? Sepúlveda, would you have permitted Saint James to evangelize your own people of Córdoba in that way?[11] For God's sake and man's faith in him, is this the way to impose the yoke of

---

[8]Roman Historian.

[9]The Romans conquered and ruled Spain.

[10]Diodorus Siculus was a Greek historian from the first century B.C.

[11]By violent means.

Christ on Christian men? Is this the way to remove wild barbarism from the minds of barbarians? Is it not, rather, to act like thieves, cutthroats, and cruel plunderers and to drive the gentlest of people headlong into despair? The Indian race is not that barbaric, nor are they dull witted or stupid, but they are easy to teach and very talented in learning all the liberal arts, and very ready to accept, honor, and observe the Christian religion and correct their sins (as experience has taught) once priests have introduced them to the sacred mysteries and taught them the word of God. They have been endowed with excellent conduct, and before the coming of the Spaniards, as we have said, they had political states which were well founded on beneficial laws.

Furthermore, they are so skilled in every mechanical art that with every right they should be set ahead of all the nations of the known world on this score, so very beautiful in their skill and artistry are the things this people produces in the grace of its architecture, its painting, and its needlework. But Sepúlveda despises these mechanical arts, as if these things do not reflect inventiveness, ingenuity, industry, and right reason. . . .

In the liberal arts that they have been taught up to now, such as grammar and logic, they are remarkably adept. With every kind of music they charm the ears of their audience with wonderful sweetness. They write skillfully and quite elegantly, so that most often we are at a loss to know whether the characters are handwritten or printed. I shall explain this at greater length in the second part of this *Defense,* not by quoting the totally groundless lies of the worst [deceivers] in the histories published so far but the truth itself and what I have seen with my eyes, felt with my hands, and heard with my own ears while living a great many years among those peoples.

Now if Sepúlveda had wanted, as a serious man should, to know the full truth before he sat down to write with his mind corrupted by the lies of tyrants, he should have consulted the honest religious who have lived among those people for many years and know their endowments of character and industry, as well as the progress they have made in religion and morality. Indeed, Rome is far from Spain, yet in that city the talent of these people and their aptitude and capacity for grasping the liberal arts have

been recognized. . . . As you see, he declares that the Indian city is worthy of admiration because of its buildings, which are like those of Venice.[12]

As to the terrible crime of human sacrifice, which you exaggerate,[13] see what Paolo Giovo, Bishop of Nocera, adds . . . "The rulers of the Mexicans have a right to sacrifice living men to their gods, provided they have been condemned for a crime."[14] Concerning the natural gifts of that people, what does he assert? "Thus it was not altogether difficult for Cortés to lead a gifted and teachable people, once they had abandoned their superstitious idolatry, to the worship of Christ. For they learn our writing with pleasure and with admiration, now that they have given up the hieroglyphics by which they used to record their annals, enshrining for posterity in various symbols the memory of their kings."

This is what you, a man of such great scholarship, should have done in ascertaining the truth, instead of writing, with the sharp edge of your pen poised for the whispers of irresponsible men, your little book that slanders the Indian inhabitants of such a large part of the earth. Do you quote to us Oviedo's *History*,[15] which bears the approval of the Royal Council, as though Oviedo, as he himself testifies, was not a despotic master who kept unfortunate Indians oppressed by slavery like cattle and, in imitation of the other thieves, ruined a great part of the continent, or as though the Council, when it approves a book, appears to approve also all the lies it contains, or as if, when the Council approves a book, it knows whether its contents are true? To this enemy you give your belief, as also to the one who is an interested party. For he possessed an allotment of Indians, as did the other tyrannical masters.

From this it is clear that the basis for Sepúlveda's teaching that these people are uncivilized and ignorant

---

[12]Venice gained prominence as a medieval trading center with a widely admired system of canals, bridges, and palaces that likened it to the *Aztec* capital *Tenochtitlán.*

[13]Las Casas dramatically shifted his audience and directed his comments directly to Sepúlveda as if debating in person.

[14]Paolo Giovio (1483–1552) was an Italian bishop and historian.

[15]References to the Crown's official historian of the conquest whose *La historia general de las Indias* (1535) was the definitive account that critics challenged. Oviedo (1478–1557) visited the Americas six times and oversaw the smelting of gold in Santo Domingo.

is worse than false. Yet even if we were to grant that this race has no keenness of mind or artistic ability, certainly they are not, in consequence, obligated to submit themselves to those who are most intelligent and to adopt their ways, so that, if they refuse, they may be subdued by having war waged against them and be enslaved, as happens today. For men are obligated by the natural law to do many things they cannot be forced to do against their will. We are bound by the natural law to embrace virtue and imitate the uprightness of good men. No one, however, is punished for being bad unless he is guilty of rebellion. Where the Catholic faith has been preached in a Christian manner and as it ought to be, all men are bound by the natural law to accept it, yet no one is forced to accept the faith of Christ. No one is punished because he is sunk in vice, unless he is rebellious or harms the person and property of others. No one is forced to embrace virtue and show himself as a good man. One who receives a favor is bound by the natural law to return the favor by what we call antidotal obligation. Yet no one is forced to this, nor is he punished if he omits it, according to the common interpretation of the jurists.

. . . Therefore, not even a truly wise man may force an ignorant barbarian to submit to him, especially by yielding his liberty, without doing him an injustice. This the poor Indians suffer, with extreme injustice, against all laws of God and of men and against the law of nature itself. For evil must not be done that good may come of it, for example, if someone were to castrate another against his will. For although eunuchs are freed from the lust that drives human minds forward in its mad rush, yet he who castrates another is most severely punished.

Now, on the basis of this utterly absurd argument, war against the Indians were lawful, one nation might rise up against another and one man against another man, and on the pretext of superior wisdom, might strive to bring the other into subjection. On this basis the Turks, and the Moors[16]—the truly barbaric scum of the nations—with complete

right and in accord with the law of nature could carry on war, which, as it seems to some, is permitted to us by a lawful decree of the state. If we admit this, will not everything high and low, divine and human, be thrown into confusion? What can be proposed more contrary to the eternal law than what Sepúlveda often declares? . . . Since, therefore, every nation by the eternal law has a ruler or prince, it is wrong for one nation to attack another under pretext of being superior in wisdom or to overthrow other kingdoms.

. . . This is not an act of wisdom, but of great injustice and a lying excuse for plundering others. Hence every nation, no matter how barbaric, has the right to defend itself against a more civilized one that wants to conquer it and take away its freedom. . . .

. . . According to his distinction, if the wise and the unwise live in one and the same political community or under the same prince or ruler, then the unwise ought to submit themselves willingly to the wiser man who governs the state, for example, the king or his laws or his governors. If they refuse to do this, it is lawful to use force against them and they can be punished, since the law of nature demands this. On the other hand, no free person, and much less a free people, is bound to submit to anyone, whether king or nation, no matter how much better the latter may be and no matter how advantageous he may think it will be to himself [*sic*]. Augustine of Ancona teaches this conclusion in this very form, that is, when the imperfect yield to the more perfect. No free nation, therefore, can be compelled to submit itself to a wiser one, even if such submission could lead to [its] great advantage. When the Philosopher advances the argument that matter yields to form, he intends to assert only that nature has produced men fitted by an inborn talent for governing others who have not been endowed with so great a natural ability. And so he teaches that such wiser men are to be entrusted with the helm of government for its preservation and welfare. Others ought to be subject to them as matter is subject to form and the body to the soul.

Sepúlveda's final argument that everyone can be compelled, even when unwilling, to do those things that are beneficial to him, if taken without qualification, is false in the extreme. For Augustine, whom he cites, is speaking of those who had promised something useful for themselves and did not keep

---

[16]The Spanish remembered wars against Moorish rulers in Iberia, and Spaniards and the Moors still raided and fought along Mediterranean coasts. Spaniards and Italians also battled the new and more imposing threat from the expanding Ottoman Empire (Turks).

their promise, with damage or injury to others. Specifically, he is discussing heretics whom the Church compels to keep their baptismal vows, not only because they are useful for themselves but especially *because they have promised and vowed them to God and, from the promise, they are bound by a certain special obligation.* For it would not be enough to argue that

the vows are beneficial to them. For we see that no unbeliever is forced to receive baptism. From the teaching of the above-mentioned Augustine the doctors conclude that one can and should be forced to do a good he has promised, but not one he has not promised. But many things will have to be discussed later concerning this.

Development of Las Casas's Views on African Slavery, from 1516 to 1552. "Petition with Remedies for the Indies"

by Bartolomé de Las Casas, 1516[17]

The remedies needed to end the damage and harm that is done in the Indies. . . .

. . . Eleventh remedy: . . . in place of the Indians that must be kept in the communities, Your Highness should maintain in each twenty blacks, or other slaves in the mines, to grow food or whatever else is necessary, and it would be much greater service and profit for Your Highness, because more gold would be collected than if you doubled the number of Indians working the mines.

. . . [So that the colonists do not take the Indians away from subsistence farming and instruction in Christianity] and without charging them anything, principally so they can engage in many profitable enterprises, Your Highness should give them license for those and grant them permission to have black and white slaves,[18] that they can bring from Castile, and that they can have herds of livestock and establish sugar mills and cane fields and wash for gold and many other things that they know to do. . . .

---

[17]*Source:* Fray Bartolomé de Las Casas, *Obras completas*, ed. Paulino Castañeda, Carlos de Rueda, Carmen Godínez, and Inmaculada de La Corte (Madrid: Alianza Editorial, 1995), vol. 13, 23, 27–28, 36.

[18]By white slaves, Las Casas was probably referring to Spain's enslaved *moriscos* and possibly people from the Balkans and northern Africa.

"Petition of Remedies for the Indies"

by Bartolomé de Las Casas, 1518[19]

Most high and mighty lord:

So that from those great kingdoms and lands that Your Highness has in the Indies, likewise the great service that to God your highness can do saving innumerable souls, that now are all lost, Your Highness can have the greatest income and the most gold and

pearls of any Christian king [I propose these remedies]. . . .

. . . Third, that Your Highness grant license to the Christians who are already in the islands that they may each have two male black slaves and two female black slaves and there is no doubt about their security, and give them the reasons for this grant [to promote mining and European immigration]. . . .

Item, that whomsoever builds a mill to make sugar Your Highness will aid with some money, because they are costly, and that Your

---

[19]*Source:* Fray Bartolomé de Las Casas, *Obras completas*, vol. 13, 49, 52–53.

Highness grant license to those that do, allowing them to import and possess twenty male and female black slaves, because with them they equal another thirty Christians who would be necessary for the work, and thus the blacks would be assured; in this way, they will build many sugar mills because this is the best land in the world for sugar cane, thus returning to Your Highness marvelous income and in less than three years. . . . Signed Bartolomé de Las Casas.—Cleric.—Protector of the Indians.

"Petition of Remedies for the South American Mainland"

by Bartolomé de Las Casas, 1518[20]

. . . Your Highness could do the same with [covering the costs of maintaining Church and military personnel] in the islands, with borrowing money and selling licenses, for there are some people who could lend Your Highness for the present expenses needed for the islands, and to those who lend money Your Highness should give license to acquire and import fifteen slaves, and there would be many who would happily lend 1,000, 2,000, or 500 *castellanos* depending on what they had. . . . Signed Bartolomé de Las Casas.

[20]The Mainland (*tierra firme*) included Panama. *Source:* Fray Bartolomé de Las Casas, *Obras completas,* vol. 13, 60.

"Letter to the Council of the Indies"

January 20, 1531[21]

Most illustrious and magnificent lord and most magnificent lords: . . .

Lords, one of the greatest causes that this land has been lost and not populated more than it has been, at least in the last ten or eleven years, is not granting freely to all who want them licenses to import black slaves, which I requested and begged of Your Highness; certainly not to have them sold to Genoese [Italian merchants] nor to other private individuals sitting here at court, and to other people whom I do not mention so as not to embarrass them, rather to have them distributed among the *vecinos* [settled property owners] and new settlers who come to these unpopulated lands, and to remedy, liberate and rescue the oppressed Indians, so that they can leave that captivity; as God had placed in my hands the remedy for them, and the settling of this land, and Your Highness granted my request. But it helped little, for the reasons mentioned, and because I did not understand this business better, may God be my protector.

My Lords and mercies are very bad servants to the King to whom I will request a grant and a license for blacks, if you knew the damage you do, and if you do not know it, inform yourselves about it; and before His Highness takes 10,000 ducats from his Chamber and grants them to whomever he will give the right to export slaves; it will do less harm to his interests to only grant licenses to import 30 black slaves [instead of granting a monopoly over slave imports]. Open the door to everyone, you do not know the harm done the King, and the land will be widely settled, and you will see the benefits that result from not selling these licenses. . . . Your servant My Lords and mercies, Signed Bartolomé de Las Casas.

[21]*Source:* Fray Bartolomé de Las Casas, *Obras completas,* vol. 13, 65, 80.

History of the Indies

by Bartolomé de Las Casas, 1552

Book I, chapter 17[22]

. . . [The Spanish King sanctioned an expedition to conquer the Canary Islands and enslave the islanders] The King gave him the men he requested and every favor and speedy dispatch. Gone to the Islands with his fleet, he subjected by force of arms three of them, Lanzarote, Fuerte Ventura, and the island they call the Hierro, making cruel war upon their natural inhabitants, with no other reason or cause than because it was their will or, to put it more bluntly, their ambition and desire to be lord over those who owed them nothing, subjugating them. . . .

Book I, chapter 25[23]

. . . Applying the reasons given [to justify war] to the prejudicial acts that the Portuguese committed against those people [west Africans], [acts] that were nothing more than cruel wars, slaughters, enslavement, and the total destruction and annihilation of many towns full of people peacefully in their homes, certain damnation of many souls that will suffer for eternity without relief, people who never threatened them [the Portuguese], never harmed them, nor made war, never insulted or damaged the faith nor even thought to impede it, and they occupied their lands justly because they never took it from others, and they lived far from the Moors who fatigue us here [in the Mediterranean], because their borders are with Ethiopia, and of their lands there is no writing or report that the people that possess them usurped the Church. Then with what reason or justice can the Portuguese justify and execute such

harm and wrongs, so many deaths and enslavement, so much scandal and the loss of so many souls among those poor people, even if they were Moors? Just because they were heathens? This was certainly great ignorance and harmful blindness. . . .

Book III, chapter 102[24]

. . . And because some of the Spaniards of this Island [Hispaniola] asked the cleric Las Casas, seeing what he was attempting [to end forced Indian labor] and because the priests from Santo Domingo refused to absolve those who had Indians, if they did not release them, if he could bring them a license from the King to import from Castile a dozen black slaves, to take the place of the Indians. Remembering this request, the cleric [Las Casas] asked in his reports that the Spanish *vecinos* of the islands be given license to bring from Spain a dozen, more or less, black slaves, because with them they could support themselves and set free the Indians. The cleric Las Casas gave this advice that they be given license to bring black slaves to these lands, not knowing the injustice with which the Portuguese take them and make them slaves; after he found out, he would not have proposed it for all the world, because they were enslaved unjustly and tyrannically from the start, exactly as the Indians had been.

All of the recommendations and measures proposed by the cleric Las Casas so that Spaniards would live in these lands without forcing Indians to labor for them, and so that they would liberate them, very much pleased the great Chancellor [the Regent Cisneros]. . . . Asked how many black slaves should be brought to the islands, the cleric Las Casas responded that he did not know, so a royal order was sent to the officials of the *House of Trade* in Seville, ordering them to meet and determine the number; they responded that for the four islands, Hispaniola, San Juan [Puerto Rico], Cuba, and Jamaica, it was

[22]Las Casas described the conquest of the Canaries, Cape Verde, the Azores and promontories on the African coast. *Source:* Bartolomé de Las Casas, *Obras completas*, ed. Miguel Angel Medina, Jesús Angel Barreda, and Isacio Pérez Fernández (Madrid: Alianza Editorial, 1994), vol. 3, 431.
[23]*Source:* Bartolomé de Las Casas, *Obras completas*, ed. Miguel Angel Medina, Jesús Angel Barreda, and Isacio Pérez Fernández (Madrid: Alianza Editorial, 1994), vol. 3, 479.

[24]*Source:* Bartolomé de Las Casas, *Obras completas*, ed. Miguel Angel Medina, Jesús Angel Barreda, and Isacio Pérez Fernández (Madrid: Alianza Editorial, 1994), vol. 4, 2190–2191.

their opinion that at present four thousand black slaves would be sufficient. Thus this came as the answer, of course somebody among the Spanish, in order to win favor, advised the governor of Bressa, who was also a Flemish gentleman[25] . . . who the King had brought with him and was part of his Council, to ask for these licenses as a reward; he asked for them, and the King gave them to him. Genoeses [merchants] then bought the license for 25,000 ducats, with the condition that for eight years the King grant no other license [for importing slaves to the Americas].

This concession was very harmful to the well-being of these islands' population, because that cleric's recommendation about the black slaves was for the common good of the Spanish [colonists], who were all poor and it was a good idea that it be given to them gratis and for free. [Instead] the Genoeses sold them the import licenses[26] and the black slaves for many castellanos and ducats, such that it is believed they profited by more then 280,000 or even 300,000 ducats, . . .and no good came out of it for the Indians, it having been ordered for their good and for their liberty, because in the end they remained in their captivity until there were none left to kill [no Caribbean Indians left]. . . .

Book III, chapter 129[27]

. . . And as the number of sugar mills grew each day, the need for slaves to work them grew, because each water-powered mill required at least eighty and the animal-powered mills thirty or forty, and

consequently, the profits for the king also grew [from licenses and taxes on slave sales]. And from this the Portuguese, having from many years back controlled the plundering of Guinea, and enslaving the blacks, very unjustly, seeing that we had such need of them and that we bought them, hastened and each day hasten to rob and enslave them, by as many evil and wicked ways as they can; likewise, as the Africans themselves see with what great anxiety they seek slaves, they begin to make unjust wars on each other, and through other illicit means they steal [people] and sell them to the Portuguese[.] In this way we ourselves are the cause of all the sins committed by both, even apart from the sins we commit by buying them.

The money from these licenses and rights that they give the Emperor, the Emperor designated for building the palace (*alcazar*) he built in Madrid and the palace in Toledo and with that money both were built. . . .

Suggested Sources:

Lewis Hanke wrote about the efforts to defend the Indians. See Lewis Hanke, *All Mankind is One: A Study of the Disputation Between Bartolomé de Las Casas and Juan Gines de Sepúlveda on the Religious and Intellectual Capacity of the American Indians* (DeKalb: Northern Illinois University Press, 1974). Missionaries and theologians linked levels of indigenous civilizations to the possibilities of conversion. See Sabine MacCormack, *Religion in the Andes: Vision and Imagination in Early Colonial Peru* (Princeton, NJ: Princeton University Press, 1991). Two films portray the disillusionment of Spanish missionaries who admired and joined indigenous society: *Cabeza de Vaca*, dir. Nicolás Echevarria (Mexico/Spain, 1990), and *Jerico*, dir. Luis Alberto Lamata (Venezuela, 1988).

Las Casas harshly critiqued Spain's Caribbean conquest in *Short Account of the Destruction of the Indies*, trans. Nigel Griffin (New York: Penguin, 1999). He refuted Spanish justifications in *In Defense of the Indians*, trans. Stafford Poole (DeKalb: Northern Illinois University Press, 1992). Jesuit Alonso de Sandoval recorded African culture, language, and

---

[25]Spain held lands in many parts of Europe. Consequently, administrators, conquistadors, and missionaries sometimes came from outside Spain.

[26]Each license was sold for 8 ducats. See Bartolomé de Las Casas, *Obras completas*, ed. Miguel Angel Medina, Jesús Angel Barreda, and Isacio Pérez Fernández (Madrid: Alianza Editorial, 1994), vol. 4, 2323.

[27]*Source:* Bartolomé de Las Casas, *Obras completas*, ed. Miguel Angel Medina, Jesús Angel Barreda, and Isacio Pérez Fernández (Madrid: Alianza Editorial, 1994), vol. 4, 2324. The chapter began by describing the 1506 introduction of sugar cane in the Caribbean and the use of first Indian and then African slaves to grow, cut, and mill it. By the mid-1500s, Las Casas calculated 100,000 African slaves were brought to Spanish America, 30,000 to Hispaniola alone.

history from years of evangelizing slaves. See *Treatise on Slavery: Selections from De instauranda Aethiopum salute*, ed. and trans. Nicole von Germeten (Indianapolis, IN: Hackett, 2008). A missionary among Aztecs, Bernardino de Sahagún recorded their history and civilization in *Florentine Codex: History of the Things of New Spain*, 12 vols., trans. and ed. Arthur J. O. Anderson and Charles E. Dibble (Salt Lake City: University of Utah Press, 1950–1982). Jesuit José de Acosta recorded native Andean history and rituals in his *Natural and Moral History of the Indies*, ed. Jane E. Mangan, trans. Frances M. López-Morillas (Durham, NC: Duke University Press, 2002).

Chapter 7

Fray Alonso de Espinosa's Report on Pacifying the Fugitive Slaves of the Pacific Coast

Charles Beatty-Medina, University of Toledo

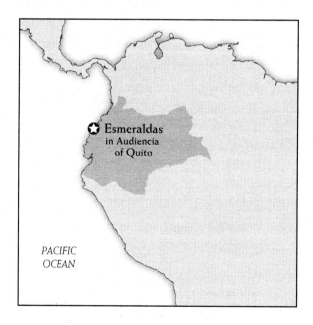

A letter from a Spanish Catholic missionary defending a group of African rebels in Colonial Latin America was a rarity. Rarer still were Spanish authorities placing those rebels at center stage in plans for territorial expansion. Such was the case, however, in Fray Alonso de Espinosa's letter to the King of Spain and the Royal *Audiencia* of Quito. Although Espinosa's letter claimed to provide an un-biased report of events from 1583 to 1585 in the coastal region of Esmeraldas, it was, in fact, a searing critique of Spanish colonization and a defense of Spain's empire. In many ways, Espinosa echoed arguments made decades earlier by Bartolomé de Las Casas, another clergyman who sought to curb Spanish greed and violence and defend Spain's role in the New World (see Chapter 6).

Numerous witnesses, like Las Casas, reported on the violence that accompanied sixteenth-century conquest and colonization. Although Crown edicts from 1512 onward ordered better oversight of Spanish colonizers, violence and physical coercion remained integral to indigenous subjugation. Esmeraldas suffered numerous unsuccessful incursions, the earliest under the command of Francisco Pizarro. As chronicled in countless Spanish reports and testimonies, European colonizers faced intense indigenous resistance. Instead, a group of African runaway slaves succeeded in establishing a small and unique colony of their own in the 1550s.

The runaways were assisted by the inability of the Spanish to settle the region. However, they faced other difficulties. They had to survive in a territory hostile to outsiders and without the benefit of external support. In time they formed what historians call *maroon* societies, the self-sustaining communities of escaped slaves. The first twenty-three escaped as the result of a shipwreck around 1553. Their struggle to survive led to intermarriage with local native communities that soon came under African leadership. Where the Spanish failed to plant a settlement, the Africans had established firm roots by the 1570s.

By that time, the *maroons* had the attention of royal authorities and the elite of Quito's society. Instead of fearing these rebel Africans, however, they embraced the idea of turning them into proxy colonizers. Much like the native *caciques*, they wanted them to become the middlemen of conquest and colonial control. Additionally, they wanted desperately to make good on a plan, hatched in the 1560s, to create a seaport in Esmeraldas that would reduce the cost to ship goods to Peru and Panama. However, the Quiteños had encountered numerous obstacles in their attempts to extend colonial control over Esmeraldas. Not only was conquest difficult, but Spaniards also eschewed settling in the humid

lowlands, and they bemoaned the scarcity of conquerable Amerindians to exploit for labor and tribute. In addition, the Crown and *viceroy* refused to permit the settlement of Esmeraldas for defensive reasons, which included the vulnerability of the coast to foreign attack.

As a result, in 1577 the Royal *Audiencia* made a bold effort to subvert the Crown's impediments and intransigence. Responding to a request for peace by one of the African leaders, the *Audiencia* sent the *maroon* leaders an official pardon and granted one of their chiefs the title of *gobernador*. The move encouraged the *maroon* leader, Alonso de Illescas, to swear his loyalty to the Crown. Along with his pledge, the *Audiencia* required Illescas to relocate his *maroons* and native allies to the coast and establish the village

In this portrait (c. 1599) by Andrés Sanchez Galque, three leaders of a runaway slave community on the Pacific coast of South America display their culture, status, and authority. They operated in a largely indigenous world in the frontier region called Esmeraldas. As the result of negotiations with royal officials, their leader, Francisco de Arobe, and two of his sons traveled to the colonial capital of Quito. There they received gifts, made assurances of loyalty, and stood for this portrait. Notice their elaborate attire. How are they portrayed to display both status and authority? What elements did the artist include to represent the three civilizations—indigenous, African, and Spanish—that informed their worldview? What might have been some of the reasons for colonial authorities to commission this portrait and send it to the royal court in Spain?

Source: Los Mulatos de Esmeraldas (1599), by Andrés Sánchez Galque (fl. 16th century)/Don Arove and his two sons, Columbia, Museo de América (Madrid).

of San Mateo de las Esmeraldas. However, like the Spanish before, Illescas failed. Internal conflict and warfare broke out on the coast, ruining the Africans' plan. Thus, instead of arriving at a resolution, Spanish-*maroon* hostilities intensified.

In 1583, Quito's royal court, or *audiencia*, attempted once again to conquer Esmeraldas. Taking advantage of the death of Peru's *Viceroy*, the lone sitting magistrate in Quito, Pedro de Cañaveral, commissioned Diego López de Zúñiga, a local *encomendero*, to enter Esmeraldas immediately without approval of the Crown. Given the commission's questionable legitimacy, he was pressed to subdue quickly the *maroons* and establish a port town at the bay of San Mateo. López de Zúñiga's tactics and lack of care over his soldiers' conduct, however, generated opposition. It is in this context that Alonso de Espinosa's letter was written, largely as a denunciation of López de Zúñiga's efforts and a supplication to the Crown to reinstate Alonso de Illescas as governor over Esmeraldas.

Espinosa's missive also reveals how racial difference was framed in colonial Latin America. Unlike notions of inherent biological makeup that came to dominate racial thinking in the nineteenth century, sixteenth-century Spanish ideas of difference were contingent on adherence to Christianity; notions of barbarism; and, finally, phenotype or appearance. Importantly, however, none of these ways of perceiving "others," in Espinosa's view, precluded the *maroons* from attaining power in Esmeraldas or from becoming good Christians. In his vision, they were not only capable but also deserving of both.

Nonetheless, Espinosa remained careful in his denunciation and reaffirmed Spain's imperial goals. Although he criticized Spanish actions, he recognized the Crown's authority. His letter, therefore, demonstrates some of the nuanced and complex ways that power relations functioned in the early colonial world. Even the lowliest friar could write directly to the Crown and its representatives, but such appeals had to be framed within Spanish terms of legitimacy and just cause. The basis in religion, ethnicity, gender, and authority for the hierarchical

foundations of society were present and understood throughout the empire.

Before delving into Espinosa's epistle, readers should also consider the writer's aims and his background. Fray Alonso de Espinosa was something of a mystery even to his contemporaries. Arriving in Quito without an appointment to one of the established missionary orders, he was an adventurer in religious robes. Given his lack of resources and connections, he may have been of humble origins. His order, the *Trinitarians*, was not even licensed by the Crown to operate in the Americas. Thus, Espinosa affiliated himself with the *Mercedarians* upon arriving in Quito. Interestingly, the *Mercedarians* and *Trinitarians* were related religious orders. Founded centuries earlier during the Crusades, they dedicated themselves to rescuing Christians captured by nonbelievers, often by offering themselves as replacements for the captured person. By the end of the seventeenth century, each order underwent major reform movements that would transform their earlier rule. We do not know if Espinosa was a party to these changes. However, his activities, both in terms of his attempt to defend the Africans and to free native people captured by the *maroons*, as well as his desire to work for those considered the lowest in the social hierarchy, provide clues. At the same time, we can detect some of the personal goals that Espinosa had in mind when he composed his report.

As readers, it is worthwhile to explore how Espinosa presented the Spanish soldiers and African rebels. It is also important to note how he narrated events that occurred on the coast. If one were to juxtapose Espinosa's view to other testimonies and letters, the comparison would yield very different perspectives. Each group—Spanish authorities, conquistadors, missionaries, and the *maroons* themselves—had competing viewpoints and proposals for Esmeraldas. Each party claimed to represent the truth, and each representation formed a different understanding of people and events. Espinosa's letter, ultimately, is a testament to both the age of conquest with its competing interests and African slave resistance that would make its own unique mark on the emerging colonial order.

Questions to Consider:

1. What was Fray Espinosa's personal aim with this letter? Did it support his desire to aid the Esmeraldas *maroons*? What was the Catholic Church's role in the relationship with the *maroons*?

2. What moved Espinosa to reject López de Zúñiga's conquest? What was the strongest evidence he presented against the Spanish governor?

3. In Espinosa's view, what redeemed the African *maroon* leader, Alonso de Illescas, and his people? Why would this be important to the Spanish Crown?

4. What view does this document provide of Africans in the wider colonial project?

Alonso de Espinosa's Letter to the Crown[1]

Report that I, Alonso de Espinosa of the order of the Holy Trinity, send to Your Majesty of the occurrences on expeditions to the Province of Esmeraldas between 1583 and 1585.

Upon the death of the *Viceroy* of Peru, Don Martín Enriquez, the Royal *Audiencia* of Quito authorized Diego López de Zuñiga for this [expedition]. He entered Esmeraldas one year earlier with eighty soldiers but accomplished nothing. They became lost and defeated and almost lost their lives before two *mulatos* born in those mountains came, gave them food to eat and recommended that Zuñiga make his way to Guayaquil and gather new soldiers because many of those with him were sick and the rest were dead. They also said that if he returned within twelve moons they would offer him their peace in the name of Your Majesty, and your governor [López de Zuñiga] followed their suggestion.

I learned that your governor went on the expedition without a priest and I asked the royal *audiencia* of Quito for permission to go on the expedition, to serve your Royal Majesty, and to aid and defend the native people. I was granted permission and with two soldiers departed along the route through the towns of Yumbos.

When the governor reached the Bay of San Mateo he sent a captain with soldiers to capture the blacks and *mulatos* at night. His intent was to torment them due to his greed and desire for gold. The soldiers were detected and your vassals escaped, and they knew that the governor had no good intentions.

I left Quito and journeyed down the river by raft. I found your vassals there, very anxious and distraught and with much sadness because your governor had burned their houses and their little *haciendas*. When they saw me, I was received with great joy and gratification. Although barbarous, they wish to live by the law of God and in service to your majesty. And due to their good spirits, I attempted to create peace and friendship between them and your governor. He placed them in my hands to do as I thought best at the time and then he fled from the land. I gave my letters to a soldier and some warlike Indians. Your governor ran into them at sea and later came to where I presented him with the land made peaceful. [The *mulatos*] served him and the soldiers for six months, giving us of their own provisions to eat. Because they neither conserved the peace much less their word given in the name of your majesty, [the *mulatos*] incited against them for the reasons I will now describe.

Don Alonso de Illescas, of colored complexion, and named governor of your subjects and vassals by the royal *audiencia* sent his son to offer peace to your governor [Diego López de Zuñiga] and tell him that within fourteen days all of them would arrive with your vassals

---

[1] *Source:* See AGI, Quito, 22, N.56, "Fr. Alonso de Espinosa sobre el estado de las Esmeraldas," Quito, 1585, fols. 2r-3v.

to reduce themselves to the service of Our Lord and your Royal Crown. The Spaniards waited ten days and never wished to stay the four more days due to their greed and desire to discover a river filled with great amounts of gold. The same greed has caused the losses and deaths of many governors and captains. And when the said Alonso de Illescas arrived to fulfill his promise no one was there to accept his surrender except a few Indians. When Illescas asked them where the governor and his men had gone, they said to find the river of gold. Illescas was angered and insulted that they disregarded him because he is the key to the land because it is under his hand and domination. These are the reasons they broke their promise and their obedience to your governor that was given in the name of your majesty. As we were now alone the governor and his soldiers returned to Quito by way of Puerto Viejo.

I returned to the province through the war-strewn land where the blacks and *mulatos* came to me once more with their subjects. They gave me their peace in your majesty's name and they wrote a letter to the royal *audiencia*. They sent me with two chief Indians so that the *audiencia* would believe the letter and their offer of peace to your majesty. The Indians came wearing skins due to the unfavorable climate they find in this city [Quito]. The *audiencia* provided each of them with a blanket and a shirt to cover them. The Indians gave me six captives, some of whom had lived with them for thirty years. I brought them all before Judge Pedro Venegas de Cañaveral who now presides in your royal court and presented the same letter that I send to your majesty. The letter pleads with the court to remember that it has been forty years since Garcilaso de la Vega, the Adelantado Andagoya, Captian Gonzalo de Olmos, Captain Juan de Olmos, Captain Carranza and Captain Peña entered this region. Your subjects captured these last two captains and ate them. Your governor Diego de Figueroa entered this region two times and governor Andres Contero and now governor Diego López de Zúñiga two times. None of

these governors or captains were able to reduce this land to your royal service due to the great disorder and agitation they caused in their greedy attempt to find gold and emeralds.

The two chief Indians came to this city [Quito] to offer their peace to your majesty and were treated badly by the Royal *Audiencia*. They were told to return to their land or wherever God would help them and they left without further consolation. What has become of them, whether they are dead or alive, I cannot tell your majesty.

They ask that your majesty grant the blacks and *mulatos* favors including a general pardon of all and whatever crimes they have committed against your crown, your subjects, and your vassals. They ask for a letter granting them and their children liberty. They ask that they should not pay tribute now nor at any time. In addition, whatever Indians come to them peacefully shall be kept safe and be free from tribute for ten years as stated in your royal orders. To *Don* Alonso de Illescas, who is the key to this government, they ask that your highness grant him the governorship over your subjects and Indians of this government. This way if his master or any other person comes to claim his liberty, he cannot be imprisoned, nor his goods sold or transferred. If your majesty grants these requests the blacks and *mulatos* will give the land fully pacified to your majesty.

When these requests from the *mulatos* to reduce these lands to the service of your royal person and our Lord reached your Royal *Audiencia*, Judge Pedro Venegas de Cañaveral [judge of the *Audiencia*] took them away because the recommendation he received was that it was better to take the region by war instead of peace and for this reason I have stopped pacifying the region.

What I ask your majesty in the name of these barbarous people is that you personally send these provisions because when *Don* Alonso de Illescas sees them with your royal signature, he will humble himself and reduce himself to your service. Equally, I ask that the subjects and vassals of these blacks may not be granted to any person other than your Royal Crown. And, that those Indians conquered henceforth by your governors or soldiers should only be granted to those who deserve them and are actively in your royal service. And this will aid the sustenance of the land and villages populated in your royal name. If Your Majesty wishes to be further informed by what I have written, grant me that the information come from a particular person and not the Royal *Audiencia*.

And because your subjects have given me their affections of their own will because I have baptized their children. Their fathers thus desire that I preach the holy gospel. The news of which will please them. This will help me understand what they know of the Holy Law which as I have said your Royal *Audiencia* had no interest in teaching them.

And so I also ask for your majesty's favor in compensation for the many labors I have undertaken to reduce this governorship, which as I said was impossible for many captains and governors. Make this province an abbey or what best serves Your Majesty as the Most Catholic and Christian King. You will do what best serves the crown and the service of God, our lord. And I say this because I do not want to see myself removed by a priest, as often happens, after having pacified the land. And because these things have occurred and truly happened, I sign this with my name in the city of San Francisco de Quito on the twenty-second of May of eighty-five years [1585]. —Fray Alonso de Espinosa

Suggested Sources:

John Leddy Phelan first published the history of the African rebels of Esmeraldas in English in his book, *The Kingdom of Quito in the Seventeenth Century* (Madison: University of Wisconsin Press, 1967). The *maroons* are also mentioned in early works on African resistance in Latin America such as Leslie Rout's *The African Experience in Latin America* (Cambridge: Cambridge University Press, 1976) and Richard Price's *Maroon Societies: Rebel Slave Communities in the Americas* (Garden City, NY: Anchor Press/Doubleday, 1973). A notable work of investigative power is Adam Szaszdi's "El trasfondo de un cuadro: 'Los mulatos de Esmeraldas' de Andres Sanchez Galque," *Cuadernos Prehispánicos* 12 (1986–1987): 93–142.

Numerous recent publications in English and Spanish have revived and revisited the history of Esmeraldas, including Charles Beatty-Medina's "Caught between Rivals: The Spanish-African Maroon Competition for Captive Labor in the Region of Esmeraldas during the Late Sixteenth and Early Seventeenth Centuries," *The Americas* 63, no. 1 (2006): 113–136; Kris Lane's *Quito 1599: City and Colony in Transition* (Albuquerque: University of New Mexico Press, 2002); and Charles Beatty-Medina's "Maroon Chief Alonso de Illescas' Letter to the Crown, 1586," ed. Kathryn Joy McKnight and Leo J. Garofalo, *Afro-Latino Voices* (Cambridge: Hackett, 2009) 30–37. For an examination of the broader dimensions of African slavery in Quito, see Sherwin K. Bryant's "Enslaved Rebels, Fugitives, and Litigants: The Resistance Continuum in Colonial Quito," *Colonial Latin American Review* 13, no. 1 (June 2004): 7–46; and Kris Lane's "Captivity and Redemption: Aspects of Slave Live in Early Colonial Quito and Popayán," *The Americas* 57, no. 2 (2000): 225–246.

Chapter 8

Blending New and Old Beliefs in Mexico and the Andes

Leo J. Garofalo, Connecticut College

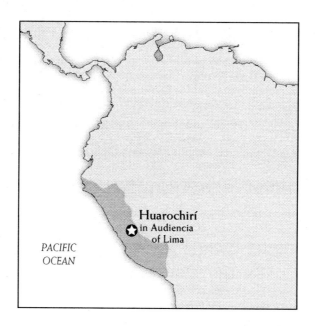

To what extent did conversion to Christianity really change indigenous people's beliefs and religious practices? Most historical evidence about conversion comes from Catholic missionaries, making it difficult to understand indigenous perspectives. However, the indigenous texts and images available suggest that the process of conversion was meaningful, but it was uneven and took generations to complete. Even after they embraced Christianity, many indigenous peoples integrated old and new religious beliefs and practices in a process that scholars try to understand as "religious *syncretism*" or "cultural hybridity." This chapter offers evidence on the process of blending religious beliefs with images of Mexico's Virgin of Guadalupe and excerpts from Peru's *Huarochirí Manuscript*.

For native peoples in Central Mexico and highland Peru, the introduction of Catholic saints followed the established practice of military victors introducing their own gods alongside the local ones. For example, in the Huarochirí region, people acknowledged the *Inca*-endorsed adoration of the Sun (a deity from the south) and Pacha Camac (a coastal oracle) as pan-Andean deities, but they kept on worshiping their own sacred beings, too. Therefore, the Spanish victors' promotion of the Virgin Mary and other saints proved quite successful because it followed the established pattern. Colonial religious authorities reinforced this understanding by locating crosses, shrines, and chapels at sites already recognized as sacred. Eventually, the Spanish drive to convert the entire population quickly faltered, and European monotheism clashed with the Mesoamerican and Andean polytheism that had for centuries allowed local peoples' deities to find a place alongside the empire-builders' gods.

Spanish missionaries split between those who advocated conversion through persuasion by building on similarities between Christianity and Mesoamerican or Andean concepts of the sacred and those who argued that true conversion required the use of force and the destruction of non-Christian idols and rituals. The advocates of peaceful conversion incorporated indigenous imagery, studied the native languages and practices, and even founded schools for the sons of native leaders (in the hopes that Catholicism would filter down). The *Franciscans'* school at Tlateloco (Mexico City) initially aimed to create a Europeanized indigenous clergy. By the mid-sixteenth century, colonizers' growing disdain for indigenous peoples and their cultures and clear examples of the continuity of indigenous beliefs and religious practices, often alongside or hidden behind Catholicism, undermined the attempts to form a native clergy and convert by creating a bridge between indigenous and European belief systems.

The changes colonialism wrought often led to violence on both sides over religion. Religious crises strengthened the hand of missionaries who wanted to remove all forcibly traces and records of the old ways. For example, *Mayan* leaders in the Yucatán responded to the need to reassert eroding legitimacy among villagers by reinvigorating traditional ritual activities. They incorporated Christian crosses and churches into their ceremonies and sacrifices, including human sacrifices. Feeling betrayed by their neophytes, the *Franciscan* missionaries carried out a brutal inquisition in 1565, torturing and killing hundreds.[1] In the central Andes, epidemic disease and demographic collapse suggested the old deities' displeasure. Depending on local circumstances, these devastating events could be used by nativists to end collaboration with the Spanish or by missionaries to encourage repentance and full acceptance of Christianity. When coupled with more onerous tribute and labor burdens in the central Andes, the epidemics sparked a nativist revival among commoners called Taqui Onqoy to reject all things Spanish and return to the old ways of worship. In response, the Spanish launched a campaign to uproot this idolatry by finding, interrogating, and punishing those involved. In both Peru and Mexico, as the sixteenth century progressed, the obstacles to a rapid and complete conversion to Christianity became more apparent and made the campaigns to extirpate idolatries a permanent feature of Church efforts in those ecclesiastic districts where supporters of a forcible approach held sway.

Although the sixteenth-century cult of Mexico's Virgen de Guadalupe initially engaged mainly the Spanish and those near Mexico City, seventeenth-century missionaries successfully built the story of this miracle and the figure of a protective female saint into a powerful tool of conversion, first, through relying on connections to indigenous beliefs and the story of a pious Indian man and, second, by creating an elaborate infrastructure and practice of worship that could draw in many and hold them for generations. According to missionary sources written much later (no historical record exists), a local indigenous inhabitant, Juan Diego, had visions of the Virgin Mary on the central Mexican Hill of Tepeyac in 1531. As proof, he offered a cloak miraculously emblazoned with an image of the Virgin Mary. Pre-Hispanic traditions associated the hill with the mother-goddess Tonantzin, who symbolized the earth as both creator and destroyer. The missionaries constructed a shrine on the hill for Our Lady of Guadalupe; cultivated a pilgrimage to the site; and developed books, images, and religious brotherhoods devoted to her story and worship. By the eighteenth century when the Mexican-born, *mestizo* painter

---

[1]Inga Clendinnen, *Ambivalent Conquests: Maya and Spaniard in Yucatan, 1517–1570* (New York: Cambridge University Press, 1987).

Miguel Cabrera made his painting, the Virgen de Guadalupe was honored throughout Mexico. His painting, featured next, depicts the Indian Juan Diego looking toward a priest who stands with eyes upturned, gazing at the now-standard painting of the Virgen de Guadalupe set into an elaborately carved and curtained altarpiece. In the early 1800s, this image would become a potent symbol of the people of Mexico in their struggles against Spanish rule.

In the Andes, sometime just before 1608, *don* Cristóbal and some of his fellow non-*Inca*, provincial elites produced the remarkable collection of writings that scholars call the *Huarochirí Manuscript*. They wrote out in *Quechua* for their parish priest, Francisco de Avila, an account of a few historical events and many of the legends, customs, and beliefs that defined who they were as a Native Andean community living on Peru's western slopes. Like his father before him, *don* Cristóbal abandoned the old beliefs and embraced the Christian religion promoted by the Spanish missionaries coming into the mountains from the colonial stronghold of Lima below on the coast. But his thoughts and dreams troubled *don* Cristóbal. Did his father remain true to the new faith, even on his deathbed? Why did the local deities and even his neighbors pressure him to continue to worship in the old ways? Even his dreams were plagued by these doubts and epic tests of his Christian fidelity.

The generation of *don* Cristóbal's late father, the *kuraka* (village chief), managed the transition to colonial religious and political life: The Spanish invaded the Andes in the 1530s when *don* Gerónimo Cancho Huaman was 4 or 5 years old; Jesuit missionaries taught literacy in his district in 1571 when he was 40 although he did not learn to write; and he represented his village at meetings of the chiefs and in court in lawsuits in 1588–1590.[2] During *don* Gerónimo's lifespan, the Spanish implemented a colonial system in the countryside that imposed a Spanish official to rule indirectly through local indigenous authorities, resettled people in villages easier to control for tribute collection and *mita* (labor drafts), and housed in each rural district a Spanish priest to evangelize the local

population. Epidemics swept through Huarochirí in the 1550s, 1580s, and 1590s, carrying off huge numbers with weak immunological defenses against diseases recently introduced into the Americas. Ultimately, the local priest, Avila, used the information collected on Native Andean society to obtain permission to launch the first campaigns to extirpate idolatry from 1609 to 1627 in Huarochirí and neighboring areas under Lima's jurisdiction.

The Mexican devotion to the Virgen de Guadalupe and the drama of *don* Cristóbal's Christian conversion and his father's ambivalence unfolded in an era of intense missionary efforts. Indigenous peoples faced a dilemma: figure out how to blend the old and the new beliefs, or embrace only one set of beliefs. Despite the violence of extirpation campaigns, many Mesoamerican and Andean peoples continued to forge compromises between Christianity and native beliefs, often incorporating Roman Catholic ritual, and eventually Christian doctrine and precepts, into their own religious frameworks.

Questions to Consider:

1. How does the image portray the Virgin Mary and the proper ways to venerate her?
2. What was the relationship between the local community's members and the *huaca*? How did the *Inca* Empire, and later the Spanish, react to this connection? Why?
3. How did the community authorities and *don* Cristóbal's family regard the *huaca* and Christianity? Why did their views change?
4. How did missionaries and their indigenous supporters seek to promote Christianity? What evidence do you see in the visual and textual sources that even the Spanish blended religious traditions to suit their own purposes? Examine some of the images in other chapters to see if they uncover evidence of cultural or religious blending.
5. If you had to choose (and this question requires you to do so!), would you say that the Spanish succeeded or failed at their efforts to convert Native Peoples to Christianity? As you construct your response, give thought to exactly what meanings you give to terms like "success" and "failure."

[2]Frank Salomon and George L. Urioste, eds., *The Huarochirí Manuscript: A Testament of Ancient and Colonial Andean Religion*, trans. Frank Salomon and George L. Urioste (Austin: University of Texas Press, 1991), 103, n. 486 and n. 490.

Miguel Cabrera's eighteenth-century painting of the Virgen de Guadalupe.

Source: Museo Nacional de Arte, Mexico City.

The Story of the Huaca Llocllay Huancupa and Its Battle with the Convert *Don* Cristóbal, 1590–1608[3]

They say the *huaca*[4] named Llocllay Huancupa was Pacha Camac's child. A woman named Lanti Chumpi, from Alay Satpa *ayllu*,[5] found this *huaca*'s visible form while she was cultivating a field. As she dug it out the first time, she wondered, "What could this be?" and just threw it right back down on the ground. But, while she was digging another time,

she found once again the same thing she'd found before. "This might be some kind of *huaca*!" She thought. And so thinking, "I'll show it to my elders and other people of my *ayllu*," she brought it back.

At that time there existed in the village named Llacsa Tampo another *huaca* called Cati Quillay, an emissary of the *Inca*. Cati Quillay was a *yanca*, one who could force any *huaca* that wouldn't talk to speak. Saying, "Who are you? What is your name? What have you come for?" he started to make the *huaca* called Llocllay Huancupa talk. Llocllay Huancupa answered, saying, "I am a child of Pacha Camac Pacha Cuyuchic, World Maker and World Shaker.[6] My name is Llocllay Huancupa. It was my

---

[3]The events involving *Don* Cristóbal occurred between 1590 and 1608. *Source:* Frank Salomon and George L. Urioste, eds., *The Huarochirí Manuscript: A Testament of Ancient and Colonial Andean Religion*, trans. Frank Salomon and George L. Urioste (Austin: University of Texas Press, 1991), 100–110.

[4]A living being venerated by Andean peoples as endowed with holiness and supernatural powers and capable of assuming multiple forms such as a person, object (stone), or place (mountain, spring, outcrop, cave). *Huacas* were interrelated through marriage, parentage, and other kinship ties.

[5]Andean peoples organized themselves into these collectivities to hold land communally and revere common ancestors.

[6]Pacha Camac was a powerful coastal *huaca* able to cause earthquakes. Pilgrims journeyed to it just south of Lima to consult with this oracle that could speak through its priests.

father who sent me here, saying, 'Go and protect that Checa village!'"[7]

The people rejoiced exuberantly, exclaiming, "Good news! Let him live in this village and watch over us." And since the enclosed courtyard at the house of the woman who'd discovered the *huaca* was a small one, they enlarged it, and all the Checa along with the Chauti and Huanri people,[8] adorned her house and courtyard with great reverence.

They made arrangements among themselves, saying, "We'll enter in to do his service according the full and waning moon, *ayllu* by *ayllu*, with the Allauca taking the lead;" and they gave him some of their llamas. At the full moon they in fact say, "It's time for his arrival," they say, "It's he who's arriving!" At the Arrival festival, in the old times, people used to dance wearing the *chumprucu* and the *huaychao* weavings,[9] just the same way as they wore them during Paria Caca's[10] festival season.

They served Llocllay Huancupa in this way for many years. At one time, maybe because people didn't take good care of him, Llocllay Huancupa went back to his father Pacha Camac and disappeared. When the people saw this happen, they grieved deeply and searched for him, adoring the place where Lanti Chumpi had first discovered him, and building him a step-pyramid.

But when they still couldn't find him, all the elders readied their llamas, guinea pigs, and all kinds of clothing [for offerings], and went to Pacha Camac. So by worshipping his father again, they got Llocllay Huancupa to return. People served him even more, with renewed fervor, endowing him with llama herders. They pastured these llamas in the place called Sucya Villca, declaring, "These are llamas of Pacha Camac." The *Inca* also ratified this practice.

They arrived to worship one *ayllu* after another, and in this fashion they served the *huaca* for a great many years. If diseases of any kind came upon them,

they would tell him and implore him for well being. Whenever any affliction or sorrow befell, or when enemies came, or there was an earthquake, people would fear him greatly and say, "His father is angry!" As for maize offerings, they gave him maize belonging to the *Inca* from the common granaries, to provide for his drinks.

Later on, at the time when a certain Father Cristóbal de Castilla was in this *reducción*[11] and when *Don* Gerónimo Cancho Huaman was the *curaca*,[12] people stopped worshiping, because both of them hated such practices. But when the first great plague of measles came, people began to worship him again in all sorts of ways. As if he were thinking, "Llocllay's sending the plague," the *curaca* ceased scolding those people any longer when they drank in the ruined buildings of Purum Huasi [old town abandoned during resettlement]. At that same time, the huaca's house caught fire all by itself, because that was God's will.

Now it's a fact that after *Don* Gerónimo died, *Don* Juan Sacsa Lliuya succeeded to the office of *curaca*, and, since this chief was at the same time a *huacsa*[13] himself, everybody began to live as they'd lived in earlier times; they'd visit both Llocllay Huancupa and Maca Uisa [another *huaca*], and they kept vigil the whole night there drinking until dawn.

Nowadays, due to the preachings of Doctor Avila, some people have converted back to God and forbidden these practices. But if it hadn't been for a certain man who converted to God with a sincere heart and denounced the *huacas* as demons, people might well have kept on living that way for a long time. We'll let you hear this story in what follows.

There was a man named *Don* Cristóbal Choque Casa, whose father was the late *Don* Gerónimo Cancho Huaman whom we mentioned before. This man lived a good life from his childhood onward, because his father bitterly scorned

---

[7]The Checa were an *ayllu* and a settlement of people living on the western slopes of the Andes parallel to Peru's Pacific shore.

[8]The Chauti and Huanri were neighboring *ayllus*.

[9]Turbans and ceremonial weavings.

[10]A snowcapped mountain peak and a *huaca* deity venerated throughout this highland region, uniting various kin and residential groups into a single ethnicity. These people authored the stories and accounts collected into the *Huarochirí Manuscript*.

[11]Spaniards used resettlements to concentrate people from outlying settlements into one place where they could more easily be taxed and Christianized.

[12]Native political lord and community leader.

[13]A person appointed to serve a term as a priest who led the worship of a *huaca*.

all these *huacas*. But when he was about to die, *Don* Gerónimo was deceived by these evil spirits and fell into this same sin. Beguiled by many ancient evil spirits, he confessed himself just before dying. As for that fellow, God only knows where he is now!

The deceased man's son, that is, the same *Don* Cristóbal we spoke of, is still alive. It was he who once saw the demon Llocllay Huancupa with his own eyes, when he was also deceived by the same ancient evil spirits because of his father's death. The story is like this. To tell it *Don* Cristóbal first swore an oath by saying, "this is the cross."

Don Cristóbal said that one night he went to Llocllay Huancupa's house while his lover was there. Cristóbal had abandoned the worship of this *huaca*, and hardly thought of him anymore. When he arrived at the dwelling he went into a little shed in the corral to urinate.

From inside that place, the spot where they've put a cross, that demon appeared before his eyes like a silver plate that, mirroring the light of the midday sun, dazzles a man's eyesight. When he saw this he almost fell to the ground. Reciting the Our Father and the Hail Mary, he fled toward the little lodging, the woman's dwelling.

When he'd walked halfway there, the demon flashed three times again. When he arrived at the room it flashed another three times, and the first time it had flashed three times also. So, all in all, it flashed nine times. Seeing that demon flash so many times, and becoming thoroughly terrified, *Don* Cristóbal reached the place where the woman slept and woke her up abruptly.

Two children were also asleep there. He was panting so hard the children got scared and said, "It's our father who's doing that!" These children and the young woman, too, were the offspring of the demon's priest. Then just as a man entering a doorway at dusk darkens the room even more, so it was that night as the demon went in and out. The demon wanted to overpower *Don* Cristóbal, making his ears ring with a "Chuy!" sound, as if he were about to demolish the house, too.

Cristóbal invoked God, shouting out at the top of his voice all the prayers he knew, saying the

doctrina[14] from beginning to end over and over again. As midnight passed, the demon was overpowering him. He thought that nothing could save him, the demon was making him sweat so. Then he invoked our mother Saint Mary, saying:

"Oh mother, you are my only mother.
Shall this evil demon overpower me?
You, who are my mother, please help me
Even though I am a great sinner;
I myself served this very demon;
Now I recognize that he was a demon all along,
That he is not God,
That he could never do anything good.
You, my only queen,
You alone will rescue me from this danger!
Please intercede on my behalf with your son Jesus.
Let him rescue me right now
From this sin of mine,
And from the hand of this wicked demon."

Thus weeping and sweating he invoked our mother the Virgin, our one and only queen.

After finishing this, he prayed saying the *Salve Regina Mater Misericordiæ* in Latin. While he was reciting it, just as he was in the middle of reciting it, that shameless wicked demon shook the house and, calling "Chus!" in a very deep voice, went out of it in the form of a barn owl. At that exact moment, the place became like dawn. There were no longer any terrors, nothing like a man entering and leaving the room.

From then on, Cristóbal worshiped God and Mary the Holy Virgin even more, so that they might help him always. In the morning he addressed all the people: "Brothers and fathers, that Llocllay Huancupa whom we feared has turned out to be a demonic barn owl."

"Last night, with the help of the Virgin Saint Mary our mother, I conquered him for good. From now on, none of you are to enter that house. If I ever see anybody enter or approach the house, I'll tell the padre. Consider carefully what I have said and receive it into your hearts completely!" Thus he admonished all the people.

---

[14]Elementary religious lessons that the priests required Indian converts to learn.

Some people probably assented, while others stood mute for fear of that demon. From that time forward, they definitely did refrain from going there. But that night, while *Don* Cristóbal was asleep in his house, Llocllay Huancupa appeared to him again in a dream. The following section describes this part of the story.

A Convert's Troubling Dreams

We've already heard that Llocllay Huancupa was an evil demon and that *Don* Cristóbal defeated him. But *Don* Cristóbal said the evil demon also wanted to overpower him in a dream. And so on the night of the very next day, the demon summoned *Don* Cristóbal from his house by sending a man. He didn't tell him, "I'm going to Llocllay Huancupa." Only when they were about to enter his house did *Don* Cristóbal catch on.

He got scared and approached an old lady, a Yunca woman,[15] who lived there in that same patio. This old woman was a Yunca woman. "Son," she said to him, "Why is it that you don't honor Llocllay Huancupa, child of Pacha Cuyuchic the Earth Shaker? It's to find out about this that he's summoned you now."

When she said this, he replied, "Ma'am, he's an evil demon. Why should I honor him?" *Don* Cristóbal was gripping a silver coin of four *reales* in his hand. He dropped it on the ground. While he was searching for it, Francisco Trompetero called him from outside: "Hey, what're you doing in there? Your father is really angry! He's calling you and he says, "He'd better come in a hurry!"

As soon as he said this, Cristóbal replied, "Wait a moment, brother, I'm coming right away" and rummaged for his silver coin in frantic haste. At the moment when he found it, when he was about to leave, the demon, just as he'd scared Cristóbal before with a silvery flash against his face, flashed out once again from inside the place where the cross was put.

Realizing that he couldn't save himself now, Cristóbal suddenly got frightened. Someone called him from inside the room, saying, "It's our father who calls you!" Saying, "All right," but deeply angry in his heart, he went inside. On entering he sat down close by the door.

Right then, Astu Huaman[16] was offering drinks and feeding the *huaca*, saying, "Father Llocllay Huancupa, you are Pacha Cuyuchic's child, It is you who gave force and form to people." As he spoke he fed him with deep veneration. The demon, unable to speak, repeated "Hu, hu" over and over again. And when Astu Huaman offered him some coca, the demon made it crackle "Chac, chac" just as a coca-chewer does.

While he was doing that, a long time, *Don* Cristóbal saw from inside the house something that looked like a painting encircling it completely in two patterned bands. It looked as a Roman-style mural painting might if it went on two levels. On one band of the painting was a tiny demon, very black, his eyes just like silver, who gripped in his hand a wooden stick with a hook. On top of him was a llama head. Above that was again the little demon and above that again the llama head. In this way it encircled the whole house in a twofold pattern.

It really scared *Don* Cristóbal that he kept seeing all these things, and he tried to recall just what he'd meant to say. Meanwhile, since the demon had finished eating, Astu Huaman made the fire blaze up again to burn all the things he'd offered.

After this was done, and when everything was quiet, *Don* Cristóbal began to speak: "Listen, Llocllay Huancupa! They address you as the animator of humanity and as the World Shaker. People say 'He is the very one who makes everything!' and all mankind fears you. So why have you summoned me now? For my part, I say, 'Is not Jesus Christ the son of God? Shall I not revere this one, the true God? Shall I not revere his word forever?' This is what I say. 'Or am I mistaken? Then tell me now! Say, 'He is not the true God; I am the maker of everything!'

---

[15]From the coastal lowlands.

[16]The *huaca*'s priest and the father of *Don* Cristóbal's lover in the last chapter.

so that from that moment on I may worship you." So Cristóbal spoke, but the demon stayed mute. He didn't say anything at all.

At that moment *Don* Cristóbal defied him, crying very loudly:

"Look! Are you not a demon? Could you defeat my Lord Jesus Christ, in whom I believe?

Look! This house of yours! Yes, you dwell surrounded by demons—should I believe in you?"

At that moment somebody threw what we call a *llaullaya*[17] at him. Regarding this thing, *Don* Cristóbal didn't know whether that demon threw it or whether it was from God's side. For, defending himself with the *llaullaya* alone, he fled from that house all the way to the corner of the count's house, always moving sideways and protecting himself with it. Then he woke up.

From that exact time on, right up to the present, he defeated various *huacas* in his dreams the same way. Any number of times he defeated both Paria Caca and Chaupi Ñamca, telling the people all about it over and over again, saying, "They're demons!" This is all we know about this evil demon's existence and about *Don* Cristóbal's victory.

On this matter: it's said that in performing Llocllay's Arrival festival in the old days, the people who celebrated used to dance first until sundown. Toward dusk, the *huaca*'s priest would say, "Now our father is drunk; Let him dance!" And he would perform a dance "as if in his stead," as they used to say. Saying, "It's our father who invites you!" he'd bring maize beer in one small wooden beaker, and put another one inside the shrine in a pot, saying, "It's he who drinks this."

Regarding this drinking: the priest, we know, would offer drinks starting from the elders, all the way down to the end of the assembly.[18] The following day he'd have them carry the leftovers and edible remains to Sucya Villca.

In the old days, the people who'd come to celebrate Llocllay Huancupa's Arrival reportedly brought the food to Sucya Villca himself. However, we know that later on, after finishing Llocllay Huancupa's feeding, people also fed Sucya Villca right at that spot. In what follows, we'll write about these food offerings to Sucya Villca, and why they fed him, and also about who Pacha Camac was.

Suggested Sources:

On the Virgen of Guadalupe and other colonial saints, see Allen Greer and Jodi Bilinkoff, eds., *Colonial Saints: Discovering the Holy in the Americas, 1500–1800* (New York: Routledge, 2003); and D. A. Brading, *Mexican Phoenix: Our Lady of Guadalupe: Image and Tradition Across Five Centuries* (NY: Cambridge University Press, 2001). On cultural and religious changes in Mexico, see Louise Burkhart, *The Slippery Earth: Nahua-Christian Moral Dialogue in Sixteenth-Century Mexico* (Tucson: University of Arizona Press, 1989); and James Lockhart, *The Nahuas After Conquest: A Social and Cultural History of the Indians of Central Mexico* (Stanford, CA: Stanford University Press, 1992). Kenneth R. Mills covers evangelization of Andean populations, traditional beliefs, and efforts to root out old practices in *Idolatry and its Enemies: Colonial Andean Religion and Extirpation, 1640–1750* (Princeton, NJ: Princeton University Press, 1997). See also Nicholas Griffiths, *The Cross and the Serpent: Religious Repression and Resurgence in Colonial Peru* (Norman: University of Oklahoma Press, 1996). Geographic isolation in Mexico's Yucatán gave local populations and missionaries more religious freedom. Refer to Nancy M. Farriss, *Maya Society Under Colonial Rule* (Princeton, NJ: Princeton University Press, 1984).

Frank Salomon and George L. Urioste, eds., provide the rest of this document in *The Huarochirí Manuscript: A Testament of Ancient and Colonial Andean Religion*, trans. Frank Salomon and George L. Urioste (Austin: University of Texas Press, 1991). Felipe Guaman Poma de Ayala also wrote about Andean history and beliefs in

---

[17]An agricultural implement or a garment.
[18]In the margin: When they finished the round of drinking, they say, the priest would bring the gourd from which the demon had drunk outside to where the guests were so they could worship that gourd.

The First New Chronicle and Good Government, ed. and trans. David Frye (Cambridge: Hackett, 2006); also available in Spanish and indexed in English online at: http://www.kb.dk/permalink/2006/poma/info/en/frontpage.htm. Huarochirí under Inca and Spanish rule is analyzed by Karen Spalding, *Huarochirí: An Andean Society Under Inca and Spanish Rule* (Stanford, CA: Stanford University Press, 1984); and Steve J. Stern, *Peru's Indian People and the Challenges of Spanish Conquest. Humanga to 1640* (Madison: University of Wisconsin Press, 1982).

Chapter 9

Patrimony and Patriarchy in a Colonial Mexican *Confraternity*

Annette McLeod Richie,
State University of New York at Albany

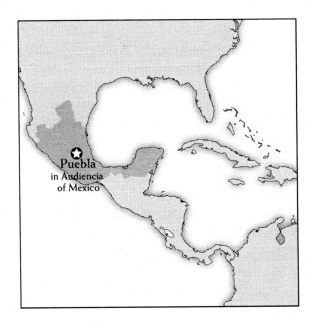

This chapter tells a story about ethnic and gender relations within a *confraternity* heavily dominated by males of Spanish descent. The story was first told from the point of view of *cabildo* members through an act of *confraternity* foundation and an amended constitution, both dating to 1605. The story continued with an *edicto* issued by the local ecclesiastic authority, addressing a complaint made by some of the indigenous members. The story of this *confraternity* old historians quite a bit about the multiethnic community where it was founded.

Confraternities united Christians along neighborhood and racial boundaries and enjoyed immense popularity in Europe. The first contingent of friars sent to New Spain brought them as part of their evangelical arsenal. They provided a dynamic social arena where diverse peoples interacted and negotiated their relative positions. Within a century of the conquest, *confraternities* were being employed to incorporate and control indigenous peoples, Africans, *castas*, and European settlers. Ecclesiastic authorities facilitated European rule by transforming indigenous communities into relatively cooperative, multiethnic parishes. In the process, some local, preconquest traditions and beliefs remained intact under a new guise. Spanish settlers embraced *confraternities* as a carryover from their Iberian way of life. In many *confraternities*, considerable room for social mobility existed for people of mixed descent.[1] Consequently, *confraternities* help historians investigate issues of domination and human agency, particularly within the scope of Church politics and gender relations.

By manipulating language and policies to be both inclusive and exclusive, confraternal leaders capitalized on the seemingly incompatible cultural values of charity and xenophobia. Elected leaders offered a rich ritual life to their constituents by promoting public expressions of piety, such as the sponsorship of orphans, widows, masses, processions, funerals, and religious images. But in the process, they also restricted their members' participation based on their ethnicity, gender, age, class, and perceived spiritual endowments. In any colonial situation, there are limits to self-expression and realization among marginalized peoples, but there are also limits to racial domination. Within rural communities, *confraternities* quickly emerged as multifaceted mediums of religious expression and civic pride that built on pre-Columbian traditions of public devotions, often taking the form of both cooperation and competition within and between *barrios* (neighborhoods). Local native identity was now expressed through the ritual pageantry of processions, dramas, the cult of saints and chapels, and *confraternities*.

In the Mexican parish of Tecamachalco, Puebla, this dynamic social experiment soon took on a life of its own. A multiethnic parish and agricultural region, Tecamachalco remained remote from major Spanish metropolises and offers a promising location to examine indigenous reactions to Christian evangelization. Between 1575 and 1743, the residents—native, Spanish, and *casta*—formed fourteen mostly contemporaneous *confraternities*, reworking the boundaries between themselves and others in the process. Using their barrios as bases, they built chapels; worshipped saints; visited sick members; and sponsored masses, festivals, and orphans. They also chose with whom they would share the privileges and responsibilities of fellowship, membership, and leadership. Inequalities in rights and responsibilities found throughout colonial society were also common in *confraternities*, contrasting Spanish and native, man and woman, rich and poor, single and married, old and young. *Confraternities'* ritual and social obligations created or solidified certain alliances, such as patron-client relationships (or employer-employee), while exacerbating other tensions or political rivalries within a community.

Despite their formulaic nature and repetitiveness, constitutions attempted to express an ideal identity and history. A comparison of constitutions to other parts of confraternal records and external documents, such as the contemporaneous *edicto*, reveal contrasts between the ideal and real practices. Amended constitutions, such as the 1605 constitution presented here, responded to changes within the sponsoring communities. While reading the document, try to identify these key concerns. To a large extent, constitutions may have been tools in the hands of elected *mayordomos* (stewards) and *diputados* (deputies), the veritable "who's who" of the local *barrio*. Constitutions reflect the pressing concerns of the day, at least in the eyes of confraternal leadership and local clergy. For example, if male confraternal leaders restricted the movements and activities of women, regardless of their ethnicity, these men may have seen themselves as protecting womanhood, but they were also reserving the best positions for themselves. This gender inequality may reveal more about how *patriarchy* (male-dominated society) operated locally. Like other religious institutions and practices, *confraternities*

---

[1]Multiethnic society also transformed other local institutions such as the *tianguiz* (market), *hacienda,* and *cabildo.*

played multiple roles in colonial society and can be fruitfully mined for a variety of insights.

Questions to Consider:

1. What appear to have been the chief concerns of the *confraternity* councilmen?
2. To what extent would you interpret the following constitution as propaganda for the preservation of colonial hierarchies?
3. How would you expect men and women who were disenfranchised or marginalized to respond to their local authorities?
4. How did this reading compare and contrast with what you are learning about interethnic and gender relations in your readings on secular life in colonial Latin America (court cases, town councils, land tenure)?

Constitution for the Arch-Confraternity of the Holy True Cross, 1605[2]

. . . These are the Ordinances of the *confraternity* of the Holy True Cross founded by the Spaniards in the church and monastery of the town of Tecamachalco. . . .

1. All who join the *confraternity* shall pay three *pesos* for their seat, three *pesos* for brethren or members of blood.[3]

   [2 *Keeping of the insignias and meeting place*]

3. Order of brethren in the procession. . . . Wearing in the procession, white tunics and cloaks, bearing insignias of the five wounds of Jesus Christ, dressed and their whips in hand so that they spill blood on their backs in remembrance of Our Master and Redeemer Jesus Christ's shedding of blood in order to save mankind. And the Ribs of Jesus are to be carried by the brethren of Light.[4] . . . Everyone is to walk with their faces and necks covered, walking with great devotion and silence, without bearing any other particular signal, lest they be recognized. The brethren of blood all walk barefoot in the procession. . . . Indian brethren penitents are to walk ahead at the beginning of the procession, without inserting themselves

nor retracing their steps with the Spanish penitents, who are there in a row behind. . . .

4. . . . The singers, who are supposed to walk in the procession, go according to practice and custom, behind the image of Our Lady. And likewise, walking behind the said image are the Spanish ladies, who because of their devotion are in the said procession, but without allowing them to pass on ahead, nor should they walk to the sides of the male penitents. . . .

5. . . . Everyone in the town shall attend the procession of Holy Thursday and other feast days. . . . If one does not attend the penalty will be one pound of white wax. . . . If a brethren fails to attend the procession, the penalty is fifty Hail Mary's and five Our Father's, . . . and one pound of white wax. . . .

6. Concerning the admission of women into the *confraternity*. . . . If some single woman wishes to be admitted as a member in this *confraternity*, she shall pay alms for her admission of three *pesos* before she will be entered into the book. . . . Wives of members, pay two *pesos*. [They cannot] be acknowledged publicly, nor are they to be admitted in the order of blood.

7. Watch over the members who are ill, or dead brethren. . . . They must go to the residence of the patient, on penalty of one pound of white wax as penitence if they are absent.

8. If one is poor, they may be registered into the *confraternity* or mass for free. . . .

---

[2]*Source:* Parish Archive of Tecamachalco (Puebla, Mexico), Asociaciones, Archicofradía de la Santa Veracruz, Book 4. Punctuation and words added for readability.

[3]An order within *the confraternity* open to adult male Spaniards.

[4]Another exclusive order within the *confraternity*.

9. An Indian with his green habit, hand bell, and a charter which states the name of the *confraternity*, so that all of the brethren shall be present at the house of the said deceased. People shall carry him to the church and monastery of this town, where he is to be buried honorably at the expense of the *confraternity*.
[*10 concerns burials, and 11–13 concern processions and masses.*]

14. Concerning the election of officials. Each year, in the afternoon after Vespers, a meeting and council of the brethren is to be held to elect one steward, two deputies and a scribe. The steward is obligated to provide clear and certified guarantees in which the property and adornments of the said Holy *confraternity* are handed over. The steward must consult with the deputies before spending more than six *pesos*. . . .
[*15 concerns deliberations.*]

16. Concerning the acceptance of offices without excuse. If elected, then they must accept the duty or the penalty of one 25 pounds of white wax. And let it be known that the Indians are not to be admitted into the council in order to vote.

17. . . . There are admitted as members some native Indians. They enjoy this privilege due only to the grace and indulgences of the said *confraternity*, to whom we exempt them.[5] . . . [They] shall not be present in the meetings and councils in order to vote in any matter, nor shall they be given any office concerned with the said *confraternity*, in order that they would bear insignias, litters, standards, staffs of government, wax torches, nor any other thing in the procession, . . .

18. The Indian member to whom the steward gives the bond of the *confraternity*, on Saturdays in the afternoon, he will be obligated so that he goes to the market of this said town and begs alms among the natives. Even though . . . they only obtain ten *cacaos* [cacao beans] that they give, and four *macoras* [handfuls] of corn. If for any personal service concerning the matters of this

confraternity, there was a need for some Indians, the steward and deputies are to pay them for their work. They can force the said Indians who are members to assist in it. . . .
[*19–26 address alms, images, masses, elections, and Palm Sunday.*]

27. Concerning Indians who made the insignias and try to walk in front of the rest. And consider that if, from this point forward, at some point, the native Indians of this town of Tecamachalco made, or wished to make, insignias and images of the resurrection of Jesus Christ Our Lord and of the Virgin Mary his mother, and intend to bring them out in procession on the morning of Easter, which until today they have not yet done so. This procession and ancient devotion of the Spanish members will be, and it is meant to be [a procession of Spaniards, not Indians]. . . . The Indians must lead in front of our banner, and with not one going from the banner to our insignias of Jesus Christ resuscitated, and the Virgin mother his most sacred mother. No other insignia shall be inserted. . . . The protection of the said procession shall be fulfilled, to protect that which until now has been customary. In no way or form shall the said Indians attempt to equal us with their insignias at our side, nor shall they occupy a better place than us because they are indecent people.
[*28–29 concern Holy Thursday.*]

30. Women shall not enter the *lavatorio* [where the holy water is kept or baptismal font]. No woman, of whatever quality she may be, is to enter into the waiting or rest area of the lavatorio, . . . if she does enter, any official can evict her.

31. No one shall lend our insignias, nor the images, their vestments, their standards, nothing, to the Indians, nor to other people, even to the friars of the monastery, even if they may be the stewards or the deputies of the *confraternity*, because they must be protected for times of devotion and they were purchased with alms.
[*32–40 concern penalties, torches, alms, Indians' work, no re-elections, and masses.*]

---

[5] Written and then crossed out.

Edict Responding to the 1605 Constitution[6]

. . . Regarding a petition which was made by the Indians of the said *confraternity* to participate in the procession and found a new confraternity. They petition to wear insignias on feast days and processions, in the manner of the Spaniards, The Spaniards wish to impede the natives from the privilege of bearing insignias and images. . . . The guardian father conceded a license to the natives so that they may appear in their processions of Holy Thursday and Good Friday, in masses for the deceased. . . . Signed Juan de Merlo. . . . The vicar cedes the privilege of wearing tunics and insignias to all brethren Indians.

Suggested Sources:

Scholars routinely try to puzzle out the meaning of religious acts and rituals. See Louise M. Burkhart, "Pious Performances: Christian Pageantry and Native Identity in Early Colonial Mexico," in *Native Traditions in the Postconquest World*, ed. Elizabeth H. Boone and Tom Cummins (Washington, DC: Dumbarton Oaks, 1996). Confraternity records sometimes show how ethnic identity can be preserved or transformed. Refer to Paul Charney, "A Sense of Belonging: Colonial Indian Cofradías and Ethnicity in the Valley of Lima, Peru," *The Americas* 54, no. 3 (January 1998): 379–407. Combining various kinds of sources on people's public activities

and performances can help paint a fuller picture of their beliefs. See Daniel O. Mosquera, "Consecrated Transactions: Of Marketplaces, Passion Plays, and Nahua Christian Devotions," *Journal of Latin American Cultural Studies* 14, no. 2, (August 2005): 171–193. Annette D. McLeod, "Sacramental and Confraternal Records from Tecamachalco's Parish Archive," in *Sources and Methods for the Study of Postconquest Mesoamerican Ethnohistory*, ed. James Lockhart, Lisa Sousa, and Stephanie Wood, *http://whp.uoregon.edu/Lockhart/McLeod.pdf*. African peoples in the Americas also used confraternities to assert individual and collective rights. See Nicole Von Germeten, *Black Blood Brothers: Confraternities and Social Mobility for Afro-Mexicans* (Gainesville: University Press of Florida, 2006).

For other confraternity constitutions, see John Frederick Schwaller, "Constitution of the Cofradía del Santísimo Sacramento of Tula, Hidalgo, 1570," *Estudios de Cultura Nahuatl* 19 (1989): 217–244, and *Nahua Confraternities in Early Colonial Mexico: The 1552 Nahuatl Ordinances of Fray Alonso de Molina, OFM*, ed. and trans. Barry D. Sell, with contributions by Larissa Taylor and Asunción Lavrin (Berkeley, CA: Academy of American Franciscan History/University of Chicago Library, 2006). The ethnographic film *Mayordomia Ritual, Gender, and Cultural Identity in a Zapotec Community* presents insights into confraternity rituals and membership (Austin: University of Texas Press, 1991). For amateur film footage of Holy Week processions, enter the search parameters "Holy Week procession," "Semana Santa," or "penitents," at *http://www.youtube.com*.

---

[6]*Source:* Parish Archive of Tecamachalco (Puebla, Mexico), *Edictos y Cordillera*.

Chapter 10

Spiritual Directions: Gender, Piety, and Friendship in Late Colonial Mexico

Karen Melvin, Bates College

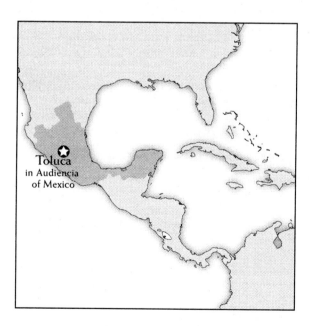

While María Josefa de la Peña's corpse lay still warm on her deathbed, a local priest kissed the hands, feet, and heart, telling all those present that he did so because the woman had possessed qualities of a saint. It was January 1784, and he was not the only one to think de la Peña saintly. During the final few years of María Josefa's young life—she died at the age of 24—she developed a reputation as a holy person in her home city of Toluca. She was said to have spent hours each day secluded in prayer, performing devotional exercises, and meditating on the life of Christ. She took the sacraments of confession and communion multiple times each week at a time when people were only required to do so once a year. She patterned much of her spirituality after a popular Spanish saint, Teresa of Ávila (1515–1582), a Carmelite nun known for her *mysticism*. María Josefa's mystic practices included fasting regularly and using painful instruments of mortification, such as a crown of thorns and a discipline of hooks (a band worn tightly around the body with the hooks facing the skin). These practices, which were to help the faithful perfect their souls and bring them closer to God, were popular among many pious women.

The reasons for *mysticism*'s popularity among women included even more than these highly valued spiritual rewards. *Mysticism* also offered women possibilities for fame, respect, and influence that they would not otherwise be able to access in the male-dominated Church hierarchy. For example, the spiritual practices of Rose of Lima (1586–1617), which included fasting, torments, and deprivations said to be so severe as to be inviting death, helped earn her an enthusiastic following during her lifetime and, later, canonization (1671) as the first saint from the Americas.

María Josefa's particular pious regimens had their origins in the strong mystic tradition of the Carmelite order. Her two *confessors* were members of this order and did much to encourage her to follow its customs and emulate its most important saint, Teresa of Ávila. They taught her how to make daily rounds of prayers, lent her devotional books, and instructed her in Teresa's writings. Although mystic practices may have set María Josefa apart from most laypersons, they were not enough in themselves to inspire a reputation for saintliness. According to Catholic belief, evidence of divine favor was a much better indicator. Only those specially chosen by God would be granted visions or miraculous favors, and according to María Josefa's supporters—including the two Carmelite priests who acted as her *confessors*—María Josefa received such gifts. Divine power had helped her heal and protect others and foretold local happenings. It also gave her the gift of

the stigmata,[1] which is why one of her *confessors* kissed the body where he did on the hands, feet, and heart. Even after María Josefa's death, some people believed that miracles continued to happen around the body. The body even emitted a sweet fragrance—a sure sign that the soul that once inhabited that body was now enjoying the glories of a heavenly reward.

Not everyone was convinced of María Josefa's holiness, however, and, at the time of her death, the Holy Office of the *Inquisition* was investigating her as a false mystic. Nor were the actions of her two Carmelite *confessors* universally accepted as appropriately decorous and *Franciscan* friars from Toluca's parish church denounced them to the *Inquisition*. In this case, the *Inquisition* was concerned not only with the *confessors*' actions themselves, but also with stopping the spread of María Josefa's fame. Mystics had long been a subject of concern for the Church hierarchy in part because of fears that false mystics might lead people astray. In addition, mystics' claims of direct connections with God undermined the institutional Church's authority by bypassing the priests who were supposed to mediate between God and the faithful. During the late eighteenth century, reform-minded clergymen sought to replace *mysticism*'s excesses with more structured and conventional devotion. Rather than approaching God through a physical, sensory piety designed to inflame the senses, reformers argued that people should use more sedate, orderly, and intellectual methods. Rather than fasts and disciplines of hooks, people should rely on reflection and quiet prayer. The *Inquisition* thus took a keen interest not only in María Josefa, but also in tracking down and reining in her network of followers.

One of those they tracked down was her good friend, María Luisa González Zepúlveda. Thanks to her close proximity to the mystic, María Luisa was able to provide a vivid picture of her friend's actions, practices, and reputation. But in the course of her testimony, María Luisa also became something of a protagonist in the story with a startling revelation: María Josefa had been acting as her spiritual director.

---

[1] The stigmata represented the five wounds that Christ suffered on the cross: nails in his hands and feet and a slash over his heart.

Although there were no official Church prohibitions against a laywoman acting as someone's spiritual advisor, it was highly unusual. Most people received their spiritual guidance from their *confessors*, who could help them search their consciences for their transgressions, assign penance for sins, and instruct them to ways of being better Catholics. Others, however, who sought to achieve higher levels of spiritual perfection might also have a spiritual director (who may or may not have been their regular *confessor*) to provide additional guidance. This person was usually a priest. For a woman, let alone a laywoman, to act as a spiritual director meant that she must have been viewed as having special gifts.

Questions to Consider:

1. Using evidence from the document, what did religion mean to people in late colonial Mexico?

2. What clues does the document offer about the reasons María Josefa might have had for following the spiritual path that she did?

3. What clues does the document offer about whether or not María Luisa was happy with María Josefa's spiritual direction? Why did she defend or not defend her friend before the *Inquisition*?

4. In what ways was María Luisa caught between the competing influences of María Josefa and Church officials? How did María Josefa's influence compare to that of Church officials? What might this suggest about connections among gender, religion, and power?

5. Compare María Josefa and her experiences with the seventeenth-century Brazilian mystic in Chapter 14.

Testimony of María Luisa González Zepúlveda[2]

In the meeting room of the Third Order of San Francisco of Toluca at 8:00 a.m. on June 23, 1784 before Father Friar Mariano José Casasola, Notary and Commissioner of the Holy *Inquisition* appeared a woman who swore to tell the truth and said her name was María Luisa González Zepúlveda (although she was known as Garduño) and she was a Spaniard, unmarried *doncella*,[3] 25 years old, originally from this city [of Toluca], and the legitimate daughter of Don Juan Manuel González Zepúlveda and Doña Barbara Rosalia Flores.

{NOTE IN THE MARGIN: This witness is known around here as a secluded doncella, inclined toward virtue, chaste in her manner of dress, and who lives in an orderly fashion and frequently takes the Sacraments of communion and confession.}

She was asked if she knows if some actions of adoration and reverence were made with any dead woman? She responded that having been present at the death of

María Josefa Piña she saw Father Friar Lorenzo, friar of the Order of [Our Lady of] Carmen whose last name she does not know, in the afternoon of the death and in the house of dead woman, adore the cadaver and kiss its feet, hands, and side. He told those present not to be scandalized by what he was about to do because that woman had died with the reputation of a saint. He pointed out to the witness [María Luisa] the sweet smell that the body was emitting, and that although she along with all those present (which were many although she does not remember who they were) claimed to smell it as well, she did not perceive any odor.

She was asked if she knew if any of the dead woman's things were distributed like relics?[4] She responded that some things, including her instruments of mortification and interior tunics, were distributed like relics to various people, who she doesn't know by name.

She was asked if they gave her any of these things? She responded that they gave her a tunic, a

[2]*Source:* Archivo General de la Nación (Mexico City), Ramo *Inquisición*, vol. 1139, exp. 3.

[3]A *doncella* was an unmarried woman, usually of a higher social status. The term implied she was a virgin.

[4]Associated with saints or holy persons, relics are objects thought to be imbued with holy or miraculous powers.

discipline of hooks, a small box filled with dust, but nothing else. She was told that the Holy Office had testimony that she had an image of the Baby Jesus that had been María Josefa's. She said that this is true but that she didn't mention it because they [the Carmelite friars who attended María Josefa's death] didn't give it to her. It had come into her possession from the Carmelite convent, which owned it, after she had asked for it for a sick woman. But she had given it, along with the other items she already declared, to the Father Commissioner as he had ordered.

She was asked what sort of esteem she gave to the tunic, discipline, and box of dust and if she knows if other people viewed the items that they took as relics? She responded that she took her things as those of a friend who she had esteemed. That she had seen Friar Sebastián de San Francisco, Carmelite, adore those that he had and carried with him, kissing them and bringing them to his chest with reverence. That this friar had asked her if she didn't perceive the smell that they emitted, but that she didn't smell it.

She was asked if she knew if the *confessors* had executed any actions with the dead woman that are worthy of concern? She responded that she only knew that they had given María Josefa permission to take Communion daily.

She was asked if she knew the method of direction that the *confessors* used with the dead woman? She responded that although she didn't know the method of direction that they used with the dead woman, she pointed out that she had been under the direction of the dead woman in matters of the spirit for a year and a half, without the approval of her *confessor*, Friar Bonifacio de la Madre de Dios, friar of the Order of Carmen. That the direction established that: María Luisa take Sacraments three days per week plus holidays and each day of the *Pasquas* [Easter, Christmas, Pentecost]; she limit her active and passive [social] visits; [she make] three hours of mental prayer on the Passion of Christ [per day], daily mortifications, common disciplines, and disciplines of blood three times per week, daily fasts, and, on three longer occasions, fasts with only bread and water.

She was asked what were her motives in following the direction of a woman? She responded that it was because she found herself without a *confessor* who she liked, and when she communicated

her distress to María Josefa, she offered to direct her. And that in this way she entered the direction of the dead woman, who she promised to obey in everything, and the dead woman took on the responsibility of directing her, although on the condition that she would test the progress of [María Luisa's] spirit for one month. Depending on how she did, María Josefa would determine whether to continue or not. That after the month passed she continued, as it seemed to María Luisa that she was improving under this direction, because it forced her to give up social visits, even though these were not bad other than the waste of time. That she maintained this method without the knowledge of Friar Bonifacio the first six months, which is when she began to loathe her direction since María Josefa opposed her consulting with any priest. She resolved to tell her *confessor*, who inquired about the method of life that she followed and reprimanded her for the frequency with which she was taking communion and for her excess of mortifications, taking into consideration that her health was so poor—other *confessors* she has consulted since then have reprimanded her for the same reasons of her health. And as it was an inconvenient hour and the witness said that much remained on this subject, the Father Commissioner ordered the continuation of this declaration be delayed until the following day.

In the city of Toluca at 8:00 a.m. on June 26, 1784 in the meeting room of the Third Order of San Francisco, María Luisa González Zepúlveda presented herself before the Father Commissioner Friar Mariano José Casasola . . . and continued her declaration under oath as made in the aforementioned manner.

She said that having advised Friar Bonifacio of what had happened in those six months, he ordered María Josefa called to the confessional, and what resulted from the answers of both [María Josefa and María Luisa] was that the Padre gave his consent, with which the witness continued her direction under María Josefa. This was done on the condition that she notify him of all that María Josefa ordered and with additional reprimands for taking communion so frequently and for excessive mortifications.

Also María Luisa said that María Josefa reacted very bitterly and badly because . . . María Luisa was having to tell her *confessor* about María Josefa's orders, and much more. María Josefa told María Luisa that her *confessor* would take away the communion and penitence that María Josefa had ordered and that if María Luisa wanted to continue under her direction, she could not share María Josefa's orders with the priest. That although he did not want her to take communion and use the mortifications in the said form, she had to do it as María Josefa had ordered. That to do this so Friar Bonifacio would not see her, María Josefa sent María Luisa to take communion at this [the *Franciscan*] parish church.

Also she said that María Josefa did not want her to have a *Padre de assiento*[5] or a [regular] *confessor* except that for purely reconciling herself[6] she was to go [confess] with Friar Bonifacio or any other *confessor*. . . .

Also she said that one time she had intended to come to confess in this Parish, seeing as how María Josefa did not like her to confess with Friar Bonifacio, but María Josefa prevented it saying that the regimen of the *Franciscans* was very distinct from that of the Carmelites. . . . That she strongly insisted that the witness write down how much had happened to her, even ordering her to do so, but she never did it. That she ordered her three times to make a vow of chastity. The first for fifteen days without any incurring of any sin; the second for twenty days with the threat of incurring venial sin; the third for one month, more or less, with the threat of incurring mortal sin.[7] That on the first two occasions she obeyed without dissent but the third caused her doubts, and so, coming to this Parish, she consulted with a [*Franciscan*] friar who told her that not for a moment should she make such a vow under these terms. And that if the Director obligated her under threat of mortal sin, then he obligated her to do the opposite under the same threat. And finally, she said that her obedience to María Josefa was such that even though her

confessor reprimanded her for the communions and austerities of fasts of bread and water and bloody disciplines, she did it so as not to lack obedience. That for this reason during one of the fasts, when the witness found herself with a serious illness, she said that she could not continue with the fast, but María Josefa ordered her *por obediencia*[8] to continue, and so she obeyed. She added that the dead woman judged her spirit as good. And that this is what she has to tell them about the direction that she had with María Josefa.

She was asked by what power or license María Josefa came to be her spiritual guide? She responded that María Josefa had said that her *confessor*, Friar Sebastián de San Francisco, had given her license to do so.

She was asked if she believed that she was following a secure path to perfection guided only by a woman's direction? She responded that she was undecided if it was going well or not, especially when she considered that the Director did not want her to consult others about her orders.

She was asked how she handled these pangs of conscience regarding the security of her soul while she remained under such direction? She responded that only by that counsel she found in her direction.

She was asked if she found any extravagances in the commands, teachings, or counsels, etc. that the dead woman gave her? She responded that other than what she had already declared, it had not seemed right . . . that María Josefa obligated her to take communion without reconciliation [confessing], as María Luisa had done various times, telling her so as to appease her concerns, that those communions remained María Josefa's responsibility. But in all else she judged that the Director proceeded properly because she offered good counsel and teachings, she reprimanded her, corrected her, and procured her advancement in virtue. That she had offered

[5] A *padre de assiento* was a priest especially valued for his maturity, experience, and wise judgment.
[6] Reconciliation, or the process of cleansing the soul of sin through confession, penance, and absolution, was required before taking communion.
[7] Venial sins were those not serious enough to prevent the soul from achieving salvation; they only hindered it. Mortal sins, if not reconciled, would prevent salvation.

[8] Literally meaning "by obedience," the phrase referenced one of the standard three monastic vows, obedience, by which the men and women religious who took it were required, under the threat of incurring of mortal sin, to obey their superiors. In this case, without vows, the threat of mortal sin would not have applied, but the concept of setting aside one's own will to comply with a superior's orders did.

perseverance in spiritual exercises and the invocation of the Sweet Names of Jesus and Mary as remedy against temptations, distractions, and weaknesses, assuring her that these were the best weapons against the Devil's temptations.

That the evening before Portiuncula[9] last year and without María Josefa's knowledge she began to confess with a Carmelite priest with whom she had had some communication, but being ashamed she didn't finish the confession. Not wanting to miss out on Holy Communion the next day, she decided to confess with Friar Lorenzo, and while she was standing next to the confessional, María Josefa arrived. She told María Luisa that she knew well that the day before she had come there with another Father, because however it appeared to her, she couldn't hide anything that she did, either for God's benefit or who knew why. She said this angrily and, stepping in front of María Luisa, told her that she would go without communion that day. At last María Luisa went to Friar Lorenzo who detained her a great while and without reason deferred absolution because she was not receiving communion that day, designating it for the next day. That afternoon the two women met in the Parish Church for the purpose of the jubilee, and María Josefa told her: well, I thought that you were not to take communion today. The next day María Josefa went to the house of the witness who told her Friar Lorenzo had designated this day to see her. María Josefa stopped her from returning to see him, and when the witness insisted, she ordered por obediencia that she not go. The same María Josefa went to see the said Father in the confessional to find out the motives for not allowing her disciple to take communion. As a result she ordered the witness never to return [to confess] with Friar Lorenzo, even though he had ordered her to appear, saying that her conferences with Friar Lorenzo were causing much confusion. He had said that she was to take great care with María Luisa because if what one or the other of them communicated to her was not consistent, he thought that it would mislead her. Nevertheless,

María Josefa was going to continue to direct her, on the assumption that she understood her spirit, provided that she declare under obediencia all that she had said and done and that she would not search for another director. After telling María Luisa all of what Friar Lorenzo had said, she added that María Luisa would not confess with another [confessor] until she allowed it, but, even though she was not confessing, she would continue taking communion on the assigned days.

She also said that Friar Lorenzo explained to María Josefa why he had not wanted María Luisa to take communion. In addition, that María Luisa, having arrived to confess with Friar Ygnacio de San Juan Baptista with license from her director and having explained that she was there because Friar Lorenzo did not allow her to take communion, Friar Ygnacio ordered her not to return to Friar Lorenzo under the threat of mortal sin. That this same friar at first disapproved that she was directed by María Josefa, but upon learning that her previous confessor Friar Bonifacio approved and consented to it, he [approved that she] continue under her direction.

Also she said . . . eventually María Josefa consented to order María Luisa to consult with Friar Ygnacio about the direction she had with her and that if he disapproved, she was to tell him that she knew that it was decreed from above by the commandments that María Josefa was receiving from God, and that if he still disapproved after all this, she was to tell him to come see María Josefa.

She was asked what commandments María Josefa had told her to tell to the priest? She responded none specifically.

And not being possible to conclude this declaration for lack of time the Father Commissioner postponed its conclusion until the following Monday, instructing the witness to search her memory, which she promised to do.

In the same meeting room on June 28, 1784 before the Father Commissioner Friar Mariano José Casasola, María Luisa González Zepúlveda reappeared. She was asked if anyone found out that María Josefa Pina was directing her spiritually? She responded that no one other than Friar Sebastián, who had given license to María Josefa; Friar Lorenzo; Friar Bonifacio de la Madre de Dios; Friar Ygnacio de San

---

[9]The popular August 2 feast celebrated in Franciscan churches when people could earn multiple plenary indulgences to lessen one's time in purgatory.

Juan Baptista; and a *Franciscan* friar, whose name she does not know because she communicated with him in the confessional. And she presumes that María Josefa told her mother and cousin, both dead now.

She was asked if she had heard about any miracles, prophecies, revelations, visions, or admirable things about María Josefa or any other person?

[*She listed more than 25 examples, most of which she had heard from Friar Sebastián but some of which came from Friar Lorenzo and María Josefa's mother. These included examples of María Josefa's intercessions with God (e.g. after María Josefa prayed to God for a couple who had been constantly fighting, the fights stopped), marvelous occurrences (e.g. after María Josefa fell in the river she came out without having gotten wet), and triumphs in the trials that the devil put in her path (e.g. when writing something for Friar Sebastián the devil took away her paper but she took the scapular*[10] *from her neck and put it around his, only taking it off when he agreed to return her paper).*]

That this is what she only learned from the word of others, but she herself was witness to some noteworthy things. The first would have been two years ago when Rafaela Garduño was extremely grief-stricken over the death of a young son, she asked María Luisa to ask María Josefa to come visit her. María Josefa went to the grieving woman's house and there she offered the usual consolations. But afterwards with María Luisa, she ordered her to tell Rafaela that she would not be able to have boys. That this came to pass. Also, even though Rafaela would have a daughter live a few days as a consolation, she, too, would die. And that this was also verified within a year or so.

That a young man not from Toluca who had gone blind stopped at the house of the aforementioned Rafaela Garduño. . . . He asked María Josefa to see him and pray to God to restore his sight because his parents were very poor and he took care of them. She had prayed to God for him, and it was revealed to her that his bodily sight did not return because it would overwhelm his soul's vision. That his sight would return for a short period and then he would die

shortly after that. María Josefa communicated the revelation to her *confessor* and by his order she told María Luisa, who affirmed the prophecy was fulfilled. . . . Shortly after [getting back his sight], the man fell back into total blindness, and having left there for his native soil, he died fifteen days before María Josefa.

Also she declared having had in her hands a small piece of paper with María Josefa's writing . . . in which she informed one of her *confessors* of her abstinence, saying that since before Lent until Pentecost[11] she had not had anything to eat because she had forgotten.

Roberta, daughter of the Embroiderer, being in María Josefa's house helping clean her room, picked up a carved crucifix in order to clean it. Its hairpiece fell off and she saw that the image was growing its own hair. . . . Another day María Josefa showed the image to María Luisa who certified the singularity of the hair, which she had seen on repeated occasions and that she has seen many times since the death of María Josefa. She knows that its hair is longer than it was last year.

She was asked if she knows the effects caused by Friar Lorenzo's actions of kissing María Josefa's feet, hands, and side [at her deathbed], by the proclamation of her doings and all the marvels that she referred to? She responded that what is evident to her is that many people take her for a servant of God and that all the people who were there at her house (which was many) from the hour that she died until the morning of the next day when they took her body to the church kissed the corpse with reverence. Because to those who came in had heard that Friar Lorenzo had adored it, kissing its hands, feet, and heart. That one Thomas Sanchez who was present, having heard of the friar's actions, adored, and kissed the same parts.

She was asked if anything else occurred to her? She responded that she had declared as much as her conscience dictated to her and that, having relieved it, she had no more to say.

Signed: Friar Mariano José Cassasola, Comisario
Friar Francisco Castellanos, Notario
María Luisa González Zepúlveda

---

[10]A piece of cloth or paper bearing a religious image or symbol and that is worn around the neck.

[11]This would have meant she fasted for a span of about 90 days. Fasting could mean complete abstinence from food or just limiting how much and what was eaten.

Suggested Sources:

Asunción Lavrin's *Brides of Christ: Conventual Life in Colonial Mexico* (Stanford, CA: Stanford University Press, 2008) provides clear explanations and vivid examples of female spirituality and pious practice in colonial Mexico. Kathleen Myers recounts the lives of some of the more famous women of the colonial Spanish Americas, including Rose of Lima, in *Neither Saints nor Sinners: Writing the Lives of Women in Spanish America* (Oxford: Oxford University Press, 2003). This work also includes selected writings from each woman. For more detail on women's spiritual writings, see Kathleen Myers and Amanda Powell, *A Wild Country Out in the Garden: The Spiritual Journals of a Colonial Mexican Nun* (Bloomington, IN: Bloomington University Press, 1999). Women's stories recorded by the Spanish Inquisition can be found in Mary E. Giles, ed. *Women in the Inquisition: Spain and the New World* (Baltimore: The Johns Hopkins University Press, 1999). Mystics and their practices figure in each of these works. For more on mystics and those judged as false mystics, see Nora E. Jaffary, *False Mystics: Deviant Orthodoxy in Colonial Mexico* (Lincoln: University of Nebraska Press, 2004). Additional information on female spiritual directors is in Patricia Ranft, *A Woman's Way: The Forgotten History of Women Spiritual Directors* (New York: Palgrave, 2000). María Josefa's story in the context of rivalries among religious orders is told in Karen Melvin, "A Potential Saint Thwarted: Religion and the Politics of Sanctity in Late-Eighteenth-Century New Spain," in *Studies in Eighteenth-Century Culture*, ed. Jeffrey Ravel and Linda Zionkowski (2007), vol. 36, 169–185.

Section III

Finding a Place within Colonial Hierarchies

Colonial hierarchies based on religious piety and lineage, gender and occupational status, and ethno-racial identity often shaped people's lives by determining their obligations and opportunities. Indigenous villagers had to pay tribute to the crown and serve in rotating labor drafts. Africans could not carry weapons and gather in public or wear fine clothing and jewelry. Only male Spaniards and nobles could carry swords. Rules barred women from many religious organizations. Therefore, colonial society is perhaps aptly considered a place with a highly stratified social structure, where rank and power were largely determined at birth. Although these limitations and rankings existed and exercised influence over how people thought and acted, individual actions, or *agency*, mattered tremendously in how people lived their lives. Indigenous and African people, in particular, forged spaces for self-determination within the limits set by the colonial state and society. Rising numbers of *creoles* developed a self-awareness, or sense of loyalty to their region and a sense of distinctness from Europeans. Even minors found ways to challenge patriarchal authority, not through outright rebellion, but by using one powerful figure against another. Africans in the Americas also sought ways to accumulate modest wealth and to distinguish themselves within their communities. This frequently took the form of using legal documents and formal membership in Church institutions to defend free status, proclaim a particular ethnic allegiance, and ensure that these benefits accrued to subsequent generations. In each case, they did this to achieve more favorable outcomes within the system rather than overturn it.

In the seventeenth and eighteenth centuries, these colonial subjects sought room to discover for themselves more comfortable ways to live within the colonial system. A desire to control their economic existence often spurred action. Indigenous people, for instance, found that living in cities and towns often freed them from fulfilling their home communities' onerous labor drafts and tribute payments. Mining operations and urban markets demanded laborers and required consumables and artisans' goods. This further spurred native migration and afforded freed and enslaved blacks opportunities to accumulate earnings. Indians, Africans, and others saw an expansion of wage labor and access to cash and kind. Large towns grew and became the focus of social dynamism and market activity. Marketplaces in particular became the domain of women outside of the Spanish elite (these elites could suffer a loss of *honor* by engaging in petty commerce), and some earned enough to live quite comfortably. Eventually, wage labor spread into the countryside, too, and agricultural production quickened to meet city dwellers' growing appetites. The events in this section took

Felipe Guaman Poma de Ayala considered Africans and their descendants capable of becoming good Christians and Crown subjects. His caption reads: "Devout black Christians from the stock of unacculturated black slaves from Africa say the rosary before an image of the Virgin Mary." He also felt that Africans' place in colonial society was far from indigenous villages, where he warned that Africans and Spanish colonists undermined the proper functioning of Indian society. He argued that colonialism exerted a morally corrupting influence that could harm African peoples, too. How did Guaman Poma emphasize the piety of black people? How did he dress the man and the woman? What did the drawing reveal about his view of colonial society?

Source: The Royal Library/Drawing 275. Guaman Poma, *Nueva corónica y buen gobierno* (1615). Devout black Christians from the stock of unacculturated black slaves from Africa ("Guinea") say the rosary before an image of the Virgin Mary.

place in these cities and towns and involved people who took advantage of these openings.[1]

Shifts in ethnicity also took place. Some people remained linked to home regions and ancestors, whereas others broke those bonds and forged new connections with people from other places or different ethnic groups. The neat division of society into Africans, Europeans, and Indians became complicated by this *mestizaje,* or cultural sharing and blending of traditions. The number of culturally and ethnically mixed people—*castas*—grew dramatically in the 1600s and 1700s, particularly in the cities and mining and trading centers that drove the economy. The spreading market activity and domestic work ensured the centrality of native and African women as key mediators between native and foreign cultures. Indeed, they helped form what became colonial cultural and daily life.[2]

Despite the limitations of colonial hierarchies and laws, the historical record provides many revealing cases of women, youth, and non-Europeans opening up spaces, gaining ground, and utilizing for various ends colonial society's institutions, commercial and legal practices, and social hierarchies. Scholars in the past few decades have been uncovering more and more stories of women and youth, poor people, and non-Europeans (even slaves and former slaves) that used colonial institutions and practices as a means to improve their own lives within the colonial system. Von Germeten guides readers through Colombian *Inquisition* records that show the diversity of Afro-Colombian experiences and identities in the colonial period. Documents

---

[1] For more on the many ways blacks survived under colonialism and engaged its institutions, see Kathryn Joy McKnight and Leo J. Garofalo, *Afro-Latino Voices: Narratives from the Early Modern Ibero-Atlantic World, 1550–1812* (Cambridge: Hackett, 2009).

[2] A good description of these broad changes in the Andean heartland can be found in Kenneth J. Andrien, *Andean Worlds: Indigenous History, Culture, and Consciousness Under Spanish Rule. 1532–1825* (Albuquerque: University of New Mexico Press, 2001).

presented by O'Toole and Kiddy offer tales of personal success, in which poor and non-European men and women found various means to overcome their humble origins. Seed's court cases demonstrate how parents and children sparred, drawing upon the Church's rules governing marriage. These primary sources and the many stories they contain will leave readers with a deeper understanding of the many ways real people tried to find a place within colonial hierarchies that structured colonial society. Together they suggest that hierarchy and agency were not always mutually exclusive, and that it was possible for individuals to work within a system designed to exploit them, sometimes finding ways to benefit and advance.

Chapter 11

African Women's Possessions: Inquisition Inventories in Cartagena de Indias

Nicole von Germeten, *Oregon State University*

Cartagena in Audiencia of Santa Fé de Bogotá

The document presented here is an *Inquisition* document and contains very little information other than lists of possessions and a few details about the sale of African women's belongings. All of the women involved in the trial suffered confiscation of their possessions as part of their punishment. Possibly the fact that some of these women had many possessions made them more suspicious to their neighbors and led to their denunciation to the *Inquisition* tribunal, which made money by auctioning off the goods. These inventories reveal the diversity of Afro-Colombian women's experiences, especially in terms of complicating the link between social class distinctions, based on wealth, and colonial hierarchies based on race or place of origin. The inventories also show the range of wealth possessed by Afro-Colombian women, documenting both sparse and lavish consumption of material goods, including objects related to religious practice. These women owned many pious images, despite the fact that the *Inquisition* accused them of denouncing the Christian religion.

The most famous Spanish institution in Cartagena de Indias, the *Inquisition*'s high court was one of only a few such tribunals in Spain's American empire. A Caribbean port city (in modern Colombia), Cartagena also served as a key maritime trading center, an important entrepôt for outgoing mineral wealth from other regions of South America and incoming European goods and African slaves. As a court of appeal for the entire Spanish Caribbean and northwest South America, Cartagena's *Inquisition* court attempted to police religious practice, beliefs, and morals. This court tried acts and beliefs that were viewed as threats to the established official religion of Catholicism. These "crimes" included: practicing Judaism or Protestantism, affronts on Catholic morality such as bigamy, and the European vision of witchcraft and sorcery. Often, *Inquisition* cases that fit into the final category dealt with popular folk practices, such as magic relating to love or health care. Although practitioners of these folk remedies usually faced light punishments, sometimes *Inquisition* officials reacted more harshly, blaming the devil's temptation for these acts.

All of the women listed in these documents were accused of witchcraft, denying the existence of God, Christianity, the Virgin Mary, and the Christian saints; making a pact with the devil; and being part of a witches' coven that called upon the devil. What the women actually did to come to the attention of the *Inquisition* court is unknown, but the accusations follow the standard language used to express an early modern European vision of crimes against Catholicism. They all suffered more or less the same punishment: an *auto de fe* wearing a robe that indicated they were witches, a year's imprisonment, confiscation of their property, and banishment from Cartagena and the surrounding area

for 2 to 3 years. Some of the women were also sentenced to public whipping.

An African woman who appeared before the *Inquisition*, from the colonial perspective, lacked *honor* due to her origins in Africa, her connections to slavery (even if freed), and her doubtful Christianity. In Cartagena, generally, slaves and free people of color filled the ranks of the poorer residents. Women in this situation might only own a few articles of clothing and collections of rags. In theory, they had no *honor* to protect and thus had no right to surround themselves with accoutrements of status and leisure they could not claim as their own. Authorities generally assumed that all African women were born out of wedlock and had children and sexual liaisons outside the bonds of marriage and, thus, denied them legitimacy and sexual *honor* and labeled them as sexually disruptive. An African woman might even be judged as less physically attractive if she did not meet European ideals of beauty. To the Spanish colonial elite, if this woman was wealthy, her possessions confused and even mocked the accepted symbols of social status, *honor*, and even the race hierarchy itself.

In Cartagena, elite status usually equated to European descent (often from the early settlers of the region); slave ownership; access to rural landholdings; ties to or involvement in mercantile or government activities; and conspicuous consumption in the form of lavish dress, horses, carriages, jewelry, and entourages. Elite status was confirmed by the public display of wealth. The elite left evidence of their material possessions and demonstrated their piety in their last wills and testaments. Often piety and wealth were intertwined through donations to churches and convents, images and portraits of saints, and jewelry such as crosses. These various material marks of conspicuous consumption demonstrated that the wealthy did not suffer hunger or endure manual labor and the dishonor that such labor conveyed. Slaves carried elite women in covered litters, and men could ride horses so they did not have to exert themselves in the tropical heat. Others made the elite's food and cleaned for them. The elite protected their *honor* and tolerated no breach in their reputation as good Catholics. One of the key elements of the *honor* code was masculine reputation, most importantly through supervising the sexuality of female relatives, including wives, daughters, and sisters. Men guaranteed their masculinity and that their wealth would pass to their biological heirs by jealously guarding women's associations with men. Men's *honor* depended on the moral reputation of the women in their family, whereas women's more limited *honor* was connected to their own moral reputation and how defensively they guarded this reputation.

Commentators such as Alonso de Sandoval (see Suggested Sources), who lived and worked in Cartagena at the time of this trial, debased non-white beauty by ascribing women of African descent strong bodies capable of work. A beautiful woman, according to his Renaissance conceptions of beauty, would not be physically capable of arduous labor. As slaves, African women's designated function in the Americas was to work, whereas European women represented purity and virtue, their beauty formulated around their wealth, *honor,* seclusion, luxurious clothes, status, and leisure. If an African woman was thought of as beautiful on these terms, she would also be considered virtuous, pure, worthy of men's protection, and of high social status, and thus not a suitable slave, free worker, or even sex object. Along the same lines of argument, characteristics associated with hard work, such as large feet or strength and endurance, became stereotypical attributes of African women. Sandoval also spoke of African slaves' nudity not offering priests much sexual temptation, because he considered their appearance bestial and because they lacked the elegant manner of speaking and *style of dress of Spaniards.* To Sandoval, clothed Spaniards appeared more attractive because of their clothing. Women of African descent were targeted as sexual objects, and viewed as lacking what was thought to be the more beauteous traits of moral purity. Despite these generalizations about beauty and adornment in the early modern era, this document demonstrates that some women of African descent actually possessed wealth and owned land, rental properties, luxurious clothing, jewelry, and slaves.

Most of the women's possessions were clothing items or other pieces of fabric, highlighting the strong tie between clothing and status at this time. Living in the tropical climate of Cartagena, the women owned a relatively small amount of bedding and warm clothing, and some had hammocks instead of beds. Demonstrating the Spanish international trade and economic power in the 1600s, many of their belongings came from outside the Spanish Empire, most commonly cloth from *Rouen,* France. The fact that most of the women owned fabric woven in France points to the Spanish dependence on other European countries for many of their luxury and even day-to-day items. The women also owned cloth described as Chinese (probably silk) and kitchenware from Japan (perhaps porcelain). These items came to Spanish America via the Manila galleon, the trading route that began in the Spanish Philippines. However, the majority of the cloth certainly came from the Americas, including cotton goods and hats made of vicuña wool (wool from a wild relative of the highland llama). Few items were dyed in bright colors, a very rare luxury at the time, but almost every article made of cloth was embroidered or trimmed. Creating this labor-intensive decoration represents one of the most important occupations practiced by women before the modern era. Considering the accusation of *denying* Christianity, it is also interesting that several of the women owned religious images specially incorporated into pieces of jewelry. Some of the women possessed a great deal of very fine jewelry, made from the region's gold, silver, emeralds, and pearls. The women both accessed the material markers of place in colonial society and challenged those hierarchies by seeming out of place.

Questions to Consider:

1. What can be learned from a list compared to other types of documents? How does this source push scholars to use their historical imagination?

2. What might a typical outfit have consisted of for each individual woman? What image were they hoping to project? How did others react?

3. How do you compare their homes and household goods with the clothing? What else can you surmise about women's lives, individually and as a group?

Inventories of African Women's Possessions[3]

{The first inventory records the possessions owned by Juana Fernández de Gramajo, a free black woman born in Cartagena de Indies, reconciled by the Inquisition court. The inventory took place on September 6, 1632.}

Her Possessions are:

A box for clothes
The bed that she sleeps in
A cedar box
A poor-quality cane mattress
A sheet
A cotton shawl
A damask pillow
An embroidered linen bodice
A cotton corset
A small, fine gold necklace
A vicuña hat
A cedar box containing the following:
An embroidered black taffeta bodice
A new black taffeta petticoat with a lining
A petticoat of yellow damask from China
A short petticoat of heavy wool, in the style made by friars
A bedspread embroidered with indigo thread
Three sheets made of *Rouen* cloth {a printed cotton fabric from *Rouen*, France}
Two rolls and a few pieces of *Rouen* cloth
One embroidered shirt
Several more pieces of *Rouen* cloth
A fine embroidered shirt
A pincushion
A pair of mules
An embroidered cloak
A small box full of a few trivial items
A Flanders-style trunk containing the following:
Jewelry with a glass pendant and five pearls

A small silver image of the *Niño Jesús* {Christ Child}
A necklace with 31 gold beads and a pearl image
String of black beads
A black *agnus* relic {an image of a lamb, symbolizing Jesus Christ}
A worn-out gold silk agnus
A few garnet bracelets with small beads
Another bracelet made of glass beads
A half-made sleeve
A napkin
A piece of *bretaña* {fine linen from Breton, France}
A gourd
A small bag with silver trim
Two roles of green taffeta
A piece of *Rouen* cloth for a sleeve
An embroidered scarf
Seven small pieces of paper taken by the secretary of the Inquisition to assess privately
China bowls
Chicorata con higueta de oro {this item includes a gold ball, although the exact English equivalent is not known}[4]
Horsehair broom
Four *reales* in cash[5]
A flask and a vial
Five large painted plates
Three small stone plates
Four small copper boxes
A brass warming pan
Two mats, one made of rattan and the other of *perate* {perhaps a local reed or other plant, see note 4}
Three pieces of old linen and *Rouen* clothcorset
A red cotton scarf
An old tabernacle of Saint Anthony
A small glass bottle
A basin of holy water
New slippers and mules

[3]*Source:* Public domain document translated by Nicole von Germeten. These summaries from the seventeenth-century Inquisition trials can also be found published in Anna María Splendiani, José Enrique Sánchez Bohórquez, and Emma Cecilia Luque de Salazar's four-volume *Cinquenta Años de Inquisición en el Tribunal de Cartagena de Indias, 1610–1660* (Bogotá: Centro Editorial Javeriano and Instituto Colombiano de Cultura Hispánica, 1997), vol. II, 297–413.

[4]Some of the words in this document have been left without translation and in italics.

[5]Four *reales* equaled a half a *peso,* a small amount of currency at the time. A farm laborer might only earn 2 *reales* a day, but mineworkers could earn 1 *peso* or more each day. A family of four might be able to live on an income of 130 *pesos* per year. The minimum cost for a basic shirt was around 1 *peso.*

A whip
A skirt of brown serge
Two chairs

{*Dated October 11, 1634, the next document records the public sale of Gramajo's goods in Cartagena's plaza. They sold for 110* **pesos.**[6] *Among the items sold were:*}

A very small, possibly gold, image of the Nino Jesús sold for two *pesos*, four *reales*.
A small plate of Chinese wood sold for six *reales*.
The brass heater sold for nine *reales*.
The vicuña hat sold for three *pesos*, seven *reales*.
The eight painted plates sold for two *pesos*, along with the various scraps of taffeta.
The necklace of gold beads, with an image and six pearls sold for twenty *pesos*.
The bracelet sold for two *reales*.

{*A September 6, 1632 inventory of goods belonging to Teodora de Salcedo, a free black woman, born in Havana, Cuba who resided in Cartagena.*}

Teodora owns the houses she lived in and a black slave woman called María Angola, who had three sons called Dominguito, Salvador and Mateo. She also has another female slave called Isabel Bran. Her houses are constructed of wooden boards and tiles. They are located in this city near Salvador de Torres' house.

In her house, she has a box containing:

White cotton cloth
Linen bed coverings
Six new embroidered shirts, one blue and the others white
Two *Rouen* cloth sheets
Four bodices
An old sheet
An old shirt
Three new cushions, one with a bolster
Two old blue pillows
An old white bodice
A necklace with 29 beads and a gold image
A necklace with 34 large and small gold beads
Two very large coral bracelets with small gold beads

Eight gold earrings with some small pearls
Eight white head kerchiefs embroidered in different colors
A colored silk corset
A scapular of blue taffeta with a shield of Our Lady of Angels, possibly gold
Some old rags

A large chest contains the following:

Hammock
A black taffeta skirt embroidered in yellow
A skirt of heavy green wool and another made of green taffeta with gold trim
A jerkin of black *realzado* [an embossed or embroidered fabric]
A bodice of gold fabric
A bodice of heavy wool embroidered in gold
A black taffeta embroidered bodice, and another brown one
A new, heavily embroidered silk cloak
Another cloak with less embroidery
Hand clothes made of Spanish linen
Two pieces of blue Guinea cloth
A letter about the sale of Teodora de Salcedo's house
A round box containing some papers
Two small round boxes
Two small, wooden, painted plates from Japan
A gourd with a green stone
A rosary
Two silver cups
Two silver spoons
Four *reales* in cash
A very small box
Coral inlaid in gold
A large silver spoon
Bone inlaid with silver
A silver image of the Immaculate Conception
A small purse embroidered in gold
Two gold amulets in a wooden box
Some strings of pearls
A vicuña hat
A brush
Four paintings
A cedar chest
Two mattresses and sheets
A cotton blanket
A pillow

---

[6]A *peso* was worth 8 *reales*, i.e., a "piece of eight." This currency was used throughout the Spanish Empire. A *peso* was meant to weigh 1 ounce of silver.

A small mattress

A brown slashed serge skirt

Two small boxes of clothes for the little black boys

Eight small plates and two large ones, all painted

A silver jug

Two clay bowls and two spoons

A small box from Flanders

Seven small plates and three bowls

A cedar vat with three small clay jars

A small green jar of sugar

Tablecloths *alimanricos* [possibly luxurious German fabric]

White underclothes

A bodice

An embroidered blue blouse

A cushion

Eight pails and a rush mat

Five cane mats

A copper pan

Ten hens, one rooster and three chickens

A small bottle of oil

Two large chairs and a stool

A small table and two seats

A jar of salt

{Dated March 26, 1634, a record of the celebration of an auto de fe in Cartagena's cathedral.}

Teodora de Salcedo was punished by being reconciled, wearing the habit, imprisonment for a year and confiscation of all of her goods. It is said that she has committed her crimes for seven years. On August 30, 1634, Teodora de Salcedo's house is put up for auction in the public plaza. Pedro de Guzman submits the first bid for 800 *pesos*, because the house is located on Pedro de Quintanilla Street, near houses Guzman already owns. Several other bidders make offers, until the house is finally sold to Pedro de Guzman for 1200 *pesos*. The rest of Teodora de Salcedo's belongings, not including her slaves, are sold for 220 *pesos*. Her black slave Isabel Bran is sold for 320 *pesos* and Maria Angola and her three sons are sold for 515 *pesos*. The fowls mentioned in the inventory stayed in the possession of Maria Angola. The documents mention that the house was rented for six *pesos* a month and also required some repairs. The slaves also required the outlay of money, due to the costs of childbirth

and the fact that one of the boys died and the women and two of the children suffered from smallpox.

{Inventory of the belongings of a free mulata, Barbóla de Albornoz, born in Barquisimeto, living at the time in western Venezuela.}

In her room was a cedar box containing her clothes and underclothes. She had no other possessions, other than:

A small gold ring

Half-made cotton petticoats

A thin cotton bodice tunic

A new *Rouen* clothsheet

A brown embroidered skirt

A heavy brown wool skirt

A thin, stiff cotton bodice

An embroidered shawl

Two pairs of sleeves

Old pillows

Embroidered headscarves

A blue embroidered kerchief

A *Rouen* cloth head scarf

Apretina con hierros de plata [A kind of belt or corset, decorated in silver]

Bloomers

A piece of muslin

Spoons from New Spain

Her letter of freedom

A taffeta scapular of the Virgin of Carmen with a small emblem made of gold and pearls

A silver ring

Two silver amulets in a wooden box

A cupping glass [for medical purposes]

A glass flask

A cedar box

A necklace with 24 gold beads and a gold and pearl pendant

Two bracelets with 15 gold beads

A canvas mattress

A black taffeta bodice

A chintz bodice with bronze buttons

A chamber pot

Old shirts and stockings

Slippers and sandals

Small gourd

These goods are deposited with the *Inquisition* because she was condemned as a heretic. *{Her jewelry sold for 25 pesos, and the rest of her goods sold for 60 pesos.}*

{Belonging of the free mulata, Ana María de Robles, born in Santo Domingo, who owned wooden houses located on San Juan Street in the Getsemaní barrio, her bed, and two boxes with:}

Four shirts
Some petticoats
A sheet
White bodices
Two cushions and an old *lerica* [perhaps a pillow]
A black undershirt
A wooden bed
A small cushion
Seven cane mats
Two tall chairs and one small one
A *bofetillo* [possibly a piece of furniture]

{Sold for less than 20 pesos. Her houses sold for 200 pesos and were said to be in bad repair. She was reconciled to the Inquisition, wearing a habit, and sentenced to one year in jail and the confiscation of her possessions.}

{Inventory of the possessions of the free black woman Juana de Mora, the widow of a black man called Constantino, identified as of the Biafara nation.}[7]

She owns two black slaves, a mother and daughter. The mother is called María Arada[8] and the daughter's name is Agustina Criolla.[9] She also owns a velvet box containing:

An old shirt with blue embroidery, as well as a new one
Some plain petticoats
A bodice
Some blouses
Linen petticoats with blue embroidery
A plain *Rouen* cloth sheet
A small white bodice
A half-embroidered piece of cloth used as a pincushion
A blue heavy wool skirt
Old bodices, one yellow and one black

An old cedar bed
A pillow
A short blue bodice
An old cotton quilt
Slippers tied with green ribbons
An old box containing a *fanega* [1.8 bushels] of corn
Two old buckets
Another fanega of corn
Seven chickens and a rooster

{Juana de Mora was sentenced to reconciliation in a habit, a year's imprisonment, and confiscation of her possessions for being a witch and an apostate heretic. Her two slaves were sold for 450 pesos, and the rest of her possessions sold for just over 20 pesos.}

{Inventory for Angelina de Nava, a black woman also called Angelina de Guinea. She owned a few houses and a small farm, as well as a black slave called Francisco Angola, who was a day laborer.}

She also has a Cedar Chest Containing her Clothes:

A lustrous shiny skirt with gold embroidered borders
A green and black jerkin with silver braid
A new blue head scarf, a white one and another small one
Black taffeta collar
A scapular of blue taffeta with a small silver insignia
A spool of blue thread from Guinea
A small box containing an agnus
A *Rouen* clothcollar
Six *varas* [a *vara* equaled .84 meters] of *puntas* [embroidered cloth]
Two documents recording the sale of the house on her farm
Small pearl choker

A trunk containing the following:

A shirt with a yellow chest
Petticoats with blue embroidery
Buff-colored silk stockings
An embroidered silk shawl
Black serge underclothes
A hammock
A cotton cloth

---

[7] A colonial label given to indicate African ethnicity.
[8] See note 7.
[9] Her name indicates she was born in the Americas.

Two old torn sheets
An old, ripped cotton blanket
A glass flask
Five small plates
A chair

{*Sold for 27 pesos. The highest bid for land was 300 pesos for the land, and 1,050 pesos for the houses.*}

{*Goods owned by Rafaela de Nava, a free black woman born in Cartagena.*}

All She Owns is in a Cedar Box in her Room:

A sheet
A blanket, half made of cotton and the half made of linen
White and blue embroidered shirts
Cotton petticoat
Blue embroidered petticoats and others embroidered with indigo thread
A thin cotton bodice lined in blue taffeta
Two headscarves, one embroidered and the other white
A pillow with two pincushions
A bag or purse
A white corset
An ebony cross in a silver case
A skirt of plain brown wool
Three cane mats and a small rush mat
A cotton sheet to cover the bed
A box containing the following:
A Chinese damask skirt, copper in color
A black taffeta bodice
A piece of white cotton
The body of a shirt with sleeves "de aijado" {*Many sleeves in this era were slashed and heavily decorated. Perhaps a style of sleeve at the time.*}
A white cotton blanket
Three white pillows, two new
Two cushions embroidered in indigo
A *Rouen* clothsheet
Small pieces of Biscayan linen
A white cushion
Two blue-embroidered pillows
A small box from Flanders with a small bone image
A small round box from Flanders with a small silver-plated image of the niño Jesús on it

Calabash containing some brass rosaries
A sash from the third order of Saint Augustine trimmed in silver
A blue head scarf
A strip of Walloon {used as underwear?}
A knife
A small box from Flanders
Two ordinary old paintings and four small ones
Slippers
Earthenware jars
A chamber pot

{*Rafaela de Nava received the same sentence as the other women and her possessions were sold for 40 pesos.*}

{*Goods owned by Dorotea de Palma, a black woman, who claimed she owned no goods whatsoever. However, the Inquisition official removed a gold necklace from her neck (with 28 round beads) and an image of the Immaculate Conception with three pearls. In the skirts of the image, was a green cross.*}

She also owns a box containing a few shirts, of no value.

A black taffeta skirt lined in heavy linen and a bodice of the same fabric
A *mantilla*
An old skirt lined in light blue taffeta
The wood and clay house where she lives in the Calle de la Cruz

{*Dorotea de Palma's husband was Juan de Padilla, a mulato slave belonging to Captain Alonso Turillo, who worked as a blacksmith. Dorotea de Palma also owned a bed, blankets, and cushions. Her husband surrendered her goods when she was charged as an apostate heretic and punished in the same way as the other women. Her house sold for 300 pesos, and the necklace for 18 pesos. The rest of her goods raised 2 pesos.*}

{*Possessions owned by the free black woman, Juana de Hortensio.*}

She Owns the Goods in her Room and a House. Her Belongings are:

A wooden bed
A white wool blanket
A mattress
A sheet
A white pillow

A silk, embroidered shawl
A white cotton quilt
Petticoats with trimmings
Petticoats of thin cotton with lace
An undershirt without pants with a yellow hem
Plain *Rouen* cloth wool petticoat
Rouen cloth sheets
Embroidered petticoats
Small white bodices
An old shirt
A hand cloth
Napkins
Shirtsleeves
Head scarf
A penitential hood
Two boxes
Wool embroidered skirt
A jerkin with silver flowers
A white bodice
Three pairs of gold and pearl earrings
Two torn shirts
Eleven chickens and one rooster
Five white pails
Three small *mejillas* [Although this word translates as "cheeks," its meaning in this context is unknown.]
Six jars
Two chairs and a silver key ring

{*Her house sold for 180 pesos. Her possessions sold for 32 pesos.*}

{*The next woman, Justa, a free mulata in service to Doña Mariana de Armas. She was charged with the crime of heretical apostasy and sentenced in 1634 to reconciliation with a habit, six years in jail, and the confiscation of her possessions.*}

She owns a box for clothing and underclothes, and nothing else.

Eight *Rouen* clothshirts, one embroidered in blue
Three petticoats, two white and one embroidered in blue thread
Two cushions
A white bodice

A small box containing:

Black wool skirt
A white lined skirt

A serge skirt
A skirt made of violet {*heavy wool, in the style made by friars*}
A black taffeta bodice
White bodice and another of black embroidered taffeta
An old embroidered shawl
A white bodice

{*These things sold for 45 pesos.*}

{*The next inventory records the possessions of Ana Suárez, a free black woman born in Zaragoza (also in New Granada) living in Cartagena. Ana Suárez owned two slaves. One slave was called Maria Angola, and she had an infant daughter called Gregoria. Ana's other slave was called Victoria Angola. Father Esteban de Amaya from Tolú (New Granada) owed her 220 pesos.*}

She has a Cedar Box Containing the Following:

A white cotton quilt
Black skirt with 15 pleats
A pleated bodice
Calabash with 16 silver *clavitos* [keys or nails?] inside it and two straps
An old ragged cloak
Six spools of copper-colored thread
A blue taffeta scapular with a small silver insignia
A piece of *Rouen* cloth
An old shirt
Hood for a tunic and a head scarf
Rouen cloth petticoat
An old piece of cotton
Two strings of coral that weigh 6.5 ounces
A silver spoon
A gold necklace with 26 beads and a gold image
A gold necklace with 32 matched beads
A necklace of small pearls with 10 pendants
Small gold chain that weighs 39 *pesos de oro*[10]
A few gold pendants
Two rings, each with an emerald
Gold and emerald earrings, each with three dangling pearls
Gold and emerald earrings with three pendants
Pearl earrings, with five pearls in the center and three pearl pendants

---

[10]Usually *pesos de oro* had the same value as a silver *peso*.

A loose earring with one small bead

An image of Our Lady with pearl pendants

Bodice of silver cloth and blue silk

Taffeta skirt with gold decoration

A shirt with slashed sleeves

A shirt with a large ruff and *barahunda* sleeves [a style of sleeve]

A *Rouen* cloth cushion embroidered in blue silk

A plot of land that belonged to Juan Bran located in the Calle de la Cruz

{Ana Suárez's jewelry sold for a total of 230 pesos. The slave woman Maria and her child sold for 370 pesos and Victoria sold for 320 pesos. The land sold for 100 pesos.}

{The next inventory records the possessions of Rufina Ortiz, a free mulata who owned some stone houses and four slaves, named Mariquilla Angola, Mariquilla Biafara, Catalina Angola and Margarita Angola. Catalina Angola was rented out as a day laborer. Rufina also owned a cedar house and Father Lorenzo de Salcedo of the Company of Jesus owed her 110 pesos.}

She Owned a Box Containing:

Seventeen shirts, some embroidered in blue thread

Five pairs of underclothes, two embroidered and three plain

Eight sheets, four embroidered and four plain

Ten cushions, seven embroidered in blue thread and three plain

A white cotton embroidered quilt

Two medium-quality tablecloths

Five bodices, four made of silk

A green and black skirt lined in blue taffeta

A brown wool skirt lined in pink taffeta

A skirt made of silver Mexican taffeta lined in heavy silk

Crimson taffeta petticoats

A black skirt

A silver carrier for chocolate

Another box, containing the following:

A cotton spread

An old serge skirt

A hand towel made of embroidered *Rouen* cloth

An old hand towel, embroidered in blue

A pincushion embroidered in blue

Two shirts and some *Rouen* cloth petticoats

Rouen cloth petticoats in pieces, embroidered in blue

Two small silver plates

Slippers with silver straps

A small silver cup

A silver-plated coconut shell and its carrier

Hammock

A small silver box, in possession of her sister Justa

Vicuña wool hat lined in black Castilian taffeta and another lined in brown taffeta

On her patio, a padlock was opened with a key and following items were found.

35 empty clay jars

Seven small empty jars

A stone and two grinding stones

Three chairs

Two stools

A broken bed made of *granadilla* [a wood from Cuba, sometimes called West Indian ebony]

Some old hammock poles

Six bundles of various sizes

Eight buckets

Six glass flasks

A green pot with two flasks and a large tumbler

Two earthenware plates from Lisbon

A small pot

A cupping glass and three glasses

A pail with eight red jars

A large pot from Santa Marta

Brass barber's bowl

A chamber pot

Two small brass pots

A small iron saucepan

Two small glazed clay pots

A bit of wool in a bucket

Two stools

{One of Rufina Ortiz's houses was rented (12 pesos a month). The slave Maria Angola, a cook and seamstress, sold for 420 pesos. The slaves Margarita and Mariquilla sold for 500 pesos. The slave Maria Biafara, who had diarrhea and typhus, sold for 100 pesos. The houses sold for 2,725 pesos.}

{The goods of Luisa Domínguez, a black woman born in Santo Domingo, who resided in Getsemaní.}

She Owns Nothing Besides a Box Containing:

Skirt and bodice of black, heavily-lined taffeta

A brown wool skirt

Old petticoats embroidered in blue thread

Three sheets, two very old, the other slightly better

Old cotton blanket

A piece of old patched cotton

An old embroidered linen bodice

Two handkerchiefs of Biscayan linen, one with embroidery

Two shirts

Three old napkins

A piece of linen

Two small loaves of chocolate

Two silver spoons

Head scarf of old muslin and another one made of *Rouen* cloth

Suggested Sources:

For background information for this document, see Lyman Johnson and Sonya Lipsett-Rivera, eds., *Faces of Honor: Sex, Shame and Violence in Colonial Latin America* (Albuquerque: University of New Mexico Press, 1998). Lance Grahn's *The Political Economy of Smuggling: Regional Informal Economies in Early Bourbon New Granada* (Boulder, CO: Westview Press, 1997) provides insights into how Cartagenans accessed material goods. Margaret Olsen's *Slavery and Salvation in Colonial Cartagena de Indias* (Gainesville: University Press of Florida, 2004) explores the Spanish perception of African bodies and Christianity. Kathryn Joy McKnight's "'En su tierra lo aprendió': An African Curandero's Defense before the Cartagena Inquisition," *Colonial Latin American Review* 12, no. 1 (2003): 63–84 investigates another seventeenth-century Cartagena Inquisition case involving Africans.

Among primary sources in English is Thomas Gage's *Travels in the New World*, ed. J. Eric S. Thompson (Norman: University of Oklahoma Press, 1958), a mid-seventeenth-century account of colonial Latin America. The Spanish naval travelers Jorge Juan and Antonio Ulloa describe the social life and customs of mid-eighteenth-century Cartagena in their *Voyage to South America* (New York: Knopf, 1964). In the 1500s, Juan Rodríguez Freile wrote *The Conquest of New Granada*, trans. William C. Atkinson (London: Folio Society, 1961) as an exposé of immorality and corruption in New Granada. Alonso de Sandoval, a Jesuit who worked in Cartagena de Indias, wrote two long scholarly books discussing Africans and Catholicism. His 1627 book has been published in English, titled *A Treatise on Slavery*, ed. and trans. Nicole von Germeten (Cambridge: Hackett, 2008).

Chapter 12

The Pious and Honorable Life of Ana Juana of Cochabamba (1675)

Rachel Sarah O'Toole, University of California, Irvine

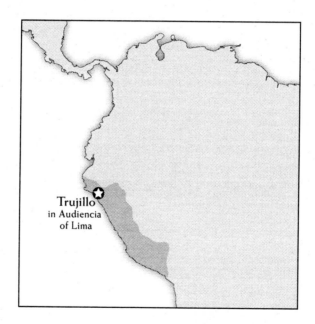

Trujillo
in Audiencia
of Lima

In the mid-seventeenth century, enslaved women and men worked as domestic servants, market vendors, textile workers, sailors, artisans, and field laborers throughout the cities and countryside of the Andes. Composing roughly 40 percent of the coastal Pacific populations, Africans and their descendants specialized in the production of the sugar, alcohol, flour, and wine that fueled an economy of silver mining in the highlands and gold prospecting in the tropical lowlands. After a midcentury hiatus, by the 1670s, the Spanish Crown contracted with transatlantic merchants who sold west central Africans and, increasingly, captive men and women from the Bight of Benin to Caribbean slave traders. From thriving colonial ports such as Cartagena, regional merchants, in turn, forcibly transported captives across the Panamanian isthmus to board sailing vessels on the Pacific coast or marched coffles southward into the coastal valleys and Andean highlands. Enslavement of African people and their descendants, thus, complemented the labor required of indigenous villagers, called the *mita*, as well as the wage work supplied by Andean migrants in mills, estates, and mines whose riches would support the hegemony of the vast Spanish Empire.

Slavery's profit to Spanish colonizers presented a formidable barrier to enslaved women and men who struggled against the impositions of bondage to free them and their kin. Individual *manumission* was a legal right of Catholic slaves in the Spanish Empire, but difficult to achieve because most slaveholders required that slaves pay for their freedom. Still, enslaved individuals pooled their daily wages (if they were permitted to contract out their labor) or earnings from the sales of bread, prepared food, or other goods with their families and friends to purchase their freedom or that of their kin. Others secured loans from wealthy patrons or owners and successfully negotiated a written agreement or a "letter of freedom" composed by a notary and signed by witnesses.

Source: The Royal Library/Guaman Poma, Nueva corónica y buen gobierno (1615) 706[720] Cómo Lleba En Tanta paciencia y amor de Jesucristo los puenos negros y negras y el uellaco de su amo no tiene caridad y amor de prógimo/soberbioso/.

Source: The Royal Library/Guaman Poma, Nueva corónica y buen gobierno (1615) [723] Cómo Los Criollos negros hurtan plata de sus amos para engañar a las yndias putas, y las negras criollas hurtan para seruir a sus galanes españoles y negros.

Slaves could only hope to defend themselves fully from physical abuse, and claim a degree of respectability and *honor*, by securing their freedom. Guaman Poma de Ayala illustrated the plight of Peru's blacks and titled this drawing (left) "Good blacks endure the abuses of their master with patience and the love of Christ." He esteemed blacks for their piety and stoicism in the face of mistreatment that he likened to that meted out to indigenous people. How was this representation of blacks positive? How did he communicate colonial power and status? Guaman Poma also feared that colonial society could strip people of all the positive qualities of morality and Christian suffering. Consider how the next drawing (right), "Acculturated blacks steal money from their masters and give it to Indian prostitutes", shows how he viewed blacks as spreading colonialism's corrupting influence.

Freed people of color and even their descendants carefully defended their status as freed people because former owners or disgruntled heirs could seek to repossess former slaves by claiming that documents were falsified or payments were missing. Seeking to establish a record of their status, former slaves registered their children's baptisms with clerics, who would list daughters and sons not only as free, but as *morena* or *pardo*. These markers of race or colonial *casta* categories also communicated that people of African descent had achieved manumitted status. By creating written documents of their families, free people of color also sought to establish their family's honorable status, even as humble laborers. Measured in gendered terms, freedom meant that men conducted their daily affairs independent from a patron's influence, and women maintained a public reputation of controlling access to their bodies. Achieving and maintaining freedom, thus, was a continual struggle involving adequate funds and social reputation.

The following document allows a rare glimpse into how one woman, identifying herself as Ana Juana, freed and then established herself, with great success, as a wealthy woman of color in the coastal Peruvian city of Trujillo. The former slave only offered hints of how she achieved freedom for herself, but she clearly detailed how slavery continued to affect her life well into her later years and, perhaps her kin, after death. Ana Juana's patronage networks, religious affiliations, and the details of her household economy also suggest how she maintained her status in a city where, as a free woman of color, she would have been in the minority among enslaved Africans and *criollos,* coastal and highland Andeans in addition to Spaniards and their descendants. Ana Juana's experiences also reveal critical realities of Spanish colonial slavery that may challenge contemporary notions of identity and solidarity as Ana Juana profited from the system of servitude after she had achieved her own *manumission.* Yet, her firm declaration that she achieved her success "from my industry and personal labor" indicates a personal pride in the security of her household.

Although clearly a unique and forceful individual, her tale provokes historians to question how respected a manumitted woman of African descent could become.

In 1675, Ana Juana paid Juan Alvarez, a notary, to record her will and testament in his books. He created a formulaic document as colonial scribes followed a standard template that included the client's full identification, proclamations of Catholic faith, funerary wishes, and declaration of debts. Yet, as a final accounting in preparation to meet God, a will was often where colonial people confessed their secrets, reviewed their life achievements, and made final statements that would be read to their family and friends after their death. The colonial will, therefore, was an intimate document that would eventually become public and, in some cases, the basis of subsequent civil cases involving inheritance. In comparison to other wills from free women of color in colonial Trujillo, Ana Juana listed a wide array of religious affiliations that alluded to her affiliations as well as suggest strategic economic choices that included extensive social networks. Wills were also meant to provide a final inventory of a person's property that, for the wealthy, could be detailed and lengthy. Thus, Ana Juana's material goods and personal loans provide the most important clues of her occupation as well as how she may have achieved her manumitted status (for indigenous women's wills, see Chapters 17 and 19). In matters of the heart, Ana Juana was surprisingly explicit, whereas in other moments she seemed to be keeping her true emotions in shadow. Even though Ana Juana chose the notary and elected to compose a will, she still may not have felt entirely comfortable exposing all aspects to her life to a non-family member. Nonetheless, a woman who identified herself with only her baptismal name rose from being a poor, enslaved woman of a highland valley town to the wealthy matron of the commercial seaport. By recording the extraordinary details of her life in a rather ordinary colonial document, Ana Juana testified to how she struggled to maintain her public reputation as a free and respectable woman of color.

Questions to Consider:

1. What clues does the document provide about how Ana Juana's gender determined how she supported herself and her husband? What were the gender distinctions within slavery during this period?
2. How does this document help us to imagine ways that free and enslaved men, women, and children maintained their kin networks in seventeenth-century Peru?

3. How might the *confraternity* have influenced Ana Juan's responses to the colonial order?
4. What were the limitations of slavery in colonial Spanish America?
5. How does Ana Juana's will compare to the Inquisition inventories in Chapter 11 (and *mestiza* and indigenous women's wills in Chapters 17 and 19)?

Last Will and Testament of Ana Juana of Cochabamba[1]

Letter of Testament of I, Ana Juana, *pardo* free *mulata* and native of the town of Cochabamba, dioceses of the Archbishopric of the city of La Plata of this kingdom of Peru, illegitimate daughter of Pascuala Flores, single woman, deceased, and my father whose name I do not remember.

[I wish] to be buried in the Cathedral of Trujillo in the circle of the Holiest Virgin of the Pure and Clean Conception—whose altar is near the main door of the entry in the middle, behind the choir—and in a *Franciscan* habit. I declare to be a sister and lay member of the said order and have a scapular and cord of my father Saint Francis. [It is my wish that] my body be accompanied by the high cross, priest, and sacristan of the Cathedral. Sing me a Mass of the body with the deacon and subdeacon present. And ten prayed Masses with their responses for my soul partitioned among poor clerics.

I am a member of the *confraternity* of the Holy Sacrament founded in the said Cathedral. And I have given and paid the dues of six *pesos* each year with much punctuality. It is the duty of the said *confraternity* to pay the costs of the Cross, priest, and sacristan.

I am a member of the *confraternity* of the Holy Christ Child founded in the parish of the Glorious Martyr Lord Saint Sebastian.

I am a member of the *confraternity* of the Mother of God of the Rosary founded in the *Dominican* [monastery].

I am a member and sister of the following *confraternities*: Saint Joseph founded in the church of the convent of Royal Saint Clara, Our Lady of Loreto, Saint Michael the Archangel founded in the Jesuit Church, Saint Nicolas *confraternity* of the *morenos* founded in the Augustinian church, Our Lady of the Snows *confraternity* of the Indians founded in the Cathedral, of the Name of the Baby Jesus founded in the *Dominican* church, Saint John of Lateran founded in the [*Mercedarian*] church. I ask the stewards and the brothers of the said *confraternities* and brotherhoods to commemorate the day of my funeral as is their obligation with the wax and insignias and that they say for me the recited Masses.

I send the required bequests that are seven. To each one I give four *reales*.

I send two *pesos* to the holy sites of Jerusalem. I declare that I am sister of the said holy sites of Jerusalem. I have given and I give alms each year [of] eight *reales* with much punctuality.

I do not owe anything to anyone that I remember. For the mercy and passion of God I do not have to pay back [anyone] nor do I owe my goods in this world to any man or woman. I wish that on the day of my death that they take out for my soul a bull of the deceased and for it I give alms of one *peso*.

[1]*Source:* Archivo Departamental de La Libertad, Protocolos, Juan Alvarez, legajo 90 (1675), #178, fols. 363–368v.

I live in a house that belongs to the *confraternity* of the Holy Souls of Purgatory founded in the parish of Saint Sebastian of Trujillo. I pay twenty-four *pesos* of rent each year. I made an agreement with the stewards of the *confraternity* according to what is written down on a paper that they will reimburse me for the improvements that I completed on the house that they have recorded as account. Accordingly, I have paid two years in advance of which I have a payment receipt.

Juan Caballero, merchant and citizen of Trujillo, owes me two hundred and seventy [*pesos*] according to a notarized document sworn before this notary due within a period of one year dated the twenty-third of January 1675.

Isabel de Cavia, wife of Blas Núñez Lozo, owes me one hundred *pesos* that I lent to her according to a document that they drew up for me before witnesses whose payment will be due on __ of October of this year 1675. Give [the amount] as alms and charity to the orphan girl Francisca Tinfasto who is placed in the house of Laureano Freyre, a merchant and citizen of Trujillo, to help her station because she is poor, an orphan, and virtuous.

My goods: A chest of *cocobolo*,[2] a new blue canopy with its bedspread, five bedspreads with one of them made of blue silk, the other of white China silk and black, [which] all together are five. Two mattresses of cotton, one embroidered and the other with fringe, four pairs of pillows each one with their pillowcase, two pincushions of silk, five pairs of sheets [with] one pair of fine *Rouen* cloth with Flemish embroidery and the rest of superfine *Rouen* cloth, plus a sheet without a match, a mattress of striped cotton with its pillow, a blanket, two skirts one of blue wool with silver point lace and the other of green camlet[3] with four braids of gold, plus two shirts of dyed red silk one with a braid of gold and the other with black point lace, plus a skirt of black camlet with its slip of crimson taffeta with gold point lace, plus a shawl of lined plush with blue taffeta with raised point lace, plus

another dyed lined shawl with raised point lace, plus another of Castilian *baize*,[4] plus three white waistcoats with large point lace, plus two handkerchiefs of chambray[5] with much embroidery, plus another six handkerchiefs of chambray with delicate embroidery, plus twelve blouses with sleeves of chambray and bodices of Brittany cloth[6] one with big, pearl buttons, plus five *fustantes* of Brittany cloth and of fine *Rouen* cloth, plus three pairs of silk stockings with three pairs without bindings, plus six pairs of stockings never worn without their sashes, plus two silk girdles, three pairs of gold earrings one pair with big pearls, plus an earring of gold without its pair, plus a pearl earring with its little golden stick, plus a [illegible] of gold with crests of pearls, plus a [illegible] with its medal of gold [illegible], plus a pair of shawls of [illegible] with pearls, another pair of wool and three ordinary ones, a string of pearls, another necklace of pearls with its pendant of a big pearl with crests of gold, another necklace of hued garnets each one with pearls, plus another of garnets with [illegible], two rings of gold, two images with their little boxes of silver, three pictures—two with black frames and one with a broken frame, two paintings of the Virgin plus a statue in Huamanga stone, plus another small statue in stone, plus one Saint John of Peata, blue two pocketbooks one of amber and the other of silver, plus two handkerchiefs, plus a large earthen jar with its sieve, a hammock and a mattress, a bronze brazier, a large kettle that makes two and a half bottles of water, plus two large trays and three small ones, a [illegible], two large chests of Panama, plus two other more worn boxes, two chairs, two stools, two little tables with one a little bigger and the other small, two little benches, two little tables one to put the little bulls for the holy days of the Mother of God, twelve pounds and six and a half ounces of worked silver of my silverware including the following pieces: a serving spoon, three forks, a large chicken plate, two little plates, a tray to hold cups and glasses, a little plate holder, a bowl of very thin metal, four candlesticks, a brazier

---

[2]*Cocobolo* or rosewood is a tropical hardwood from the southern Pacific coast of Mexico and Central America.

[3]Camlet is a woven fabric made of goat's hair and silk or of wool and cotton.

[4]*Baize* is a coarse, woolen (or cotton) cloth.

[5]Chambray is a soft fabric woven of colored and white yarns.

[6]Cotton cloth from Brittany.

with its pommel, a little box, a gourd with its yoke of golden silver, a little pitcher of silver.

A slave [named] María de la Encarnacion of *casta conga*, between eighteen and nineteen years old purchased in the city of Panama.

In the said town of Cochabamba where I am from, being a single woman and a slave of *doña* Ysidora de Arroyo, I had for a son Joseph who, today, would be about twenty-four years old. When I left my home, he was a boy and a slave owned by his mistress, *doña* Ysidora de Arroyo. At this time I do not have news of him—whether he is alive or dead, free or enslaved— [still] I declare him to be my illegitimate son so that there is someone to whom he belongs according to his right [and] with which I discharge my conscious. That which belongs to him will stay in the power of my executor and bondholders until the said, my son, comes to collect that which belongs to him or has it remitted to him if he is able because he is a slave. In case he is dead without direct heirs and is not capable of receiving my goods, I wish and it is my will that the portion that belongs to him is joined and consolidated in a chaplaincy[7] and memorial that is founded from the base of my goods to say Masses for my soul in the form that seems appropriate and executed by my executor and bondholder.

I declare that after I was freed and having the said Joseph as my illegitimate son, I married in Cochabamba to a poor man, Juan, a native of Lima over twenty years ago. We married, both destitute, and thus I declare that I did not bring anything to the marriage. We came to this city of Trujillo and after some time, he left my company, about fifteen years ago and I do not know or do I have news of where he is as of this day. The said husband never had the capacity or the intelligence to know how to look for ordinary sustenance for him or for me. He left my company, as I said, and during our marriage we did not have any children. I declare this to be so and that all the goods that I have declared and established I have and acquired with my industry and personal labor. [My goods] have done well for me [and] for my freedom and [in] serving some people and especially my master the ex-bishop of Panama, *señor don* Sancho Pardo de Cardenas who gave me

some alms and all the good that I could do for me in life and in death, he did for me for the service that I did for him in this city of Trujillo when he was dean of this holy church and afterwards in Panama.

I do not have obligatory heirs, relatives or descendants. My universal and only heir is my soul . . . for which I declare a chaplaincy and foundation of the gospel . . . including recited Masses perpetually for my soul, those of my parents and son Joseph, relatives, and do-gooders and people who it could be helpful for and for the blessed souls in Purgatory that be served and prayed in the parts, churches, and altars chosen by the appointed clerics. . . . They should say the recited Masses on the days and the holidays chosen by the clerics with one of the Masses to be said precisely on the day of the Mother of God of the Pure Conception that is the eighth of December . . . including two *pesos* for the wine, wax, and hosts . . . and it would please me that this cleric is not subjected to an inspection or a seminary because with this gravity of its foundation and institution and I have established it as such. I name as my first cleric as Joseph de Usinaga, boy of about fourteen years, illegitimate son of my niece, Teodora de Usinaga, citizen of Lima, to serve it and say the Masses . . . and after the death of my nephew, I name the clerics who are poor and virtuous of the Order of Saint Peter with which if there were any debt or blood relative related to me, I would [still] prefer him. The patron of the chaplaincy is Licenciate don Antonio de Saabedra y Leyba, dean of the Cathedral of Trujillo.

Executors: Licenciate don Antonio Saabedra y Leyba, dean of the Cathedral and Licenciate Antonio de Castro, cleric and head sacristan of the Cathedral.

Trujillo August 3, 1675.

She did not sign, because she does not know how to write.

Witnesses were Francisco de Soyna Alvarado, Pedro de Ortega Solarsano, and Gerónimo de Vederuela.

Suggested Sources:

An introduction to the position of free women of African descent in the colonial Andes is Christine Hünefeldt's *Paying the Price of Freedom: Family and*

---

[7]A charitable sponsorship of a cleric.

Labor among Lima's Slaves, 1800–1854 (Berkeley: University of California Press, 1994). Free women of color manumitted themselves and their families in the United States and Brazil. See Kimberly Hanger, *Bounded Lives, Bounded Places: Free Black Society in Colonial New Orleans, 1769–1803* (Durham, NC: Duke University Press, 1997); and Kathleen J. Higgins, *'Licentious Liberty' in a Brazilian Gold-Mining Region: Slavery, Gender, and Social Control in Eighteenth-Century Sabará, Minas Gerais* (University Park: Pennsylvania State University Press, 1999). Free women's labor became part of their family structures and identities. See David Barry Gaspar and Darlene Clark Hine, eds., *More Than Chattel: Black Women and Slavery in the Americas* (Bloomington: Indiana University Press, 1996); and Jennifer Morgan's *Laboring Women: Reproduction and Gender in New World Slavery* (Philadelphia: University of Pennsylvania Press, 2004).

Published primary sources regarding free women of color in the Andes are growing, especially Nancy E. van Deusen, *The Souls of Purgatory: The Spiritual Diary of a Seventeenth-Century Afro-Peruvian Mystic, Ursula de Jesús* (Albuquerque: University of New Mexico Press, 2004). For a historical novel that paints characters whose intertwined identities meld and clash with colonial discrimination in urban colonial Peru, see Lucía Charún-Illescas, *Malambo*, trans. Emmanuel Harris II (Chicago: Swan Isle Press, 2004).

Chapter 13

Obeying the Heart and Obeying the Church

Patricia Seed, University of California-Irvine

The engagement of a young couple would not seem to merit more than a passing notice in today's society. Whether a family approves or disapproves of a match remains a private matter to be settled behind closed doors. Relatives, close friends, and pastors try to help the family come to an agreement. Should a couple's relatives continue to object to a union, no institution formally judges their motives.

However, when parents clashed with their children over choice of a marriage partner in seventeenth-century central Mexico, a powerful institution officially investigated the reasonableness of both sides' positions. In the case of irresolvable conflicts, the Church intervened in a wholly unexpected way, enforcing a culturally defined set of norms of reasonable and unreasonable objections to a marriage. In short, it sided with children if they could provide evidence that their parents or other relatives were preventing the marriage in ways or on grounds that the Church deemed unacceptable. Unpalatable means included physical threats or intimidation, and objectionable motives covered parental financial interests. After receiving testimony from witnesses that such actions or motives existed, Church officials essentially allowed the couple to marry in secret. Church judges also assisted very determined couples who deliberately became pregnant and then enlisted the Church's support to override parental objections and marry.

The specific reasons behind such exceptional actions lay in the recent past. At the Catholic Church's Council of Trent held in Europe from 1545 to 1563, the right of parents to interfere with their children's choice of a marriage partner was hotly contested. In previous centuries, a couple could marry simply by promising to marry and consummating the relationship. In this way, parents and other parties had no way of interfering. Arguing that this secret system led to marriages that violated many Church prohibitions (called impediments), officials at Trent debated several strategies to prevent such future occurrences. But strong national differences emerged among the clergy attending the Council. French clerics wanted parents to have the right to an absolute veto over their offsprings' matrimonial preferences (for any reason, including parental financial gain). Spanish clerics endorsed a more moderate position, requiring prior notice of a marriage, called banns, to be posted or announced publicly for 3 weeks, allowing time to uncover any impediments. Furious French clergy denounced the compromise and refused to make the Council of Trent's decrees compulsory for the Catholic Church in France, so intent were they on asserting authoritarian parental control over matrimony. The more moderate Spanish Church, however, adopted the decisions at Trent almost as soon as the Council concluded its business.

Understanding that parents could easily abuse their power over their children's legitimate matrimonial choices, out of greed, self-interest, and ambition, Spanish clergy adopted a compromise that allowed couples to avoid inappropriate interference. They would allow the pair to marry secretly and post public notice (the banns) only after the ceremony in case any legitimate ecclesiastical cause appeared to prevent a marriage. The couple was forbidden to consummate their marriage until after the final public announcement had been made.

In the following case taken from the National Archives of Mexico, the young man was the son of one of Manila's leading families, and the daughter, a wealthy Mexico City heiress.[1] The young woman belonged to a well-to-do but historically unknown family; by contrast, Miguel Legazpi came from a historically prominent family, possessing a last name that appears to this day on streets and towns throughout the Philippines. Legazpi was a relative of the Spanish expeditionary leader who captured the islands and subjected their inhabitants to Spanish rule in 1565. Miguel Legazpi arrived in Mexico City by a tortuous route. The son of a government official, Miguel was born in Spain and accompanied his father, who was sent to help govern the Philippines, only to return to New Spain several years later.

Few of the cases appearing in ecclesiastical courts involved such well-known historical figures; nevertheless, many came from the middle and upper levels of Spanish society in the New World. Merchants, bureaucrats, and sometimes silversmiths and tailors appeared in these Church courts. Most often they were Spanish, but sometimes the partners were of mixed ancestry, and occasionally African American, including a handful of slaves. Masters were forbidden from interfering with their slaves' matrimonial plans; therefore, the boldest among the slaves sought Church help, eventually forcing a reluctant master to sell a slave to the spouse's owner.

Opposition to a marriage also emerged for a variety of other reasons—conflicts over money, pride, long-standing feuds between families, disparities in social standing, and *honor*. It is impossible to know how often such conflicts arose, let alone how often couples appealed to the Church, because complete records failed to survive. During the era when these episodes occurred, the Catholic Church still occupied a prominent and influential position in colonial

---

[1]Spain controlled the Philippines, and trade blossomed between Mexico and Manila.

society. Such power may seem intrusive and despotic today. However, in their actual functioning, historical institutions often appear more grey than black and white. On the one hand, the Church in this era helped the Spanish King, Philip II, to imprison and execute those who appeared to practice Judaism. On the other hand, in this other arena, the Catholic Church was more moderate, more understanding of human foibles, and challenging rather than supporting traditional "patriarchal" values.

Even though it lacked police powers, Church officials could call on the government to assist it in carrying out ecclesiastical decisions. This independent authority would begin to wane not long after this case, starting a steady downward spiral that would increasingly leave power in the hands of the government alone. The state, unlike the Church, would defend *patriarchal* authority. But as will appear in this case, the seventeenth-century Church enjoyed considerable power to sanction and protect individual choice and freedom to marry (within reasonable limits).

Questions to Consider:

1. How long did the courtship take place and what are the banns of marriage?
2. Based on the document evidence available, was *don* Joseph Legazpi a fortune hunter or did he genuinely love *doña* Juana de Rivera?
3. What is consanguinity? Affinity? Why was *doña* Juana quizzed about such ties?
4. Countless best-selling books continue to repeat the erroneous idea that defending a couple's right to choose their marriage partner is an exclusively modern development. Why are they wrong? Does this document challenge previous images of the Church? What cultural assumptions underlay the Catholic Church officials' actions in this case?

Petition for Permission to Marry before a Church Judge, April 27, 1630[2]

Captain don Joseph de Legazpi Echevarria, born in the city of Valladolid in the kingdom of Castile, legitimate son of Geronimo de Legazpi Echevarria, *oidor* (senior judge) in the *audiencia* (high tribunal) of the Philippines, and of *doña* Mariana de Velasco:

Declare that I have tried to marry *doña* Juana de Rivera y Arevalo, native of Mexico City, daughter of Alonso Ortiz (deceased) and *doña* Juana de Rivera according to the rules of the Holy Mother Church. Both of us are willing to marry. We have known each other for many days, and we have promised to marry each other. If this marriage comes to the attention of said *doña* Juana de Rivera, her mother, Doctor Ortiz, and Pedro de Ortiz, brothers of said *doña* Juana de Rivera, and other relatives that she has in the city, they will impede and disrupt [this marriage] and it will not take place. The reason is that said *doña* Juana [her mother] is taking advantage of the paternal inheritance of the aforementioned, which is a considerable sum.

So that said marriage takes place, I ask and beg your Excellency [the archbishop] to receive the information that I will offer on the freedom [to marry] for both of us, our lack of impediments. [I beg that] you undertake the dispensation of the banns of marriage ordered by the Holy Council [of Trent] and give permission that any regular or secular clergyman of the Cathedral of Mexico City (where we are parishioners) marry us without the banns preceding [the marriage]. [Signature]

MARGINAL NOTE: Send what is asked for in this petition to the provisor and Vicar General of this Archbishopric so that he ascertains what would be just. His Excellency Don Francisco Manso Zuñiga Archbishop of Mexico my lord. {I approve.}

In the city of Mexico on the 28th of April 1630, señor doctor Luis de Cifuentes, official provisor

[2]*Source:* Archivo General de la Nación, Mexico, Ecclesiastical Section, Marriages, box 15.

judge and Vicar General of this city and the entire Archbishopric, having seen this petition sent by His Excellency [the Archbishop]===said [that] I have ordered and order said don Joseph de Legazpi to bring [witnesses] before any of the notaries of this city to prove the information put forth in said petition. So I do order. [Rubric]

Declaration of the Other Party

In the city of Mexico on the fifth of May in the year 1630, I, the notary, received the sworn statement of a Spanish woman who said her name was *doña* Juana de Rivera Arevalo and that she was the woman mentioned in this petition. Toward this end I received her declaration in the matter of the marriage that she wants to contract with *don* Joseph de Legazpi. Making a sign of the cross in proper form and promising to tell the truth according to Our Lord God. ===Asked if she is or has been married, or had made of vow of chastity or religion, or had promised to marry someone else, or is in any way a relative by consanguinity or affinity with *don* Joseph Legazpi whom she wishes to marry, if she has any other public or secret impediment [such] that she could not marry, and if she wishes to marry of her will, and if anyone has forced her to marry== She said that she is not married nor has she been married, nor does she have any of the impediments about which she was asked, and she is free to marry. She wants this marriage to take place of her free will and with great pleasure and is not being forced by anyone. And this she declared to be the truth and signed [this declaration]. She said she did not know her age. By her appearance she seems to be thirty. [Signature]

Witness Testimonies

1. Bartholomew Nieto

In the city of Mexico on the seventh of the month of May of 1630. Because of the marriage that he wants to contract with *doña* Juana de Rivera, *don* Joseph Legazpi has offered information and presented as a witness a Spanish man who said his name was Bartholomew Nieto, single, and resident of this city, no occupation, and living in the Maldonado Inn. In the small plaza for fruits, I the notary, received a sworn statement. Making a sign of the cross in proper form and promising to tell the truth according to Our Lord God, being asked about the petition.

He said that for the past nine years he has known *don* Joseph de Legazpi, who is presenting him as a witness. The entire time he has communicated and dealt with him in the city of Manila where he [Legazpi] was a captain. And he [Nieto] had been in the home of his father, His Excellency don Geronimo de Legazpi, senior judge (*oidor*) of the city and its Royal Tribunal (*audiencia*). And this year this witness and don Joseph Legazpi came to this kingdom [of New Spain] from the city [Manila] and the Philippines in the flagship named Saint John the Baptist. And the witness has always known that said *don* Joseph is single and never married. And people in the city of Manila also hold this opinion of him, without the witness [Nieto] having heard anything to the contrary. And he holds him [Legazpi] as a person who is free to marry as he wishes. This he said to be the truth and swore to it. Said witness did not sign [the document] because he did not know how, and declared that he was thirty-six years old, more or less.

2. Felipe Vasquez Cortes

In the city of Mexico on the self-same seventh day of the month of May of 1630, I aforementioned notary of aforesaid presentation for said information received the sworn statement of Felipe Vasquez Cortes single, resident of the city of Mexico living in the city's storehouse in the company of *don* Juan de Quevedo. Making a sign of the cross in proper form and promising to tell the truth according to Our Lord God, being asked about the petition.

Said that he has known [the] *doña* Juana de Rivera Arevalo contained in this petition for the past eight years more or less. The entire time he has communicated and dealt with her and has always believed her to be single and free to marry without having heard anything to the contrary. And she can marry the aforementioned person, *don* Joseph de Legazpi. And this present witness holds as certain and has no doubt that if [news] of this marriage reaches *doña* Juana de Rivera [her mother] she will impede and disrupt it, and [the marriage] will not

take place because she is benefiting from the paternal inheritance of *doña* Juana which is a considerable
sum. And [also] she [the petitioner] lives under the
authority of her mother. It will be a service to our
Lord God, if the banns were dispensed because of the
grave inconveniences of making them public. And
he said this was the truth. And to ratify the sworn
statement, he signed [the statement] and said he was
over twenty-five. [Signature]

3. Pedro Mexia

[*Third witness, Pedro Mexia, single, resident of Mexico
City, who lives in the house of Captain Luis Vela in front
of the entrance to the Convent of Saint Clare, was sworn in
according to the protocols described above.*] For the past
twelve years which is the time that he [Legazpi] has
lived in Manila in the Philippine Islands he has
known the *don* Joseph Legazpi contained in this petition. And this witness accompanied his father *don*
Geronimo de Legazpi Echevarria senior judge of the
High Tribunal of Manila, when he left Mexico City
for Manila twelve years ago. *don* Joseph de Legazpi
left this city when he was a young boy, and this witness accompanied him [to Manila] and returned
with him to this province of New Spain in the flagship that came from said islands [the Philippines]
this year. [*He swore to the statement, signed and said he
was thirty-four more or less.*]

4. Juan Valentin

[*Fourth witness, Juan Valentin, a tailor, single, and living in Mexico City. He worked in the shop of Francisco de
Guevara, master tailor who lived on Eagle Street. He was
also sworn in according to the protocols described above.*]
"For the past seven years he has known the *doña*
Juana de Rivera Arevalo described in this petition,
who lives in her mother's house in the San Geronimo
neighborhood of this city. He has always held that
she is single and free to marry without having heard
anything to the contrary. And this witness maintains
that if the banns for this marriage were made public
for this marriage that aforementioned [*doña* Juana de
Rivera] wishes to undertake, the marriage would not
occur. The mother and a brother who is a priest
[Doctor Ortiz] who live in the same house will

hinder it in order not to turn over the estate that she
inherited from her father, which has a great deal [of
money]. And because the mother and brother are
powerful people they can seek numerous ways to disrupt the marriage. So that the marriage takes place,
it would be a service to God to dispense the banns.
And he said this was the truth and signed it [saying
he was] nineteen years old. [Signature]

[*Here follows a sworn statement by don Joseph de
Legazpi Echevarria declaring that he is single. The statement follows the identical format as the statement made by
doña Juana de Rivera Arevalo, omitting only the information previously given about his willingness to marry.*]

The Verdict is Rendered

Act: In the city of Mexico on the eighth of May
1630, señor doctor Luis de Sifuentes, official *provisor*
judge and Vicar General of this city and Archbishopric having seen what *don* Joseph de Legazpi has requested as well as the information provided to this
effect. Regarding the license to marry *doña* Juana de
Rivera Arevalo, [namely] to dispense with the
banns: Said that he has ordered an order that a
license to marry be issued such that the priests of
this Holy Cathedral Church of this city or any other
secular or regular cleric can act without the banns
ordained by the Holy Council [of Trent] [preceding
the ceremony]. His Grace dispenses the banns for
said *don* Joseph de Legazpi and *doña* Juana de Rivera
Arevalo, who must be notified that they may not
join together [consummate the marriage] until after
the said banns are made public in the Cathedral.
[They must not join together] under pain of excom-
munication and a fifty *peso* fine. In case the marriage
does not take place before one of the priests of the
Cathedral, the clergyman before whom the marriage
is contracted must certify the marriage with the day,
month, and year on the reverse side of this license
and send [the certification] to the priests [of the
Cathedral] so that the banns are made public and the
marriage is registered also in their parishes. Thus I
order and sign. [erasure Ortiz de Rivera Arevalo]
[Signature Doctor Luis de Cifuentes] Before me [sig-
nature Alonso de Carvajal]

Suggested Sources:

This case forms part of the story told in Patricia Seed, *To Love, Honor, and Obey in Colonial Mexico* (Stanford, CA: Stanford University Press, 1988). To understand how attitudes changed regarding the seriousness of engagements and how young men employed the language of seduction, see "Marriage Promises and the Value of a Woman's Testimony in Colonial Mexico," *Signs* 13, no. 2 (1988): 284–293; and "Narratives of Don Juan: The Language of Seduction in Seventeenth and Eighteenth Century Hispanic Literature and Society," *Journal of Social History* 26 (June 1993): 745–768. Sexual and marriage politics can also be studied in Asunción Lavrin, *Sexuality and Marriage Choice in Colonial Latin America* (Lincoln: University of Nebraska Press, 1989). The Manila galleon carried Mexican silver to East Asia. Two introductions to the galleon are Dennis Flynn, Arturo Giráldez, and James Sobredo, eds. *European Entry into the Pacific: Spain and the Acapulco-Manila Galleons* (Burlington, VT: Ashgate, 2001); and William Lytle Schurz, *The Manila Galleon* (New York: E. P. Dutton, 1939). Pictures of the ships that sailed from Acapulco to Manila appear at *http://www.treasureexpeditions.com/The-Manila-Galleons.htm,* and images of the treasures of a sunken Manila galleon from the government of Guam's Web site: *http://ns.gov.gu/galleon.*

Chapter 14

Black Hierarchies and Power in Colonial Recife, Brazil

Elizabeth W. Kiddy, Albright College

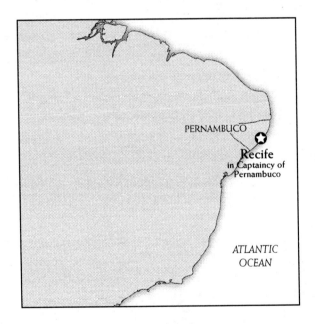

Slavery and the slave trade shaped the demographics of Brazilian society during the colonial period. The Portuguese had engaged in the slave trade since the middle of the fifteenth century, and after the "discovery" of Brazil in 1500, Africans from across West and Central Africa were carried to sugar plantations, gold mines, and to the urban centers of Brazil to work at every conceivable type of labor. A huge number of Africans died as a result of the harsh working conditions. Some Africans, however, especially in the urban centers, were able to gain their freedom and labor as free men and women while maintaining ties to others from their African "nations."[1] Rather then simply remaining at the bottom of the Portuguese social ladder as

---

[1] Slaves gained their freedom through purchase, owners' wills, and favors to mistresses and their children. From the beginning of slavery in Brazil, the number of freed people of color continued to grow. See A.J.R. Russell-Wood, *The Black Man in Slavery and Freedom in Colonial Brazil* (New York: St. Martin's Press, 1982).

Brazilian slaves work in a cobbler's shop. One raises his hand to receive a punishment. The cobbler's wife, or possibly a *mulata* nursemaid, appears in a doorway to the adjoining house. Skilled labor typified Brazilian slavery just as much as manual labor. Women worked in the manual labors but rarely in skilled professions. Female slaves in cities worked more frequently as servants or wet nurses. What other differences appear? How do the images relate to the documents?

Source: Cobbler's workshop, 1834 engraving by J. B. Debret. Biblioteca National do Rio de Janiero Brazil/Picture Desk, Inc./Kobal Collection.

"slaves," "Africans," or "blacks," Brazil's laborers worked to organize these differences within their own communities by creating complex hierarchies.[2]

From the northeastern port of Recife in the captaincy of *Pernambuco*, the late eighteenth- and early nineteenth-century documents in this selection represent one such system. They reveal both a common way that blacks organized themselves in hierarchies, the *confraternity* system, linked to the highly unusual practice of blacks being granted government "commissions" to lead their African nations and labor groups. The first successful captaincy in the colony of Brazil, *Pernambuco*, along with *Bahia*, boasted one of

the longest lasting sugar economies. Both ports *Bahia* and Recife experienced great diversity in their African and African-descended populations due to the constant influx of slaves from different regions. Recife alone in the late eighteenth century received an average of 2,300 Africans who arrived every year from central West Africa and the Bight of Benin. Portuguese authorities recognized the differences among these blacks, as the commission letters show, and for many years legitimized their self-governance.

African nations in Brazil emerge as an important theme in these selections. Rather than referring to a nation in the modern sense, or even a birthplace, the nations reflected group identities reformulated by the slave trade. Torn from local communities, captives searched for ways to make sense of their new world, aligning with one group or another along the way. This process began a realignment of group identities, which continued even after captives arrived in Recife and elsewhere. These alignments emerged in the colonial documentation as *nações* (nations or ethnicities), which can be understood to reflect alliances that captives forged during long and dehumanizing journeys and after their arrival. They even maintained these identities even after winning or buying their freedom.[3] Throughout Brazil the main divisions in the African community were between slaves from the *Mina* Coast, which roughly corresponds to the Bight of Benin of West Africa, and those from Congo and *Angola* in western central Africa. Portuguese monopolized trade in several ports in the Bight of Benin, and they secured a colony in *Angola* since the fifteenth century. Therefore, slaves from these regions predominated.

One of the Portuguese social structures that Africans used to organize these differences was the *confraternity* system. They were lay organizations that were officially under the umbrella of the Catholic Church but which remained separate from the Church. They were founded, organized, and run

[2]See Elizabeth W. Kiddy, "Kings, Queens, and Judges: Hierarchy in Lay Religious Brotherhoods of Blacks, 1750–1830," in *Africa and the Americas: Interconnections during the Slave Trade*, ed. Renée Soulodre-LaFrance and José Curto (New Brunswick, NJ: Africa World Press, 2005), 95–125.

[3]Joseph C. Miller, "Retention, Reinvention, and Remembering: Restoring Identities Through Enslavement in Africa and Under Slavery in Brazil," in *Enslaving Connections: Changing Cultures of Africa and Brazil during the Era of Slavery*, ed. José Curto and Paul E. Lovejoy (Amherst, NY: Prometheus/Humanity Books, 2004), 90–91.

by laypeople, and their chaplains were *confraternity* employees. Both the state and the Church had some rights to oversee their books, but for the most part *confraternities* enjoyed a significant degree of independence. *Confraternities* took responsibility for many of the social services of Portuguese and Iberian society, both religious and secular. For example, they buried the dead and distributed charity among the poor. Some black *confraternities* promised to buy their members' freedom. They built their own churches, hired their own chaplains, and celebrated the feast days of their patron saints. As early as the late fifteenth century, *confraternities* of blacks were founded in Portugal and subsequently in Portugal's colonies in Africa and Brazil. The most widespread of these was the *confraternity* dedicated to Our Lady of the Rosary.[4]

The first document presented is from the 1782 statutes of the rosary *confraternity* of the blacks located in the neighborhood of Santo Antonio in Recife. The rosary *confraternity* in Recife officially began in 1654, and the members built their own church from 1662–1667. The 1782 statutes were a revision of a seventeenth-century document that had limited the membership of the *confraternity* to Africans from *Angola* and *crioulos* (Brazilian-born blacks). By 1782, however, the African population of Recife had grown much more complex, and Chapter 28, reproduced in part later, takes up the issue of the increasingly diverse membership of the organization. The *confraternity* had always had a king and queen, as many rosary *confraternities* did. This chapter offers insight into an even more complex system of ethnic orientation and organization as it defines the roles of the different nations within its membership.

The ethnic hierarchy in itself was not that unusual; in fact, many *confraternities* divided along ethnic lines. What made the situation in Recife unusual was the use of government commissions (*patentes*) to legitimize the positions of governors, of which four

examples appear later. The books of commissions in *Pernambuco* from 1776 to 1802 include dozens of entries naming governors both of African ethnicities and of black professions.[5] These commissions appear to be unique to colonial Recife and its environs. Successive governors of the captaincy of *Pernambuco* in the second half of the eighteenth century issued these commissions to the blacks of the colony, blacks who in almost all of the cases had already been either elected or named to the position by people in their group. Three commission letters even name women to head groups of street vendors and peddlers in the region around Recife.[6] The commissions were then duly entered into an official book of government military commissions as well as into the brotherhood books.

The commission letters and the brotherhood document reveal an interrelated web of formal hierarchies formed by the black community and sanctioned by the Portuguese government in the captaincy. The brotherhood system linked to both the ethnic groups and to a form of organized labor through these formal hierarchies. The letters themselves demonstrate some of the reasons why whites accepted the system. However, early nineteenth-century changes threatened this system and eventually either destroyed it or pushed it underground. The Haitian Revolution (1789–1804) and a series of slave uprisings in the captaincy of *Bahia* put slave societies throughout the Americas on alert. In 1804, a new governor, Caetano Pinto de Miranda Montenegro, arrived in *Pernambuco* who was determined to put an end to what he saw as the abuses of power in the captaincy, especially the hierarchies of blacks. The last document is a letter from Miranda Montenegro to his colleague in the neighboring city of Olinda, responding to the request to outlaw all gatherings of blacks, including religious feast

---

[4]Compromisso da Irmandade de Nossa Senhora do Rozario dos homens pretos erigida nesta Villa de Santo Antonio do Recife (1782). Universidade Federal de Pernambuco, Divisão de Pesquisa Histórica, AHU Pernambuco, Códice 1293, Capítulo 28.

[5]Arquivo Público do Estado de Pernambuco (APEPE), Patentes Provinciais (Pp), books 2–10.

[6]On urban labor, see Mary C. Karasch, *Slave Life in Rio de Janeiro, 1808–1850* (Princeton, NJ: Princeton University Press, 1987), 185–213; João José Reis, "'The Revolution of the *Ganhadores*': Urban Labour, Ethnicity and the African Strike of 1857 in Bahia, Brazil," *Journal of Latin American Studies* 29 (1997): 355–393.

day celebrations. Although Miranda Montenegro urged caution, he clearly wanted to end what he saw as the abuse of privilege practiced by the blacks. Blacks, too, responded to new limitations placed on their freedom. In 1814, Pernambucan authorities uncovered plans for an uprising in Recife. Conspirators belonged to these interlocked hierarchies of blacks; in fact, evidence suggests that the conflict had more to do with interethnic conflict than with conflict with white society. In 1814 and 1815, blacks in Alagoas, then a part of *Pernambuco*, were also found to be plotting (see the final document).[7] As a result of the new social tensions, the system of interlocking hierarchies of Recife receded into history as a new era of intolerance opened in late-colonial Brazil.

----

[7]Luiz Geraldo Silva, "'Sementes da Sedição': Etnia, Revolta Escrava e Controle Social na América Portuguesa (1808–1817)," *Afro-Ásia* 25–26 (2001): 32–39.

Questions to Consider:

1. How many different ways appear in the documents of blacks differentiating among themselves? (see also Chapter 12) What assumptions about race were operational in the documents?
2. In the commissions, what were the reasons that the governor gave for naming a particular person to the post? What do those motivations reveal?
3. In what ways would Portuguese-dominated colonial society benefit from allowing blacks to form their own governance system? Who supported these opportunities and who opposed them? Compare this case to Cuban militiamen in Chapter 30 and *maroon* leaders in Chapter 7.
4. What are were some of the challenges to society that such practices represented? Would these challenges secure individual or collective benefits?

The Confraternity Statutes of the Confraternity of Our Lady of the Rosary

of Black Men, Founded in This Neighborhood of Santo Antonio in Recife (1782)

Chapter 28[8]

There will be a King of Congo, and a queen, both will be listed in the election book and each one will give a donation of 4 *mil-réis*.[9] The king will be one of the members of this *confraternity* from the Kingdom of *Angola*, free from slavery, married, of good habits, and God-fearing.[10] On the feast day of Our Lady both the king and queen will give the donation listed above to help to offset the cost of the festival. To help with the work on the Church, the

king will be obligated to go to ask for alms along with others of his nation on the four feast days of the year that this *confraternity* celebrates. He is also obligated to name a governor from each nation, who will be inaugurated in our church. The king, on the day of his coronation, will be met at the church with the ringing of the bells and our chaplain will crown him in the main church in a solemn act, when the king will give the customary

----

[8]*Source:* Compromisso da Irmandade de Nossa Senhora do Rozario dos homens pretos erigida nesta Villa de Santo Antonio do Recife (1782). Universidade Federal de Pernambuco, Divisão de Pesquisa Histórica, AHU Pernambuco, Códice 1293, capítulo 28.
[9]*Mil-réis* were currency in colonial and imperial Brazil, literally one thousand *réis*.

[10]The title of the kings in many of the rosary brotherhoods was King of the Congos, no matter what the particular "ethnicity" of the officeholder. This practice may be related to the conversion of the King of the Kingdom of Kongo, in Africa, in the late fifteenth century. See Elizabeth W. Kiddy, "Who is the King of Congo? A New Look at African and African-Brazilian Kings in Brazil," in *Central Africans in the Atlantic Diaspora, 1500–1850,* ed. Linda Heywood (Cambridge: Cambridge University Press, December 2001), 153–182.

donation as well as the wax for the candles on the altar. Our secretary will make sure that everything is done according to the rules laid out here, and will make a note of the proceedings in our books. The inaugurations of the governors will also take place with all solemnity, and they will turn in their commissions to the King to be recorded in the appropriate book, after which they will each pay the secretary two *patacas*.[11]

Documents 2–5: The Commissions

Document 2

Simião da Rocha, Governor of the Blacks of the Nation Dagomé[12]

José César de Menezes of the Council of Your Majesty, Your Governor and Captain Major of *Pernambuco*, Paraiba, and other neighboring captaincies, etc. Let it be known to all that would see this commission letter that the blacks of the nation Dagomé informed me that they unanimously elected the black Simião da Rocha as their governor. Because the members of that nation have always behaved well, and Simião da Rocha has all of the necessary requirements for that job and I expect that he will completely satisfy the obligations that fall to him, I hereby name the above mentioned black Simião da Rocha to the position of Governor of the Blacks of the Dagomé nation, who split from the Sabaru nation with whom they had previously been joined.[13] He will hold the position for the customary time, while behaving as he should, and enjoying all of the privileges that are due him. I order that the King of Congo and other officials to recognize, honor and esteem him, recommending peace to him, and demanding that he govern his subordinates; who I also order to obey him and to fulfill his orders relative to the good of the public, as they should and are obligated to do . . . José César de Menezes 3/February/1776

Document 3

Ventura de Souza Graces, Governor of the Black Ardas of the *Mina* Coast[14]

José César de Menezes of the Council of Your Majesty, Your Governor and Captain Major of *Pernambuco*, Paraiba, and other neighboring captaincies, etc. Let it be known to all who would see this commission letter that I learned of the good behavior of the black Ventura Graces of the Nation of the Ardas, of which he is presently a Lieutenant Colonel. I further learned that the ruling board of the black Ardas of the *Mina* Coast elected him the post of the Governor of that nation after the resignation of the present Governor Ventura Vas Salgado, who stepped down because of his advanced age. It is my hope and expectation that he [Ventura Graces] will fulfill the obligations that pertain to him, keeping peace among the blacks of his nation. I therefore name the above mentioned Ventura de Souza Graces to the position of Governor of the Nation of Ardas of the *Mina* Coast, which he will exercise for the customary time, and will enjoy all the jurisdiction that pertains to him with the preference of seniority that belongs to that nation . . . José César de Menezes 7/April/1776

Document 4

The Black Manoel Nunes da Costa, Governor of the Black Markers of Sugar Boxes[15]

José César de Menezes of the Council of Your Majesty, Your Governor and Captain Major of *Pernambuco*, Paraiba, and other neighboring captaincies, etc. Let it be known to all that would see this commission letter that I learned that the black markers of sugar boxes of this city elected the *crioulo* Manoel Nunes da Costa to be their governor. In order to conserve the peace that they should always keep among themselves at work, evicting all disorders that might occur, and with the hope and expectation that he will entirely satisfy all of the obligations that pertain to the above mentioned position, I hereby name the above mentioned black *crioulo* Manoel Nunes da Costa to the position of the governor of the black sugar merchants of this plaza, which he will exercise

---

[11]A coin worth 320 *réis*.
[12]APEPE, Pp 02, folha 114v, 3 February 1776.
[13]Dagomé and Sabaru both refer to places on the Mina Coast, the Bight of Benin.

[14]APEPE Pp 2, 133v, 7 April 1776.
[15]APEPE Pp02, 198, 13 September 1776.

while behaving and he is enjoying the rights that are his in the named position. And by this letter, I order that the King of Congo and other officials to recognize, honor and esteem him, he who has been put in possession of that position, recommending to him peace, and demanding that he should have of the loyalty of his subordinates who I also order to obey him, to fulfill his orders relative to the good of the public and the royal service, as they should and are obligated to do . . . José César de Menezes 13/September/1776

Document 5

The Black João da Assunção, Governor of the Fishermen[16]

. . . I have learned that João da Assunção has the necessary qualities to exercise the position of governor of the fishermen, which serves to prevent disorder and allows them to do their work in good harmony, and to be ready for the call to Royal Service when the opportunity arises. I expect that he will completely fulfill this obligation as he should. Therefore, in accordance with Chapter 20 of the rules of this government, I hereby name the above mentioned João da Assunção to the position of Governor of the Fishermen of this Town, which is vacant because of the troubles caused by Tomás Francisco who previously held the post.[17] The position does not have any pay, but enjoys all of the privileges, and exemptions, that pertain to it . . . I order all of the fishermen to obey you and fulfill your orders . . . José César de Menezes 22/September/1784

Document 6: Changes in the Early Nineteenth Century, 1815

Letter to the General Council of Olinda, in response to his letter.[18]

I received your letter of the 18th of this month, in which I found reflections that might have been correct if they had been based on the example of

Bahia only. . . . But theories should match the facts, and not the fact the theories. You have been in *Pernambuco* only four months, while I have governed the captaincy for twelve years and I should, perhaps, be familiar with the insubordination and lack of respect of the blacks of Recife and Olinda. The blacks of *Bahia*, because they come from warlike nations, perhaps do not have kings and governors who by their letters of commissions name secretaries of state, generals, lieutenants, Admirals, Brigadiers, Colonels, and all of the other military posts—all of which we have in *Pernambuco*, along with the trappings of majesty and nobility that they embrace—this is the insolence here which must be stopped.

I have worked a long time to destroy these errors and abuses. . . . I have revoked many of the black commissions, and I have warned and threatened the blacks, but only in this past year do I see them being more submissive. Many blacks also saw the swift measures that I took whenever there was some sort of disorder. It is necessary, in fact, to break them of all these habits, and tear out all of these abuses by the roots. Nevertheless, we should give them some time to become accustomed to this greater submission and wait to see the result of the uprisings in Alagoas; and it will be necessary that in Recife and Olinda that we do the same [that they do], because if too much freedom is given in one region, it is not surprising that any restriction becomes hated in another.

24/December/1815

Caetano Pinto de Miranda Montenegro.

Suggested Sources:

The following is the only collection of documents on slavery in Brazil available in English. See Robert Edgar Conrad, *Children of God's Fire: A Documentary History of Black Slavery in Brazil* (University Park: Pennsylvania State University Press, 1994). Thomas Ewbank lived in Rio de Janeiro in the mid-1800s and wrote *Life in Brazil* (New York: Harper and Brothers, 1856). Henry Koster described early nineteenth-century life in and around Recife in his *Travels in Brazil* (London: Longman, Hurst, Rees, Orme, and Brown, 1816).

---

[16]APEPE Pp05, 6–6v, 22 September 1784.
[17]Referring here to the rules of the government of Pernambuco of 1670. Chapter 20 gives the governor the right to name people to military posts. APEPE, Ordens Régias, 04, 171.
[18]APEPE, Ofícios do Governo 15, 160.

In addition to the sources listed in the footnotes, for rosary brotherhoods in Minas Gerais, see Elizabeth W. Kiddy, *Blacks of the Rosary: Memory and History in Minas Gerais, Brazil* (State College: Pennsylvania State University Press, 2005). Elizabeth W. Kiddy examines black hierarchies in Pernambuco, Minas Gerais, and Rio de Janeiro, Brazil, using some of the documents included in this selection. For "Kings, Queens, and Judges," see note 2. A.J.R. Russell-Wood provides a foundational text on free blacks in *The Black Man in Slavery and Freedom in Colonial Brazil* (New York: St. Martin's Press, 1982). "*Xica*," dir. Carlos Diegues (New York: New Yorker Video, 1976) offers a carnivalesque look at the true story of a slave in the eighteenth-century diamond-mining district of Brazil who gained freedom and wealth. You can view videos of Brazilian confraternity processions if you enter the search parameter "hermandades" at http://www.youtube.com.

Section IV

Challenging Colonial and Cultural Norms

The activities and relations that people engaged in every day tell historians and students an immense amount about the norms governing behavior, and how commoners and authorities interacted with one another. Daily events sometimes even reveal what people may have thought about themselves and about others, a topic that became increasingly important as colonial cities and rural towns gained prominence. As cities and towns grew in size and population they became centers of market and cultural activity, and they held people from the core population groups now inhabiting the Americas: Native Peoples, Europeans, and Africans. These distinct groups had to figure out ways to relate to one another and to live their lives in multiethnic environments. Many rural indigenous communities remained relatively homogeneous, and traditions sometimes survived more intact in Indian hometowns. By contrast, in the urban centers people were culturally and ethnically more mixed; not even one ethnic group prevailed among Native Peoples. Language and other indicators of ethnic difference also divided people within the Iberian and African populations. One group might become dominant, but it was never alone or unchallenged. These interactions and evidence of material life help reveal how this diversity functioned within colonial society, in particular the kinds of challenges it posed to secular and Church authorities anxious to govern these mixed populations.

Cities and towns, therefore, became the birthplaces of the multiethnic and mixed-heritage societies that characterize Latin America to this day. Despite the blurring of some ethno-racial lines, hierarchies endured; nobles enjoyed privileges denied commoners, Europeans in general outranked Africans and Indians, and men dominated women. But it was not always clear how to apply these hierarchies to individuals within an increasingly complex society. In this section on mature colonial society, a core question is how state and Church institutions and individuals and groups marked difference and status. The chapters will make more sense if readers keep in mind the ways Spaniards understood race and difference in this age of Iberian power and empire building.

Beliefs about "racial" identities and their relative fixity or fluidity developed in tandem with overseas conquests and commerce in Africa and the Americas and with the opportunity to enslave or rule over the conquered. This historical juncture blended religious notions with the realities of power, domination, and profit. Iberian attitudes about difference, or racial thinking, originated in medieval Christians' prejudices and conflicts with Jews and believers in Islam. Victorious Iberian Christians came to rely on a fundamental distinction between Old Christians with *limpieza de sangre* (purity of blood) and New Christians whose descendants would forever be marked by an association with non-Christian practices. These

The Hispanicized native Andean chronicler, *Felipe Guaman Poma de Ayala*, depicted, starting on the left, a Spanish *corregidor* toasting an indigenous commoner seated across from him, calling him "sir *kuraka*" in Spanish. The Indian responds in the native Andean language *Quechua* "Sir, great sir, I will serve you." Next are a *mestizo* and a *mulato*. *Guaman Poma* called all three lowly people. In the foreground, an Indian boy or an Indian servant brings a wineskin. Directed to the Spanish king in 1615, he hoped his letter would persuade the king that indigenous people could be good Christians if Spanish abuses ended. *Guaman Poma* worried about socially disruptive influences of outsiders such as these in Indian towns. How did *Guaman Poma* depict each of these men—their station and their interactions? What did he hope to communicate to the King?

Source: The Royal Library/Felipe Guaman Poma de Ayala, Nueva corónica y buen gobierno (1615), fol. 505 [509].

converts and their lineages lacked the *limpieza* or purity of Old Christians.

Iberian officials also commonly recorded *casta* or *calidad* of origin or lineage. As Africans were incorporated into Iberian society from the 1450s forward and the transatlantic movement of Old World peoples began in earnest in the sixteenth century, Africans became marked as a *casta* lacking *limpieza* or Old Christian status.[1] The pope allowed the wholesale enslavement of Africans and their shipment overseas to ensure Africans' Christianization. Thus, for many people, religious status or *calidad* (honor and reputation) became linked to human bondage, and both conditions were passed from one generation to the next. In their classificatory writings and in missionary practice on all three continents and in Asia, missionaries established hierarchies based on cultural and religious characteristics rather than on supposedly "biological" differences. Although spared in most cases from the stigma of chattel slavery (unless captured in war), Native Peoples in the Americas were also marked forever as newcomers to Christianity and, therefore, not pure and by nature lacking Spanish honor. Nevertheless, to distinguish one person from another in court or on the street, these identities based on descent and religious heritage still relied on the ethnic markers: hairstyle and dress, language and religious practice, occupation and residence, and so forth. The importance of these markers, along with legal documents to prove lineage and local reputation, allowed racial identities to shift.[2] In the course of daily interactions or during a person's lifetime, race was socially defined using these ethnic markers.

Thinking and governing in terms of ethno-racial status took hold during the development of Iberia's imperial traditions. Portugal and Spain

[1] Magnus Mörner, *Race Mixture in the History of Latin America* (Boston: Little, Brown, 1967).
[2] David Cahill updates the discussion of race and shows it in action in the colonial world. David Cahill, "Colour by Numbers: Racial and Ethnic Categories in the Viceroyalty of Peru, 1532–1821," *Journal of Latin American Studies* 26, no. 2 (May 1994): 325–347.

formed powerful monarchies and governing institutions in an era of unprecedented expansion of European trade, conquest, and settlement overseas. The Spanish Empire heavily emphasized settling colonists, administrators, and missionaries in towns and cities on the North and South American continents. From these centers, they could directly exploit populous indigenous societies and imported African workers. These empires and their values took shape and became realities as the monarchies' representatives tried to manage affairs overseas and established royal courts. Subjects and recently subjugated populations began to use courts and colonial-style documents to resolve conflicts and claim rights in cities, workplaces, and markets. The empire became real in people's lives when subjects both recognized the authority and legitimacy of the monarchy and the Church, and in return claimed rights, protection, and membership in colonial society.

Colonial Latin American cities and towns were at once intermixed and highly stratified according to racial and social status. The chapters in this section use primary-source documents to illustrate that even though the Spanish elite held ultimate power, racial hierarchies were often blurred in practice, and some non-Europeans gained significant personal power. Although Spanish immigrants enjoyed many privileges relative to non-Europeans, Owensby's chapter uses an anonymous Spaniard's poem to introduce the fact that many young men from Spain faced lives of uncertainty about whether they would achieve their goals or ever again see their homelands. Likewise, Spanish women struggled against and within colonial *patriarchy*, as illustrated in excerpts from documents authored by the nun Sor Juana Inés de la Cruz and the cross-dressing Catalina de Erauso. Documents in chapters on *mestiza* and Indian women by Mangan and Garofalo focus on the development of multiethnic identities in urban centers: Mangan explores the life of a *"mestiza en hábitos de India"*—a *mestiza* woman who dressed (and lived) as an Indian in Potosí, and Garofalo examines informal power structures through the life of a native Andean healer in Lima. Melton-Villanueva brings *cacicas* (female indigenous rulers) into view, introducing readers to *doña* Ana María de la Cruz Alpizar, whose will problematizes the notion that only Spanish or indigenous men exercised political power. The core documents in this section bring alive the vibrancy and complexity of living in colonial Latin American cities and towns.

Chapter 15

A Romance of Early-Modern Mexico City: Self-Interest and Everyday Life in Colonial New Spain

Brian Owensby, University of Virginia

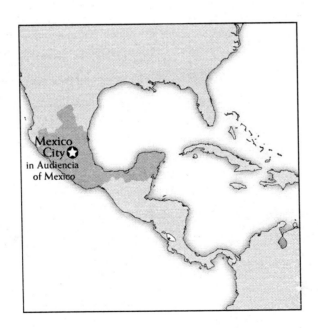

The colonial Mexican social order is often assumed to have been immobile, an ossified hierarchy of entrenched positions offering scant hope of social mobility. In theory, people suffered little anxiety over gaining or losing status. Scholars once supposed that great forces sweeping Europe during the sixteenth and seventeenth centuries—a growing sense of individual fate among ordinary people, a deepening sense of social competition, an expanding sense of aspiration and anguish over the possibilities of social mobility—did not buffet the New World. In the faraway Americas, allegedly separated from the historical forces so often identified as having given rise to modern individualism, the social world has been characterized chiefly in terms of the tense and intimate relations among different ethnic groups—Spaniards, Indians, blacks, and *castas*, or people of mixed race. There is no denying the importance of these labels or the role these groups played in colonial Mexico. This anonymous poem, however, suggests that for many, perhaps especially transplanted Europeans, early-modern Mexico may have been no less a place of social competition and personal anxiety than early-modern Europe.

From 1500 to roughly 1650, Spain underwent a cultural shift in which individuals began to think that they could—and had no choice but to—act alone to get by in the world. Spaniards of this period did not imagine themselves completely apart from others, for they remained creatures of a society defined by estates and hierarchies. But they did nurture a slowly unfolding sense that individual actions could affect the world in their favor, even as they understood that their aspirations could just as easily founder. In an early seventeenth-century play by Calderón de la Barca, one of the principal characters expressed both pride and anxiety over self-autonomy saying that he was "king and kingdom unto myself, I live alone with myself, with myself alone content."[3]

In effect, Calderón was commenting on a more general cultural phenomenon in Spain and the rest of Europe, from the late sixteenth century forward— the universal hunt for prestige, material reward, and social power. This hunt made life an anxious contest. According to contemporary writers, personal life was lived on a war footing. Christóval Suárez de Figueroa lamented that "our life is but a continuous and perpetual war, without any sort of truce or peace."[4] Saavedra Fajardo claimed that among the Spaniards "people arm themselves against each other, and everyone lives in perpetual distrust and

suspicion."[5] Around the mid-seventeenth century, Jerónimo de Barrionuevo worried about the broader consequences of so thoroughly individualistic an approach to life: "each pursues his own business and not the common and good of all, as a result of which everything goes wrong." In the process, "some enrich themselves, making others poor."[6] These were the wages of a generalized sense among ordinary people that they had no choice but to determine their own destinies in the world.

This attitude appears to have been no less pronounced in the New World, a place where common folk could more readily play out their dreams than in the Old World (Europe). One of Cortés's soldiers, Bernal Díaz, noted in his chronicle of the conquest that settlers came to Mexico in good measure "because there was wealth."[7] Toward the mid-seventeenth century, Juan Solórzano y Pereira, in his treatise on the law of the Indies reaffirmed the point, noting that money and status, more than religion, brought Spaniards to the Americas.[8] Of course, it is an old story that Spanish emigrants to the New World sought opportunity because social mobility was limited in Spain and Europe. In the Americas, even a petty trader with no capital could prosper modestly. And when trying to persuade a nephew to join him from Spain, a merchant could write of "the ease you will have here."[9]

At the same time, as in Spain, an atmosphere of struggle and confusion pervaded everyday life in Mexico, inspiring personal and moral anxieties. It was from deep within this context that an anonymous poet penned these verses, probably sometime in the early seventeenth century. Written to be read out loud, possibly at *tertulias*—sessions of drinking and conversation among friends, *romances* of this sort were common, perhaps the most popular poetic

---

[3]Pedro Calderón de la Barca, *Darlo todo y no dar nada*, Diogenes's first speech, Act I, *http://www.trinity.edu/org/comedia/calderon/darlot .html*.

[4]Christóval Suárez de Figueroa, *El pasagero: advertencias utilísimas a la vida humana* (Madrid: Biblioteca Pensamiento, 1913), 360.

[5]Diego Saavedra Fajardo, *Idea de un príncipe político-cristiano representada en cien empresas* (Murcia: Universidad de Murcia, 1985), 291 (empresa 43).

[6]Jerónimo de Barrionuevo, *Avisos* (BAE, CCXXI), vol. I, 100.

[7]Bernal Díaz del Castillo, *Historia verdadera de la conquista de la Nueva España* (BAE, XXVI), 312.

[8]Juan Solórzano y Pereira, *Política indiana* (Madrid: Biblioteca Castro, 1996), vol. I, 105 (I, VIII, 25, and 28).

[9]James Lockhart & Enrique Otte, *Letters and People of the Spanish Indies: Sixteenth Century* (Cambridge: Cambridge University Press, 1976), 143–146.

form of the day.[10] There was a sarcastic, mocking tone to these stanzas that covered up a deep angst over the circumstances of life in Mexico City at this time. The protagonist began by remarking on the glitter of high society, followed by a note of worry that some rise while others fall in life. As a narrative, the poem is straightforward. A young man thinking about his Spanish homeland was swept away by the vibrancy, wealth, and beauty of Mexico City. Drunk on his thoughts, he was forced to account for himself and in a moment of honesty laid bare his status anxiety. He closed the poem with a melancholy riff on the role of self-interest in the colonial world he now called his own.

This scene from Eugene Delacroix's painting *Amadis de Gaule* (1860) in which Amadís rescues Olga during the siege at Galpan's Castle depicts the chivalry amidst chaos that characterized the late fifteenth and sixteenth centuries in the Old World and the New. What can this painting suggest about the ideals of manhood that Spanish men sought to live up to? According to the poem, what was changing that made it harder to uphold and live by these ideals?

Source: Eugene Delacroix's painting *Amadis de Gaule* (1860). Courtesy of the Virginia Museum of Fine Art, Richmond, Virginia.

Although only a single poem, this *Romance* suggests that many Spanish men in early-modern Mexico experienced the uncertainty of wondering whether they would rise or fall in life, and lived with the vertigo of knowing that in some ways they were on their own in a world where people armed themselves against each other in distrust and suspicion— even kinsmen might lie to one another—each pursuing his own business and not the common and good of all. And for many of them, relations with women—actual or imagined—was a crucial measure of success or failure.

Although this poem may have been written by a *peninsular* Spaniard, it could just as easily have been the work of a *creole*—a Mexican-born Spaniard mocking the exaggerated pretensions of those more recently arrived. Either way, it is a sharp commentary on the conditions of people who lived in a world of success that could not accommodate all those who aspired to status.

Questions to Consider:

1. What were gender relations like in the *Romance*? How and why did gender relations add to the protagonist's social anxiety in the poem? Why did the author express his worries through his encounter with women?

2. In what passages did the author use sarcasm? What does this reveal about the author's views and purposes in writing the poem? How would the interpretation change depending on whether a peninsular Spaniard or a *creole* wrote the piece?

3. When the author asserted that "self-interest accomplishes all," what did he mean? What standard(s) of conduct and morality seemed to be falling by the wayside, at least in the author's mind?

4. What did the centrality of "self-interest" in everyday life mean for the protagonist? What speculations might be hazarded about the author's personal circumstances by reading the poem?

[10]See Ruth Hill, "Caste Theater and Poetry in 18th-Century Spanish America," *Revista de Estudios Hispánicos* 34 (2000): 3–26.

Romance to Mexico City

by Anonymous, ca. 1600[11]

Yesterday afternoon, while I was
Contemplating my mischance
Struggling with the memory
Of my homeland distant,

A great speech came to mind
Which I had borne within me
Amidst the silence
Of this laudable city:

So many gallant gentlemen,
Many gracious women
Who the city adorn, ennoble,
Exalt and illumine;

A great number of merchants
Who, though they have no rival
Like the weights of a clock,
Some rise while others fall;

Many doctors with tassels
Many scholars famous,
And canon lawyers who
Would outdo Bartolus[12];

Theologians who preserve
Conscience against lapse,
University graduates, and lawyers,
More than in Salamanca perhaps.[13]

Among these ten excellencies
Are those who raise up this city,
On the foundations of
Rome, Spain, France, and Italy.

Silver, cattle, and wheat
Illustrious bridges and plazas,
Beautiful and famous temples
Fountains, horses, and casas.

With these thoughts,
And the pleasure they occasioned,

I entered a house
Boasting of discretion,

Where sat four women who
Like the light of dawn shone.
And at the threshold
A modest greeting I intoned.

Among them there was one
Who fourteen years had not attained
She asked of me some questions—
"What kinds of towns hath Spain?

"Whom serve you, from what do you live?
"Who are you, what are you called?
"Are you a bachelor, what is your estate?
"Are you to a lady enthralled?

"How goes it for you in this land?
"What are its excesses, what does it lack?"
And under my breath I murmured,
"May the devil keep this child back."

Then I raised my voice and said:
"Dear girl of my soul,
"A bachelor I am and have no master.
"They call me Jeronimo.

"All the estate I have
"My cape will cover,
"And I hope its service
"You soon discover.

"About this land I feel that
"My life and my aspirations
"Are gallant clothes I use,
"Costly attire rich in inspiration.

"Jewels and rich emeralds,
"Fine nacre, snow white,
"Divine judgments
"Which with the senses take flight.

"They say that in this land
"It is Venus who reigns.
"This is false. For of success
"Few feel the flame.

"For from what I have seen
"And what happens in this land
"What love does not attain
"Self interest can command.

---

[11]*Source*: Biblioteca Nacional (Madrid), MS 19387.
[12]Bartolus de Saxoferrato, an Italian law professor and one of the most important jurists of medieval Europe.
[13]"Salamanca" refers to the great University of Salamanca in Salamanca, Spain.

"He is a handsome young fellow
"Narrow waisted with long shirt.
"Gold and brocade he wears,
"Wrapped in fine cloaks.

"Brave, wise and discreet
"He dances well and sings,
"Pays courtly compliments,
"Though he doesn't say a thing

"His great power encloses
"All the sun sees and heats.
"With his powerful arm
"He wrecks, subjects, and decrees.

"Kings, princes, and marquises,
"Dukes, counts, and monarchs,
"Among Christians and infidels,
"Self interest hits the mark.

"This wicked poison
"Of self interest so pervades
"Our lives that no man
"Can avoid its face.

"Men live without faith
"Sans God, and law, and soul.
"And he who knows the most
"Deceives, adulates, cajoles,

"In order to make his kinsman
"Think himself on a sinking ship,
"So the deceiver can deflect his own woes
"Northward of his missteps.

"For everything shows that in the end,
"In the plaza and the hinterland,
"What love cannot attain
"Self interest can command.

"Amidst these lasses,
"Who on proud wings glide,
"The vain and spoiled man
"Across their lovely laps lies.

"Some hold with an iron grip.
"Others use men for their deceits.
"Young girls call it life.
"'*My soul*,' older women entreat.

"My gift is the widows,
"My glory other men's wives.
"All of the biddies deny it,
"Because they are soft and lie

"In fallen gardens
"Like wizened, unripe fruit.
"Long live love, love live long!"
I told my ungrateful beaut.

So that a stranger not enjoy
Such outcast beauty,
The ladies listened rapt
To the words of my soliloquy.

Almost with mercy, these dears
Were about to grant my wish,
When my enemy said, "Your words
Are trifling and mawkish."

"Come, sit and converse,
Take the cards and deal."
But I, in my garments,
Did not have a penny to wield.

I blushed so deeply
That anyone on their guard
Would have known my game
Without seeing my cards.

So I stood and told them,
"If you ladies will wait
I will go fetch some money
For I am dying to play."

That is how I left them
Engulfed in the flames of their stare
Damning my debt,
My disgrace, and my despair.

It is in my interest
To take matters into my own hands,
For if you'll excuse me, there is nothing
Self interest cannot command.

The End.

Suggested Sources:

For an introduction to eighteenth-century plays and poems about daily life, see Ruth Hill, "Caste Theater and Poetry in 18th-Century Spanish America," *Revista de Estudios Hispánicos* 34 (2000): 3–26. For indigenous people confronting their circumstances through law, see Brian Owensby, *Empire of Law and Indian Justice in Colonial Mexico*

(Stanford, CA: Stanford University Press, 2008). Castile sent the most people to the Americas, especially the region of Extremadura. Ida Altman analyzes their motivations in Ida Altman, *Emigrants and Society: Extremadura and America in the Sixteenth Century* (Los Angeles: University of California Press, 1989).

Letters between family members and friends in Spain and the New World provide an excellent source on the expectations and realities of immigration in this era. See James Lockhart and Enrique Otte, eds., *Letters and People of the Spanish Indies: Sixteenth Century* (Cambridge: Cambridge University Press, 1976). For one of Golden Age Spain's best-known playwrights, see Pedro Calderón de la Barca, *Eight Dramas of Calderón*, trans. Edward Fitzgerald (Urbana: University of Illinois Press, 2000). For one of his most

notable plays, see Pedro Calderón de la Barca, *Life is a Dream*, trans. Edward Fitzgerald (Studio City, CA: Players Press, 1992). Bernal Díaz del Castillo chronicled the disappointments of conquest and settlement in *The True History of the Conquest of New Spain*, trans. J. M. Cohen (Baltimore: Penguin Books, 1976). The Jesuit Juan de Mariana (1565–1624) wrote a tract describing the duties and virtues required of a king. See Juan de Mariana, *The King and the Education of the King (De Rege et Regis Institutione)*, ed. and tr. George Albert Moore (Washington, DC: Country Dollar Press, 1948). The online versions in Spanish of Felipe Guaman Poma de Ayala described Spanish immigrants' dress and demeanor, *http://www.kb.dk/permalink/2006/poma/info/es/frontpage.htm*, and *The Encyclopedia Britannica's* online version of Guaman Poma's *Letter to a King*.

Chapter 16

Ambitious Women in a "Man's World"

Leo J. Garofalo, *Connecticut College*

Sor Juana Inés de la Cruz is Mexico's most famous female poet, and yet she wrote and published in an era when women were barred from the university. Societal norms discouraged, and the Church even forbade, women like Sor Juana from engaging in literary, intellectual, or public discourse. Sor Juana flaunted these norms as the following poems and essay demonstrate. She even delved into theology, which was unheard of for a woman! Sor

Juana's elite Spanish origins and her time in a convent made her similar to another remarkable woman who left her family and the possibility of marriage behind in order to pursue a career reserved only for males. Catalina de Erauso strapped on a sword; boarded a ship for the Americas; and made a name for herself as a soldier, a fortune-seeker, and a brawler in the Andes. Unlike Sor Juana who lived openly as a woman and challenged for a time some of society's dictates for elite women, de Erauso escaped these limitations by hiding her female identity and disguising herself as a man.

Social conventions held that elite Spanish or *creole* women either married their social equals or entered a convent with a substantial dowry. Elite women's decorum and station helped determine family *honor* and social status. A culture of *honor*, shame, and *patriarchal* power developed in colonial Hispano-America, and both of the women featured in this chapter grew up in this gendered *honor* system. This shared culture affected elite men and women differently, and commoners developed their own codes of *honor* that were in dialogue with this elite culture but fundamentally different. In very basic terms, gender refers to what being a man, or being a woman, meant in a particular culture at a particular time. In Iberia and Ibero-America during the colonial era, *honor* accrued to elite men who demonstrated personal forcefulness, ruled over a household (a *patriarch*), and commanded respect in public for their social rank. This elite, male code required that men project an aura of command, receive displays of submission from others, and exercise control over the women in their household, especially over women's movement outside of the house and their sexuality. Sexual conquests outside the home often brought respect for men but dishonor or even disgrace to elite women. The elite code of *honor* for women dictated a sense of shame, self-enclosure and isolation, submissive postures of obedience and respect toward authorities who presided over them within the home and in the Church, and a fierce regard for sexual propriety (virginity for girls, fidelity for wives, and abstinence for widows). This code was most meaningful for elites because they possessed the resources to cloister women (keep them out of public view or under surveillance) and avoid the dishonor of manual or public occupations or buying and selling. Living from rents and office holding bestowed more *honor* on elite men and women than did engagement in commerce or practicing a skilled profession. Poor women could not live up to the elite culture of true womanhood: Poor women could not be cloistered, protected from sexual freedom or exploitation, or shielded from the necessity of manual labor and/or work outside the home. The ultimate beneficiaries of the whole system

were the elite, male *patriarchs* who exercised considerable power over the women around them, servants and employees, and even lesser elite males.

Subaltern versions of the gendered *honor* code focused less on lineage and female enclosure and more on individual dignity and rights. Male commoners knew that they could not compete with elite men because the aura of household authority was tied to lavish consumption, strict female cloistering, and vertical social contacts with subordinates. Instead, subaltern men redefined the code to value manly courage and an individual's acts (meting out physical and psychological abuse, contesting humiliation, and cultivating a reputation as a man who stands up against threats). A subaltern woman's *honor* rested less on her ancestors and religious beliefs and valued more her actions. She gained *honor* through displays of physical courage as a moral guardian of her community (riots or protests to authorities), affirmation of her individual dignity, and contesting the subaltern men in her own family circle. For female commoners, a commitment to honorable consensual union (monogamy) as opposed to elite code of marriage was itself proof of honorable respectability in a sexual sense. With both the elite and subaltern codes of gendered behavior, variations and human manipulation of the system appeared, giving historians evidence of women claiming a voice and some freedom of movement and thought within a man's world.

Many elite families in the Iberian world sent girls to convents for religious instruction and a cloistered existence in anticipation of future marriage or a decision to profess as a nun. Elite women and girls could preserve the high public opinion of their families and even enhance the families' reputation for piety by entering convents. A sizeable monetary dowry was required of women and girls entering a convent to become formal, decision-making members of the cloistered community. Many poorer women and girls lived and toiled in the convents as servants or slaves of the elite nuns. Convents in the Americas also wielded some important economic power: They decided how to invest the accumulated dowries. Thus, convents in many regions offered access to family *honor*, religious standing, and credit.

Not all elite female youth and women who entered the convent, however, conformed to these expectations of obedience to authority, silence, and an existence completely cut off from the outside world. As exceptions to the rules, ambitious women in a male-dominated world fought conventions to find their own way in life. Both Sor Juana Inés de la Cruz (1651–1695) and Catalina de Erauso (1592–1650) stood out for their extraordinary courage in flaunting the highly restrictive norms of elite female behavior and accomplishments. Their lives and writings, therefore, open a window for understanding both the rigidity and flexibility of colonial society and gender norms.

Born in 1592 on the northern coast of Spain in San Sebastian to a large and prosperous Basque family, Catalina de Erauso's role as a lesser noblewoman was to uphold her family's position in society. It is possible that her father served as a soldier in the Americas, and that her older brother Miguel had been there since she was 2 years old seeking fortune in commerce or glory in battle. Three more brothers would also make the voyage to engage in commerce and soldiering. Motivated by the same goal of building family *honor*, the family sent the five daughters to the town's convent to be educated for religious life or marriage if a good match appeared. Except for Catalina, who ran away after completing the novitiate before professing as a nun, the investment paid off: One sister married, and the other three took their vows and became nuns. In the accounts she and others gave of her life, Catalina de Erauso explained that she fled the nunnery to escape beatings by another nun.[1] She cut her hair, refashioned her garments into a man's outfit, and found work as a page. Still disguised as a boy, she made her way onto her uncle's galleon bound for the Americas as a ship's boy in 1603. In Panama, she jumped ship and began working with a Spanish merchant with whom she traveled to Peru, where her adventures continued, as seen in this chapter's excerpt from her autobiography.

Catalina de Erauso's career in Peru gained her fame, first in the Bishop of Humanga's 1617 letters back to Spain written when he discovered her true identity, and later in published accounts that she herself gave. Upon returning to Spain, she successfully petitioned for a military pension from King Philip IV. Pope Urban VIII gave her dispensation for her violent crimes and permission to dress in men's garb. Both the King and the Pope enjoyed curiosities such as the virgin, warrior nun, and she gained celebrity status in Seville and Rome drawing crowds, receiving dinner invitations from the nobility, and sitting for at least two portraits (Francisco Pacheco painted one in 1630). She eventually tired of being treated as a spectacle and set sail for the Americas again in 1630, apparently dying there in 1650.[2]

Like Catalina de Erauso, Sor Juana Inés de la Cruz's fame—for intellectual virtuosity rather than swordplay—won her powerful friends and a degree of freedom unavailable to most other elite women. Born in 1651[3] to an unmarried mother from an influential Spanish *creole* family in Chimalhuacán, Juana Ramírez y Asbaje enjoyed both access to privileges—like her grandfather's library and being able to receive an education instead of working from an early age—and faced the limitations of her illegitimate birth. When she moved to the viceregal capital of Mexico City at age 8 to live with her aunt and uncle and enjoy their library and better tutoring, this child prodigy came to the attention of the Spanish *Viceroy* and his wife, who made her a lady-in-waiting in 1664. This patronage and her position in court helped her overcome the stigma of her birth and gave her greater exposure to both art and science, but it did not eliminate the pressure for her to marry or follow a religious vocation as she matured. Her learning and a dowry from the *viceroy* allowed Juana Ramírez some choice in convents. After 3 months in a strict convent, she began her career as Sor Juana, a nun in the less rigorous convent

---

[1] Catalina de Erauso's two 1626 petitions to the King for a military pension also emphasized her desire to serve the Crown as a soldier as a motivation for fleeing the abbey. Mary Elizabeth Perry, "From Convent to Battlefield: Cross-Dressing and Gendering the Self in the New World of Imperial Spain," in *Queer Iberia: Sexualities, Cultures, and Crossings from the Middle Ages to the Renaissance*, ed. Josiah Blackmore and Gregory S. Hutcheson (Durham, NC: Duke University Press, 1999), 394–419.

[2] Stephanie Merrim, "Catalina de Erauso: From Anomaly to Icon," in *Coded Encounters: Writing, Gender, and Ethnicity in Colonial Latin America*, ed. Francisco Javier Cevallos-Candau, Jeffrey A. Cole, Nina M. Scott, and Nicomedes Suárez-Aráuz (Amherst: University of Massachusetts Press, 1994), 177–205.

[3] A baptismal record suggests that she may have actually been born in 1648.

of San Jerónimo (1667). Sor Juana continued to write, publish in Spain, stage plays and literary and scientific readings, and correspond widely with other writers and scientists.[4] Two successive *viceroys* valued her fame and literary talent. They saw themselves in Spain and Mexico as patrons of the arts and as such friends of the intellectual and artistic elites of their time.

This openness to new ideas, beauty, and even accomplished women in public clashed with the goals of reformers within the Church who considered society corrupt; in particular, they considered convents mired in laxity and a neglect of true devotion to prayers. The Church reformers feared the new ideas being explored in literature, public discourse, and the nascent field of scientific inquiry. Eventually, in 1681, her confessor, a male authority to whom every nun rendered accounts, advised that Sor Juana dedicate herself to prayer. She replaced

Commissioned to document a family's connection to a prestigious convent or a convent's connection to a famous nun, these portraits show a nun in the habit of her religious order and accompanied by the symbols and images associated with her particular convent. If she was saintly or caused miracles, this might be depicted as well. More often a nun's portrait was painted at the moment of her death, and she was shown grasping the wax flowers and flowered crown worn when taking her vows as "a bride of Christ" at the beginning of her religious career. How does Sor Juana's portrait conform to these norms of representation? What symbols or items are associated with her? Does the painter present her as a saintly, pious, or mystical figure?

Source: Museo de America.

A 1772 copy of a famous seventeenth-century portrait of Sor Juana reminds viewers of her renown and the admiration Mexicans felt for her. How is she portrayed in this image? How can it be contrasted with the first painting? What items and surroundings appear? What do these features tell viewers about who Sor Juana was and how she was seen?

Source: Demetrio Carrasco (c) CONACULTA-INAH-MEX. Authorized reproduction by the Instituto Nacional de Antropologia e Historia/ Dorling Kindersley Media Library.

---

[4]Stephanie Merrim, *Early Modern Women's Writing and Sor Juana Inés de la Cruz* (Nashville, TN: Vanderbilt University Press, 1999).

him. Her former supporter, the Bishop of Puebla, launched a more formidable attack in 1691 under the assumed name of Sor Filotea (Sister Filotea), accusing her of worldliness and intellectual activity unbefitting a woman and a nun (she had published a commentary on theology). An excerpt from her thirty-page response is included in this chapter. Sor Juana's position continued to erode; she lost the protection of the current *Viceroy* and the reforming Archbishop targeted her personally. When the reformers gained the upper hand, they forced Sor Juana to renounce her studies at 42, give away her books and scientific instruments, and assume a life of service and prayer in 1694. She died a year later caring for the other nuns during a smallpox epidemic. Despite this defeat, the writings of these two remarkable women have outlived them, describing their lives and views in their own words.

Questions to Consider:

1. In what ways did Catalina de Erauso and Sor Juana Inés de la Cruz transgress society's norms, and in what ways did they reinforce them?
2. On what grounds did the disguised Catalina de Erauso resist marriage? On what grounds did Sor Juana Inés de la Cruz reject marriage?
3. How did Catalina de Erauso describe and act out being a man? How did she portray women and their actions and their options?
4. How did Sor Juana critique male attitudes toward women? And how did she defend her studies and forays into the male world of literature and theology?
5. How did Sor Juana's description of her youth help explain what she was trying to convey in her poetry?

Two Poems by Sor Juana Inés de la Cruz, a Cloistered Nun, 1689[5]

Untitled, 1689

World, in hounding me, what do you gain?
How can it harm you if I choose, astutely,
Rather to stock my mind with things of beauty,
Than waste its stock on every beauty's claim?

Costliness and wealth bring me no pleasure;
the only happiness I care to find
derives from setting treasure in my mind,
and not from mind that's set on winning treasure.

I prize no comeliness. All fair things pay
to time, the victor, their appointed fee
and treasure cheats even the practiced eye.

Mine is the better and truer way:
to leave the vanities of life aside,
not throw my life away on vanity.

---

[5]*Source:* Originally published in Madrid in the first edition of volume 1 of Sor Juana's works in 1689. Sor Juana Inés de la Cruz, *A Sor Juana Anthology*, ed. and trans. Alan S. Trueblood (Cambridge, MA: Harvard University Press, 1988), 95, 97, 111, 113.

"Philosophical Satire," 1689

Silly, you men—so very adept
At wrongly faulting womankind,
Not seeing you're alone to blame
for faults you plant in woman's mind:

After you've won by urgent plea
the right to tarnish her good name,
you still expect her to behave—
you, that coaxed her into shame.

You batter her resistance down
and then, all righteousness, proclaim
that feminine frivolity,
not your persistence, is to blame.

When it comes to bravely posturing,
your witlessness must take the prize:
you're the child that makes a bogeyman,
and then recoils in fear and cries.

Presumptuous beyond belief,
you'd have the woman you pursue

be Thais when you are courting her,
Lucretia once she falls to you.[6]

For plain default of common sense,
could any action be so queer
as oneself to cloud the mirror,
then complain that it's not clear?

Whether you're favored or disdained,
nothing can leave you satisfied.
You whimper if you're turned away,
You sneer if you've been gratified.

With you no woman can hope to score;
whichever way, she's bound to lose;
spurning you, she's ungrateful;
succumbing, you call her lewd.

Your folly is always the same:
you apply a single rule
to the one you accuse of looseness
and the one you brand as cruel.

What happy mean could there be
for the woman who catches your eye,
if, unresponsive, she offends,
yet whose complaisance you decry?

---

[6]Contrasting the sultry courtesan Thais who accompanied Alexander on his Asian campaign with the chaste Roman noblewoman Lucretia, who, after she was raped, killed herself to preserve the family honor.

Still, whether it's torment or anger—
and both ways you've yourselves to blame—
God bless the woman who won't have you,
no matter how loud you complain.

It's your persistent entreaties
that change her from timid to bold.
Having made her thereby naughty,
you would have her good as gold.

So where does the greater guilty lie
for passion that should not be:
with the man who pleads out of baseness
or the woman debased by his plea?

Or which is more to be blamed—
though both will have cause for chagrin:
the woman who sins for money
or the man who pays money to sin?

So why are you men all so stunned
at the thought you're all guilty alike?
Either like them for what you've made them
or make of them what you can like.

If you give up pursuing them,
you'd discover, without a doubt.
you've a stronger case to make
against those who seek you out.

I well know what powerful arms
you wield in pressing for evil:
your arrogance is allied
with the world, the flesh, and the devil!

Sor Juana's Defense of Women's Education and God-Given Intelligence, 1691[7]

. . . I was not yet three years old when my mother sent off one of my sisters, older than I, to learn to read in one of those girls' schools that they call Amigas. Affection and mischief carried me after

---

[7]*Source:* Sor Juana wrote "La Respuesta" in 1691, but it was published for the first time in 1700 in Madrid in the first edition of volume 3 of her works. Sor Juana Inés de la Cruz, *The Answer/La Respuesta*, ed. and trans. Electa Arenal and Amanda Powell (New York: The Feminist Press, 1994), 49, 51.

her; and when I saw that they were giving her lessons, I so caught fire with the desire to learn that, deceiving the teacher (or so I thought), I told her that my mother wanted her to teach me also. She did not believe this, for it was not to be believed; but to humor my whim she gave me lessons. I continued to go and she continued to teach me though no longer in make-believe, for the experience undeceived her. I learned to read in such a short time that I already knew how by the time my mother heard of it. My teacher had kept it from my mother to give delight with a thing all done and to receive a prize for a thing done well. And I had kept still, thinking I would be whipped for having done this without permission. The woman who taught me (may God keep her) is still living, and she can vouch for what I say.

I remember that in those days, though I was as greedy for treats as children usually are at that age, I would abstain from eating cheese, because I heard tell that it made people stupid, and the desire to learn was stronger for me than the desire to eat—powerful as this is in children. Later, when I was six or seven years old and already knew how to read and write, along with all the other skills like embroidery and sewing that women learn, I heard that in Mexico City there were a University and Schools where they studied the sciences. As soon as I heard this I began to slay my poor mother with insistent and annoying pleas, begging her to dress me in men's clothes and send me to the capital to the home of some relatives she had there, so that I could enter the university and study. She refused, and was right in doing so; but I quenched my desire by reading a great variety of books that belonged to my grandfather, and neither punishment nor scoldings could prevent me. And so when I did go to Mexico City, people marveled not so much at my intelligence as at my memory and the facts I knew at an age when it seemed I had scarcely had time to learn to speak.

I began to study Latin, in which I took fewer than twenty lessons. And my interest was so intense, that although in women (and especially in the very bloom of youth) the natural adornment of the hair is so esteemed, I cut off four to six fingerlengths of my hair, measuring how long it had been before. And I made myself a rule if by the time it had grown back to the same length I did not know such and such a thing that I intended to study, then I would cut my hair off again to punish my dull-wittedness. And so my hair grew, but I did not yet know what I had resolved to learn, for it grew quickly and I learned slowly. Then I cut my hair right off to punish my dull-wittedness, for I did not think it reasonable that hair should cover a head

that was so bare of facts—the more desirable adornment. I took the veil because, although I knew I would find in religious life many things that would be quite opposed to my character (I speak of accessory rather than essential matters), it would, given my absolute unwillingness to enter into marriage, be the least unfitting and most decent state that I could choose, with regard to the assurance I desired of my salvation. For before this first concern (which is, at the last, the most important), all the impertinent little follies of my character gave way and bowed to the yoke. These were wanting to live alone and not wanting to have either obligations that would disturb my freedom to study or the noise of a community that would interrupt the tranquil silence of my books. These things made me waver somewhat in my decision until, being enlightened by learned people as to my temptation, I vanquished it with divine favor and took the state I so unworthily hold. I thought I was fleeing myself, but—woe is me!—I brought myself with me, and brought my greatest enemy in my inclination to study, which I know not whether to take as Heaven-sent favor or as a punishment. For when snuffed out or hindered with every [spiritual] exercise known to Religion, it exploded like gunpowder; and in my case the saying "privation gives rise to appetite" was proven true.

I went back (no I spoke incorrectly, for I never stopped)—I went on, I mean, with my studious task (which was to me peace and rest in every moment left over when my duties were done) of reading and still more reading, study and still more study, with no teacher besides my books themselves. What hardship it is to learn from those lifeless letters, deprived of the sound of a teacher's voice and explanations; yet I suffered all these trials most gladly for the love of learning. Oh, if only this had been done for the love of God, as was rightful, think what I should have merited! Nevertheless I did my best to elevate these studies and direct them to His service, for the goal to which I aspired was the study of Theology. Being a Catholic, I thought it an abject failing not to know everything that can in this life be achieved, through earthly methods, concerning the divine mysteries. . . .

Catalina de Erauso's Adventures Disguised as a Man in Seventeenth-Century Peru[8]

Chapter 3: From Panama she travels with her new master, Urquiza, the Trujillan merchant, to the port of Paita and the village of Saña.

I left Panama with new master, Juan de Urquiza, aboard a frigate bound for the port of Paita, where he was expecting a large shipment. But as we neared the port of Manta, we were overtaken by such foul weather that the ship capsized in a squall, and those who could swim—myself, my master, and some others—made it to shore. All the rest drowned. In Manta, we managed to find passage on one of the king's galleons, for a princely sum, and we headed for the port of Paita, where my master found his shipment as expected in a vessel belonging to a Captain Alonso Cerrato. He then charged me with the task of sending on the shipment in numerical order, and went on ahead.

I set myself to the task I had been given, unloading the goods and sending them on in the proper order. All the while my master was receiving the stuff in Saña, some sixty leagues away, and when I had finished unloading everything, I set out from Paita with the last few items to rejoin him.

When I arrived in Saña, my master gave me a warm welcome, delighted with the work I had done and with the deal itself, and straightaway he gave me two new outfits, one black and the other brightly colored. He set me up in one of his shops, placing in my care a great deal of property in the form of both goods and cash, all in all more than one hundred and thirty thousand *pesos'* worth, and then he wrote down in a book the various prices of the items and how I was to sell them. He left two slaves to assist me, and a black woman who was to cook for me, and indicated I was to spend three *pesos* on daily expenses, and having done this, he loaded up the rest of the goods and took them on to Trujillo, some thirty-two leagues away. . . .

Who would have guessed those tranquil days were numbered, or that trouble lay just around the

next corner! One Sunday, when I had gone to the theater and pulled up a chair to enjoy the show, a certain Reyes showed up, and placed his chair squarely in front of mine, and so close up I couldn't see a thing—I asked him if he wouldn't mind moving a bit to the side, he responded in a nasty tone, and I gave him back a little of the same. Then he told me I'd best disappear, or he'd be forced to cut my face wide open. Seeing as how I was weaponless, except for a short dagger, I made my exit, more than a little enraged, and with a couple of friends at my side who followed along trying to calm me down.

The next morning, a Monday, I was in the shop doing business a usual when I saw Reyes walk past the door, first one way and then the other. I closed the shop, grabbed up a knife, and went looking for a barber to grind the blade to a sawtoothed edge, and then, throwing on my sword—it was the first I ever wore—I went looking for Reyes and found him where he was strolling by the church with a friend.

I approached him from behind and said, "Ah, señor Reyes!"

He turned and asked, "What do you want?"

I said, "This is the face you were thinking of cutting up," and gave him a slash worth ten stitches.

He clutched at the wound with both hands, his friend drew his sword and came at me, and I went at him with my own. We met, I thrust the blade through his left side, and down he went.

I ran straight into the church, followed just as quickly by the sheriff, *don* Mendo de Quiñones, a knight of Alcántara, who dragged me out and carted me off to jail—the first I was ever in—and clapped me in irons and threw me in a cell. I got word to my master, thirty-two leagues off in Trujillo, and he came at once and spoke to the sheriff and, by dint of one thing or another, managed to get the irons removed. He continued to plead my case and I was returned to the church, and three months later, after

[8]*Source:* Catalina de Erauso, *Lieutenant Nun: Memoir of a Basque Transvestite in the New World/Catalina de Erauso*, trans. Michele Stepto and Gabriel Stepto (Boston: Beacon Press, 1996), 10–13, 16–17, 26, 28–29.

numerous appeals and maneuvers on the part of the head bishop, I was free to go.

At this point, my master told me he had figured out a way for me to get out of this mess without the law banishing me, or Reyes or one of his friends killing me, and it was this—I should marry *doña* Beatriz de Cardenas, whose niece was married to that no good Reyes himself, whose face I had cut up. Do this, he said, and everything would calm down.

Now, it should be noted that *doña* Beatriz de Cardenas was my master's mistress, and that what he had in mind was to hold on to the both of us—me for business and her for pleasure. And they must have worked the whole thing out between them, because after I had been taken back to the church I used to sneak out at night to the lady's house, and there she would caress me, and implore me, supposedly for fear of the law, not to go back to the church but to stay with her. Finally one night, she locked me in and declared that come hell or high water I was going to sleep with her—pushing and pleading so much that I had to smack her one and slip out of there.

I lost no time in telling my master this marriage just wasn't going to happen, that there wasn't any way in the world I was going to have a thing to do with it. He begged and pleaded and promised me mountains of gold, reminding me of the lady's beauty and talents, and how this would put an end to all that business with Reyes, and he mentioned other things too—still, I held my ground. Once he saw this was the case, he said I should go to Trujillo and set up shop there—and that is exactly what I did.

Chapter 5: From Trujillo to Lima.

With Trujillo behind me, and having traveled more than eighty leagues, I came to the city of Lima, capital of the opulent kingdom of Peru. . . .

At my master's bidding, I presented the letter to Diego de Solarte, a wealthy merchant who today is the chief consul in Lima. He received me in his house in a most kind and gracious manner, and a couple of days later put me in charge of his shop, with a yearly salary of six hundred *pesos*, and there I worked, much to his satisfaction and content.

But at the end of nine months, he told me I should think about making my living elsewhere, the reason being that there were two young ladies in

the house, his wife's sisters, and I had become accustomed to frolicking with them and teasing them—one, in particular, who had taken a fancy to me. And one day when she and I were in the front parlor, and I had my head in the folds of her skirt and she was combing my hair while I ran my hand up and down between her legs, Diego de Solarte happened to pass by the window, and spied us through the grate, just as she was telling me I should go to Potosí and seek my fortune, so that the two of us could be married. Solarte went to his office, called for me a little while later, asked for the books, took them, fired me, and left.

I found myself in a sticky spot, with no work and no friends. At that time in Lima, they were raising six companies to fight in Chile, and I joined one, signing on as a soldier, and immediately received the allotted salary of two hundred and eighty *pesos*. . . . I had a mind to travel and see a bit of the world.

And so, assigned to the company of Captain Gonzalo Rodriguez, I left Lima in a troop of one thousand six hundred men under the command of the field master Bravo de Sarabia, on the way to the city of Concepción, some five hundred and forty leagues off.

[*Catalina de Erauso joined the war against the Mapuche during her years in Chile and earned the military rank of lieutenant. She also killed a fellow soldier and a colonial official during a tavern brawl, and she mistakenly stabbed her brother fatally as a second at a nighttime duel, forcing her to flee Chile and head towards what is today Argentina.*]

Chapter 7: She leaves Concepción for Tucumán.

I set out along the coast, suffering a good deal, especially from thirst, for there was no fresh water to be had for miles around. Along the way, I fell in with two other soldiers, deserters both, and we continued on our way together, determined to die rather than let ourselves be arrested. We had our horses, our swords, our firearms, and the guidance of God on high. We ascended into the mountains, climbing for more than thirty leagues, and in all of them and the three hundred more we travelled, we didn't meet up with a single mouthful of bread, and only rarely some water or a clump of rough herbs, or some small animals, and now and then a gnarled root to keep us alive, and now and then an Indian who fled before us. [*The horses and her traveling companions died, and she was rescued on the other side of the Andes by ranch hands who took her, still disguised as a man, to their mistress's ranch.*]

The lady was a half-breed, the daughter of a Spaniard and an Indian woman, a widow and a good woman. When she saw how broken and friendless I was, she took pity on me, gave me a decent bed to sleep in, a good meal, and told me to rest—after which, I felt much better. The next morning, she fed me well, and seeing as I was so entirely destitute she gave me a decent cloth suit, and went on treating me handsomely, making me small gifts of this and that. The lady was well-off, with a good deal of livestock and cattle, and it seems that, since Spaniards were scarce in those parts, she began to fancy me as a husband for her daughter.

After I'd been there for eight days, the good woman said she wanted me to stay on and manage the place. I let her know how grateful I was, seeing how I was penniless, and told her I would serve her to the best of my abilities. And a couple of days later, she let me know it would be fine by her if I married her daughter—a girl as black and ugly as the devil himself, quite the opposite of my taste, which has always run to pretty faces. Still, I pretended to be overcome with happiness—so much good fortune, and for one so undeserving!—and I threw myself at her feet, telling her I was hers to dispose of as she pleased, as one she had snatched from the jaws of ruin, and I went on serving her as well as I knew how.

The woman tricked me out like a dandy and gave me full run of the house and the lands. After two months, we went into Tucumán for the wedding, and there I remained for another two months, delaying the thing on one pretext or another until, finally, I couldn't take it anymore and I stole a mule and cleared out—and that was the last they ever saw of me.

It was during this time in Tucumán that I had another adventure of the same sort. In the two months while I was putting off the Indian woman, I struck up a casual friendship with the bishop's secretary, who made quite a fuss over me and more than once invited me to his house, where we played cards and where I met a certain churchman, *don* Antonio de Cervantes, the bishop's vicar-general. This gentleman also took a fancy to me, and gave me gifts and wined me and dined me at his house until,

finally, he came to the point, and told me that he had a niece living with him who was just about my age, a girl of many charms, not to mention a fine dowry, and that he had a mind to see the two of us married—and so did she.

I pretended to be quite humbled by his flattering intentions. I met the girl, and she seemed good enough. She sent me a suit of good velvet, twelve shirts, six pairs of *Rouen* breeches, a collar of fine Dutch linen, a dozen handkerchiefs, and two hundred *pesos* in a silver dish—all of this a gift, sent simply as a compliment, and having nothing to do with the dowry itself.

Well, I received it all gratefully and composed the best thank-you I knew how, saying I was on fire for the moment when I would kiss her hand and throw myself at her feet. I hid as much of the stuff as I could from the Indian woman, and as for the rest I led her to believe it was a gift from *don* Antonio, something on the occasion of my marriage to her daughter, whom that gentleman had heard of and thought the world of—especially considering I was so crazy about her myself.

This is how things stood when I saddled up and vanished. And I have never heard exactly what became of the black girl or the little vicaress.

[*Her adventures continued in Potosí and other parts of Peru: she fought bandits, managed a train of llamas and Indian porters, raided Indian villages seeking gold dust, and ran afoul of the law many times for fighting. Her pride in her origin in the Basque region with its own language and culture brought fellow "Basqueros" to her aid several times. However, she was eventually cornered in Huamanga and escaped hanging for murder only by revealing her true identity—a woman and a runaway nun—to the local bishop. He claimed religious jurisdiction over her and returned her to a convent in 1617. Eventually news arrived from Spain that she had never professed as a nun and was thus free to leave. She left the life of a nun and returned to Spain in 1624.*]

Suggested Sources:

Catalina de Erauso's story fits into a larger story of Spanish outmigration and return told by Ida Altman in *Emigrants and Society: Extremadura and America* in the Sixteenth Century (Berkeley: University of California Press, 1989). Kathryn Burns and Elisa Sampson Vera Tudela explain that convents reproduced Spanish-dominated society. See Kathryn Burns, Colonial Habits: Convents and the Spiritual Economy of Cuzco, Peru (Durham, NC: Duke University Press, 1999); and Elisa Sampson Vera Tudela, Colonial Angels: Narratives of Gender and Spirituality in Mexico, 1580–1750 (Austin: University of Texas Press, 2000). On a nun who developed entrepreneurship, see Susan Soeiro, "Catarina de Monte Sinay: Nun and Entrepreneur," in Struggle and Survival in Colonial America, ed. David G. Sweet and Gary B. Nash (Berkeley: University of California Press, 1981). For gender and honor norms in the colonial world, see Lyman L. Johnson and Sonya Lipsett-Rivera, eds., The Faces of Honor: Sex, Shame, and Violence in Colonial Latin America (Albuquerque: University of New Mexico Press, 1998).

The remarkable life and writings of the convent-slave-turned-mystic Ursula de Jesús again demonstrate the power and protection that fame and a religious career could provide. See Nancy E. van Deusen, The Souls of Purgatory: The Spiritual Diary of a Seventeenth-Century Afro-Peruvian Mystic, Ursula de Jesús (Albuquerque: University of New Mexico Press, 2004). Octavio Paz offers a biography and analysis of Sor Juana in Sor Juana, or, The Traps of Faith, trans. Margaret Sayers Peden (Cambridge, MA: Harvard University Press, 1988). Director María Luisa Bemberg produced an excellent historical film of Sor Juana's life base on Paz's book and titled Yo, la peor de todas [I, the worst of all] (Argentina, 1990). Catalina de Erauso's story also found its way into film, most famously in Emilio Gómez Muriel's film starring María Félix as Catalina in La Monja Alférez [The Lieutenant Nun] (Mexico, 1944). The cross-dressing Lieutenant Nun as an icon of transgression and homoerotic desire is documented by Sherry Velasco in The Lieutenant Nun: Transgenderism, Lesbian Desire, & Catalina de Erauso (Austin: University of Texas Press, 2000).

Chapter 17

A "*Mestiza* in the Clothes of an Indian:" The Social Significance of Female Dress in Colonial Potosí

Jane Mangan, Davidson College

In late 1631, in the mining city of Potosí, Peru, Juana Payco fell ill, quickly worsened, and died suddenly, without leaving behind a will. Her personal assets were sizeable, and two different churches battled her grandnephews to inherit her estate.[1] To safeguard her belongings

during the legal wrangling, city officials conducted an inventory of the goods in her household. The legal

---

[1] A 1631–1633 lawsuit between the convent of San Agustín and the convent of the Company of Jesus over the ownership of the goods left by Juana Payco.

battle tells much about Church and family power dynamics; however, the inventory is most intriguing because it also reveals the politics of identity and material culture in seventeenth-century society. As with the poor Spaniard in Chapter 15, identity alone was no clear indicator of economic status. Despite being a property owner and having a modest estate, Payco was no Spanish *doña*;[2] rather she was a woman identified as a *mestiza en hábitos de india*, a rare category that linked gender and race.[3] Translated literally this term signified a woman who was a *mestizo*, born of Spanish and indigenous ancestry, but donned the "habit" of an indigenous woman. Payco's case revealed a woman of some means who chose to be identified (through dress and lifestyle) as someone in a theoretically lower station—an Indian woman. Why would she want to do that?

The dress of Potosí's indigenous women was remarkable. In 1600, a visiting Spanish priest, Fray Diego de Ocaña, described the female members of the *Jesuit cofradía*, or religious brotherhood, of the Niño Jesus: "[They] dressed in very fine silk patterned with velvet, and underneath the *azú* [*acsu*] a skirt better than the Spaniards'. The 'liquidas' [*llicllas*]—which are what they wear over their shoulders like shawls—of velvet and damask; and the *ñañaca*, which is the clothing that they wear over the head, of the same; the *chumbes*, which are what cinches the waist, are of their wool of many colors."[4] Clothing served as an unmistakable part of identity for these women, just as it comprised a distinctive part of Payco's inventory. Female garb drew heavily from pre-conquest tradition and consisted of an acsu (tunic), lliclla (shawl), chumbe (belt), and ñañaca (head covering). Naming the components of dress in *Quechua* reinforced their Andean identity. Prior to Spanish conquest, the

Andes had a highly developed system of textile production. A different quality cloth and distinct designs indicated status.[5] Clothing held intimate links to identity, both male and female. In the colonial era, the specialized definitions of clothing remained. Urban women of indigenous descent not only used style and quality of dress to identify themselves, but they also used clothing and textiles as a way to accumulate and preserve wealth. To Ocaña's surprise, these women wore a style of dress both sumptuous *and* distinctly non-European. Non-European garb that could be equated with relative economic status in a colonial city caught Ocaña's eye.

Throughout colonial Spanish America, material culture more generally served as an important marker of identity. What people wore, what people ate or drank, what people chose to adorn or fill their homes suggested links to European, indigenous, or African cultures. Programs of social control, whereby Spanish rulers dictated how indigenous peoples worked and lived based on their ethnic identity, relied on dress. Some changed their identity by changing their dress. Indigenous men who hoped to avoid paying Indians' mandatory tribute, for instance, changed clothing to appear *mestizo* or Spanish. For women with some Spanish blood, dressing as an indigenous woman could have its benefits in the marketplace. *Mestiza* women who passed as indigenous women would gain exemption from the royal *alcabala*, or sales taxes, on goods they sold.[6]

This was especially important in the context of colonial Potosí, which had a large Indian population and a booming market due to the silver mines there. Potosí in this era was one of the New World's most extraordinary cities, growing as an urban center from 1545 onward to 160,000 by the

---

[2]An honorific title showing respect to an elite, important, or high-born woman.

[3]On these categories, see Jane E. Mangan, *Trading Roles: Gender, Ethnicity, and the Urban Economy in Colonial Potosí* (Durham, NC: Duke University Press, 2005) 129, 152–154.

[4]Fray Diego de Ocaña, *Un viaje fascinante por la América hispana del siglo XVI*, ed. Fray Arturo Alvarez (Madrid: STVDIVM, 1996), 200.

[5]For instance, *cumbi* (also spelled *cumbe*) referred to an expertly woven cloth of the finest, softest wool worn by the ruling elite.

[6]On the issue of nonpayment of *alcabalas* by indigenous traders, see Martin Minchom, *The People of Quito, 1690–1810: Change and Unrest in the Underclass* (Boulder, CO: Westview Press, 1993), especially chap. 5, 62–63.

early 1600s.[7] After the discovery of silver in its Rich Hill at some 13,000 feet of altitude, the city bustled and boasted markets, churches, and a variety of domestic dwellings ranging from impressive two-story stone homes with imposing facades to small, thatched huts. Potosí's location in the heart of the Andean Altiplano and use of indigenous laborers for mine work bestowed indigenous influence in the city. This example also draws attention, as does the Otomí case in Chapter 23, to the fundamental role of indigenous labor and identity in colonial cities, even though urban sites typically connoted Spanish identity. In Potosí's markets and stores, in the neighborhoods, and in cultural institutions like *cofradías*, indigenous networks were powerful, providing the city with significant social differentiation among indigenous people. Ultimately, Potosí's thriving economy and cultural norms worked to complicate the powerful draw of Hispanicization. Potosí's unique context allowed women, especially well-situated indigenous women like Payco, to lead productive lives.

Several more details about Payco emerge in the lengthy judicial case that accompanied the inventory. Payco was native to Potosí, with parents *and* grandparents buried there. She owned a well-furnished house in a central location close to the main market.[8] She was a member of two *cofradías* and, at one time, made a monetary donation to the Jesuits' Niño Jesus, the very *cofradía* observed by Ocaña. Between 1624 and 1627, Payco held the important position of prioress of the *cofradía* of Nuestra Señora de la Soledad. During her tenure, she oversaw the collection of 1,500 *pesos* worth of alms. Although Payco had no husband and, at least

as far as this record reveals, no children living in 1631, she created a strong kin network. She raised her two nephews, Thomas and Salvador Quispe, in the absence of their mother. In addition, Payco's household included orphans she welcomed; some worked for her as servants. All of these individuals held her in esteem. Further, Payco served as a godmother for two of Juana Arnanca's daughters. Not surprisingly, numerous men and women came and went from her home to pay respects during her brief illness.[9]

Evidence in the documents shows involvement in the urban economy, especially related to textiles. Pawned items, again in cloth, suggest business activity.[10] Moreover, Payco's niece, Madalena Taquima, recounted that she assisted her aunt in buying and reselling goods. The link between her identity and her economic roles and successes in a colonial city is a critical one. In Potosí, *mestiza* women who engaged in the urban economy drew on indigenous identity not only for the right to claim tax exemptions, but also because the urban economy served as the domain of indigenous women. Spanish women ran taverns (*chicherías*) or grocery stores (*pulperías*), but they did not, in Potosí, engage in large-scale market transactions of subsistence goods, the mild stimulant coca leaf, clothing, or wax. Indigenous women did, and they thrived financially.

The example presented in this primary document complicates assumptions that racial passing or acculturation functioned primarily as processes that help individuals assimilate with the dominant social and racial groups. Scholars argue that the adoption of Spanish clothing, jewelry, and hairstyle "became destabilizing practices that blurred the social classifications imposed by the colonial order" because skin tone could not function as an automatic determinant of race, especially between Spanish and *mestiza* women.[11] Non-Spaniards could use dress to challenge social

---

[7]Seventeenth-century population estimates drawn from: "Descripción de la villa y minas de Potosí. Año de 1603." In *Relaciones Geográficas de Indias*: Perú, edited by Marcos Jiménez de la Espada. Vols 183–185 of BIBLIOTECA DE AUTORES ESPAÑOLES DESDE LA FORMACION DEL LENGUAJE HASTA NUESTROS DIAS. Madrid: Atlas, 1965, p. 377–378; Bartolomé Arzáns de Orsúa y Vela, *Tales of Potosí*, ed. R. C. Padden, trans. Frances M. López-Morillas (Providence, RI: Brown University Press, 1975), xxiv; Dr. Don Joseph Baquijano, "Historia del descubrimiento del Cerro de Potosí," *Mercurio Peruano* 7 (January-April 1793): 28–48.

[8]ANB.EC, document 1633.4: fol. 36–36v.

[9]ANB.EC, document 1633.4, fol. 67v.
[10]ANB.EC, document 1633.4, fol. 67v.
[11]María Melendez, "Visualizing Difference: The Rhetoric of Clothing in Colonial Spanish America," in *The Latin American Fashion Reader*, ed. Regina A. Root (New York: Berg, 2005), 24. See also Melendez, 25–30.

An indigenous man and woman at work in a mid-eighteenth century blacksmith shop in Trujillo, Peru. The bishop commissioned the watercolor paintings by local artists as a way to better understand and govern his district. What did the painting tell viewers about Indians' work and about men's and women's economic roles? What about their manner of dress when compared to Juana de Payco's dress from an earlier era and a city far to the south? What other ethnic markers are associated with these Indians?

Source: *Forge*, 1783 watercolor by Jaime Martínez Compañon. Picture Desk, Inc./Kobal Collection.

in a culturally indigenous manner and wearing the acsu and lliclla, offered a life experience with elements of relative power and prestige including leadership of a *cofradía*, significant social networks, property ownership, and impressive savings of silver *pesos*. Her inventory challenges the common wisdom about the politics of race and gender in seventeenth-century Potosí and elsewhere in colonial Spanish America. And, when viewed alongside the examples of Sor Juana Inés de la Cruz, Catalina de Erauso, Juana de Mayo, or *doña* Ana María, it highlights the diversity of experiences even for those who shared gender or ethnic identity. Only by studying this remarkable diversity of identities and experiences alongside the shared laws and power structures can historians glimpse the workings of colonial society.

Questions to Consider:

1. Analyze the clothing and textiles in this inventory according to item, type of cloth, and quantity. What was the significance of these items as markers of ethnic identity?

2. Find additional examples of colonial material culture. What did Juana Payco have in her home at the time of her death and what clues do those possessions offer about how she lived and worked in a colonial city?

3. Consider the relationship between the inventory and Juana Payco's identity as a *mestiza en hábitos de india*. What was the relatedness of gender and ethnicity in this particular category? How does this unique category highlight the experiences or choices of individuals or categories unanticipated within colonial power structures?

4. How did Juana Payco's inventory relate to the assertion of this section that "despite the blurring of some ethno-racial lines, hierarchies endured?" As you ponder these questions, consider the inventory along with the *Romance* or *doña* Ana María's will in order to think comparatively about race and hierarchy in colonial Latin America.

structure by "moving up." Juana Payco's lived experience, as read through her inventory, allows us to rethink this notion. If one possessed some characteristics identifiable as *mestiza*, supposedly higher up the social ladder than *india*, why move "down" as it were, into the indigenous sector of the population? For a *mestiza* like Juana Payco, living

Lawsuit between the Monastery of San Agustín and the Jesuits over the Ownership of Goods Left by Juana Payco, Called the *Lunareja, mestiza* en *habitos de india,* Who Died Without Leaving a Will in Potosí[12]

In the Villa of Potosí on December 27, 1631 don Fernando de Saavedra Monsalve, magistrate and judge of the estates of the deceased in this Villa, said that it has come to his attention how Juana Payco who was called La Lunareja *mestiza en habitos de india* died intestate without leaving a will.[13] And to know and verify the estate and heirs that she left, I order the present scribe with Juan Martin Navarro, interpreter, go to the house of the aforementioned and take inventory of the estate of the aforementioned, and [that] they place the estate [goods] in deposit with a reliable person who, obviously, will hold them until something else is ordered, and as such I order and sign, *don* Fernando de Saavedra Monsalve, before me Antonio de Jaen Orellana your majesty's scribe.

In the Villa of Potosí on the said day, month, and year named in the compliance of the said act in the houses of residence where Juana Payco, *india* deceased, died, in front of me the present scribe and witnesses, Juan Martin Navarro, interpreter, inventoried the goods of the aforementioned in the following form and fashion.

- First a canopy of sackcloth
- A wooden bed frame
- Two mattresses
- Two blankets
- Another blanket
- Four wax statues
- Three of said {wax statues} half-finished
- A broken mortar
- An altar with statues and two painted canvases
- A cinched cloth containing raisins

- Another two blankets
- Two old green skirts[14]
- Three old shirts[15]
- One chumbe[16]
- One sack of peanuts
- Three sacks of corn
- One-half sack of *chuño.*[17]
- Also, one closed box that did not appear to have a key. It was opened and the following was found inside
- Three small bags with silver and 492 *pesos* were found inside
- A bedspread of blue *cumbe*[18]
- A black Indian cloak[19]
- A new acsu[20] of new cotton
- A lliclla[21] of the same
- An acsu of old cumbe and a striped lliclla
- Two black lliclas striped with colors
- One black acsu striped with colors with a lliclla of Jauxa[22]
- Another black acsu and lliclla
- Four nanacas[23]
- One brown lliclla
- One cotton acsu
- One purple velveteen cloak
- One white striped shirt[24]
- One old blue skirt[25]

---

[12]*Source:* Archivo Nacional de Bolivia. Expedientes Coloniales, document 1633.4. *Lunareja* was a nickname for a person with several moles on her face. *Quechua* words in the original have been left in *Quechua* and designated with (Q). All other words in the document were written in Spanish and have been translated to English.
[13]Minor punctuation changes made in order to make the document more readable. Brackets are used for any inserted words.

---

[14]*Faldellines* in the original.
[15]*Camissas* in the original.
[16]Textile belt, typically wool (Q).
[17]Freeze-dried potatoes (Q).
[18]Finely woven native textile, also spelled *cumbi* (Q).
[19]*Manta,* a Spanish term, in the original.
[20]Basic dress worn by native Andean women in the form of a long tunic (Q).
[21]Shawl worn by native Andean women (Q).
[22]Jauxa or Jauja refers to cloth produced in modern-day Junín, Peru.
[23]Head covering worn by native Andean women (Q).
[24]*Camiseta* in the original.
[25]*Faldelin* in the original.

- A bale of Quito cloth[26]
- One cloth sack and in it thirty colored skeins of wool large and small
- Also two chumbes of colored wool
- Another white chumbe
- Three silver *topos*[27] with their bells
- One pillow with its old cushion
- One black cumbe acsu
- Also, a box was opened with a key that Juan Marcos de Vargas gave, and in it the following was found
- In a small trunk, two *topillos*[28] with gold enamel with their bells, the one with a small emerald.
- Another golden *topillo* with blue enamel
- Glasses with their box of gilded silver in a velvet bag
- A purple silk chumbe
- Small pearls and an eagle of blue glass
- Also two small silver topos with their bells were found
- One silver bowl and cup
- A small silver clamp, broken
- Three *pesos* in *reales* of eight
- Two women's shirtfronts embroidered in black silk
- One pillow and pillowcase embroidered in black silk
- Five lliclllas of colored *abasca*[29]
- Two ñañacas abasca
- Another ñañaca of the same
- Two acsus of old abasca
- Four acsus of cumbe
- Half acsu of cumbe
- Four ñañacas of cumbe
- One black llicla adorned with stripes
- One woman's blouse of white cloth
- Seven and a half *varas* of *Rouen* cloth
- One *Rouen* bedsheet
- Some old cloth sleeves[30]

- Also, another box was opened with a key brought by the aforementioned and in it was found the following:
- Two cups, one large and the other small
- A woman's shirt
- One Indian shirt[31] of abasca
- Colored glass beads
- Also, a small box was opened and in it was found the following
- A bracelet of pearls and blue garnets
- Five medals of Our Lady of Copacabana
- Five medals of Our Señor, two golden and three lame.
- A small sack and in it 28 *pesos* and one-half *real*
- Three skeins of colored wool
- Also, a blanket was found in the said house
- Also, in one room three sacks of oregano were found
- Two and a half loads of magueys
- Eleven limbs for rafters
- All of which said goods were impounded and hidden on behalf of the said Juana Payco, Indian deceased, and deposited with Agustin Guaman, Indian *ladino* in Spanish tongue, professional silk dealer. . . .

Suggested Sources:

To help expand readers' analysis of the Juana Payco inventory, see publications on Potosí, indigenous women's colonial experiences, and the meanings of dress. An anthropological study of 1980s Arequipa, Peru, and the nearby Colca valley discussed the cultural and political significance of women's traditional dress (*bordados*). See Blenda Femenías in *Gender and the Boundaries of Dress in Contemporary Peru* (Austin: University of Texas Press, 2005). Kimberly Gauderman's *Women's Lives in Colonial Quito, Gender, Law, and Economy in Spanish America* (Austin: University of Texas Press, 2003) provides a broad study of the legal, cultural, and economic situation of women under colonial patriarchy. For Potosí's history and the function of

---

[26]From Quito.
[27]Pins, typically made of silver, used to fasten the *llicla*, or shawl, of native Andean women (Q).
[28]See previous note, *topillo* is a small version of the same pin.
[29]*Abasca* (Q) was a common woolen cloth produced in the Andes and distinguished from the finely woven *cumbi*, or *cumbe*, by its coarse nature.
[30]*Mangas*.

[31]*Camiseta*.

gender and ethnic identity in markets, see Jane Mangan, *Trading Roles: Gender, Ethnicity and Economy in Colonial Potosí* (Durham, NC: Duke University Press, 2005). On gender and race in the conquest, see Karen Powers' work emphasizing indigenous and *mestiza* women, *Women in the Crucible of Conquest: The Gendered Genesis of Spanish American Society, 1500–1600* (Albuquerque: University of New Mexico Press, 2005). An innovative analysis that moves beyond static colonial labels of identity is found in Stuart B. Schwartz and Frank Salomon, "New Peoples and New Kinds of People, Adaptation, Readjustment, and Ethnogenesis in South American Indigenous Societies (Colonial Era)," in *The Cambridge History of the Native Peoples of the Americas*, vol. III, pt. 2 (Cambridge: Cambridge University Press, 1999).

Primary source materials related to colonial Potosí and to the long-standing theme of Andean market women offer distinct perspectives. A 1551 discussion of Potosí and its markets appears in Pedro Cieza de León's travel account. See Pedro Cieza de León, *The Incas*, ed. and intro. Victor Wolgang von Hagen, trans. Harriet de Onis (Norman: University of Oklahoma Press, 1959). Bartolomé Arzáns de Orsúa y Vela, an eighteenth-century native of Potosí, wrote about his beloved hometown in Bartolomé Arzáns de Orsúa y Vela, *Tales of Potosí*, ed. R. C. Padden, trans. Frances M. López-Morillas (Providence, RI: Brown University Press, 1975). Sofía Velasquez's autobiography offers a source on twentieth-century market vendors. See Sofía Velasquez with Hans Buechler and Judith-Maria Buechler, *The World of Sofía Velasquez: The Autobiography of a Bolivian Market Vendor* (New York: Columbia University Press, 1996). The PBS Television Americas Series (Program 4 "Mirrors of the Heart") features the *pollera*-style dress of indigenous women in La Paz in a discussion of identity in the modern day.

Chapter 18

To Change the Fate of All Women: Charges of Witchcraft against Juana de Mayo

Leo J. Garofalo, Connecticut College

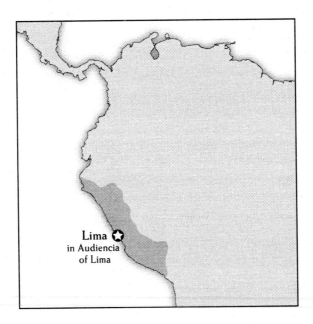

Lima
in Audiencia
of Lima

The Indian woman Juana de Mayo had heard that people were speaking badly of her to the ecclesiastical investigators. The investigators were busy holding hearings in her neighborhood with anyone who could help them expose superstitious or idolatrous beliefs and root out the ritual use of coca leaf in Lima's multiethnic parishes. To clear her name and ease her conscience about a few

questionable acts she had witnessed and even participated in, she voluntarily appeared before investigators and explained the rituals she had viewed. She
described how the other women sent her out to buy
the mild stimulant coca leaves for these clandestine
gatherings usually involving only a couple of other
women. This testimony given in Spanish was
recorded by scribes along with the testimony given
by other Indian, Spanish, and *mestiza*[1] women already under arrest and being held in the Church
investigator's jails.

Eventually several women pointed to Juana de
Mayo as the ringleader, a skilled ritual specialist
who ran these gatherings. They insisted that she
was not a peripheral figure; they claimed she was
an herbalist renowned for cleansing and preparing
materials with magical properties. Juana de
Mayo's local reputation brought many women,
and occasionally a man, to her for help. After her
arrest on charges of superstition and practicing
witchcraft, the investigating judge interrogated
her, and she gave fuller accounts of these ceremonies and other ritual acts. Juana de Mayo and
the other women who were questioned along with
her provide voices not usually heard in the historical
record or in the history text.

Andean and *mestizo* people—and women in
general—speaking about their experiences under
colonialism and about life in colonial cities can be
hard to find. Historians struggle to find people in
the past who left some record of what they
thought, explained the motives for their actions,
or gave hints about how they understood and
crossed class and ethnic lines. High indigenous
nobility and their *mestizo* or bicultural children
wrote or dictated some important accounts in the
early colonial period: The leader of the *Inca* resistance, Tito Cusi Yupanqui, and the *mestizo*
Garcilaso de la Vega (who called himself "the
Inca") figure prominently among the elite native
Andean males who succeeded in making their

voices heard.[2] Non-nobles are harder to find. Two
remarkable exceptions date from the early 1600s:
The Christian indigenous chronicler Felipe
Guaman Poma de Ayala wrote a book-length letter
to the king in Spanish and *Quechua* and anonymous
authors in an Andean town recorded local customs
and stories in *Quechua* in the *Huarochirí Manuscript*
(see Chapter 8). Guaman Poma created an unparalleled history of *Inca* rulers, Spanish conquest, and
colonizers' abuses. While requesting reforms and
an end to bad government, Guaman Poma lent insight into how people under colonial rule felt torn
between the new faith and the old ways. In a similar fashion, the authors of the *Huarochirí Manuscript* documented local history, myths, and
villagers' struggles to fully embrace the new religion and let go of the old allegiances. In both
cases, the authors are men and members of the
local elite, maybe even *kurakas* (ethnic chiefs), or
at least they are aspirants to these positions of formal political power. *Witchcraft* trials and the
campaigns to extirpate *idolatries* bring more fully
into view both elite and common indigenous
people, males and females.

If read with care and while developing a sense
for the most likely distortions and fabrications,
sources from the ecclesiastical investigations and the
Spanish *Inquisition* can be incredibly revealing of
both official beliefs and fears and the thoughts and
actions of those accused and questioned. The much
more secretive Spanish *Inquisition* technically held
no jurisdiction over Indians as relative newcomers to
the faith; in Lima, the *Inquisition* prosecuted those
accused of secretly practicing Judaism, *witchcraft*,
bigamy, blasphemy, Protestantism, solicitation in
the confessional, and popular Christianity. The local
bishops authorized and supervised the ecclesiastical
investigations into the beliefs and practices of all
people living within selected parishes, including

[1]A *mestiza* woman or a *mestizo* man possessed both European and
indigenous heritage. In seventeenth-century Lima, ethnic, rather
than purely biological, markers categorized people.

[2]Holding out in the mountains against Spanish domination, Tito
Cusi Yupanqui described the brutality of the conquest and his
reasons for resisting Spanish rulers and their *Inca* collaborators in
a letter he dictated to a Spanish priest. With an *Inca* noblewoman
as a mother and a Spanish conquistador as a father, Garcilaso de la
Vega became a Renaissance gentleman, writer, and warrior in
Spain against the *moriscos*.

Indians. These investigations, called the "campaigns to extirpate *idolatries*," usually struck rural areas such as Huarochirí, where the parish priest-turned-investigator used the information recorded in the manuscript to investigate and punish his Indian parishioners (and build a successful career in the Church). However, ecclesiastical investigations could focus on urban centers or reach into them in pursuit of the accused and their associates. Such was the case in the 1660s, as investigators began their work in Lima, giving us an unparalleled view of urban men and women's roles, interactions, and thoughts.

In these investigations and in the *Inquisition* trials, ritual specialists like Juana de Mayo appear in each of the ethno-cultural groupings present in the Americas: Iberians, Africans, and native peoples. They played a special problem-solving role at the local level in their neighborhoods and towns and within their networks of relatives, acquaintances, and clients. People often looked to them to find ways to bridge and blend these traditions that encompassed beliefs about the supernatural, practical medicine, medicinal plants, incantations, and prayers. Although quite specialized as the document that follows shows, their work drew upon and improvised within the body of popular culture. As such it often clashed with official practices and Church dogma, and it could threaten the authority of elites and officials and state institutions to intervene to mediate conflicts or control knowledge and power. Thus, wherever it appears, "*witchcraft*"—or whatever is labeled as *witchcraft*—usually exposes the innerworkings of society; the sources and beneficiaries of formal and informal power become visible.

In a chapter on sorcery, Indian chronicler Felipe Guaman Poma de Ayala labeled these: sorcerer of dreams, sorcerer of fire, and the sorcerer who sucks (out the illness or magic). By the 1600s, the Christianized Guaman Poma viewed the Spanish extirpators as too harsh and motivated more by greed or feuds with parishioners than by true Christian fervor. Why does he label these ritual specialists in this way and depict them as he does? Which elements of the drawings seem European and which seem Andean? How do they relate to the Juana de Mayo's case that follows?

Source: The Royal Library/Felipe Guaman Poma de Ayala, *Nueva corónica y buen gobierno* (1615). Drawing 109. *Llulla layqha umu*, deceitful sorcerers and witches fol. 279 [281].

Questions to Consider:

1. Explain what parts of the testimony seem believable and what parts might be distortions. What can be learned from the distortions or silences in the document?

2. Using these testimonies and the summary of the charges, what can be said about the ways men and women and people from different ethno-racial groups interacted?

3. What authorities called *witchcraft* could be deemed the last resort of those with no influence or power in society, or it could be seen as an informal or officially illegitimate form of influencing others and exercising real power. What evidence for both sides can be found in these excerpts? Which is more convincing in this case?

Case of Witchcraft against Juana de Mayo and Her Collaborators[3]

Juana de Mayo Comes Before the Ecclesiastical Court to Clear Her Conscience

In Lima, on October 31, 1668, Juana de Mayo, an Indian native of the village of Ica and widow of the late Ignacio de Lesus, appeared before *don* Juan Sarmiento de Vivero, ecclesiastical judge and investigator. She lives in front of the Hospital of the Holy Spirit [sailors' hospital] in the house of *doña* Mariana de Espinosa. As a God-fearing and Christian woman in order to clear her conscience she came to declare that she allowed a *mestiza* named María de la Cruz to cast spells and practice superstition in her house. She allowed her to chew coca in her house, and she went to buy the herbs for the baths given [to other women] by the *mestiza* Maria de la Cruz who is now under arrest in the jail of the *visita* [ecclesiastical investigation]. And the herbs were *mastranto* and rue with basil.[4] And she also went for *aguardiente* and wine, and she left the women shut up in her room.[5] And she went outside to sow. [Asked who she left shut up in her room.] She said the *mestiza* Marota and a young Spanish woman named *doña* Josepha to receive the baths. [Asked for how long she had been shutting them in.] She said for one year. Asked for what effect they gave the baths with these herbs. She said Maria de la Cruz said that they were so that the men would love the women bathed. Asked if she knows of any other acts of superstition by the *mestiza* Maria de la Cruz. She said she knows of nothing else. She is more or less sixty years old. She does not know how to sign her name. She adds that once when she was going in company of Maria de la Cruz and a *zamba* [Afro-indigenous person] Maria Nicolasa who is also in jail, and the zamba was accompanied by a young soldier named *don* Fernando, whose surname

she does not know, they captured a lizard. They smeared the lizard's blood [document's paper is broken] on Maria Nicolasa and *don* Fernando saying that it was good against scrofula.[6] And she swears that everything she said and declared was true.

She does not sign.

Juana de Mayo Returns to Denounce Others and Herself

In Lima, on November 11, 1668 before *don* Juan Sarmiento de Vivero . . . Juana de Mayo, a *ladina* Indian woman who understands Spanish so she does not need an interpreter, made a declaration to relieve her conscience. [She swears to tell the truth.] She declares that more or less a year ago a woman called *doña* Josepha de Araja . . . introduced her to a woman called *doña* Andrea who lived with her in a room, and that *doña* Andrea asked Juana de Mayo for some powders to make the men love her. As she did not know anything about spells she gave *doña* Andrea cheese with ground avocado [pit] to please her and received a chicken in exchange for the powders. And *doña* Josepha gave her some powders made from red seashells they call *mollo*[7] so that men would desire her. And asking her how they gave the women the powders, and why she gave them to *doña* Josepha. She said she gave them to her innocently so that the men would desire her. And she declared that *doña* Josepha gave her a magnet to decorate, and she decorated it with pearls, coral, small pins, a half *real*, two grains of white corn, and two of dark corn. She asked her to conjure with it, but she did not because she does not know how to conjure. Asked why she decorated it. She said that she decorated it so that men would desire *doña* Josepha. She declared that when *doña* Josepha and the *mestiza* Maria de la Cruz

---

[3]*Source:* Archivo Arzobispal de Lima. Hechicerías. L. 6. Exp. 8. "Causa de hechicería contra Juana de Mayo, India, nativa de Ica, viuda de Ignacio de Lesus," 1668-6, Lima, 63 fols.
[4]Mastranto was any one of the aromatic plants of the *labiadas* family used for medicine and against parasites.
[5]*Aguardiente* was sugarcane rum.

[6]A tubercular swelling of the lymph nodes in the neck considered curable by the touch of royalty.
[7]The reddish spondylus shell, or spiny oyster, from warmer seawaters to the north was a prized Native Andean ceremonial item used in rituals and sacrifices.

who is at present in the [ecclesiastical court's jail] sent her to buy coca, so that they would not steal something from her she told them to stay out of the belongings in her room because she had a snake that would tell her if they took anything. She declared that she only said this to scare them because she cannot look at snakes, not even dead ones. She also said that she tricked a *mulata* called Anita who belongs to a nun from the Santa Clara convent with the avocado pit powders because she came to ask her for them, and she gave them to her so that men would want her if she threw the powders on their heads. She showed a piece of stick that she said she had given women to boil in water to apply with *alumbre*[8] to tighten their lower parts. Depending on what she gave them, they paid her a one-once silver coin, four *reales*, or two *reales*. The *mulata* Anita gave her four *reales*. . . . She stated that she has nothing more to declare and that this is the truth and is common public knowledge as she promised to tell the truth. She affirmed it and ratified it after it was read to her. She is sixty years old more or less and cannot sign.

The Declaration by the *Mestiza* Maria de la Cruz

[*After reviewing the declaration of Juana de Mayo, the judge decided that she was not telling the full truth. He resolved to question Maria de la Cruz about the life and habits of Juana de Mayo. De la Cruz was brought from the jail and sworn in on January 17, 1669.*] Asked if she knows a woman named Juana de Mayo. She said that she knows the woman named Juana de Mayo who is an Indian. And that is what she gave for an answer. Asked where the Indian woman named Juana de Mayo lived. She said that the Indian Juana de Mayo lived in the Street of the Holy Spirit [Hospital] just past a blacksmith shop as if we are going to the Plaza. Asked how long she knew Juana de Mayo. She said since she was thirteen or fourteen years old, and she knows her because she is her aunt although she does not know where the family connection is because she

was brought as a little child from her *tierra*[9] and raised among the nuns until she was thirteen or fourteen years old. Asked if she sometimes shut herself up in the house of Juana de Mayo to chew coca leaf. She answered that as a Christian she wanted to tell the truth about what she was asked. Once in her aunt *doña* Maria de Borja's bedroom, she met Juana de Mayo, and she took Maria de la Cruz to her house, where she met a man who made her fall [had intimate relations with her] and then left her there and went away. And since it was her first communication with the man, she felt bad that he had left her.

Coming and seeing her sad and weighed down, Juana de Mayo told her not to worry that she would remedy her and to give her two *reales*. Maria de la Cruz gave her the two *reales*, and Juana de Mayo took her to the San Sebastian neighborhood to a house where they sold coca, and she bought two *reales* of coca. They returned together to Juana de Mayo's house and spreading a reed mat on the floor and bringing a *real* of wine, Juana de Mayo divided the coca in two, placing half beside Maria de la Cruz and half beside her. They chewed the coca, and at about twelve midnight Juana de Mayo told her not to be afraid because she was going to ask for signs, and that if she was not interested she could go to bed. She said she was not afraid, with that Juana de Mayo that they should see all the signs. She asked for signs that the man, who was called Martin, would come back. The signs could be the braying of a mule, the neighing of a mare, the crowing of a rooster, sounds like castanets on the roof, or a stone thrown at the door [she heard all of these sounds, and Juana de Mayo promised Martin would return the next day]. And although it was true that the man Martin did not return the day after they read her fortune, he came a day later and stayed with her for eight days and then left and never returned.

Asked if on some day Juana de Mayo shut herself up in her house to chew coca with a Spanish woman named *doña* Josepha. She said that Juana de Mayo never got together with *doña* Josepha to chew coca at her house. What happened was that more or less a year ago being broken and destitute for having spent three

---

[8]Folk remedies recommended *piedra alumbre* (aluminum and potassium sulfate) to remedy the loss of virginity.

[9]Hometown or home region.

years sick in bed she [Maria de la Cruz] went one day to find Juana de Mayo. She met Juana de Mayo a block after the street where they sell the cloaks, and she told Juana de Mayo that she had gone to find her to remedy her many misfortunes because they said she was bewitched. Juana de Mayo answered that she could not do anything then because she was going to the house of a *señora* to tend to her because Juana de Mayo had raised her and called her daughter. Juana de Mayo persuaded her to come along. [*They went to the house of doña Josepha, a twenty-five-year-old Spanish woman with a crippled hand.*] Upon entering *doña* Josepha's room, she heard her say to Juana de Mayo, "Mamita, you're here. I've been waiting hours." Juana de Mayo asked her if they had gone to the market and if they had it there. *Doña* Jospeha responded that she had not bought it, but that she would send the slave flying to get it while they sat down to lunch. And she saw how *doña* Josepha sent a black slave boy to the house of a female barber (*barbera*) who sold coca for two *reales* worth of coca. *Doña* Josepha served them a lunch of roast meat and preserves, and when the slave brought the two *reales* of coca in a basket hanging from his arm, they sat down to chew the three of them and another woman who she does not know. Juana de Mayo said that first they must [read the signs] for *doña* Josepha and for the other Spanish woman, and they sent for one *real* worth of wine which Juana de Mayo sprinkled on the coca leaves. Juana de Mayo made a ball out of the coca leaves and put them in her mouth, and Maria de la Cruz heard her say that *doña* Josepha was very dirty like a pig and that she must be cleaned meaning that she was bewitched. And she heard *doña* Josepha talking with Juana de Mayo saying, "yes Mamita, I see. What cure will I need?" And Juana de Mayo responded that a bath was necessary. She saw *doña* Josepha give Juana de Mayo money to buy what was needed for the bath.

Juana de Mayo went to the Plaza [*Lima's main market was in the main square*], and when she returned from the Plaza she had a little bundle of flowers, a half *real* of white corn, *junquillo* [*an herb*], apples, and a new clay basin. The next day they borrowed a mule and went to the Valley of Surquillo on mule back, and they gathered herbs from the fields of diverse kinds among which she recognized *mastranzo* and *tapatapa*. They returned to Juana de Mayo's house

where she boiled the six kinds of herbs she brought home in a special pot for that purpose with a *real* of new, unseasoned wine and the flowers, apples, and junquillo that she bought in the plaza the day before. And from this potage Juana de Mayo gave her [Maria de la Cruz] a little bit and told her to wash her face with it. And she washed her face with it. Asked why she washed her face with the potage. She said she washed her face with it to remove the curse placed upon her and that she had to wash not only her face, but also her arms, thighs, and secret parts. . . . She went back to Juana de Mayo's house and begged her to cure her, and Juana de Mayo shut her in her house for a month. They chewed coca in the corral, and before chewing the coca that sometimes was a *real* and a half's worth and other times two *reales* of coca, Juana de Mayo conjured it putting the coca on her lap and speaking some words that she did not understand. Even though she begged Juana de Mayo to teach her, Juana de Mayo did not want to teach her, saying it was not the time, that she was too young.

. . . Asked if she had seen or heard Juana de Mayo perform magic other than that she performed for her or for *doña* Josepha de Araya. She said that one day Juana de Mayo was angry at her daughter because she said her soul was condemned to the inferno because she had done harm to an Indian *barbero* [*barbers cut hair, shaved, and let blood*] called Juan Ramos because he had fought with Juana de Mayo's daughter named Maria de la Assension [Ascent to God] and with Juana de Mayo's son-in-law called Nicolas. . . . She had done harm to Juan Ramos at her daughter and son-in-law's behest that he would be destroyed, have to sell his shop, and work for others like the poorest of artisans. [*And it came to pass according to Maria de la Cruz.*] Asked if she had seen on other occasions that Juana de Mayo committed other acts of superstitious *witchcraft*[10] or conjured with some words. She answered that once when she was a young girl and in the company of Juana de Mayo she met a woman named *doña* Geronima whose surname she does not know but who lived in the San Lázaro neighborhood. Juana de Mayo gave Maria de

---

[10]The interrogating judge invents a word here by combining *supersticiones* (superstitions) with *hechicerias* (witchcraft) to create "supercherias."

la Cruz some powders in a paper to take to *doña* Geronima, and she put them in the food and gave it to her husband, her mother-in-law, and her father-in-law. Juana de Mayo told her this was so something bad would happen to *doña* Geronima's husband so he would be sent to Chile.[11] As for the conjuring and the words that she heard Juana de Mayo say, she begged Juana de Mayo to tell her the words she spoke to the coca when she conjured. Juana de Mayo told her that the words she said to the coca that she had to chew were, *mama palla linda mia* [*my pretty Indian noble lady*]. And she told her there were even more important words [*but she would not tell her*]. . . . She promises that what she declared is the truth given under oath and she affirms it and ratifies it having read it. She is more or less twenty-three years old. She cannot sign her name.

[*The case continued with testimony being taken from the Spanish woman doña Josepha and the Indian woman Ana de Oserin. Along with Maria de la Cruz, they pointed to Juana de Mayo as the knowledgeable ritual specialist in the group. On January 30, 1669, the Judge investigator Sarmiento ordered de Mayo's room searched. They found nothing suspicious, but they arrested her and brought her to jail for interrogation anyway, leaving a key with a neighbor to care for the chickens in her courtyard corral. She was charged with being a witch, superstitious, and an idolater.*]

Juana de Mayo Defends Herself but Admits Some Guilt

In Lima, on February 8, 1669, in order to give her confession an Indian women held prisoner in this jail was brought before Señor Licenciate *don* Juan Sarmiento de Vivero, investigating ecclesiastical judge looking into the idolatries committed in Lima's archbishopric. [*Being ladina the interpreter was dispensed with. The lawyer assigned to defend Indians remained involved in the case. She was sixty and the widow of Ignacio de Jesus. Her daughter Maria Cano lived with her husband Nicolas de Herrera.*] Asked if she has used superstitions or *witchcraft*, divining to foretell the

things to come. She denies being a witch and using *witchcraft* and superstitions. . . . She denies seeing coca chewed in order to boil it for superstitious ends or to spit out to tell fortunes or giving baths. She only confesses to having seen the *mestiza* Maria de la Cruz chew coca and boil chewed coca in wine and aguardiente and that this confessant accompanied her because she was in Juana de Mayo's house. . . . She denies knowing that what Maria de la Cruz did by chewing the coca and then boiling it with wine and aguardiente was bad.

. . . Asked about how she knows the *mulata* Anita slave of the nun from the Santa Clara Convent. She said that does not deny knowing the *Mulata* Anita because she came to her in need. She told her [Juana de Mayo] that she needed help because the men she had gave her no money. And she told Anita if she wanted she would give her some powders of the Madre Celestina[12] and a very nice bath, that there were no better baths than the ones she gave. The *mulata* Anita asked how much she would have to pay. And she said that she could pay what she wanted and that she would give her a nice bath. Anita said that she wanted a good bath and that she would pay. Anita paid four *reales*, and she made her a bath of cooked mastranto, rue, *eneldo*, basil, and orange tree leaves. And with this bath she bathed Anita *Mulata* one morning some six months ago. This bath [and] some powders of *mollo* shell with ground avocado pit so that after the bath she could apply these powders to the skin, the neck, and the face, in order to have much better luck.

. . . [*She admitted to knowing doña Josepha de Araya who came looking for her and persisted even though Juana de Mayo avoided the stranger at first. Juana de Mayo explained what happened next.*] *doña* Josepha came to her house at night and finding her there said *mamita mia* [*my little mother*] I must speak with you here, and saying that *doña* Josepha pulled a hen from under her arm and sweets wrapped in paper. She gave them to her saying that she came to beg something of her and not to be angry with her. She

---

[11]Authorities regularly banished people convicted of crimes to Chile's garrisons and frontiers.

[12]The Madre Celestina, or Mother Celestina, referred to the character Celestina in the popular *Tragicomedia de Calisto y Melibea*. The old lady Celestina served as a go-between for lovers. Juana de Mayo could also simply mean to say the powders were magical.

said that she was not going to be angry and what was she going to beg for. *doña* Josepha told her that she wanted Juana de Mayo to make impotent [*ligase*] a young married man she knew named *don* Sebastian whose surname she forgets because she had heard that Juana de Mayo knew how to cure. And that she brought the semen of this *don* Sebastian on a rag that she gave Juana de Mayo. She responded that she did not know how to do those things because God would punish her for such a sin, and that what she would do for her was give her some very good baths, and that there were no baths like hers. And she would also give her some powders to daub herself with so she would have luck and many men would like her and she would not miss that *don* Sebastian. *Doña* Josepha asked her to come to her house [*where she lived with doña Andrea. Juana de Mayo went the next day, was received in person and served wine and sweet-breads and given a peso to buy what was needed for the bath. Most of it she spent on food—goat meat, hot peppers, and tomatoes, but she also bought a ceramic basin.*] And at night *doña* Josepha came to her house so she could be bathed in the water she had boiled the mastranto, orange tree leaves, basil, and rue. . . . After the bath she rubbed her skin with the powder and told her with this you are sure to win a lot of money. And *doña* Josepha presented her with a shawl and a fancy skirt that she could put on in her name. [*Doña Josepha invited her by the next morning and gave her chocolate and bread, and Doña Andrea gave her a big guinea hen in exchange for some of the powders.*]

. . . She said that she gave an Indian woman named *doña* Ana de Guzman, also known as de Ozerin, a little blue cloth bag, and she gave roots of the *tapatapa* herb, salt, garlic, and *contrayerba* to *doña* Ana to put in the bag, so that her husband would not mistreat her. She also confesses that she gave her a bath with water of mastranto and *siempreviva* from the hill, and that they went together to pick it.[13] She gave her the bath so that her husband would love her. Asked if women with their faces covered with veils [*tapadas*] went to find her at night and in the daytime. She admitted that they did,

and she confesses that when *doña* Ana de Guzman asked what those women came looking for, she responded that they came seeking their fortune, the powders of the Madre Celestina. But she did not tell her that some came to ask for other important favors like taking a letter to a man.

. . . Asked if *doña* Ana de Guzman or Ozerin has a *comadre*[14] in Lima's port Callao or if she knows this confessant. She said that *doña* Ana de Ozerin has a comadre who is an Indian woman living in Callao, and she confesses that she knows the comadre who is called Francisca. The comadre Francisca has two married daughters, one with a shoemaker and the other with a fisherman, whose names she does not know. And asked if she wanted to carry out some superstitious acts or spells for the daughters of the Indian Francisca. She confessed to having made the *hechizo* [*spell or withcraft*] of a mixture in a pot of strong vinegar, human excrement, and *yerba de vidrio*.[15] They needed it to use against a *negra criolla*[16] from Panama who is now deceased. One day much afflicted, the Indian Francisca told Ana de Oserin that the husband shoemaker had beaten her daughter. Ana de Oserin told her not to be upset because Juana de Mayo knew how to make a water that would drive away his girlfriends because she had seen it done for a black woman so that her boyfriend tired of his girlfriend. Thus it was that a big jug of *guarapo*[17] was smashed at the door of that girlfriend's house, and the man returned to his woman whose name was Catalina. *Doña* Ana de Oserin said to her comadre that it was necessary to add yerba de vidrio to the water [*they also added hot chile peppers*]. . . . They poured it into a gourd vessel, and Ana de Oserin herself dumped the water on the doorstep of her daughter's competitor under Juana de Mayo's supervision.

. . . [*The investigating judge questioned her about intervening in another case of infidelity.*] She confessed to giving a little jar of water to a *mestiza* named Maria

---

[13]Juana de Mayo gave the common names of herbs and plants used in home remedies. For example, *siempreviva* was a perennial found growing among rocks, sold in the local market, and used in medicine.

[14]Godmother of her child. The parents and godparents become co-parents, *compadres* and *comadres*.

[15]Sexual rivals or those hoping to shame somebody publicly threw these odious *aguas fuertes*, or strong waters, against somebody's door or on their doorstep.

[16]American-born black woman.

[17]Undistilled sugar cane drink made and consumed primarily within the Afro-Peruvian population.

de la Concepción who was married with an Indian named Diego de Guzman, brother of *doña* Ana de Oserin. The water in the jar was cooked with the herb *tapatapa* so she could sprinkle the bed and the place where he sat in order to soften his heart and stop his beatings. Asked who requested the water or to whom she gave it. She confessed to having given it to *doña* Ana who went about trying to keep her brother from mistreating his wife. . . . Ordered to say the commandments of God's law she admits that she does know them. She cannot sign her name.

Prosecutor's Summary of the Charges

The Ecclesiastical Prosecutor for the general investigations of this city and its Archbishopric in the criminal case initiated and continued against Juana Mayo Indian for being a superstitious witch . . . accuses the said Juana Mayo with being accustomed and habituated to casting spells and committing superstitious acts with little fear of God Our Lord and in great harm to her soul. Most seriously she appeared twice before Your Mercy [the judge] to make fictitious declarations and to make it understood that she was not nor had been a witch. She only admitted to allowing others to chew coca in her house hiding her own guilt for being a witch and coming forward to testify only because she heard that others had accused her before Your Mercy. They availed themselves of her ability to use magic in order to remedy their jealousy and to have luck with men and so that the men would love them and give them money. And this can be verified in the testimony of *doña* Josefa de Escobar the accusation that she made against herself the 18 of October of the past year 668 and the first declaration made by the said Juana Mayo was on the 31 of the said month and day. . . . And on folio 17 is the declaration of the said *doña* Josefa de Escobar to whom [the accused Juana Mayo] gave some red powders to bring luck. [Escobar] saw her give some red powders to bring luck to a woman named *doña* Andrea de La Fuente for the said effect, and in addition to this superstition she gave the said *doña* Josefa an herbal bath so that she would have luck, and she prepared a [piece of] magnetite with a half *real* coin and brooches of

fine cloth pearls and coral to carry with her so that men would give her money. And in this same manner she gave an herbal bath to *doña* Ana de Oserin so that her husband would love her. [She bathed Oserin] stark naked in a washtub and that in addition to the herbs the bath contained apples white and black corn gold and silver leaf. And to the said woman she gave a little bag with superstitious items which she could not look at and that were to make her husband love her. And she confessed having given the said little bag of plain blue cloth and that she told *doña* Ana to put in it the root of the *tapatapa* herb salt garlic and contrayerba. And she ordered her to put in the said little bag all the things mentioned so that her husband would not mistreat her. . . . And in addition she should be charged for giving some powders of a dark color to the said *doña* Ana Oserin to put in her husband's food. . . . And she also divined the future in a superstitious way in a porcelain basin filled with water and coca leaves one small and another large for the daughter of an Indian woman named Francisca who works in Callao and doing a superstitious ceremony walking around the said porcelain basin. And in her declaration the said Juana de Mayo I mean *doña* Ana de Oserin said and declared that wanting to confess she unstitched the said little bag to see what was inside, and in it she found some small bones some white powders in a paper white dark and red corn and in a paper green and red feathers. . . . And also for having given another superstitious bath of herbs and roots three apples cut into pieces, gold and silver leaf, perfume to a woman who had left twelve *reales* the night before with the said *doña* Ana de Oserin. And thus I charge her [Mayo] with all the other acts and superstitious actions . . . being so many and diverse I will not list them in this document except to mention that they are sufficient to merit the punishment of Juana Mayo who answered all with a denial of being a witch even though her acts and public fame and investigations show her to be a great witch and a superstitious person. And she who denied being a witch admitted everything making it necessary to torture her to verify the superstitious acts she did for her daughter. And also throwing the powders in the face of the *mestizo* Marselo is a crime worthy of investigation because it is prejudicial superstition and indicates a demonic pact. And also to investigate why she went with *doña* Maria de Huarochirí an Indian from Huarochirí to the town of Huarochirí at the time her daughter wished to marry because the said *doña* Maria de Huarochirí has a reputation as a witch. . . .

Bachiller Juan Berau y de Vargas [Signed]

The Sentence

[*On October 10, 1669, the Archbishop of Lima Doctor don Pedro de Villagómez found Juana Mayo (Indian, ladina, native of Villa, widow, more or less 60 years old), Maria de La Cruz (migrant to Lima, mestiza, 23), doña Josefa de Escobar (Spaniard, widow, 25), and Ana de Ozerin (Indian, muy ladina, native of Callao, widow, 40s) all guilty of idolatry and superstition. Each must pay a 10-peso fine. In jail since the 5th of January, 1669, Juana Mayo was considered adequately punished with the addition of the fine.*]

Suggested Sources:

The less powerful in Mexico turned to *witchcraft* to influence the behavior of the more powerful people in their lives. See Ruth Behar, "Sexual Witchcraft, Colonialism, and Women's Powers: Views from the Mexican Inquisition," *Sexuality and Marriage in Colonial Latin America*, 2nd ed., ed. Asunción Lavrin (Lincoln and London: University of Nebraska Press, 1989), 178–206. Martha Few found that some women exploited the fact that the clergy considered women closer to the supernatural powers in *Women Who Live Evil Lives: Gender, Religion, and the Politics of Power in Colonial Guatemala* (Austin: University of Texas Press, 2002). Irene Silverblatt argues that Lima's Inquisition and other state institutions created an image of women as witches and Indians as idolaters in *Modern Inquisitions: Peru and the Colonial Origins of the Civilized World* (Durham, NC: Duke University Press, 2004). Nicholas Griffiths and Kenneth Mills provide detailed analysis of Peru's campaigns to extirpate idolatries. See Nicholas Griffiths, *Cross and the Serpent: Religious Repression and Resurgence in Colonial Peru* (Norman: University of Oklahoma Press, 1996); and Kenneth Mills, *Idolatry and Its Enemies: Colonial Andean Religion and Extirpation, 1640–1750* (Princeton, NJ: Princeton University Press, 1997).

To read original Inquisition cases translated into English, try *Spanish Inquisition, 1478–1614: An Anthology of Sources*, trans. and ed. Lu Ann Homza (Indianapolis, IN: Hackett, 2006). Indigenous notables wrote about enduring traditions and changing beliefs in *Huarochirí Manuscript: A Testament of Ancient and Colonial Andean Religion*, trans. from the Quechua and ed. Frank Salomon and George L. Urioste; and Felipe Guaman Poma de Ayala, *The First New Chronicle and Good Government*, ed. and trans. David Frye (Indianapolis, IN and Cambridge, MA: Hackett, 2006). Available indexed but unabridged online at *http://www.kb.dk/permalink/2006/poma/info/es/frontpage.htm*.

Chapter 19

On Her Deathbed: Beyond the Stereotype of the Powerless Indigenous Woman[1]

Miriam Melton-Villanueva,
University of California, Los Angeles

[1]For their inspiration and commentary I thank José Enciso Contreras, James Lockhart, David Martinez, Margarita R. Ochoa, Susan Schroeder, and Kevin Terraciano.

It is common to assume that the violence and oppression faced by indigenous women today reached its peak in the colonial era, as if the economic deprivation and social exclusion imposed after conquest fully succeeded. After all, both women and men traditionally held high positions in Mexico City's central market, until the Spaniards gained control and excluded women from serving as formal, official leaders.[2] But does that mean that indigenous women thereafter lived in silence and powerlessness? This stereotype restricts people to narrow roles, in many cases ignoring the way native women advanced the interests of their families and communities. *Doña* Ana María's testament allows readers to question women's supposed insignificance in building colonial Latin America.

On her deathbed, *doña* Ana María de la Cruz y Alpízar dictated her last testament in an unnamed indigenous tongue, probably Otomí. She hired the *notary,* witnesses, and interpreter. Latin American colonies relied on notaries to legalize all kinds of events. In these common transactions, women entered the historical record, especially here when the local deputy filled in as *notary.* In this testament, readers discover that *doña* Ana María is a *cacica.* *Cacica* and *cacique* are, respectively, the female and male titles of indigenous hereditary nobility.[3] Although historians tend to define *cacicas* as simply the wives of *caciques, doña* Ana María's husband does not carry even an honorific title of *don,* much less a hereditary title of ethnic nobility.[4] In this case, *doña* Ana María held the title in her own right.

The testament clearly illustrates her ability to bequeath, own, invest, and manage property. It also links property with social position. *Doña* Ana María

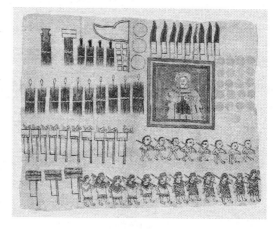

This document, submitted as evidence in a legal case, records the way communities defended their interests 10 years after the Conquest in 1531. The early colonial pictorial styles informed their later swift adoption of Roman script; as part of the colonization process, young men from elite groups were trained and became notaries for their communities. In this codex, using indigenous writing traditions, communities complained of excessive tribute payments (noted as bundles of reeds, coins, workers, and porters represented as feet above bundles). They included a banner with the Madonna and Child. Spanish colonialism blended indigenous and European elements. How does this codex show that combination? How does the image shape views of indigenous populations' ability to act and react to European colonialism? Do successful actions such as this one, which ended in a legal victory for the people of Huejotzinco, mean that indigenous people also generated colonial history?

Source: Landmark Native Legal Victory, Huejotzingo Codex. Mexico: 1531. Harkness Collection, Manuscript Division, Library of Congress (87).

---

[2]Susan Kellogg, "From Parallel and Equivalent to Separate but Unequal: Tenochca Mexica Women, 1500–1700," in *Indian Women of Early Mexico,* ed. Stephanie Wood Susan Schroeder, Robert Haskett (Norman, OK: University of Oklahoma Press, 1997).

[3]James Lockhart, *The Nahuas after the Conquest: A Social and Cultural History of the Indians of Central Mexico, Sixteenth through Eighteenth Centuries* (Stanford, CA: Stanford University Press, 1992; reprint, 2005).

[4]*Don* and *doña* are honorific titles. *Doña* is the female form, like lady, dame; and *don* the male form, like lord, sir.

was called a *cacica,* but scholars cannot tell from this one document the nature of her title. Consequently scholars must ask: What did her status mean in her community? For what kind of decisions might she have been consulted? Did she represent her community to colonial authorities? A legal petition in which she is also named might provide concrete information to address just such questions. In this case, legal categories for land provide important clues to *doña* Ana María's status. The particular type of land described a "land grant" of vast size, a *sitio de ganado menor*, used for raising small livestock, especially sheep and goats. After it had been in existence for a while, the land grant became in effect a ranch or even an *hacienda*, or at least a major component of one. That she owned a sitio de ganado menor suggests she inherited a formal title of nobility along with this land. So even though researchers cannot definitively tell whether the title *cacica* was used here in a formal way based on legal colonial title and/or decree or simply in an informal way based on community usage, one can discuss the implications of contextal clues. Because *doña* Ana María owned a sitio de ganado menor, and the deputy district magistrate recognized *doña* Ana María as a *cacica*, one could argue that she may have held this title formally, in the sense of it being recognized by the colonial government. At the very least, one might argue that she carried out important informal work in her community. For example, a reader can describe the kind of things *doña* Ana María refers to doing in her testament (bequeathing various other properties, establishing a chaplaincy, calculating the agricultural yield of specific property, for example) in a local context. The fact that this record exists at all is a function of skills *doña* Ana María used to negotiate the Spanish legal system.

This would not be the first time new research finds that indigenous women commanded influence in the colonial period. *Doña* Ana María's actions are easier to recognize when understood in the context of several studies demonstrating that native women held authority in a variety of public roles. *The Testaments of Culhuacan* collected early colonial *Nahuatl*-language testaments in which indigenous women were not only given official titles but also were called on as witnesses.[5] Kimberly Gauderman found that indigenous women in Quito, Ecuador, played a dominant role in the marketplace.[6] *Indian Women of Early Mexico* describes the life experiences of a wide variety of women as active participants in colonial society, bequeathers, property owners, rebels, and sometimes leaders.[7] In general, native women's authority was not recognized by the colonial government and therefore was not formal or official. However, women's actions that shaped the lives of their families and communities may be defined as leadership, even if those actions were unrecognized in documents written by colonial authorities.

Questions to Consider:

1. What evidence suggests that *doña* Ana María held the position of *cacica* on her own, as opposed to arriving at noble rank through marriage? Define her leadership by including social details that suggest *doña* Ana María's political, social, and economic networks.

2. To broaden the scope of the first question, add a description of how a legal struggle over Juana Payco's belongings (see Chapter 17) might further define the kind of status and authority these two indigenous and *mestiza* women enjoyed in the Spanish colonies. How did these women contribute to the life and prosperity of their communities into the late colonial period?

3. How did *doña* Ana María describe her land? Cite details suggesting her managing or participating in agricultural and economic processes. Describe how these details imply her status in the community.

4. Describe some limitations of working with this testament. How mediated was it by others who influenced *doña* Ana María's account? How might this and other factors restrict what researchers can know and say about this testator?

[5]For example, see Document #38, Lucia Teicuh's Testament, in which Ana Xoco is named as one of many female witnesses, is a widow, and holds the title *cihuatepixqui*. S. L. Cline, and Miguel Leon-Portilla, eds., *The Testaments of Culhuacan* (Los Angeles: UCLA Latin American Center Publications, 1984).

[6]Kimberly Gauderman, *Women's Lives in Colonial Quito: Gender, Law, and Economy in Spanish America* (Austin: University of Texas Press, 2003).
[7]Susan Schroeder, Stephanie Wood, and Robert Haskett, eds., *Indian Women of Early Mexico* (Norman, OK: University of Oklahoma Press, 1997).

Testament of Doña Ana María de la Cruz y Alpízar, 1703[8]

In the settlement they call del Cuescomate,[9] the *hacienda* of *doña* Ana María de la Cruz y Alpízar, *cacica* and *principal*, and widow of Diego Sánchez Barba Coronado, citizens of this jurisdiction of Xilotepec, on the tenth day of the month of December of the year 1703. I, Manuel Lorenzo de Tejeira, deputy *alcalde mayor*[10] in this jurisdiction, for the captain don Andrés de Lamora the *alcalde mayor* and military captain in this province and its boundaries for His Majesty, say that I was summoned by said *doña* Ana, whom I attest that I know, whom I found sick in bed. Even though she is competent in Castilian,[11] Antonio Lorenzo de Tejeira being present, he executed the office of interpreter, and he swore to faithfully and legally perform to the best of his ability said office of interpreter. And I, said deputy, being in her presence, she said that it must be more or less four years ago that she made her testament before *don* Bernardino Muñoz, former deputy of this said settlement of Xilotepec, and because so much time has passed, and because certain reasons now move her, it is her will and desire to make another, annulling the last, that only this one should be valid. In said conformity, I, said deputy, acting as delegated *juez receptor*[12] with two witnesses present, for lack of a royal or public notary,[13] the proprietor of the title of notary being ten leagues from this said town, executed said testament which the said testator issues in the following form and manner.

In the name of our lord God, may all know who should see this instrument of last will and testament that I *doña* Ana María de la Cruz y Alpízar, *cacica* and *principal* of this jurisdiction of Xilotepec and widow

of Diego Sánchez Barba, my deceased husband and former citizen of this jurisdiction, being ill and bedridden for many years now, but of sound judgment, memory, mind, and will, just as our lord God was served to endow me, believing as I do in the mystery of the most Holy Trinity, father, son and Holy Spirit, and choosing as my advocate and intercessor the queen of the angels María our lady and the glorious lord patriarch Saint Joseph, and all the male and female saints of the heavenly court, under whose protection, shelter, conviction and faith I say that I order and grant this, my testament, in the following form and manner:

First of all, I send and commend my soul to our lord God who made, created, and redeemed it, and the body to the earth from which it was formed.

Also I order that my body be buried in the parish church of San Pedro and San Pablo of said settlement of Xilotepec in the place and site which should seem best to my children and executors, arranging everything in accordance with their means. And may they arrange the funeral, masses, and offerings as they see fit.

Also, I declare that I was married according to the decree of the holy mother church sixty years ago, more or less, to Diego Sánchez Barba, my deceased husband, within which marriage we had and engendered twelve legitimate children: the first [obscured in margin], and Magdalena, María, Mateo, Diego, Manuel, Pedro, Nicolás, Juan, Felipe, Angela, and Esteban, of whom the following are presently alive: Nicolás, Juan, Esteban, María, a widow, and Angela.

Also, I declare that at the time of my marriage the only thing I brought into the control of my husband[14] was a site for small livestock, which is where we have lived and to this day is occupied by my said children to whom I have pointed out the places and lands which each one possesses and has settled. With this understanding let them carry on and live in peace and tranquility without doing

---

[8]*Source:* Testamento de Ana Maria de la Cruz Alizpar, Jilotepec I, #2, 1703: Archivo General de Notarias, Estado de Mexico, Leg. 2, Ca. 1, Fs. 1-4.
[9]*Cuescomate* is a *Nahuatl* word meaning "of the granary," or "of the corncrib."
[10]The *alcalde mayor* is the chief magistrate of a sizable district, often provincial.
[11]*Castilian* is the Spanish language.
[12]The *juez receptor* is an official who receives evidence that may be used in court.
[13]A *notary* legalized transactions by keeping a written record of events. Official notaries purchased their positions.

[14]The implication here is that this was the only property included in her dowry.

harm to each other; rather, let them enjoy it with God's blessings and mine.

Also I declare that within said site [for small livestock] I have reserved one piece of land which is on this side [of the river], on the river bank, which is irrigated. And in this said piece of irrigated land there can be sown two loads of wheat or one *fanega*[15] of maize. It is my will that every year my said children will cultivate and sow it, and that from the proceeds they have the masses said that it would suffice to pay for. And if there is not money for it, I order them to separate the good grain from the bad, paying attention to the fact that I am dedicating it to the good of my soul and that should serve me in the same way as a chaplaincy.[16]

Also, I declare that said site, as attested to by titles and papers which are in my control, extends to the other part of the river and abuts on some lands that today are occupied by the Castillos within the jurisdiction of the town of Xilotepec. May this piece of land always be recognized as mine, it is generally called La Manzanilla. As to this aforementioned area of Manzanilla, many years ago, as my said children know, I have had it dedicated to and intended for a benefactor of mine, my nephew Julián de Artiaga y Almáraz, legitimate child of Magdalena de Alpízar and Miguel del Almáraz, to which said Julián I find myself very grateful for the help in the form of alms and good deeds which I have received. In order to repay him the love and attention which he has always given me, it is my will from now on and forevermore to make as I do make him a free donation of said piece of land so that he may enjoy it, he and his heirs and descendants, with the blessing of God and mine, to which purpose I ask my said children to approve it, and that they not trouble or disturb him, rather they defend him in whatever suit people might want to bring against him, because it is my last will, and I make said donation good, pure, perfect, and irrevocable, this the law calls a donation

between the living, for which reason let him take and secure possession, and let a copy of this clause be made and given to him whenever he should ask for one.

And I declare that I have a house lot which is in this settlement of Xilotepec, in front of the door [could be gate] for the horses, next to the fount [could be water trough], where Ana, nicknamed Anota ["Big old Ana"] lives and is provided for by me. One half of it belongs to me; the other half [belongs to] the heirs of Martín de Alpízar, my brother, now deceased. I declare this for the record.

Also I declare that my children and executors should give two *reales*[17] each to the mandatory bequests.[18]

Also I declare that no one owes me anything, nor do I owe anything to anyone.

And to fulfill and pay for this my testament I leave and name as testamentary executors Esteban Sánchez and Julio my sons, whom I ask to remember my soul. And as of this moment I retract and annul any and all testaments, bequests and codicils which I should have made and issued legally or extralegally before this so that they are not valid, but only this present one, because it is my last will. And I, said deputy, for better validation and confirmation interpose in it all of my judicial authority that by law I can by virtue of my commission so that it will be valid and credible in and out of court, because the person concerned has issued it before me. And so I certify and attest that it was done on this said day, month, and year, and I said deputy signed, because *doña* Ana María de la Cruz did not know how to sign. With interpreter and witnesses, to which I attest.

Manuel Lorenzo de Tejeira
interpreter: Antonio Lorenzo de Tejeira
witness: Julio Sánchez García[19]
witness: Joseph de Avila

---

[15] A *fanega* is a unit of grain often said to have been approximately equivalent to a bushel and a half.

[16] In practice, people used a chaplaincy, or *capellanía*, as an investment, to protect individual and family assets.

---

[17] 1 *real* was one-eighth of a *peso*.

[18] *Mandas forsosas* were mandatory bequests, of which the most common was the fund for the Holy House of Jerusalem. Everyone was sparing with these, usually half a *real* or 1 *real*.

[19] Julio Sánchez García is doubtless the son who is named executor.

Suggested Sources:

For primary documents by and about indigenous persons, see Matthew Restall, Lisa Sousa, and Kevin Terraciano, eds., *Mesoamerican Voices: Native-Language Writings from Colonial Mexico, Oaxaca, Yucatan and Guatemala* (Cambridge: Cambridge University Press, 2005). For collections of testaments, see S. L. Cline, and Miguel Leon-Portilla, eds., *The Testaments of Culhuacan* (Los Angeles: UCLA Latin American Center Publications, 1984); and Caterina Pizzigoni, ed., *Testaments of Toluca* (Stanford, CA: Stanford University Press, 2007). Stephanie Wood's Virtual Mesoamerican Archive provides links to a comprehensive range of digitized sources, as well as research-based articles, Web sites, and teaching materials, *http://whp.uoregon.edu/VMA_Preview/about.lasso*. In addition, the 1974 ethnographic documentary "The Spirit Possession of Alejandro Mamani" shows family conflict during the making of a will in the Andes.

Various scholars have analyzed testaments made in indigenous communities. See Susan Kellogg and Matthew Restall, eds., *Dead Giveaways: Indigenous Testaments of Colonial Mesoamerica and the Andes* (Salt Lake City: University of Utah Press, 1998) for additional themes about which to write. For articles based on testaments, see Frank Salomon, "Indian Women of Early Colonial Quito as Seen through Their Testaments," *The Americas* 44, no. 3 (January 1988): 325–341; and Miriam Melton-Villanueva and Caterina Pizzigoni, "Late Nahuatl Testaments from the Toluca Valley" *Ethnohistory* 55, no. 3 (Summer 2008): 361–391. An environmental context of the region covered in this testament can be found in Elinore Melville, *A Plague of Sheep* (Cambridge: Cambridge University Press, 1994).

Section V

The Age of Reform

The War of Spanish Succession (1700–1714) ended centuries of rule by Hapsburg monarchs and ushered in a new era in which the victorious princes of the Bourbon dynasty introduced French administrative practices in Spain and Portugal. In order to rebuild the economy after the war, strengthen the power of the new monarchies, and obtain the resources needed to confront new powers like Britain, rulers of Spain and Portugal used new administrative practices modeled on French absolutism. The new rulers implemented political and economic innovations first in Iberia and then later in the Americas, particularly in the second half of the eighteenth century. Hapsburg rule had been characterized by negotiation among competing interests, a partnership with the Church, and considerable flexibility and regional variation in the application of royal policy. The Bourbons strove to remove the element of negotiation from imperial rule, subordinating the increasingly powerful and wealthy Church to Crown officials and imperial goals. To retain their imperial status and overseas dominions, the Bourbon kings of Spain and Portugal believed that they had to make royal government more centralized, more standardized, more efficient, and absolute. A mounting tide of reforms swept Spain and Portugal in the eighteenth century and reached the American colonies increasingly after 1740. Bringing many changes in colonial jurisdictions, imperial personnel, and taxation, each of these "*Bourbon Reforms*" favored strengthening the new Bourbon monarchs' power over colonial subjects and revenue.

In the Americas, many of these Bourbon measures felt like a second—and very unwelcome—European conquest for Spanish colonists and colonized groups alike. From the 1740s into the 1780s, Bourbon reform measures tightened royal control and extracted greater profits by implementing higher taxes, new monopolies over trade, and establishing more customs houses. In particular, imperial reformers sought to replace American-born officials with Iberians whose primary loyalty they hoped would remain with the monarch. American-born Spanish colonists often proved more loyal to family and business ventures in the colonies than to the Crown. Consequently, Spanish reformers took aim at the large number of *creole oidores* (judges) in the *audiencias* (royal courts). They enlarged the *audiencias* and appointed mostly *peninsulares* (Spaniards from Spain) to these new posts. Reformers followed the same pattern of favoring *peninsulares* over *creoles* at all levels of colonial administration, causing *creoles* to lose considerable political power. Fiscal reforms soon followed political reforms. After the British defeated the French and Spanish in the Seven Years' War (1756–1763), the Bourbons attempted to make the American colonies pay for their own defenses. They raised taxes, established more customs houses, and built more American forts, garrisons, and naval vessels, particularly in the Caribbean; in many years colonial defense consumed 40 percent or more of annual treasury income. In order to make the colonial administration more answerable to the king and to promote local economic activity, reformers began placing new regional governors, *intendants*, throughout the empire. They charged *intendants* with finding ways to make the colonial population produce more and pay more taxes and duties on that production. *Intendants* reported directly to the Minister of the Indies, circumventing the established administrative channels and the possibility of local interference.

The reformers also tried to follow new economic trends rather than ignoring or resisting them as in the past: In Spanish America, they expanded the volume of official trade by improving the fleet system, opened up more ports in Iberia and the Caribbean to trade, and created new jurisdictions in places where smuggling siphoned off resources. For example, Portuguese traders sold slaves to Buenos Aires without paying the royal fifth and violating monopolies for supplying slaves to Spanish America; and, along the Caribbean coasts of what is today Colombia and Venezuela, planters sold their crops to French, British, and Dutch smugglers in exchange for cheaper and better-made manufactured goods. In both cases, colonial subjects circumvented customs duties and the monopoly system designed to force Latin Americans to export raw materials to Spain and to buy manufactured goods only from Spanish merchants. To better control these once peripheral agricultural export regions and frustrate French, British, and Dutch encroachment on this increasingly valuable trade, reformers placed *viceroys* in Santa Fe de Bogotá (*Viceroyalty* of Gran Colombia)[1] and Buenos Aries (*Viceroyalty* of Río de la Plata). In general, Spanish colonists and the colonial populations approved of measures like better defenses against British raids and more ships and ports participating in transatlantic trade. However,

others weakened local autonomy and violated the way things had always been done, and they did so at a time of social and economic change.

The potential and threat of political and economic reform in Ibero-America came at a time of considerable social change in American society. Populations in Gran Colombia and Río de la Plata grew, particularly the numbers of European and African descendants. In addition, their economic importance grew as exports expanded rapidly for indigo dye, sugar, cocoa, and cow hides. In the original core, colonial regions of Spanish America like Mexico and Peru, the indigenous population remained the majority depending on the region, but American-born colonists became more numerous and vastly outnumbered Europeans among those enjoying a Spanish social status (also a legal category). The *mestizos*, *mulatos* (called *pardos* in Venezuela), and other peoples of mixed heritage (*castas*) grew even more quickly and constituted an even larger minority than the Spanish. This increasingly complex society and an expanding economy created more opportunities for social mobility (changing economic status or the ethno-racial category a person occupied or could claim). For some this mobility was a welcome chance to move up in a hierarchical world and turn economic wealth into social status, where *honor* had once prevailed as the primary arbiter of rank. For colonial elites, especially Spanish *creoles* worried about threats to their status and privileges, this mobility threatened to further blur the lines separating those of European heritage from the rest. Spanish *creoles* seemed especially concerned about those descended from former African slaves assuming a greater role in colonial society with more access to education, government office, and military rank. Furthermore, the royal reformers expressed scorn for the colonists, and the new brand of colonial official sent directly from Spain with a mandate to shake up local government, heightened *creoles'* fears. Some Crown policies even opened the door to slightly greater *casta* participation in government, education, and commerce. Thus, social, economic, and political forces on both sides of the Atlantic

[1] Today's Venezuela, Colombia, and Ecuador.

converged in the 1700s to create a volatile but dynamic age of reform.

Alongside the administrative and economic consolidation, conflict over racial privilege and, to a lesser extent, gender norms took place propelled by both local social pressures and the new Crown and Church laws and practices. The primary sources presented in this section link these imperial processes with the struggles over race, gender, and status within local society. In particular, local *creole* elites who enjoyed Spanish legal status opposed many changes, whereas other social sectors embraced them as new opportunities for mobility and inclusion.

Officials and colonial residents attempted to makes sense of the changing reality around them in many ways, including the fascinating paintings featured in the first chapter in this section depicting ethno-racial categories. Unlike other sections in which images appear in many chapters, this section's first chapter collects all the images in order to address key questions of visual representation and sources for the era of reform. In the second chapter, a public letter highlights colonial elites'

hostility to mixed-race *pardos* and newly empowered Spanish-born officials. Cope offers documents exposing the persistence of traditional notions about proper market practices and the difficulty of enforcing rules—new and established—in the face of popular resistance. Tutino's chapter introduces an Otomí Indian poem from eighteenth-century Mexico, in which Indians clearly claim that it was their labor that led to great achievements in the colonial city of Querétaro. Church reformers recognized the explosive nature of societal change in this period, and Manuel Abad y Queipo's report to the king encouraged the use of parish priests' local influence to maintain indigenous and *casta* loyalty and avoid unrest. Social and economic volatility made the second half of the eighteenth century both an exciting and a troubling time in which to live. Elites and subalterns jostled to figure out how they fit into changing societies and a changing relationship with foreign rulers who now seemed more distant than ever. The chapters in this section will lead readers through the streets, markets, and courts in some of the cities and regions that became flash points in late colonial history.

Chapter 20

Official Paintings Seek to Classify People in a Complex Society

Leo J. Garofalo, Connecticut College

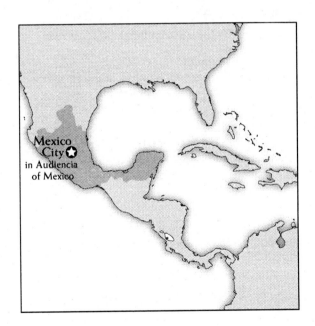

By 1700, two centuries of marriage and coupling between members of the main cultural groups—Spanish, Indian, and African—resulted in a population of *castas* and *mestizos* that was continuing to grow rapidly. A 1792 census for Peru showed 27 percent mixed (including blacks), 13 percent Spanish (both European and American-born), and 56 percent Indian. Estimates made for early nineteenth-century Mexico or New Spain showed 22 percent mixed parentage (including blacks), 18 percent for Spanish, and 60 percent Indians. What role or place did and should people of mixed descent have within colonial society? Did their presence reinforce colonial Spanish rule, or threaten to undermine colonial order? Such questions were of dire importance to Spanish and *creole* elites; they benefited from a colonial system in which rights and obligations were largely determined by one's belonging to a specific cultural group. Painters and bureaucrats both strove, each in their own way, to classify the diverse peoples found within mid- and late colonial society. These so-called *casta* paintings represent one place that officials' legal categories came together with local painters' attempts to render accurate representations of the people whom they saw living around them. Colorful canvases depicting families made up of two parents of different ethnic identities and their further mixed offspring appeared in Mexican painters' workshops, in colonial homes, and on ships headed for a Spain hungry to learn more about an increasingly complex Mexican society.

The *creole* elite appeared at the center of controversies over the growing *casta* population. *Creoles* vastly outnumbered Spaniards, Spanish officials spurned *creoles*, and opportunities for social mobility opened up for *castas* and *creoles* alike. Among those considered Spanish, the American-born or *creoles* dominated. *Creoles* even included some people of mixed parentage, further confounding simple classification. This mixed parentage, coupled with the Crown's desire to tighten control of colonial governance and revenues, fueled royal officials' disdain for *creoles*. In addition to physiognomy, social ranking depended very heavily on a combination of reputation and appearance determined by such factors as parents, place of residence, occupation, marriage partner, language, dress, and haircut. Thus, an Indian married to a *mestizo* and living and working among them in an occupation associated with *mestizos* would most likely be taken as *mestizo*. Wealthy *mestizos* able to obtain an education and marry into *creole* families could eventually become *creoles* in the eyes of the local community and sometimes even before the law. Not surprisingly, those enjoying the privileges afforded Spanish status (e.g., exemption from tribute and labor drafts, better treatment in court, access to education and official positions) worried about movement within their own ranks and the expansion of those ranks to include people formerly excluded.

The *casta* paintings offer a glimpse into these discussions of hierarchy and the richness of colonial society.

Departing Spanish officials commissioned many of these paintings, most often as a single canvas showing between sixteen and eighteen combinations, or as a series of canvases each showing an idealized version of one of these couples and their children. Although not all Mexicans felt that the canvases portrayed their society in a positive light (for instance, showing violence or domestic quarrels), the painters were Mexicans, and they often treated their subjects with dignity and sympathy, creating powerful portraits. This empathetic view is particularly evident in the paintings by the Mexican *mestizo* artist Miguel Cabrera, who in 1763 painted all but the first and last images in this chapter. Andrés de Islas painted the first and last scenes in 1774. Along with portraiture, *casta* paintings offered colonial artists a genre of secular art outside the more constrained imagery and stories dictated by the religious art that occupied most of their time and talent. The images collected in this chapter feature seven individual canvases taken from two collections (each with sixteen canvases) that show the archetypes of each *casta* permutation. Both series begin with a canvas labeled **"From a Spanish man and an Indian woman, a *mestizo*"** and end with a canvas labeled **"Gentile Indians"** shown with bows and arrows and loincloths.

The first canvas (**"From a Spanish man and an Indian woman, a *mestizo*"**) shows a walk in the countryside with a Spanish man richly dressed in European clothing, wearing a wig and tri-corner hat, beside an Indian woman clothed in very fine Spanish-style bodice with lace and full skirt made of traditional indigenous fabric, a gauzelike garment in the shape of an Indian woman's *huipil*, and an Indian woman's folded cloth headpiece. Their *mestizo* son wears the same clothing as his father. The second image (**"From a Spanish man and a *mestiza* woman, a *castiza*"**), by Miguel Cabrera, shows a Spanish man in a market with a tri-corner hat, orange embroidered waistcoat, and a white wig gazing at a medium brown-skinned *mestiza* woman in a fitted floral pattern dress with crisscross embroidery who holds a similarly dressed *castiza* (Spanish and *mestizo*) daughter eating a banana. The third painting

("From a *castizo* man and a *mestiza* woman, a *chamiso*"), set inside a cigarette maker's workshop, features a *castizo* man, his *mestiza* wife, and their *chamiso*[2] son with a pile of coconuts in the foreground. The fourth panel ("**From a *negro* and an Indian woman, a *china cambuja*"**) begins to include black African lineage with a black man (labeled *negro*), with his Indian wife wearing a white huipil, and their *china cambuja* daughter in a European-style costume. The next portrait ("**From an *albarasado* man and a *mestiza* woman, a *barsino*"**) is set in a dark interior with the boy holding a bowl of beads and a candle and the girl holding out a coin. The *mestiza* mother grooms her daughter, perhaps suggesting the removal of lice eggs. The father's red pants are slipping down to reveal his undergarments. The sixth image ("**From an Indian man and a *barsina* woman, a *zambayga*"**) shows a family sharing tamales in the street with two large water urns with carrying lines in the foreground. The last scene ("**From a Spanish man and a black woman, a *mulata*"**) shows a well-dressed Spanish man without a wig fighting with a humbly dressed *negra* in a kitchen filled with numbered and labeled fruit and a daughter dressed liked her mother.

Certainly these scenes of work, rest, and love and the kinds of people depicted in them existed around the Mexican painters and the officials and elites who commissioned their work, but it is doubtful that terms like *coyote, albarasado,* and *barsino* meant anything in daily life, in local social status, or even in elite-dominated courts. The broader categories such as *mestizo, mulato,* Spanish, and Indian combined with other factors such as property, occupational skills, and family connections meant far more. These factors, rather than increasingly narrow categories, determined how colonial people saw themselves and lived their lives. Thus, *casta* paintings represent both legal fiction and social reality; and governing in a society characterized by both posed the greatest challenge to colonial authorities (Chapter 22 shows Mexican authorities trying to control city markets).

Questions to Consider:

1. How do the first two images in this chapter compare and contrast? What is similar, and how can the differences be explained?
2. Look closely at the paintings as a whole. What significance is there in the way Indians, Spaniards, *mestizos,* men, and women were portrayed?
3. What differences in skin tone do you notice in the various paintings? Given your observations, how important did color seem to be in determining one's status in these paintings?
4. What are the multiple ways that status and rank were communicated in these paintings? What can this series of paintings teach us about Mexican society, and what lessons seem to be either missing or misleading?

"From a Spanish man and an Indian woman, a *mestizo.*"
Source: Museo de America.

---

[2]*Chamiso* was a term for the racial mixture being described. Along with the terms *china cambuja, barsino, albarasado,* and *zambayga* below, *chamiso* was rarely, if ever, used in daily life in Mexico.

"From a Spanish man and an *mestiza* woman, a *castiza*."

Source: Museo de America, Madrid/The Bridgeman Art Library, London/New York/The Bridgeman Art Library International.

"From a *castizo* man and a *mestiza* woman, a *chamiso*."

Source: Museo de America.

"From a *negro* and an Indian woman, a *china cambuja*."

Source: Museo de America.

"From an *albarasado* man and a *mestiza* woman, *barsino*."

Source: Museo de America.

"From an Indian man and a barsina woman, *zambayga*."
Source: Museo de America.

"From a Spanish man and a black woman, a *mulata*."
Source: Museo de America.

Suggested Sources:

Focusing on Mexico City, Ilona Katzew traces the eighteenth-century shifts in ideologies of race and ethnicity and creole identity in *Casta Painting: Images of Race in Eighteenth-Century Mexico* (New Haven, CT: Yale University Press, 2004). Magali M. Carrera identifies a mid-century transition to backgrounds of specific interior spaces and public city spaces and the addition of numbers and notations in *casta* paintings in *Imagining Identity in New Spain: Race, Lineage, and the Colonial Body in Portraiture and Casta Paintings* (Austin: University of Texas Press, 2003). Several scholars offer strategies for interpreting these sources in Ilona Katzew, ed., *New World Orders: Casta Painting and*

Colonial Latin America (New York: Americas Society, 1996). Social historians show how elites and government officials in this era attempted to control Mexico's popular subculture and to classify and punish petty crime. See Gabriel Haslip-Viera, *Crime and Punishment in Late Colonial Mexico City, 1692–1810* (Albuquerque: University of New Mexico Press, 1999); and Juan Pedro Viqueira Albán, *Propriety and Permissiveness in Bourbon Mexico*, trans. Sonya Lipsett-Rivera and Sergio Rivera Ayala (Wilmington, DE: Scholarly Resources, 1999).

María Concepción García Saíz authored a catalogue in which fifty-nine sets of *casta* paintings can be viewed. See *Las castas mexicanas: Un género pictórico americano* (Milan: Olivetti, 1989). Several *casta* paintings and other period works by Cabrera and other artists can be viewed at the Web site for the Museo de América, *http://museodeamerica.mcu.es/*. Alexander von Humboldt collected population data, described social and political conditions, and noted salient economic activities and trends in North and South America. On Mexico, see his *Political Essay on the Kingdom of New Spain* (New York: Knopf, 1972). In addition, a 1774 account of Mexico can be found in Pedro Alonso O'Crouley, *A Description of the Kingdom of New Spain*, trans. Seán Galvin (San Francisco: John Howell Books, 1972).

Chapter 21

Creole Town Councils Fear Change from Above and Below

Leo J. Garofalo, Connecticut College

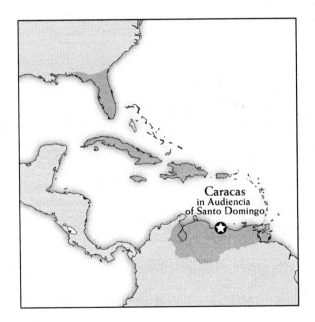

Caracas
in Audiencia
of Santo Domingo

The Spanish *creoles* of the Caracas *cabildo* (city council) met in extraordinary sessions in 1795 and 1796 to debate, and eventually protest, royal measures meant to reform colonial administration and reinvigorate Spanish imperial power in the Americas. Even though the profits earned by Venezuela's exports of plantation crops like sugar were rising steadily and the number of *creoles* in the colony had never been higher, the *creole* elites felt threatened, and they wanted their King to know about it. They took the bold measure of writing directly to the King; they justified their act by stating that all loyal subjects must speak up whenever royal policies and officials seemed misguided about the reality on the ground and certain to upset the local social order. In their view, the Bourbon monarchs' reforms had created a political crisis.

The spark that provoked the *cabildo* to complain was a *cédula* (a royal decree) issued by the *Council of the Indies* allowing non-Spanish people to pay a fee in order to claim Spanish or "white" status and the privileges it offered. Only men enjoying Spanish legal status could enter the clergy, study in the university, or hold government office. Now Crown officials threatened to upset the local social hierarchy and reduce the privileges enjoyed by *creole* elites with its *cédula de gracias al sacar* granting a legal dispensation from non-Spanish status in exchange for about 188 *pesos*.[1] Even though historians have shown that relatively few people took advantage of the offer to raise their social status by paying the fee, the measure and the imperious way it was implemented greatly upset local power holders.

The *cabildo* members already felt under attack from above and below. *Cabildos* served as town councils responsible for municipal affairs and market regulation in the city and its hinterland. American-born Spanish colonists, the *creoles*, dominated the *cabildos* (in the Indian towns, indigenous people and, occasionally, *mestizos*, ran the *cabildos*). As *Bourbon Reforms* began to take hold, Crown policies pushed *creoles* out of most other government offices, especially the royal courts called *audiencias*.[2] *Creoles* increasingly saw their interests opposed by the Spanish-born *peninsular* officials who were replacing *creoles* in the colonial government. Local elites felt more of a bond with *peninsulares* who married into local families and bought property and engaged in business; the *cabildo* of Caracas carefully identified *creoles* and *vecinos* (prominent citizens and property owners residing in a city or town) as sharing the same interests and opposing any expansion of the "white class" as the

complaint termed it.[3] The *cabildo*'s report refers to *creoles* as "Naturales blancos" (white natives), "Naturales de esta ciudad" (natives of this city), and "Naturales de las Américas" (natives of the Americas). The choice of the label "naturales" (literally native to the land) to describe a subgroup of people enjoying Spanish legal status departed from the more common use of the term in previous centuries to refer to Native Americans. These labels suggest a strong elite identification with their home region. Bourbon officials seemed unaware of the intricacies of local distinctions or unwilling to be bound by them. New Crown agents and their attitudes toward the colonial population threatened the established "colonial pact" that bound the ruled to their rulers.

The *cabildo* had already discussed and critiqued a series of royal measures that opened the way for challenges from below. For instance, the councilmen opposed new licensing laws that would allow minors (males younger than 25) to obtain the right to practice as *notaries*, attorneys, town councilmen, doctors, and surgeons. Now the *cabildo* complained about new avenues for status available to peoples of non-European descent, whom they likened to male minors.[4] In both cases, the *cabildo* hoped to limit mobility despite royal reforms that threatened to loosen elite *patriarchal* power. Royal law once barred those labeled "people of color" from all white privileges, including education; but the *cédula* and the militias now threatened the authority and exclusivity of white status. After the Spanish defeat in the Seven Years' War (1756–1763), the militarization of the Americas intensified, and Crown officials recruited more *creoles* and *castas*—including *pardos*—into militias. The Crown needed more robust

---

[1]Roughly equivalent to the cost of a good horse or three times the annual wages of a muleteer or other unskilled worker. In 1801, the Crown reduced the fee to 88 *pesos*.

[2]An *audiencia* was a high court of royal justice with administrative functions located in several administrative centers spread throughout Spanish America.

[3]*Vecinos* usually referred to prominent citizens and property owners residing in a city or town; these could be American- or European-born, and local usage often meant that even non-Spanish and non-elites who owned property in a city or town might be labeled *vecinos* by their neighbors and others who knew them. The *cabildo* in Caracas seemed to use the term *vecinos* to refer primarily to European *creoles* and Spaniards residing permanently in the city and sharing *creoles*' interests. Under the colonial system, indigenous and other non-European people were legally considered minors.

[4]The *cabildo* complained about *pardos* and *mulatos* (people of Spanish and African ancestry) and *zambos* (people of African and Indian heritage).

defenses, especially in the Caribbean region. Militia membership gave *pardos* access to less discriminatory military courts (*fuero militar*), local social status, and sometimes wages.[5] In Venezuela, both *creoles* and *pardos* coveted the legal protection of the *fuero* and the distinction of a military rank. To neutralize these threats from above and below, the *creole* councilmen appealed to the venerable colonial concept of *obedezco pero no cumplo* (literally: "I obey but do not execute"): the *cabildo* and the colonial officials would recognize and obey the royal will while refraining from implementing any measures that local circumstances would render detrimental to Crown interests and governability in their

---

[5]These courts might be more likely to defend militia members' interests, insist on solid evidence for conviction, and impose lower fines and less brutal punishments.

district. *Creoles* sought to limit change and win the Crown back to their side. *Bourbon reform* of the imperial system was hammered out this way among competing interests in each region and each locality.

Questions to Consider:

1. What were the three principal requests that the City Council of Caracas mad, and why was each so important to the council members?
2. How did the council describe and explain the relationships among the *peninsulares*, Spanish *creoles*, and the non-Spanish classes?
3. What do these demands and class and ethnic relationships tell you about Spanish *creoles'* sense of identity and interests?

Caracas's Cabildo Writes to the King to Denounce a Royal Decree, 1796[6]

[*The Cabildo began by noting the dates of the Royal Decree, the mounting opposition, and the duty of loyal vassals to inform their monarch of the harm caused by Crown law or by royal officials.*]

Sire, . . .

The *Cabildo* believes that the dispensation of the status of *Pardos* and *Quarterones*[7] offered by the Royal Decree is capable of expanding what is allowed them because of their nature: it allows a *Pardo* freed from his low status to qualify for all the functions that the Laws of the Kingdom prohibit, and for all of those reserved until now for white men of pure blood in these Indies; so that a *Pardo* leaving his inferior class, with your Majesty's dispensation will be treated as a member of the white class.

---

[6]*Source:* José Félix Blanco, ed., *Documentos para la historia de la vida pública del libertador de Colombia, Perú y Bolivia* (Caracas: Imprenta de "La Opinión Nacional," 1875) vol. 1, 286–288.
[7]People defined as having one-quarter black ancestry.

This transformation that the Royal Decree considers so easy and grants for such a small sum of money is regarded with horror by the *vecinos* and Natives of America [Spanish *creoles*] because they alone know because of their birth [in America] or because of the passage of many years [in America] the immense distance that separates the Whites and the *Pardos*: the advantages and superiority of the one and the lowliness and subordination of the other. The *pardos* would never have dared believe possible the equality promised by the Royal Decree if there had not been somebody who by protecting them humiliates and insults the white creoles and *vecinos* and invigorates and favors the [*pardos*] with the hope of absolute equality and with an opportunity to acquire the honors and offices that until now had been reserved exclusively for the Whites.

This misfortune, the root of many others in the Americas, originates precisely in the lack of knowledge among the majority of

European officials, who arrive in America prejudiced against the character of the native-born white *vecinos* and worried by false and mistaken ideas about the reality in the country. Unable to discern things with impartiality and rectitude, they mistake and misunderstand what they see, despite what the examples and experiences show. All of these resolutions, projects, and operations come animated with the same defect, and obstinately closing their eyes to the clear reality, they only succeed in using the means their authority makes available to oppress and ruin those whose defense depends on Your Majesty's bounty and justice.

One [of the misfortunes] that affects this Province is [royal officials'] protection of the *Mulatos* and other inferior people who know of the decree because of the very public way equality was introduced, and [they] strengthen this favor by providing officials with personal service [and divisive and false stories]. . . .

The *Pardos, Mulatos* or *Zambos* (whose differentiation is not commonly known, or is negligible) descend directly from the Black slaves introduced into this Province to work the land. Necessity made licit an expedient censured in the past and detested today as inhumane; slavery was adopted and protected by the kind of rigor, harshness, and segregation with which slaves are treated in order to preserve the subordination by the same means with which it was established, because it is impossible that a man accept being a slave if he does not fear that they will punish the desire to recover his lost liberty as a crime.

In addition to the infamy of their origin, they have the obscenity of the illegitimacy, because it is rare for the *Pardo, Mulato,* or *Zambo* in this province to have legitimately married parents to free him from being a bastard; and it is rarer yet that he not have parents, grandparents, or close Relatives that are slaves or have been slaves, or serve as servants of some family of *vecinos* or white *creoles.* You ordinarily see *Pardos,* or *Mulatos* dressed [in finery] in

violation of the Laws[8] but with a brother who works as somebody's servant; or they have a magnificent fortune but also a good number of enslaved nephews and relatives.

Ask yourself Your Majesty, how is it possible for the *Vecinos* and White *creoles* of this Province to allow at their side and to mix with as a person of their same class a *Mulato* descended from their own slaves or those of their parents or ancestors, a *Mulato* with relatives still in slavery, or a *Mulato* disfigured by being chained to bastardy and dim-wittedness?. . .

[The Cabildo warned that the Pardos would now aspire to more, and their disorders and subversion would have to put down by force.]

[Another problem] is the power that the *Pardos* have acquired with the establishment of militias regulated and commanded by officers of their same economic class. Adopted as a well-founded measure, experience shows that it will be the ruin of America, because being incapable of resisting a foreign invasion by a powerful enemy and the Whites' militias being more than enough to contain the slaves and the peace within the country, the *Pardo* militias only serve to foment the arrogance of the *Pardos* giving them an organization, leaders and weapons to facilitate a revolution, and to confuse people. Often an officer adorned with his uniform, epaulets, and sword and with a little color in his face receives undeserved deference that elevates his thoughts to other higher aims. And occupied in the cities and towns with military exercises, they scorn cultivating the fields, abandoning the agriculture to the Whites and the Black slaves. They depend on artisan skills for their subsistence, and because they arbitrarily assign prices for their work, they never seek to improve their work. In old age or with any other impediment, they descend into idleness, begging, and misery.

---

[8]Sumptuary laws reserved the use of expensive jewelry and fine clothing for the Spanish (including the American-born Spanish *creoles*). People of non-Spanish status frequently violated these rules governing clothing and food, causing *cabildos* to spill much ink and threaten all manner of punishments.

It is impossible to believe the sad state of this Province. The European Spaniards who are not *vecinos* judge it necessary to occupy the official positions in order to earn a living, and because of this they remain idly seeking a post until they are given preference in a position without any other merit. The American Spanish or *vecinos* are destined to labor in the countryside suffering the fatigues and tasks of this occupation. Or they go along dissipating their force and talent in the lazy vanity and corruption of the cities ignorant of their interests and victims of contempt. The *Pardos* and free *Mulatos* dedicate themselves to the mechanical arts, which many now disdain thinking it indecorous to be both a soldier and a shoemaker or barber. . . . The result of this is that no white man applies himself to these arts in order to avoid being taken for a *Pardo*. And the *Pardos* do not work in the countryside in order not to mix with the slaves. In a word, they all want to be gentlemen in the Americas, to hold offices, and live from public salaries, or at society's cost without contributing to it.

If the origin of this calamity is sought it will be found without doubt in the lack of compliance with the Laws and in the little interest in the country shown by those charged with executing the laws. . . . The Magistrates are impeded by that natural laxity with which a man regards the interests of others and of a country in which he only finds himself in passing. And they are only driven by the desire to acquire enough wealth to finish their careers in their own country or in another place. . . . Many times the Europeans themselves let slip that . . . their lack of application or their difficulty in imposing order and remedying the problems is motivated by nothing more than the fact that they do not have to remain here, and that planning to leave America, they care little about the destruction of the Americas and even less if *Mulatos* become confused with the Whites.

It is not the *Cabildo*'s goal that all public offices be conferred only on the *Americanos* and the Europeans residing in the Americas. . . . Instead, a perfectly indispensable alternative could be generally adopted to divide the official posts between the two so that they would communicate with each other and cooperate to enforce the Laws adapted to the country's circumstances. . . . Otherwise, if it continues as it now is, there can be no order, justice, and tranquility with the no-longer secret and public struggle that unfortunately exists between the *vecinos* and the officials; the officials believe all the negative things they have been told or have imagined, and the *vecinos* are convinced that no good can come from prejudiced judges who ignore the *vecinos*' rights. . . .

. . . At the present time, the separation of your vassals cannot be good for Your Majesty. . . . With so many foreign enemies clearly visible and desiring to rival the riches, size, and glory of the Spanish colonies . . . and envying these possessions, it is necessary to eliminate the impediments to our security by making unshakeable the sincere love that the *Creoles* and Spanish *vecinos* of this Province feel for their Kings. . . .

In this situation and in order to hold onto this part of your dominions, Your Majesty needs no more than the loyalty of the Spanish *creoles* and *vecinos*, who, because they are married here and have their property here, try to live in peace according to the religion and subordinate to the Crown just as they were born. They only ask that Your Majesty preserve their ancestors' *honor* and their precursors' traditions, without subjecting them to the insult that results from the association with *Pardos* elevated to equality by grace of the Royal Decree. . . . Under no circumstances is it good that the *Pardos* for a small amount of money, and without an outstanding history of serving the state, become Whites and obtain, or become capable of obtaining, the honors and distinction afforded those who have had the immense task of preserving their *limpieza* though legitimate descent. . . .

They will have informed Your Majesty that the Province is full of mixed families, that many of the *Pardos* enjoy the same possessions as Whites, that there are innumerable legal battles over *limpieza*,[9] and that it is ill-advised to favor distinctions in the Americas. . . . These reports are wrong, superficial, and malicious. Even if it is true that there are one or two families whose origins are in doubt, or who are vulgarly said to be as dark as *Mulatos*, . . . these families live on the edges of the city and exercise no influence or power generally or in the public sphere.

It is also true that there are many lawsuits by *Pardos* trying to gain recognition as Whites, but this disorder, of which there are very few examples prior to 1790, is caused by the *oidor Don Francisco Ignacio Cortínez* who had private motives to loathe the *creoles* for their boldness, and was declared the [*Pardos'*] protector. . . . He convinced the other Ministers of the *Audiencia* to protect them, persuading the judges with slanderous reports. . . . [Thus] Cortínez is the author of such repugnant pretensions, and the ruin of the orderly hierarchy of families. . . .

. . . It is shameful and above all inopportune [to allow *Pardos* to enter the white class] considering that the Province enjoys the capacity and means to keep the *Pardos* subordinated, as they should remain, without any need for the Law to confuse them with the Whites who abhor and detest this union and mixture. . . . They are convinced that this is an arbitrary measure invented to subordinate them and undermine their authority under the false pretense that this promotes Your Majesty's interests.

. . . The security of the Metropole's rights is united with that of this province. . . . *Mulato* students will swarm into the schools. They will try to enter the Seminary. They will bid for and obtain the seats in the city council. They will serve in the public offices and in the Royal Treasury. They will learn about all the public and private business. The disinterest and retreat of the decent White people will follow. *Pardos'* greater numbers will encourage

the *Pardos*. The [whites] will abandon these offices with regret and out of contempt [for the *Pardos*]. The families that conquered and populated the Province with their blood and enduring great hardships will disappear. The names of those loyal vassals who remained loyal to the rule of the Kings of Spain will be forgotten. Even the memory of their surnames will be erased. And the sad day will come when Spain will be forced to depend upon *Mulatos*, *Zambos*,[10] and *Negros* whose suspect loyalty will cause violent upheavals, without having anyone who—in order to protect his own interests and honor, his purity of blood and public name—will risk his life, calling upon his sons, friends, relatives, and Countrymen to contain the vile people and defend the common cause and his own.

[Your Majesty will find fidelity] precisely among the *Creoles* and *Vecinos* in America who venerate Spain as the origin of their nobility, purity of blood, and *honor*. They read the histories of the exploits and loyalty of their Ancestors. They have plentiful possessions to defend. And they desire to live peacefully with the comfort of their Christian Religion, and the security that they have in the power and valor of the Spanish Nation.

. . . Is it possible that they will mix the *limpios*,[11] distinguished, and honorable Vassals with men of lowly and detestable lineage? What crime have they committed that new members of their class will be created, members whose loyalty will always be shaky? Can it be believed that Your Majesty's intention is to trust and give rights to men who, far from looking to Spain as the center of their happiness, fix their gaze on the dark inhabitants of Africa, from where they came, and who will patronize them and raise them up against the Spanish from whom they say they have received a thousand abuses. Can the new Whites be more loyal than the old?. . . Who has

[9]"Purity" (i.e., Spanish and Christian) of the family's lineage.

[10]*Zambos* referred to people of African and indigenous heritage.
[11]"Clean" as in *limpieza*—literally free from the "stain" of non-Christian ancestors. See note 9.

erroneously persuaded [Your Majesty] that the *Pardos* do not admire the *Negros*, from whom they inherit their defects, an inclination odious to the Whites, to whose status the *Pardos* aspire in order to insult and discredit the Whites? The *Mulatos* regard the *Negros* with affection, and the Whites with loathing.

[What Your Majesty has been told] is very different from the reality in the Province; to the way of thinking of the distinguished families of pure descent, . . . who remain totally separate from interaction and commerce with the *Mulatos* or *Pardos*, and who consider it a grave affront to have it said they rub shoulders with [*Pardos*] or that they enter their houses, it is impossible to erase this distance even if it is imposed by Law, as a reward, or the royal grant. . . .

This is not opposition to this class of people participating in the benefits of society. . . . The Province's *Mulatos* and *Pardos* are the ones who live without working, enjoy their rest, and reap the benefits without responsibility, and without contributing anything to the public good and the Royal Treasury. . . . Those who live in the cities, villages, and towns . . . try to alter their state out of hatred for the Whites; while the few who are in the countryside live content in their poverty and idleness, or by thievery. . . .

Those *Pardos* living in town are generally enlisted in the Militias and therefore they are free from the correction and vigilance of the *alcaldes ordinarios*,[12] the only judges who for the good of the country could apply the law to the *Pardos'* conduct. Their military chiefs only take care that they attend the military exercises, . . . and that the ordinary magistrates do not touch the Militiamen, protecting the disrespect and mockery of the magistrates, . . . and turning the military exemption from civilian prosecution into cover for every disorder and crime. This is another reason for the

presumptuousness of the *Mulatos* because no matter how ragged and poor they look when they appear before a judge, they have the nerve to raise their voice. . . .

The [*Pardos*] are made up of those who live in an indigence that brings laziness in its wake, others are blacksmiths, carpenters, silversmiths, tailors, masons, shoemakers, butchers, slaughterhouse workers, . . . They are the arbiters of how much they work, they mix the metals according to their whim, and they charge what they want for their goods, and they can trick everyone. Complaints are not heard and the harm is not remedied because the magistrates . . . and military judges are not interested in any of this. They look upon the Province as an inn, content to suffer the problems for the short time that they have in the Province. . . . Because of this disorder the mechanical arts do not improve . . . and their goods have to be accepted no matter how badly made, whenever they are completed, and at the price they demand.

From what they earn, they contribute not a single *maravedí*[13] to the Royal Treasury, to the City's income, or to any other establishment; . . . the whole weight of the taxes falls upon the farmers and merchants; such that the *Mulatos* and *Pardos* of this Province (except a few here and there who have farm lands, and subsist honestly by working the land, or in some trade) live in the greatest ease and freedom in their little houses, working only the hours that they want to earn their daily bread, without wanting to apply themselves to other labors. The *Pardos*—especially the ones who are officers, corporals, or sergeants in the militias—hold in low regard cultivating the land or working for those who own lands. Even those who are not employed and work as day laborers are so dishonest, crooked, and arrogant that they escape without repaying the loans given them by the *hacendados*.[14] And for any reprimand they

---

[12]Leading members of the *cabildo* were named *alcaldes ordinarios*, and they served as magistrates within a city's jurisdiction.

[13]34 maravedís equaled one silver *real*; 8 *reales* made a *peso*.
[14]Owners of large, landed estates called *haciendas*.

abandon the work, endangering the crops and damaging the agriculture and commerce. They do this every day saying that they are free, safe in the certainty that their commanders will not make them pay. . . .

The remedy for these problems is not to foment the arrogance of the *Pardos*, or dispel the hatred that they feel towards the Whites by raising their status. Instead they should be obliged to work in the fields, prevented from living idly in the cities, obliged to improve their artisan crafts, placing an official price on their work, and their arrogant thoughts should be suppressed on every occasion. . . . [The magistrates] should reduce the militias of Whites and the militias of *Pardos* to detached companies to muster when there are disturbances. They should reward the *Pardos* who work and cultivate the immensity of fertile lands that the inaction of so many arms leave uncultivated and deserted in this Province.

. . . It is impossible to achieve the order and regulations that this *Cabildo* desires for the preservation of these domains, the glory of Your Majesty, and the happiness of your American vassals without replacing the current ministers in the *Audiencia* Real. They are widely hated by the public, especially the *oidor Don* Francisco Ignacio Cortínez,[15] whose hostility to the country's *vecinos* and *Creoles* is frequently manifested particularly to distinguished persons. . . . Lastly, they openly and scandalously protect the *Mulatos*, or *Pardos* and all the vile people in order to lessen the regard for the distinguished and honorable old families.

One of the greatest improvements Your Majesty could make in this Province is to remove those ministers whose ideas and maxims (when they are not at root delinquent) are in effect pernicious to the public good, protection of rights, and the administration of justice. . . . It seems a kind of curse that each magistrate here wants to be superior to the others and absolute, each usurping the others'

powers. They are wrapped up in competition and discord: nobody thinks of anything except to expand his jurisdiction, enlarge his authority, grow conceited, and demand undeserved gifts. . . . And for this reason they patronize the *Mulatos*, *Pardos*, and inferior people who serve them without pay, and who falsely adulate them, and flatter them in terms that the distinguished and honorable white people cannot.

. . . So that the seditious discord and multitude of embroilments in this Province cease, the Ministers who at the moment compose the Real *Audiencia* should leave. Their places can be occupied by others more zealous in promoting the interests of Your Majesty and the honor and property of the *vecinos* and *Creoles* of this country who will bless Your Majesty for such an important benefit. And the care that Your Majesty takes to preserve the *honor* of your vassals assenting to their humble and fervent pleas will give them a very powerful obligation to remain firm in their loyalty.

May God protect Your Majesty's Royal Person. Chapter Hall of Santiago de Caracas. November 28. 1796.

[*Signed by eleven city councilmen.*]

Suggested Sources:

The sense of a uniquely American identity and the formation of a set of interests at odds with imperial goals developed slowly but gained great currency and force by the end of the 1800s in many Spanish American regions. See D. A. Brading, *The First America: The Spanish Monarchy, Creole Patriots, and the Liberal State, 1492–1867* (Cambridge: Cambridge University Press, 1991). Elite angst over an increasingly complex social structure found expression in how painters employed the body, dress, and occupation to visually express subalterns' lineage and race, at times showing empathy for their subjects. See Magali M. Carrera, *Imagining Identity in New Spain: Race, Lineage, and the Colonial Body in Portraiture and Casta Paintings* (Austin: University of Texas Press, 2003). As in other eighteenth-century societies, elites such as the *cabildo* members brought discussions

---

[15] An *oidor* served as a judge on the royal courts (*audiencias*).

of honor and sexuality into how culture and race intersect in daily life and define political and economic rights. Ann Twinam situates the *cédula de gracias al sacar* within this discussion. See Ann Twinam, *Public Lives, Private Secrets: Gender, Honor, Sexuality, and Illegitimacy in Colonial Spanish America* (Stanford, CA: Stanford University Press, 1999). During the 1700s, the Spanish royal courts system made up of the *audiencias* in the Americas (cases could be appealed to the Council of the Indies in Spain) gained strength and increasingly enforced Crown policies even when faced with fierce local opposition. Refer to Mark A. Burkholder and D.S. Chandler, *From Impotence to Authority: The Spanish Crown and the American Audiencias, 1687–1808* (Columbia: University of Missouri Press, 1977). Increasingly *peninsular* officials made careers, and fortunes, for themselves in the colonial administration. See Mark A. Burkholder and D.S. Chandler, *Politics of a Colonial Career: José de Baquíjano and the Audiencia de Lima*, 2nd ed. (Wilmington, DE: SR Books, 1990). Scarlett O'Phelan Godoy examines the goals and impact of the new colonial policies developed in Europe during the Enlightenment and implemented in the Americas in her *Rebellions and Revolts in Eighteenth Century. Peru and Upper Peru* (Köln: Bohlau, 1985). John Leddy Phelan provides a detailed study of how popular protests escalated into a rebellion against *Bourbon Reforms* such as new taxes and more *peninsular* officials less willing to bend to local custom even as the rebels pledged loyalty to the king ("Death to Bad Government and Long Live the King," they cried), *The People and the King: The Comunero Revolution in Colombia, 1781* (Madison: University of Wisconsin Press, 1978).

Chapter 22

The Politics of Petty Commerce: Who Defines the Public Good?

R. Douglas Cope, *Brown University*

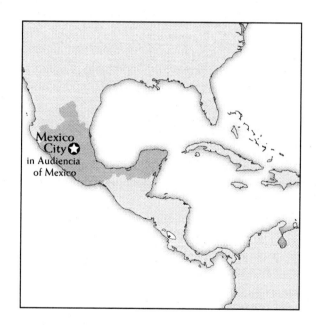

In a monarchical system, implementation of the law might seem straightforward: The king commands, and everyone else obeys. Yet in colonial Spanish America, even under more strict Bourbon rule, matters were not so simple. Archival sources reveal complex debates among government officials over how to achieve their aims, and how to deal with a recalcitrant populace. This chapter presents two instances of such discussions: a 10-year debate over regulating the bread trade, and debates over guild regulations. Both documents show how economic policies, in particular, provoked prolonged discussions, because they had such far-reaching effects. Government bureaucrats kept a close watch on everyday economic activity. Merchants and manufacturers in urban centers such as Mexico City operated within tight regulatory constraints.

The craft guilds that brought together the craftsmen who produced most of the city's goods had to meet exacting standards, spelled out in printed ordinances approved by the city council and the *viceroy* (this parallels the Caracas *cabildo*'s concerns over the quality and pricing of *pardo* artisans' work in Chapter 21). The candle makers' *ordenanzas*, for example, stipulated different kinds of treatment for different kinds of wax and also distinguished between ordinary candles and those created for specific holidays. The *cabildo* attempted to ensure the supply, quality, and reasonable price of other key goods (such as meat) by creating monopolies. Prominent local men bought the exclusive rights to sell beef and mutton in the city but had to follow detailed rules that not only specified the sale price, but also prescribed the entire supply process. In the case of bread, the *cabildo* set prices and mandated specific profits for bakers and vendors. When it came to regulating taverns, city authorities decreed how, when, by whom, and to whom *pulque* (the native intoxicant made from the maguey plant) should be sold. The documents featured in this chapter show how the *cabildo* deliberated, inspected shops, and filed reports and testimony. The royal court, attorneys, and the artisans themselves also intervened and left records of their positions in the debates. These excerpts show how actors in the city markets interacted with different levels of the colonial government.

Colonial authorities did not establish this dense network of regulation to maximize the economy's efficiency or productivity. Instead, they sought larger social and political goals: the maintenance of domestic order and the promotion of the "public good" (*bien común*). Taverns, for example, provided relaxation, recreation, and solace to the urban poor—but for that very reason, they posed a threat. As gathering places for large numbers of *castas* and Indians, they became, in elite eyes, sites of crime, social disorder, sexual misbehavior, and possible sedition. The government addressed this dilemma by permitting taverns to exist but within certain constraints. They could only operate during daylight hours, and they could not serve food (which encouraged customers to linger and drink more). In addition, the government mandated separate establishments for men and women. Such attempts to impose order posed both practical difficulties—plebeians often evaded prohibitions[1]—and policy headaches. Economic imperatives and desired social outcomes could easily conflict. Indigenous women dominated the marketplace in the central plaza, purveying vital foodstuffs to the city's poor, whereas elites shuddered at their promiscuous intermingling with men in a public venue. The authorities encouraged Indians to adopt artisan trades, even though this drew them into the Hispanic economy, undermining the ethnic segregation that supposedly structured colonial society.

Still, government officials persisted in using legislation to fine-tune social behavior. They drew upon a "natural law" doctrine stating that all human beings share certain fundamental understandings, precepts that have been divinely implanted in their souls. This enables them to form workable political communities. Yet social harmony is easily disrupted, for humanity's sinful nature often leads it astray. The task of ensuring that natural law is observed falls to the sovereign; only he can rise above petty private concerns and guarantee the common good. The Crown delegated this responsibility to local officials, who rendered judgments on a case-by-case basis, struggling to balance the conflicting claims of interested parties while still preserving the welfare of the entire community.

What exactly did the "public good" mean when it came to the economy? Mexico City officials placed the greatest emphasis on protecting consumers, especially Indians and the urban poor. Above all, they worked to ensure a steady supply of affordable foodstuffs. Authorities had a justified fear of plebeian wrath: As one judge put it, "everywhere a hungry people are the most formidable hammer in the world."[2] The Mexico City *tumulto* (disturbance) of

---

[1] Over half Mexico City's taverns operated without the necessary viceregal license in the late eighteenth century, according to Michael C. Scardaville, "Alcohol Abuse and Tavern Reform in Late Colonial Mexico City," *Hispanic American Historical Review* 60, no. 4 (1980): 653.

[2] Archivo General de las Indias, Seville, México, legajo 781, fol. 518r.

1692, still a vivid memory well into the eighteenth century, had begun as a classic corn riot.[3] Officials also saw the poor as victims, easy prey for knowledgeable and cunning merchants. On the one hand, commerce was necessary and even beneficial in promoting exchange among different regions. Long before Adam Smith, colonial elites grasped the supply and demand mechanism and understood that price fixing could have negative consequences. On the other hand, merchants and producers often gave in to greed and recklessly pushed prices up at the expense of consumers. In the final analysis, the merchant's essential task remained transporting goods from where they were available to where they were needed. If the transportation component was missing, then the merchant was merely engaging in "reselling" (*regatonería*), buying cheap to sell dear. This practice represented the epitome of socially irresponsible commerce. Small-scale trading offered many opportunities for such malfeasance.

Regulating daily market activity thus presented a difficult challenge. The poor had to be protected, yet too heavy a hand might impede production and make matters worse for everyone. The first set of documents in this chapter concerns a decade-long debate among government officials over the regulation of Mexico City's bread trade. Various officials—and the bakers themselves—had definite ideas about the problems affecting the trade, but they had trouble reaching any consensus on a solution. Did plebeians need fine bread, or would larger amounts of lesser quality serve them better? Where should marketplaces be located? Could market incentives alone maintain orderly practices, or should the government intervene on a daily basis? In other words, simply deciding what constituted the "public good" could prove problematic. Ultimately, the government made no sustained, sweeping reforms. The second set of documents, dealing with various guild matters, suggests an even greater (and constant) difficulty

for the authorities: simply enforcing the existing regulations. Here, guild *veedores* (inspectors) struggle to control illegal production and sale of goods. Only licensed masters could employ journeymen and apprentices and sell their wares in legally recognized shops. However, a 1736 investigation found some forty "corner tailors" (many of them journeymen) violating guild restrictions; 30 years later, the city's tanners complained of an inundation of illegal shops. By the eighteenth century, gaping holes rent the regulatory web. The Bourbon officials would go farther than their predecessors in attempting to crack down on illicit activities—for instance, by ordering a thoroughgoing reform of marketplaces in the 1780s and 1790s. Nevertheless, as the documents that follow suggest, they faced serious obstacles in bringing "order" to the plebeian economy or to wider colonial society. Many studies point to the challenges faced by mid- to late eighteenth-century reformers attempting to overturn the established ways people lived and interacted with government and the Church in the colonial Americas.[4]

Questions to Consider:

1. What did public officials see as the root cause of the bread trade's problems? What objections would they have made to the notion of a free-market economy?

2. In what ways did the councilmen claim to be upholding public welfare with their regulation of the bread trade? Did such government regulations actually promote the "public good"?

3. Why did eighteenth-century Mexico City have a thriving "illegal" or "informal" economy? How did it differ from the "official" economy?

---

[3]R. Douglas Cope, *The Limits of Racial Domination: Plebeian Society in Colonial Mexico City, 1660–1720* (Madison: University of Wisconsin Press, 1994), 125–160.

[4]Pamela Voekel, "Peeing on the Palace: Bodily Resistance to Bourbon Reforms in Mexico City," *Journal of Historical Sociology* 5, no. 2 (1992): 183–208; and Juan Pedro Viquiera Albán, *Propriety and Permissiveness in Bourbon Mexico*, trans. Sonya Lipsett-Rivera and Sergio Rivera Ayala (Wilmington, DE: Scholarly Resources, 1999).

Dilemmas of the Bread Trade[5]

Councilmen's First Attempt to Impose Order on Trade

The district administrator and city councilmen provide new legislation for the bread trade.

We order first, that since [previous] orders and measures have not sufficed to exterminate the pernicious abuse of excessive profits, especially those that the bakers give to the storekeepers . . . the bakers cannot send bread to the storekeepers, but that the latter must bring, transport, and buy it from whatever bakers they please, as they do with all other goods they sell, under penalty of fifty *pesos* for the first offense, and for the second, privation of their trade; and this prohibition includes the bakers of Tacubaya, who can sell their bread only in the Plaza. . . . Second, no one, not even the so-called *Tlacuperos*,[6] will make deliveries of bread, for it is prohibited henceforth to sell bread in the streets, or in storefronts, since this is clearly the practice of resale. . . . Third, be heedful that only day old bread be sold in the Plaza.[7] . . . Fourth, that henceforth the bakers cannot work, nor make dough at night, because of the damage this causes to the neighborhood, as well as the workers, under penalty of fifty *pesos*[8] for the first time, and loss of their trade for the second = and finally, it is ordered that from now on, no one can open a new bakery, or transfer the title of one already erected, without license from this court . . . bakeries must be at least four hundred *varas*[9] apart in the future; and those erected in the present must be sold to the most immediate bakery, or business, so that once their effects and equipment are sold, they will no longer serve as bakeries, nor can they continue in this trade, which will impede the damage and competition of one [bakery] against the other, and the pernicious industry that one undertakes to produce more dough than the others, without keeping good order . . . to the detriment of the public.

Months Later Councilmen Again Grapple with Trade

[*Several months later, the district magistrate and the city councilmen continued to lament:*] the very grave damage that the common people of this republic feel, with the excessive profits, which day after day the bakers and storekeepers have introduced, the one selling and the other receiving the bread, fomenting innumerable sins this way . . . making bread of bad quality, and with inadequate grains, and even selling underweight loaves to achieve such profits, and doubling without necessity the amount of dough, burdening the workers and servants, robbing them not only of their corresponding daily pay, but even of their deserved rest, making them work day and night.

Don José Antonio de Areche, city attorney:

the low quality [*bajo*] bread has never been regulated, nor is it now, but instead the bakers have always given as many ounces as they like, and in proportion to the increase in ounces their sales improve.

As for the proposal that all bread come to the Plaza, without question this would be economical, because of the small expense and great exercise of the one who leaves from the outskirts of the city to obtain bread, for by the time he arrives at the Plaza it will be supper time, and he will have saved breakfast and dinner.

Mexico City, like all cities, is composed of two estates, Noble and Plebeian, and two kinds of

---

[5]*Sources:* Archivo General de las Indias, Seville, México, legajo 2779, sin número, 7 July 1772; Ibid., 4 February 1773; Ibid., 26 October 1770; Ibid., 28 November 1770; Ibid., 22 September 1770; Ibid., June 15, 1770, 26 Sept, 1776; Ibid., 24 September 1770; Ibid., 12 September 1780.

[6]*Tlacuperos* sold small amounts of bread and other items on the streets and accepted *tlacos* (store tokens given out as change) in payment for their wares.

[7]So that sales in the plaza would not compete with those in other, favored localities.

[8]This would represent about 1 week's profit for the average baker.

[9]A *vara* is equivalent to approximately 33 inches.

people, rich and poor; and in all, the plebeian and poor abound, but attention must be given to the feeding of all, for all are Members of the Republic . . . good government demands that the noble, delicate, and rich have a good, fine, and beautiful bread, and that the plebeians and poor do not lack bread, and that this be increased in ounces: this can be achieved by the production of two breads, fine and *bajo* . . . separately made in separate bakeries, and purchased by separate subjects . . . the reason for this is, that with this method, the [bakeries] will not use up so much wheat flour, and their provision will last longer . . . poor people would supply themselves with large amounts of the bread they crave, using *tlacos* and *quartillas*,[10] from the stores, rather than taking small amounts of finer bread . . . it should be prohibited, as the ordinances do, that high quality bakeries produce low quality bread; this way they will not buy inferior grain, nor have occasion to give "dirty" bread, dark, full of garbage. . . .

The Bakers Testify to the Council

Don Domingo Hernández Tejada, baker:

He says that it is true that he has made bread defective in quality and quantity because of the scarceness of wheat, and that his prices have not conformed to the government regulations . . . and he has given the storekeepers excessive earnings, such as two *reales*,[11] two-and-a half *reales*, and perhaps four in every *peso*, as a bonus, though the guide fixes the profit at one *real* for every *peso* = Question: does the bakery owner have the same cost . . . in preparing eight *cargas* of dough and ten? He says: that while there is a difference, it is of little significance, since it does not exceed one *peso* = Question: How many *cargas* of flour do you manufacture daily? He says: he makes about seven-and-a-half or eight *cargas*, which he believes is among the largest amounts of dough made in this City.

Don Antonio Larralde, baker:

It is impossible to give eighteen ounces of good bread, given the price of wheat and its scarcity, so that even with ready money one cannot find it . . . it is a rare baker who has quality flour reserved. No one can meet his expenses because of the great number of bakeries; when I entered this trade . . . about thirty years ago there were no more than thirty bakeries . . . in this city and then they produced bread of good quality, and the community was sufficiently supplied, without the abuses that are experienced today because of the enlarged number of dealers . . . who number more than seventy.

Bakers' representatives:

We have information that in times of abundant harvests many bakers give [the storekeepers] two or three *reales* of earnings in every *peso* and they could not do this without mixing wheat of bad quality and seeds into their flour dough, and committing other abuses in order to sustain such profits. . . . Currently, because of the increased costs of wheat, they are only giving a half *real* of earnings per each *peso*, and some give one *real*.

The High Court Comments on the Dispute

The High Court comments on regulations proposed in 1780:

Wheat of poor quality should not be mixed with good wheat, neither by the bakers nor the millers; the former should be used in low quality bread, the latter in the high quality . . . the two masses of dough should be made separately. . . . Neither one nor the other should be resold. . . . [The dough] should not be taken out of the bakeries until seven in the morning. . . . No baker may sell bread in his establishment . . . but all must go to the plazas, streets, and other public locations where it will be reweighed. . . . [Selling in the plaza] would facilitate the daily inspection of the judges to review and reweigh the bread put in these public places . . . and without the inconvenience and trouble of forcing people to frequent distant bakeries. . . .

---

[10]Another token, worth less than a *tlaco*.
[11]A basic monetary unit; 8 reales made up 1 *peso*.

A purchaser who is limited to one or a few bakeries, because they are the only ones at hand, will find that in the plazas . . . he can choose what he wants from among many bakers, and the latter will take great care to make [their bread] of the best quality. . . . [Bakers] may not give illicit earnings to the store-keepers. . . . [Banning the sale of bread in stores would] avoid frauds and illicit pacts among traders because to ensure the greater retailing and daily consumption of bread, the bakers advance their sales by making agreements with the storekeepers to give them preferential credit, with exorbitant profits, usury, and other condemned means. But . . . this Royal Audiencia grasps the need for bread to be retailed in stores because of the means they offer . . . in the bakeries the miserable poor with only a half *real* [apiece] cannot supply themselves with the various goods that sustain them at any given time . . . [But the storekeeper would have to] buy it [bread] freely in the plazas and other public places where it must be sold by the bakers and by no means in their bakeries.

The Struggle to Control the Market[12]

Regulating the Hatters, Tailors, and Dyers

The attorney for Juan Félix de Gálve for Juan Bautista, Baltasar de Santiago, Blas de la Cruz, Juan Diego, Gabriel de la Cruz, Juan Gregorio, Marcos de la Cruz, and the other Indians of the hatter's trade:

I say . . . that María Francisca, an Indian widow has taken up (along with other exercises) the mak-ing of hats, buying very considerable quantities of wool [and] having against the provision of the ordi-nance employed workers, journeymen and appren-tices, making use of the Indian Francisco de la Cruz through whose intervention she has [gained] the majority of the trade in selling hats, causing grave damage and prejudice to the said my parties who are the legitimate hat makers and who because of the said María Francisca's interference are not able to find work. . . . Neither is *don* Pedro Ramírez an official hat maker, [yet] he also has begun to employ workers and journeymen = Tomasina de la Rosa, an Indian women who says she is unmarried also has workers and journeymen . . . and at present her [true] occupation is selling *pulque* = Juan Antonio also has a worker, and his employer (with two journeymen) is an Indian bread maker named Maria de Zárate = Juan de Dios . . . sells bacon = Diego de Santiago is not a guild member.

The response by María Francisca:

Although [the plaintiffs] pretend a zeal to eliminate frauds and damages, and poor jobs, this is not the fundamental matter, when one can observe that the best and finest work is that done by my employees; but their well known desire is to achieve their own convenience, and theirs only, while the rest can per-ish, without paying attention to the common good and public utility, and so much the worse for him who does not have the wherewithal to gain [formal] training, as they give to understand when they are eminent in their offices, and the said ordinances should not be invoked when they go against custom and ancient laws, in which my workers were always exempted.

Ventura Serrano and Domingo de Maya, alcaldes and veedores of the tailor's guild:

We say that . . . many people within the *plaza mayor* of this city, and other vendors in the streets or thieves' market go about selling clothes in contra-vention of that disposed by the said ordinances and likewise [there are] many journeymen of the said guild who occupy themselves solely in making the said prohibited clothing.

---

[12]*Sources:* Archivo de Ex-Ayuntamiento de la Ciudad de México, Fiel Ejecutoria – Veedores de Gremios, vol. 3832, expediente 1, fols. 69, 71, 18 April and 26 April 1690; Ibid., exp. 3, fols. 1r-2v, 16 October and 19 October, 1706; Ibid., vol. 3833, exp. 64, fol. 1r, 19 November 1750; Ibid., vol. 3834, exp. 35, fols. 1r-2v, 22 March 1766.

Inspection of the Stands in the Plaza del Volador [also known as the "thieves' market"]

Juan Hernández Chapas
López Laporas
Antonio de Morales
José de Guzmán
Bartolo de Salazar
Juan Antonio de Córdova
Miguel Samudio

Inspection of Homes

José Ramírez, journeyman tailor
Agustín de la Puente

Don Francisco de Estrada, and Don Antonio de Mascareñas, examined masters and veedores of the dyers' guild:

We say that the trade is so deteriorated . . . that it could not possibly be worse; and this proceeds from the bad manner in which many manage it, weighting the silks and doing other wicked things . . . the principal authors of these excesses being those who without being examined nor having any ability, jump into opening public dye shops and to work in them, and the majority keep them private and in the barrios, so they are not impeded. *Don Domingo Borica and don Francisco Sanaez, veedores, petitioning the High Court*:

We say that this city is inundated with *asesorias* [apartments] and stores where they sell hides in prejudice of the public, the guild, and good government . . . we request that you order the closing of the asesorias and stores where they sell hides, pieces of leather, goatskins, and sheepskins. . . . The damage to the public from these asesorias is that there they generally sell poor hides . . . from which it results that the shoes [made from them] are not very durable, and the public suffers. The trade or guild suffers an intolerable damage, for because of these asesorias, the tanners' shops do not have the outlet they should, nor the corresponding commerce . . . because these asesorias are at the entrance of the tanners' *barrio*, and the customers come into the neighborhood . . .

[and] in these asesorias they give a greater quantity of leather for a *real* than in the tanneries, perhaps twice as much, and the shoemakers gravitate toward what is cheap, without considering the quality, or worth of the good. . . . [For the tanners] it is necessary, in order for them to make a living from their trade, to give the same amount or more as that of the asesorias, and to do this it is indispensable that they not give the correct treatment to the skins and this causes damage to the public. The seventh ordinance prohibits the purchase of hides for resale on pain of loss of the goods . . . in order to avoid the pernicious crime of resale, and that is what the asesorias encourage and commit, for they either buy the hides in the tanneries to resell them in the asesorias, which is encouragement, or they buy them elsewhere to resell, which is regatonería . . . even guild journeymen are prohibited from having shops and selling goods.

Suggested Sources:

The literature on petty commerce in colonial Latin America remains rather sparse and scattered. Jay Kinsbruner's studies, *Petty Capitalism in Spanish America: The Pulperos of Puebla, Mexico City, Caracas, and Buenos Aires* (Boulder, CO: Westview Press, 1987) and *The Colonial Spanish American City: Urban Life in the Age of Atlantic Capitalism* (Austin: University of Texas Press, 2005) are fundamental. R. Douglas Cope, *The Limits of Racial Domination: Plebeian Society in Colonial Mexico City. 1660–1720* (Madison: University of Wisconsin Press, 1994) explores the economic and social lives of plebeians in midcolonial Mexico City. The classic novel by José Joaquín Fernández de Lizardi, *The Mangy Parrot: The Life and Times of Periquiilo Sarniento*, trans. David Frye (Indianapolis, IN: Hackett, 2004) provides picaresque vignettes of the hand-to-mouth existence of the urban poor. Recent scholarship focuses on non-Spanish market women. See Jane E. Mangan, *Trading Roles: Gender, Ethnicity, and the Urban Economy in Colonial Potosí* (Durham, NC: Duke University Press, 2005). Roger Horowitz, Jeffrey M. Pilcher, and Sydney Watts, "Meat for the Multitudes: Market

Culture in Paris, New York City and Mexico City over the Long Nineteenth Century," *American Historical Review* 109, no. 4 (October 2004): 1055–1083, places the Mexico City meat trade in historical perspective and highlight the Native American contribution. William B. Taylor, *Drinking, Homicide, and Rebellion in Colonial Mexican Villages* (Stanford, CA: Stanford University Press, 1979) documents the significance of *pulque* consumption. Richard L. Garner (with Spiro E. Stefanou), *Economic Growth and Change in Bourbon Mexico* (Gainesville: University of Florida Press, 1993) offers a fine overview of Mexico's eighteenth-century economy, including the bread trade.

Chapter 23

Indians Do Prodigious Things, Indians Make Everything: The Otomí of Querétaro, 1738

John Tutino, Georgetown University

How did indigenous peoples understand their lives as colonial subjects? The Otomí of Querétaro composed a song in which they proclaimed themselves the builders of the colonial order. This chapter examines that song, written in 1738, as part of a festival celebrating the construction of a great aqueduct. Querétaro was a major city in eighteenth-century New Spain. A center of commerce and transportation, of cloth making and irrigated cultivation, it was a key urban link between Mexico

City—the pivot of colonial government, financing, and oceanic trade—and the rich mines of Guanajuato, Zacatecas, and San Luis Potosí to the north. Querétaro was also a center of worship—its plaza dominated by a great *Franciscan* church; its heights marked by the College of Santa Cruz, which sent so many missionaries to Texas and California; and its outskirts marked by the chapel of Our Lady of Pueblito, the Virgin honored by nearly everyone from the powerful few to the native majority.[1]

Yet Querétaro was also different from other major colonial centers. It was founded after the conquest, not by Spanish conquerors, but by Otomí people taking advantage of the fall of their historic *Mexica (Aztec)* overlords to press northward into the rich bottomlands known as the Bajío. Around 1500, that basin was a frontier contested by Mexica and *Tarascan* states to the south and to the north by warrior nomads denigrated by *Aztecs*, Otomí, and Spaniards as *Chichimecas*—sons of dogs. The post-conquest incursion was led by Connín, an Otomí who had served the Mexica as a trader and a tribute collector, living and working across contested political and cultural borders, integrating what others saw as worlds in conflict.

As the Mexica fell to powerful outsiders, Connín organized groups of Otomí settlers in the late 1520s or early 1530s to drive northward and settle. A few *Franciscan* missionaries accompanied them, creating a Christian-Otomí incursion into the lands of the *Chichimecas*. Querétaro was Connín's most important and enduring foundation. By 1550 it was a place of *huertas* (intensively cultivated, irrigated urban gardens), wheat farms, and a gristmill, with Old World livestock grazing all around. Connín, baptized *don* Fernando de Tapia, was the leading wheat grower and stock grazer, a ruling lord who repeatedly served as governor of the *República de Indios* (Republic of Indians) that exercised local government. He built personal power and brought advantages to Otomí settlers by combining astute entrepreneurship and political intrigue. Neither a traditional native lord,

nor the favored dependent of Spanish conquerors, Connín led a community working rich *huertas* in an urban environment along the banks of a river. In short, the town was an Otomí foundation under Spanish rule.

The discovery of silver at Zacatecas and Guanajuato to the north and west in the 1540s brought Spaniards, indigenous migrants, African slaves, and vast herds of livestock northward in prodigious numbers. They invaded the lands of the *Chichimecas* beyond Querétaro in ways so disruptive that the second half of the sixteenth century was defined by *Chichimeca* wars. Connín (*don* Fernando de Tapia) and his son *don* Diego de Tapia organized and led Otomí forces to fight beside Spaniards against *Chichimecas*. Querétaro's Otomí cultivators sustained the fight and the new settlements pressing north.[2]

By claiming essential roles defending and provisioning the silver economy that shaped New Spain, the Tapias negotiated their way to remaining key lords, landlords, and entrepreneurs at Querétaro in a time when most indigenous rulers were pressed toward subordinate roles. The Tapia family's power also helped the Otomí majority retain lands and water rights that sustained families and fueled prosperous trades. As fighting waned in the 1590s, *don* Diego de Tapia emerged as the most powerful entrepreneur and governor between Mexico City and the northern mines. He operated vast landed properties, he ensured that the Otomí who had joined him in the fight against the *Chichimecas* kept the rich huertas along the river—and he welcomed the arrival of Spanish merchants and grazers, and the founders of a new textile industry, as long as they recognized the Tapia family's eminence and the rule of the Otomí republic. From 1590 to 1650 Querétaro became the key center of trade, textiles, and cultivation north of the capital.

Otomí power, however, did not endure without contest. The first threats came from within. The Tapias had used eminence in Otomí society to claim power and profit in a Spanish commercial world. *Don* Diego's only heir was a daughter, *doña* Luisa. After 1600 he founded and she led the Convent of

---

[1]This introduction summarizes the detailed treatment of the history of Querétaro in John Tutino, *Making a New World: Forging Atlantic Capitalism in the Bajío and Spanish North America* (Durham, NC: Duke University Press, forthcoming).

[2]Phillip Wayne Power, *Soldiers, Indians, and Silver: The Northward Advance of New Spain* (Berkeley: University of California Press, 1952).

Santa Clara, endowing it with all the Tapia lands and water rights. That Otomí-Christian foundation became the leading mortgage bank in the Bajío. It funded the expansion of Spanish commercial cultivation through the seventeenth century. The sisters at times challenged Otomí cultivators' rights to the water essential to their huertas. The Tapia legacy became a Spanish convent-bank. Then in 1655, the Spanish entrepreneurs who had profited in trade and textiles since the *Chichimeca* war gained rights to create a Spanish council. It did not replace the Otomí republic but left it to rule the Otomí majority, focused in the San Sebastian parish north of the river among the huertas. After more than a century of colonial life, Querétaro would be ruled by dual powers—one Otomí, the other Spanish.

The eighteenth century brought an explosive revival of mining at Zacatecas and Guanajuato, driving another wave of commercial expansion at Querétaro. Trade, cloth making, and irrigated cultivation expanded to the profit of Spanish entrepreneurs—and to the lesser benefit of Otomí cultivators still ensconced in their huertas. The boom proved so prosperous that rich entrepreneurs like the *Marqués* de la Villa del Villar del Águila moved north from Mexico City to make Querétaro his home and base of operations. At Querétaro, too, *don* Pedro Romero de Terreros began the life of trade, mining, and landed investment that would make him Conde de Regla, the richest man in New Spain, perhaps the Atlantic world.[3] Profit and concentrating wealth shaped Querétaro in the 1720s and 1730s. The Spanish center of the city, home to rich entrepreneurs, great churches, and elegant convents needed water. So the *Marqués* organized the Spanish Council to lead the construction of a great aqueduct.

It would claim a portion of the flow from the springs that fed the Querétaro River in the canyon west of the city. Water that historically irrigated Otomí huertas would be diverted to supply the palatial homes and convents of the Spanish center. In a political-ecological assertion of colonial power, the aqueduct, over a mile long and 50 yards high, marked the urban landscape and proclaimed the eminence of Spanish rule. Two centuries after its Otomí foundation, Querétaro appeared a Spanish city. The descendants of the city's founders had been reduced to "Indians." Or had they?

The festivities inaugurating the aqueduct in 1738 were recorded by a *Jesuit* priest, Francisco Antonio Navarrete, in a text published as the *Relación peregrina*—a pilgrim's account. He wrote to honor the Marqués who had come from Mexico City to Querétaro and built the aqueduct that would ensure the city's health and wealth into the future. Yet the Otomí did not acquiesce in their long-developing subordination. The indigenous republic organized a parade as part of the celebrations and Navarrete recorded the long song of praise in which they supposedly "honored" the Marqués and asserted their own distinction, making it unmistakably clear that the Otomí, not the Marqués, built the aqueduct—and everything else that made Querétaro a flourishing colonial city.

Questions to Consider:

1. Based on Father Navarrete's prologue, what did the Jesuit admire about the Otomí? What did he condemn?

2. In the song of praise, the Otomí referred to themselves and other native peoples with many terms. List these terms and explain what they suggest—separately and together.

3. How did the Otomí characterize their religious lives, past and present?

4. How did the Otomí portray work and the importance of water?

5. The Otomí emphasized their past power, their embrace of Christianity, and their colonial subordination. How did they see their moral relationship to the Spaniards who ruled? What might the Otomí have hoped to gain by this public assertion of eminence?

---

[3]See Edith Couturier, *The Silver King: The Remarkable Life of the Count of Regla in Colonial Mexico* (Albuquerque:University of New Mexico Press, 2003).

Description of the Indian Procession[4]

The same Thursday [October 18, 1738] in the afternoon we witnessed the campaign of a magnificent squadron of soldiers, composed of the *República de Indios*, the natives of the city. Kettledrums and trumpets led the way, their noise inviting our ears to turn our eyes to the amusing spectacle. A large squad of indigenous infantry followed, armed with bows and arrows, naked except the coverage necessary for modesty. Their bodies were painted in many colors, making their minimal dress acceptable, their nudity decent. From time to time they hollered shouts so sharp and fearsome accompanied by the rude tone of the *teponaztles* (log drums) that as they passed they brought to mind the warfare of their gentility,[5] filling hearts with pleasant surprise, calling to mind the deeds of their heroic ancestors who found the valor to defeat the indomitable pride of their barbarity.

Next marched a disciplined cavalry of *indios principales* (native notables), dressed extravagantly in the style of Romans with rich plumage, harnesses, and saddle blankets. At the rear of the squadron on a beautiful mount rode the native Governor, carrying a banner and a shield that read: *VICTOR EL SEÑOR MARQUÉS DEL VILLAR DE LA ÁGUILA.* The Governor's majestic imperial robes were carried aloft by twelve Indian footmen, dressed as their ancestors would when they marched to the flags of uncivilized gentility.

---

[4]*Source:* Francisco Antonio Navarrete, *Relación peregrino* (1739; reprint: Querétaro: Gobierno del Estado, 1987). The translations are mine, from pp. 86 to 90 of the Querétaro edition.

[5]Navarrete refers to the Otomí before their conversion to Christianity as *gentiles*, a term without the strong tone of condemnation that might have been suggested by potential alternatives such as "pagan." Still, he quickly turns to an assertion of barbarity.

The Indian Guild's Praise

The American Guild
in its native dress
parades with pleasure
proclaiming its joy.

A gathering grounded in antiquity
clothed by design
to remember the ancient past
and display its parallels to our times.

In our gentile past
we served the Devil,
and offered him adorations
across valleys and on cliffs.

We knew not the great God
venerated by Christianity,
wasting all our worship
on false sacrifices.

We attributed power and meaning
to false deities,
making rocks and trees
magnets of our solicitations.

We spilled innocent blood
of beautiful infants,
conceding bloody sacrifice
to the ferocious Devil.

For today's celebration
we parade in traditional costumes,
showing off the great opulence
we enjoyed for centuries.

The mines gave us
gold for our robes,
the air gave us birds and their feathers
for our brilliant headdresses.

The land gave us cotton
to make balls of thread,
and from them
we wove our clothing.
The water gushed pearls
in numbers so great,
that to be paralytic,
was not an illness but a vice.

It is astonishing
that so many souls lived in shackles,
without corroding the falsehoods
that were truth to our unfortunate ancestors.

Finally, the time of joy came,
when God, so compassionate,
gave them the light to see
the stains of their sins.

The light came in water,
so all could see the prodigy
that water was the oil
in which light's splendor shined.

As a remedy for all,
God gave, because he chose to,
water as the medicine
of baptismal fonts.

They received by water
the essential cure for the soul
in those first days of light,
and in the centuries since.

Water is the shared refuge
of the soul, and of the body,
washing stains,
irrigating the land.

With our souls and bodies
rejoicing in water,
mulatos and blacks, Spaniards and
Indians offer thanks to God.

Of all the miracles of water,
we proclaim that
in imitation of water,
Indians do prodigious things.

They have been to this day,
the people who keep everything flowing,
they sustain what everyone is and has been,
for the benefit of all.

The Indians plant the fields
the Indians harvest wheat,
the Indians bake bread,
the Indians make everything.

It is certain that
if these dominions lacked Indians,
everything would be scarce
because Indians are the fifth element.

And because the world knows
how much is made possible
by the delivery of water,
it is important that we celebrate today.

From beginning to end,
the Indians alone,
at the cost of hard work
gave water to distinguished citizens.

They built the reservoir,
risking danger,
they built soaring arches and vaults,
they made buttresses, bricks, cement.

And while the work was paid,
we know that
without our work
the cost would be much greater.

As so, if water is the fountain
in which Indians washed away
the sins and crimes of
their ancient blindness.

Now all the natives
are so grateful,
we return to the Spanish
a river of water, clean and pure.

To Indians, water gave
life free of
cruelties and rudeness,
of impurities and of sorceries.

Today, we return the favor,
because we understand,
that if purity reigns,
it is because Spaniards live free of vice.

So we Indians march
to proclaim, in strong voices,
that with water the city
will become a beautiful paradise.

The white flowers, the roses,
the jasmine and the lilies,
now transformed into stars,
by conversion to Christianity.

Because if water is the mirror
in which we see our ancient slovenliness,
who on seeing water so pure,
will not erase their sins.

We owe this river of grace
to the always invincible gentleman,
who turned his riches
into a pilgrimage of good work.

This is the Lord, the Marqués del Villar,
to whom in unity,
Chichimecas and Otomí,
give a thousand thanks, as children.

And because our clamorous voices,
our log drums and flutes,
reach to heaven,
as one we shout: Huzza!

This is the Lord, the Marqués del Villar,
to whom in unity,
Chichimecas and Otomí,
give a thousand thanks, as children.

And because our clamorous voices,
our log drums and flutes,
reach to heaven,
as one we shout: Huzza!

Suggested Sources:

The sixteenth-century history of the Bajío, including the participation of the Tapias and the Otomí, is covered in Philip Wayne Powell's *Soldiers, Indians, and Silver: The Northward Advance of New Spain* (Berkeley: University of California Press, 1952). James Lockhart details the complex participation of indigenous notables and communities in regions just south of Querétaro in *The Nahuas after the Conquest* (Stanford, CA: Stanford University Press, 1992). Entrepreneurship in Querétaro during the eighteenth century is explored through a biography by Edith Couturier, *The Silver King: The Remarkable Life of the Conde de Regla in Colonial Mexico* (Albuquerque: University of New Mexico Press, 2003). Ellen Gunnarsdótir examines religious life during the same period in *Mexican Karismata: The Baroque Vocation of Francisca de los Angeles, 1674–1744* (Lincoln, NE: University of Nebraska Press, 2004). A history of Querétaro, emphasizing Otomí foundations and later Spanish assertions, is part of my *Making a New World: Forging Atlantic Capitalism in the Bajío and Spanish North America* (Durham, NC: Duke University Press, forthcoming).

Few primary sources in English illuminate indigenous communities in eighteenth-century New Spain. For early periods, *Letters and People of the Spanish Indies: Sixteenth Century*, ed. and trans. James Lockhart and Enrique Otte (Cambridge: Cambridge University Press, 1976) offers a broad array of perspectives. For the early seventeenth century, *Annals of His Time: Don Domingo Anton Chimalpahin Cuauhtlehuanitzin*, ed. and trans. James Lockhart, Susan Schroeder, and Doris Nomala (Stanford, CA: Stanford University Press, 2006) offers a Nahualt-speaking intellectual's vision. A rare English voice on the interior of New Spain and other regions of Spanish America was published in 1648 by the English friar, Thomas Gage. There are many editions; easily accessible is *Thomas Gage's Travels in the New World* (Norman: University of Oklahoma Press, 1985). And a broad sampling of native perspectives from across New Spain from the sixteenth through the eighteenth century is now available in Matthew Restall, Lisa Sousa, and Kevin Terraciano, eds. and trans., *Mesoamerican Voices: Native Language Writings from Colonial Mexico, Oaxaca, Yucatán, and Guatemala* (Cambridge: Cambridge University Press, 2005).

Chapter 24

High Clergy Warns the Crown of Popular Discontent

Leo J. Garofalo, Connecticut College

Viceroyalty of New Spain

earing an upheaval in the countryside and widespread disaffection among parish priests, a reform-minded bishop boldly counseled the Spanish king to reverse royal policy. Well-conceived reforms strengthened the monarchy, reasoned the bishop; ill-conceived changes diminished subjects' loyalty. After the mid-1700s, Bourbon monarchs sought to change the relationship between the Church and the state. Charles III (1759–1788) in particular discarded the Habsburg idea of a partnership in which Christianization justified Spanish rule in the Americas in favor of the absolutist idea of the Church as a servant of the state. Reformers expected the Church to serve as a loyal ally in pastoral and spiritual affairs, without interfering in political, economic, and judicial affairs. This Spanish regalism favored absolute Crown power and tighter central control over commerce, courts, and governance. Tighter control over the Church derived not from Enlightenment's anticlericalism and freethinking, but from a desire to assert the Crown's supremacy. The Crown attempted to redirect the clergy's energies back to spiritual duties and away from politics and developing the Church's property and wealth. Manuel Abad y Queipo's 1799 report responded to these royal efforts at ecclesiastical reform and proposed some alternative social and economic reforms designed to diffuse explosive social tensions and to stimulate agriculture and industry in rural Mexico. This chapter opens a window on the negotiation of a new relationship between the Church and the imperial state.

The stakes were high on both sides in this negotiation. The French Revolution (1789) had swept through France, destroying both Church and royal power. The Haitian Revolution (1791–1804) had ended slavery in the colony and showed that even the most downtrodden of colonial subjects could overthrow their imperial masters. Absolutist monarchs had expelled the *Jesuit* religious order from their empires in Portugal (1759), France (1764), and Spain (1767) because of resentment of its autonomy; its international reach and allegiance to the pope; and its control of American schools and universities, *haciendas*, and mission areas. Royal patronage already gave the Crown the power to control priests' and missionaries' movement to the Americas and to appoint and remove clergy at will, especially the powerful archbishops and bishops. Below the higher levels of the Church hierarchy, many parish priests and sacristans and even some members of the religious orders struggled with inadequate pay, low levels of education, and frequently a lack of devotion to Christian labors. According to the Crown, they were not doing their job of delivering sermons and administering the sacraments to parishioners. All this occurred in a highly stratified society swept by economic insecurity for many and opportunity for social mobility and wealth accumulation for a few. Abad y Queipo aimed to renew both the clergy and flagging royal legitimacy by charting a course between reform and a defense of historic privileges.

Although a staunch royalist, Abad y Queipo (1751–1825) could be called an enlightened bureaucrat because he believed in progress and using Enlightenment reasoning to solve social and economic problems. He advocated rolling back ecclesiastical reforms, in particular reinstating the clergy's right (*fuero*) to be tried in Church courts rather than by secular authorities.[1] Abad y Queipo frequently mentioned the distinction between the regular clergy and the secular clergy. The regular clergy belonged to religious orders (e.g., *Dominicans* and *Franciscans*) governed by their orders' specific rules and answerable to a superior back in Spain. The need for missionaries to evangelize the indigenous population and the continued need for qualified priests to minister in all sorts of parishes, however, brought the friars out of their monasteries and under local bishops' control and Crown oversight in the Americas. Initially few in number, secular clergy were the ordained priests and sacristans under a bishop's jurisdiction; they labored as parish priests, private chaplains, or attached to specific endowed chapels. By the late eighteenth century, many of both the secular clergy and regular clergy living outside their monasteries suffered a similar plight; they either could not find a permanent appointment and benefice (property) and living (income) provided in exchange for pastoral duties, or what they received was wholly inadequate to maintain them or sustain them in a dignified state. Furthermore, they served a population legally divided among Spanish, *castas* or *mestizos*, and Indians; however, these categories were increasingly blurred by trade, intermarriage, and movement out of legally circumscribed communities, neighborhoods, and occupations. By this point in colonial history, social position and cultural markers more than exclusively racial designations distinguished Indians from *castas*, or even *castas* from people enjoying "Spanish" legal status. In short, class played a greater role in society than in the past. According to Abad y Queipo, the divisions created by wealth and poverty linked the plight of the clergy to that of the general populace. Both cried out for remedy.

---

[1]Royal law historically conferred specific rights, privileges, and immunities on special groups of subjects such as the military, nobility, clergy, or Indian communities as rewards or paternal protection. Reformers targeted these exemptions and privileges.

Consequently, many issues found their way into Abad y Queipo's report to King Charles IV (1788–1808) warning against ending legal immunity for the clergy and explaining the causes of popular discontent. Sent to Mexico in 1786, Abad y Queipo offered his views on Indians' communal landownership, how to raise the common people out of poverty, how to make agriculture and textile mills more productive, and how to fill royal coffers with tax revenue. In the same breath, Abad y Queipo tried to benefit his fellow clergymen and advise the King on how to avoid social upheaval.

Questions to Consider:

1. How did Abad y Queipo both call for reform and resist change? Was his proposal a radical position in his time or a conservative defense of the status quo?

2. On what grounds might the King and his counselors have found Abad y Queipo's argument persuasive? On what grounds might they have considered his proposals a challenge to royal authority?

3. Did the social classes and tensions described in late eighteenth-century Mexico confirm or contrast with the relationships among Indians, *castas* (*mestizos*), and Spanish described in earlier eras (in previous chapters, such as Chapters 11, 15, and 17)?

4. In what ways did this report present a "view from above?" How do you compare this perspective on social tensions and the relationship between rulers and the ruled to other perspectives presented in this section or in the preceding sections?

The Bishop Defends the Clergy against Royal Reforms and Warns of Social Tensions in Mexico, 1799[2]

. . . With greater reason still the American clergy can claim the title of preserving the conquests and educating the conquered peoples. The clergy settled the Indians in towns, they taught them Castilian Spanish, the Catholic and moral faith and civilized them to the extent possible in those times, as is credited in the municipal history of each province and in the general history of these kingdoms. The clergy worked incessantly to separate them from their errors and vices, the clergy taught them their first letters and artisanal arts and professions. The reverend Quiroga,[3] first bishop of this diocese, to whom we owe the establishment of the majority of the Indian towns and all of the hospitals, established

in each town its own artisanal craft creating interdependency among the towns, so that communication and commerce would be created among them. Three centuries later his memory is preserved in the hearts of the Indians. In the early days the bishops and the rural priests were the Indians' defenders against the oppression of the *encomenderos, hacendados* and *alcaldes mayores*,[4] in this way they motivated many of the royal decrees favoring Indians in the *Reales Audiencias* [Royal Courts] and the Supreme *Council of the Indies*. Since then they have continued with equal zeal to instruct the Indians and aid in the time of epidemics and scarcity. And finally, Sire, the American Clergy is the only class that, because of its beneficence in the spiritual and civic matters, retains any regard and appreciation in the common people's heart. This consideration is more important than you think and in order to make it clear it is necessary to provide here an idea of the actual state of the

---

[2]*Source:* Manuel Abad y Queipo, "Escritos del obispo electo de Michoácan Don Manuel Abad y Queipo," in *Obras sueltas*, 2nd ed., ed. José María Luís Mora (Mexico: Editorial Porrúa, 1963), 204–212. This collection of documents was originally published in Paris in 1837.

[3]The *Franciscan* Bishop of Michoácan, Vasco de Quiroga, wrote in 1535 that America's native peoples lacked what Europeans defined as civil society; thus, the Americas could be occupied and colonized by people capable of establishing civil society and a government.

[4]Originally called *corregidores*, these regional royal officers enforced royal law and collected taxes at the local level. The *intendants* later replaced the *alcaldes mayores*.

population of this kingdom and its secular and ecclesiastical government.

The Moral and Political State in which the Population of New Spain is Found in 1779

We already said that New Spain is composed of close to four and a half million inhabitants,[5] that are divided into three classes: Spanish, Indians and *castas*. The Spanish constitute a tenth of the population and they own most of the property and wealth in the kingdom. The other two classes, that make up nine-tenths, can be divided into two thirds of *castas* and one third of pure Indians. Indians and *castas* are occupied in domestic service, in agricultural work and in the ordinary jobs of commerce and works as artisans. This is to say, that they are first-rate employees, servants and day laborers. Consequently between them and the first class there is a conflict of interests that is common between those who have nothing and those who have everything, between the dependents and the masters: envy, robbery, poor service on one side; contempt, usury, and harshness on the other. These results are common all over the world to a certain extent. But in America they reach a high level, because there are no gradations or middle [classes]; everyone is rich or miserable, nobles or infamous.

In effect, the two classes of Indians and *castas* are found in the greatest dejection and degradation. The color, ignorance and misery of the Indians place them at an infinite distance from a Spanish person. The favor of the law helps them little and in everything else causes them much harm. Circumscribed within the circle that forms a radius of six hundred rods [approximately 1,800 feet], that marks the legal boundary of their towns, they have no private lands. The community lands that they are forced to farm without any immediate benefit, must be for them an even more odious burden, because the difficulty of profiting from the products they produce increases each day. Urgent problems cannot be resolved because

of the new form of government established by the *intendant* system,[6] no decision can be made without recourse to the superior junta of the Real Hacienda [Royal Treasury] in Mexico City. Prohibited by law from living together with the other *castas* and dealing with them, they are denied the enlightenment and help that they should receive from communication and trade with them and with other people. Isolated by language and by their government, the most tyrannous and useless, they continue their customs, ways and gross superstitions, that eight or ten old Indians manage to mysteriously maintain in each town, who live without working at the expense of others' sweat, dominating them with the harshest despotism. Barred by law from making a work contract, from borrowing more than five *pesos* and in a word from trading and making contracts, it is impossible for them to improve their instruction, to better their fortunes, they cannot even take a step forward to lift themselves from their misery. [Legal scholars] are amazed at the hidden cause that made harmful the laws meant to benefit them. But it is more amazing that they have not perceived that the cause of the harm is in the privileges themselves. They are the same offensive arm that a resident of another class injures his opponent with when serving as an official for the Indians, without ever defending them. This conjunction of causes puts the Indians in a truly apathetic state, inert and indifferent about the future and about almost everything that does not immediately stir the grosser passions.

The *castas* are held to be infamous by the law because they descend from black slaves. They pay *tribute*, and as the census counts are executed with such exactitude, tributary status becomes for them an indelible mark of slavery that they cannot erase with the passage of time, not even by mixing with other races in successive generations. There are many who because of their color, their physiognomy and conduct would be elevated to the Spanish class, if it were not for this impediment for which they are kept

---

[5]In reality, it was closer to six million at that time.

[6]Placed throughout Spanish Americas between 1782 and 1790, these new provincial governors were charged with improving efficient administration and increasing royal revenue by relieving *viceroys* of some of their responsibilities and encouraging improved crops, mining techniques, and infrastructure projects.

down in the original class. This class is, thus, denigrated by law, poor and dependent, it lacks a useful education and retains some coloring from its origin; in these circumstances it is of low spirits and allows itself to be carried away by the strong passions of its fiery and robust temperament. This class frequently commits crimes. But it is a marvel that it does not commit more crimes, and that in this class there are many individuals known for their good conduct.

The Indians like the *castas* are governed locally by the district magistrates, who have contributed in no small part to the situation the Indians find themselves in. The *alcaldes mayores* are considered merchants rather than judges, authorized with an exclusive privilege and the power to execute it themselves, to monopolize commerce in their province and derive from it in a five-year term between 30,000 and 200,000 *pesos*. Their usurious and forced *repartimientos* [forced sales of goods to Indians] cause great humiliation. But in the middle of all this, two favorable circumstances usually result: one, they administer justice with disinterest and rectitude in the cases to which they are not a party; and the other, they promote industry and agriculture in the areas that matter to them. To remedy the abuses of the *alcaldes mayores*, they were replaced by sub-delegates, who are rigorously barred from all trade. But because they were not granted any salary, the solution was infinitely worse than the problem itself. If they only rely on the legal tariffs, among the poor who only engage in crime, they will starve. By necessity they will prostitute their jobs, defraud the poor, and make a business out of crimes. For the same reason it is extremely difficult for the *intendants* to find ideal people for these posts. The only ones who apply to serve are failures or those whose conduct or talents do not allow them to subsist in society's other careers. In such circumstances, what benefits, what protection can these ministers of the law dispense to the two classes mentioned? By what means can they reconcile benevolence and respect, when injustice and extortion are necessary?

By contrast, the priests and their deputies, dedicated solely to the spiritual service and temporary aid for these miserable classes, earn their affection, gratitude and respect. They visit and console them in their illness and their work. They act as doctors,

they prescribe medicine, [and] they pay for and sometimes apply the remedies themselves. They also act as lawyers and intercessors with the judges and those who charge them. They also help them resist the oppression of the magistrates and the powerful property owners. In a word, the people have nobody they can trust, except the Clergy and in the superior magistrates, who are harder to reach.

In this state of affairs, what interests could possibly unite these two classes with the first and bind all three to the law and the government? The first class has the greatest interest in obeying the laws that protect their lives, honor and their property or their wealth against the insults of the envious and the assaults of the miserable. But the other two classes that do not have property, *honor*, or anything else that would provoke an attack on their lives and person, what regard do they have for laws that only serve to measure the punishments for their crimes? What affection, what benevolence can they feel for the ministers of the law, who only exercise their authority to send them to jail, the whipping post, to the frontier fort or the gallows? What ties can these classes strengthen with the government, whose beneficence they are incapable of comprehending?

Will it be said, that to keep any people subordinate to the laws and government, fear of punishment was enough? . . . Let the modern legislators come and show, if they can, a means that can keep these classes subordinate to the law and the government other than the religion, preserved in the bottom of their hearts by the preaching and advice from the pulpit and in the confessional by the ministers of the Church. They are the true custodians of the laws and the guarantors of its observance. . . .

. . . We are not attempting to impede the sovereign judgment of Your Majesty or the wise counsel of your devoted ministers. We only seek to lay bare the results of acts that perhaps are not as well known there as to us. . . . In any case, Sire, we give testament of our desire for the happy success in Your Majesty's glorious endeavor.

It seems to us of the greatest importance, first, the total abolition of the *tributes* paid by the Indian and *casta* classes. Second, the abolition of the legal infamy that affects these *castas*; that they be declared honest and honorable, capable of obtaining civil posts that do not require noble status, if they deserve them for their good customs. Third, the distribution without charge of Indian community lands among all the residents of each town. Fourth, an agrarian law similar to that of Asturias and Galicia, that by means of leases and conveyances of twenty or thirty years, in which the *alcabala* [royal sales tax] is not collected, permits the people to farm the large property owners' uncultivated lands, at a just assessment in the case of disagreements, with the condition that they fence them and anything else that seems necessary to preserve unharmed the right to the property. The province's *intendants* will oversee all of this in the first instance, with rights to appeal to the district's *audiencia*, as in any other civil suit. Sixth, permission for all the classes, Spanish, *castas* and Indians from other towns to settle in Indian towns and build houses and buildings there if they pay for the plots. Seventh, pay a salary to all the judges, except the *alcaldes ordinarios* [town council magistrates], who should serve without pay as part of their council duties. If you add the freedom to build cotton and wool mills, it will give greater impetus to the people taking the first step towards their happiness. Mills are already permitted in general, but only with a special license from the *viceroys* or governors; but this unnecessary obstacle should be removed for the poor and all other charges, except the sales tax on the importation and export of merchandise.

We realize that the proposition to abolish *tribute* in the Crown's time of need will surprise many. But if in the arithmetic of the treasury there are times when three plus two is not five, the present case is certainly one of them. And with a calculation approximating the reality, it will be demonstrated that with the abolition of *tribute* and the other provisions referred to, far from hurting the royal treasury, will expand in less than ten years to three or four times what is today generated from *tribute*. . . .

Now the population of New Spain [Mexico] rises to 4,500,000. Subtract the tenth that is the Spanish class, the wealthy class that consumes the most, leaving the other two classes numbering 4,050,000 souls; at five per family, they make up 810,000 families. Some of these families are out of poverty because of their industriousness, they go about well dressed, with shoes and are better fed

than the rest; they can be compared in this regard with Spain's lower class. A fifth are in this state. But suppose they were a third leaving 540,000 families in the lowest state. The families that are best off in this last class are the peons on the *haciendas*; they each consume 50 *pesos* annually on the highland estates and 72 *pesos* annually on the lowland estates, averaging 61 *pesos* annually. A family in the highest third spends at least 300 *pesos* for food, clothing and shoes, compared with the 61 *pesos* that is the annual consumption of the best-off families in the lowest two thirds, resulting in a difference of 239 *pesos*, that, spent on items of consumption, should produce 14 pesos of *alcabala* revenue. According to this calculation, if the 540,000 families of the lowest two thirds increase their consumption at the same rate as the wealthiest third, the annual *alcabala* revenue will increase by 7,560,000 *pesos*. That is to say, the royal treasury will earn six times what it earns from *tribute*. Thus, by the means set forth above these two thirds of the population should be lifted from their poverty and increase their consumption to the level of the top third of their class; by which it is seen that although royal charges are lowered, it always results in tripling or quadrupling what is earned from *tribute*, to the great benefit of the treasury, people's customs, agriculture, commerce and the government. . . .

Returning to our main theme, and insisting on the principle that individual interests produce and reinforce the links within society, or, in other words, the first are proportional to the second; we find that when applied to the Clergy one reason alone, when there is no other, would suffice to preserve unchanged the *fuero criminal*[7] [legal exemption] just as prescribed in our ancient laws. The interests of the Clergy vary depending on the religious order or class; and there is an even greater variety of interests among the individual members within each religious order or class. They are all loyal to the government, but not all to the same degree. A parish priest and a sacristan receive benefits from Your Majesty, and both receive from

---

[7] As a way to limit Church power and assert the supremacy of royal law and Crown officials, Bourbon reformers targeted the clergy's exemption.

Your Majesty and your laws the prerogatives that they enjoy in their profession and their salaries. But being greater the prerogatives and powers of the first greater than the second, so too is greater its gratitude to its benefactor [the Crown] and its interest in observing the laws that allow it to enjoy these greater benefits. The gradual differentiation of the benefits produces another gradual differentiation in the sentiments of the beneficiaries. There is also a different level of adherence between one sacristan and another and between one priest and another. The loyalty among the Church cannons is greater than among the priests and sacristans, because their rewards are greater. The loyalty of the bishops exceeds all the others, because their rewards from Your Majesty exceed in number and excellence. They are your natural counselors, they enjoy military honors like the field marshals, they are frequently seen heading Your Majesty's supreme councils in government affairs and commissions of the greatest importance; they are treated with a sublime and affectionate decorum; their persons and dignity are recognized and protected by law; and in short, they owe their promotion as Bishops and all of the prerogatives of this position apart from the divine ones to Your Majesty. This accumulation of benefits aligns them and identifies them with Your Majesty, such that all your interests they view as their own and they can never separate themselves from this view.

But the rest of the clerics without high position who do not have these benefits and subsist only from the small stipends of their office, receive nothing from the government that distinguishes them from the other classes, if it is not the privilege of the fuero [legal exemption]. In this situation, are found eight tenths of the secular clergy in America; at least that is the case in this bishopric. All the regular clergy is in the same situation. Some are like the priest's auxiliaries, they are the ones who preach the most and take confessions and most frequently and closely work with and control the lowest two classes of society. For this reason they have a greater influence over the hearts of these classes. Therefore the clergy's fuero is the only special link that aligns it with the government. Consequently, if the clergy's fuero is abolished, it will break this link and loosen the government's link to the lowest classes. Prudence and politics dictate that this [privilege] not be altered, given that it causes no harm.

Sire, we are dealing with the natural order of things; we write of ordinary cause and effect; of the reasons and motives that ordinarily govern the human heart. . . . The clergy are men, and their hearts are also sensible to self-preservation, *honor* and their own well being, that, as it is said, is the first principle of allegiance to the government. Experience proves this principle and logic true. And so we see in the *Correo de Europa*, that the regular clergy in France, that for years had been in the most contemptible state and scorned and part of the secular clergy that, for its poverty, found itself in the same state, abandoned the ship when the first waves of the storm battered the ship of the monarchy; but all the other members of the Clergy fought until the end to save it. . . .

We also demonstrated the intimate relationship of the ecclesiastic immunity and the Spanish Clergy's prerogatives with our monarchical government, the links and reciprocity of interests among all its members and parts. And analyzing them one by one, we demonstrated that the evidence shows these cause no harm to the common good of Your Majesty's subjects, nor impede in the least the exercise of your sovereign power. Thus in effect, the immunity from local prosecutors cannot have the least influence over the frequency of crimes; nor in America do they cause any harm to the common good, nor does the Clergy's immunity from royal officials harm the treasury. . . . The time is past, when the bishops could change the sentences of the secular tribunals. We are at the other extreme. The secular tribunals change the judgments of the bishops and they change them even in cases dealing with purely spiritual matters. . . .

We believe, Sire, that we have done Your Majesty the most important service in putting forward the facts in this matter. For the rest, we confide in the great virtues of Your Majesty and especially in your very pious inclination towards the Church, for the religion and for your ministers. . . . We throw ourselves upon your clemency and we redouble our prayers to the Almighty, to illuminate Your Majesty's understanding when formulating the new legal codes and in the administration of your vast dominions and to guard your royal and Catholic person in happiness and glory for the many years that the Church and your kingdoms need you. Valladolid de Michoacán, December 11, 1799.

NOTE.—The Illustrious Señor *Don* Fray Antonio de San Miguel, my renowned predecessor, and the very illustrious and venerable dean and council of this church commissioned me to write this report, and they saw fit to adopt it as their own and elevate it to the throne via the Supreme *Council of the Indies* in its original form, without any changes whatsoever. In the exposition of the proofs of the principal issue I found good reason to propose to the government for the first time liberal and beneficent ideas in favor of the Americas and its inhabitants, especially those withoutproperty and in favor of the Indians and *castas*; and I proposed eight laws: . . . the general abolition of the *tribute* paid by Indians and *castas;* the abolition of *castas'* infamous legal status; the free distribution of Indian communities' lands among Indians as private property; an agrarian law that confers upon the people the equivalent of the unused lands held by great landowners by means of twenty- to thirty-year leases . . .; free permission for non-Indians to settle and build in Indian towns, buying their housing plots or renting them; providing the necessary funds to territorial judges; and free rights to set up cotton and wool mills. The agrarian law offers the only way to unite as a single society a divided population, without which it is impossible to give good customs, civilization or culture to the general mass of the people. It can be seen that these laws constitute the principal basis for a liberal and beneficent government Since then I have not ceased to amplify and expand on these ideas, promoting them with zeal and energy through all means possible and as can be seen in the writings that followed.—Manuel Abad y Queipo.

Suggested Sources:

William B. Taylor provides a detailed account of the efforts to transform the Mexican Church's functions in the late colonial period. See William B. Taylor,

Magistrates of the Sacred: Priests and Parishioners in Eighteenth-Century Mexico (Stanford, CA: Stanford University Press, 1996). On the economic and political impact of Bourbon reforms, see John R. Fisher, Allan J. Kuethe, and Anthony McFarlane, eds., *Reform and Insurrection in Bourbon New Granada and Peru* (Baton Rouge: Louisiana State University Press, 1990). Bourbon Reforms, including tighter control of the clergy and Church property, began in Spain. See John Lynch, *Bourbon Spain, 1700–1808* (New York: Blackwell, 1989).

The Spanish Crown commissioned reports on the state of affairs and defenses in its American holdings. Two Spanish military officers assigned to accompany a scientific expedition produced one in 1749. See Jorge Juan and Antonio de Ulloa, *Discourse and Political Reflections on the Kingdoms of Peru, Their Government, Special Regiment of Their Inhabitants, and Abuses Which Have Been Introduced into One and Another with Special Information on Why They Grew Up and Some Means to Avoid Them,* ed. John J. TePaske, trans. John J. TePaske and Besse A. Clement (Norman: University of Oklahoma Press, 1978). German traveler and naturalist Alexander von Humboldt described the social and political state of various Spanish colonies. See an abridged English version: Alexander von Humboldt, *Political Essay on the Kingdom of New Spain,* trans. John Black, ed. Mary Maples Dunn (New York: Knopf, 1972). The full-length work is also available: Alexander von Humboldt, *Personal Narrative of Travels to the Equinoctial Regions of America, during the Years 1799–1804,* trans. and ed. Thomasina Ross (London: H. G. Bohn, 1852–1853).

Section VI

The Age of Transformation and Revolt, 1780–1825

The age of transformation and revolt stretched from 1780 to 1825, beginning with peasant and slave revolts that offered radical alternatives to the European colonial systems (best represented by slaves taking over in the new nation of Haiti). The era culminated with *creole*-led forces seizing power in one region after another in order to establish independent republics and forestall a complete overthrow of the colonial political, economic, and social systems. This was an era when imaginings of nationhood, citizenship, and political rights began to appear, motivating debate, political and military leaders, and mass movements. Over the course of decades, people from a wide array of class and ethnic backgrounds chose to replace centuries-old empires and imperial subjects with nations and citizens. However, not everything changed with independence: Iberian-descended *creoles* retained many of the colonial-era hierarchies in the new republics, and the economies continued to depend on the exploitation of indigenous people, *castas*, and slaves. In fact, access to courts and legal rights to land, property, and control of children declined for indigenous people and women with the creation of independent nation states in Ibero-America.

This era of change and warfare sprang from a prolonged period of rising class-race tensions and economic hardship. Between 1772 and 1776, Spain's Bourbon monarchy raised the *alcabala* (sales tax) from two percent to four percent and then to six percent. Furthermore, tax collectors installed new customs houses along the Spanish colonies' principal trade routes and began to collect these levies more vigorously. Because the collectors ignored local exemptions and extended the taxes to indigenous-style products—like corn and textiles—for the first time, they angered most colonial residents. Royal courts and officials failed to resolve vigorous protests over the new fiscal measures and *corregidores'* (local tax collectors and magistrates) increasingly frequent practices of imposing their cronies and other outsiders on indigenous communities. Indians, *castas*, and even Spanish *creoles* began to unite more frequently in revolt against policies that they all recognized as "bad government." Peasant rebellions also increased in both New Spain (Mexico) and Peru: In central Mexico, at least 142 short-term uprisings occurred, mainly in native villages, between 1680 and 1811, and native Andean people rose violently against colonial authorities over a hundred times between 1720 and 1790.

As revolts intensified and grew in size toward the turn of the century, a sense grew within both elite and popular sectors that the government should be responsive to the demands of the populace. Dissatisfied subjects often identified their primary loyalties with administrative regions that would later become nation states. They imagined different ways that politics might be structured and some envisioned breaking away from Spanish rule altogether. Some of the earliest examples of the potential of these new movements and ways of thinking appeared in Peru. North of Potosí, an illiterate *Aymara* Indian peasant leader, radicalized by repeated abuses, drew on democratic communal customs of decision making to fight back. In *Cuzco*, Tupac Amaru II, an educated and Hispanicized indigenous elite, and his wife, Micaela Bastidas, drew on a colonial revival of enthusiasm for the pre-Hispanic *Incas* to rally Indians and non-Indians both to fight the imperial state's impositions. Garofalo's chapter presents the correspondence among revolutionary leaders and their attempts to forge a multiethnic alliance. Divided loyalties, however, led royalist Indian nobles, terrified *creoles*, and Spaniards to combine forces to defeat the rebels. Nevertheless, Andean peoples continued to imagine alternatives to foreign domination. The chapter by Marión demonstrates that, even in the very regions where indigenous leaders and their allies were defeated in the 1780s, non-elite Andean peoples' ongoing participation in politics led them to fight against foreign rule in later struggles.

Along with the revolt that Tupac Amaru II and Micaela Bastidas started in Peru, the Haitian Revolution (1791–1804) exemplifies the potential and transformative nature of these early movements. The revolution in the French Caribbean plantation colony of Saint Domingue (later Haiti) played a huge role in how Iberian *creoles* and people of African heritage viewed independence. With the outbreak of the French Revolution (1789), French colonists on the island fell to fighting each other over the ideas of the revolution. These divisions provided slaves and ex-slaves an opportunity to revolt in 1791; they cast off the chains of servitude and demanded rights as French citizens, destroying the plantation system in the process. Eventually the military and political leadership of Pierre Dominique Toussaint L'Ouverture and Jean Jacques Dessalines helped Haitian rebels to end definitively slavery and defeat the slave owners and a succession of European powers, securing full independence by 1804. Haiti became the second republic in the Americas and the first one ruled by non-Europeans (albeit mostly those of middle-class or elite sectors). For slave owners and *creoles*, Haiti represented the explosive potential of revolt from below and the danger of elite divisions,

opening the way for radical revolution. Although Haiti promised hope for many former slaves, Reid Vazquez's chapter in this section explains why royal, Afro-Cuban militiamen took great pains to condemn the Haitian revolutionaries and prove their own steadfast loyalty. Throughout the Americas, including the United States, political and economic decisions were influenced by these hopes and fears. These first anticolonial rebellions in the Andes and the Caribbean proved to be the most radical, and they shook the colonial world.

The wounds were barely healed from these wars when new events in Europe shattered Iberia's imperial power and forced people of varying ethnic and class backgrounds across the Americas to act decisively in the first years of the nineteenth century. French dictator Napoleon Bonaparte occupied Portugal in 1807 and Spain in 1808, forcing out the Bourbon monarchs in both kingdoms and placing his brother Joseph on the Spanish throne. *Creoles* rejected Napoleon's brother and claimed that sovereignty revert to the people. Resistance grew in places like Buenos Aires and Caracas, where provisional governments were set up in 1801 claiming to govern for the deposed king. In Caracas, the famous *creole* leader, Simón Bolívar, persuaded a congress in 1811 to declare full independence; for the next 15 years he fought and defeated royalist forces, setting up *creole* rule in the republics that would eventually become the nations of Venezuela, Colombia, Ecuador, Peru, and Bolivia. Chapter 27 in this section examines Bolívar's pronouncements and plans for government and nationhood. These documents allow readers to follow Bolívar's thinking about how to treat different groups in society, which influenced several republics' new "social contracts" with their citizens.

In Mexico, the 1808 Napoleonic invasion had a divided impact. On the one hand, Spanish and *creole* royalists seized control of the colonial government on behalf of the deposed King. On the other hand, critics of monarchal rule began to plot the overthrow of imperial power. One group of plotters included the *creole* priest Miguel Hidalgo; when his fellow conspirators were detected and captured, he rang his church bells and called on his

Dated July 20, 1810, this watercolor depicts *creole* revolutionary general and statesman Simón Bolívar (1783–1830) literally liberating slaves. Initially, Bolívar saw no contradiction between independence from Spain and continuing slavery, but he changed his mind by the second half of the 1810s. Bolívar offered male slaves liberty if they joined his rebel army, but many slaves refused to pursue this perilous route to freedom. After the independence, he expressed fears that Afro-Latin American demands for equality would impose non-white rule and exact revenge on *creoles*. Nevertheless, Bolívar advocated gradual emancipation, resulting in abolition in Venezuela, Peru, and Ecuador in the 1850s. Full emancipation required an extended struggle, involving slave resistance, to overcome the opposition of slave owners and merchants. How is the liberation of the slaves portrayed here? What is the relationship between the slaves and the liberators? What message might this work of art have conveyed in 1810? How does that message relate to the actual progress of slave emancipation in Ibero-America?

Source: Casa-Museo 20 de Julio de 1810, Bogota, Colombia/The Bridgeman Art Library International.

parishioners to join him in launching a rebellion. Mexican *campesinos* (rural farmers and agricultural workers), long frustrated with late colonial policies, were primed to come together under a leader and take advantage of the apparent division among *creoles*. Thus it was that in 1810 central Mexico's indigenous and *mestizo* peasants rose up first under the banners of Father Hidalgo and then continued fighting under the command of a *mestizo* parish priest, José María Morelos. Chapter 26 on Morelos focuses on the leader's vision for an alternative to Spanish rule that he hoped would appeal to both progressive *creoles* and poor *campesinos*. A coalition of militias commanded by *creoles* and Spanish officers eventually suppressed the revolt in 1815, but resistance in many areas was never fully stamped out.

Brazil followed a different path to independence. First, the colony provided a refuge for the Portuguese monarchy and court, fleeing Napoleon; from 1807 until 1821, the Portuguese Crown ruled its empire from Rio de Janeiro. During this time, commerce flourished with the opening up of trade, and the colony developed key institutions like banks, universities, and printing houses. Brazilian *creoles* welcomed these changes, although they resented the British domination of trade. When in 1808 the French were driven from Iberia, an assembly of Portuguese liberals wrote a new constitution demanding the return of the monarchy, the reinstatement of Lisbon's trade monopoly, and rolling back Brazilian autonomy. Brazil's landowners and urban professionals opposed this "recolonization" and succeeded in persuading the prince regent, *Dom Pedro*, to remain in Brazil. They convoked a Constituent Assembly and created an independent monarchy in Brazil (1822–1889). In the following years, debates over many issues continued, among them slavery and the status of free people of color. Schultz's chapter brings to life one of the Assembly debates in 1823 over race and citizenship in the Empire of

Brazil. Although some fighting occurred, Brazil avoided the protracted and destructive wars fought in Mexico and the Andes. Furthermore, Brazil's *creoles* prevented any fundamental change in the socioeconomic structure in the new nation.

The letters, decrees, and accounts collected in this section reveal how political thought and actions functioned at many levels of society and how many people within these American societies ceased to think in terms of subjects and empires and began to think and act as citizens of nations. Military service in *creole*-led independence movements allowed many *mestizo* men to secure status as citizens alongside their *creole* commanders. Indians, women, and blacks, however, fared much worse, because colonial-style hierarchies endured and became central organizing principles in the new Latin American republics. As the colonial period waned and anticolonial and independence struggles spread, indigenous, *creole*, and

mestizo elites began to envision politics and society after European rule. Race relations loomed large in their thoughts, and most independence leaders called for an end to colonial racial divisions and the establishment of equality before the law. In practice, however, independence prolonged legally sanctioned racial inequalities, despite the existence of more egalitarian alternatives. The groups that defended alternative national visions continued their struggles by resisting elite impositions. Historian John Tutino summed up this shift by stating "As the colonial rule ended the contested process of nation-building began."[1]

---

[1] John Tutino, "The Revolution in Mexican Independence: Insurgency and the Renegotiation of Property, Production, and Patriarchy in the Bajío, 1800–1855," *The Hispanic American Historical Review* 78, no. 3 (August 1998): 367.

Chapter 25

Indian Leaders Tupac Amaru and Micaela Bastidas Fight to End Spanish Rule

Leo J. Garofalo, Connecticut College

Cuzco
in Audiencia
of Lima

ighteenth-century Indian leaders wrote to each other to coordinate military strategy and to the *creoles* and Spaniards, whose power they challenged in order to explain their cause. Risking everything, and often losing it, these men and women rose up in arms to end a colonial system based on the exploitation of indigenous communities and the impunity of Spanish officials. Taking the name Tupac Amaru II after the last *Inca* king executed in 1572 for resisting Spanish rule, the *cacique* (ethnic chief) José Gabriel Condorcanqui and his wife, the mestiza Micaela Bastidas Puyucahua, a *cacica* (female ethnic chief recognized by the colonial state), denounced the indifference of foreign rulers to the

219

plight of all people living in the Andes.[2] At first, following a pattern common since the 1740s, they only rebelled against unjust or corrupt Crown officials. Only later did they openly break with the king; these leaders had to articulate their goals, find ways to win and hold popular support, and negotiate with the non-Indian defenders of cities and the Spanish commanders of forces marching into the mountains to fight the rebels. Unusual in that it survived this brutal counterinsurgency campaign, the correspondence gathered here shows male and female leaders shaping the course of a major anticolonial insurrection.

The son of a prominent *cacique* in the town of Tinta just south of the important colonial center of *Cuzco*, Condorcanqui claimed descent from an *Inca* royal family, and he and the other rebel commanders were well established within colonial society. The *Jesuits* educated Condoranqui at their school in *Cuzco* for the sons of indigenous nobles, and he was related to the prominent indigenous, *mestizo*, and *creole* families which had intermarried in the region. Condoranqui and Micaela Bastidas were wealthy by Andean standards: They owned hundreds of mules, which they used to transport goods up and down the Andes, and they invested in mines and growing the mild stimulant coca leaf for market. Like other native Andean elites involved in the neo-*Inca* revival that bolstered their regional status and legitimacy within indigenous peasant communities, Condoranqui and Bastidas sometimes dressed in *Inca* garb, used sun images and the Quechua language, invoked connections to the *Incas*, collected *Inca*-style *keros* (drinking goblets), and commissioned paintings of themselves dressed as *Incas*.[3] Like colonial elites everywhere, Condoranqui's ambitions were stymied by colonials' subordinate position within the empire. At the local level, competing indigenous families supported by the *corregidor*,[4] Antonio Arriaga, blocked Condoranqui from assuming

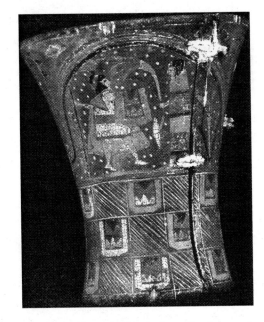

Indigenous nobility and native Andean elites in general collected *Inca*-style drinking goblets, called *keros*, and many other items of clothing, paintings, banners, and royal headgear to publicly link themselves to a precolonial past dominated by *Inca* rulers. When Andean people rebelled, the *viceroy* banned these items. The colonial-era *kero* pictured here shows a man dressed as an *Inca* and a woman dressed as a *coya*, or *Inca* queen, presenting him with flowers representative of *Inca* nobility. How was each represented and dressed? What symbols can be distinguished, and what might they represent?

Source: Museo de America.

ethnic leadership; and in the viceregal capital Lima, he failed repeatedly to secure official recognition of his family's claims to serve as *caciques*.[5] These leaders' family resources, their local standing, and their extensive trading networks aided them tremendously when they finally chose to violently resist colonial rule.

---

[2]David T. Garrett, "'In Spite of Her Sex:' The Cacica and the Politics of the Pueblo in the Late Colonial Andes," *The Americas* 64, no. 4 (April 2008): 547–581.

[3]*Inca* portraits adorned many private homes, churches, and other institutions in the *Cuzco* region.

[4]*Corregidores* were royal magistrates and tax collectors at the local level, and they were the first targeted along with customs houses in colonial tax revolts.

---

[5]*Caciques* or *kurakas*, *cacicas* if they were women, served as the local authorities of their indigenous home communities. Ideally *caciques* enjoyed local legitimacy because they belonged both to the ethnic group they governed and to hereditary families of indigenous nobles endorsed by the imperial state as useful partners in ruling the indigenous majorities.

The *Bourbon Reforms* brought economic hardship to Tinta and the southern Andean region in general and provoked additional conflicts over leadership within indigenous communities in the late 1700s. In particular, the *corregidores* forced communities to accept commoners, *mestizos*, and even *creoles* as *caciques* precisely because these interlopers would not defend a community's interests. The *corregidor* Arriaga in Tinta generated considerable local opposition. He imposed the Indians' tribute and *reparto* obligations in a heavy-handed manner,[6] and he clashed with the principal indigenous families by intervening in the naming of *caciques* in order to install people who would cooperate with his collection of taxes and forced sales of commercial goods. In addition, he violated the jurisdiction of local clergymen so often that the local bishop of *Cuzco*, a friend of Condoranqui, excommunicated the arrogant royal official. Not surprisingly, the rebels began their revolt by capturing and executing Arriaga on November 10, 1780, before some 4,000 onlookers (stripping him of the symbols of office, personal *honor*, and Christian standing) and utilizing the arms and money confiscated from him to mobilize an army of thousands. On November 17, 1780, in the town of Sangarará, the rebels soundly defeated the royalists and slaughtered hundreds of *creole* and indigenous troops sent from *Cuzco* to suppress the uprising. This victory brought thousands more fighters to the anticolonial cause, and the rebellion spread from Tinta to Lake Titicaca and the *Aymara* rebels in the south, where peasant leaders had already been fighting colonial authorities on their own.

The rebel army reflected the region's diversity and followed the hierarchies of *Cuzco's* colonial society. Family members formed the inner circle directing the war, with Bastidas as Tupac Amaru's chief adviser and heavily involved in gathering supplies and weapons. After the rebels' defeat, the people executed by the Spanish as leaders included nineteen Spanish and *creoles*, twenty-nine *mestizos*, seventeen

Indians, and four blacks; they were landowners of large estates or members of the middle sectors of colonial society.[7] Prominent *creoles*, *mestizos*, and native Andeans commanded the army, below them served *mestizos* and native Andeans as officers, and indigenous commoners made up the vast majority of the rank and file.[8] Support for Tupac Amaru spread quickly among local *caciques*, kin, and muleteers, but he failed to gain adherents beyond his and his wife's network of connections. This failure to recruit more ethnic leaders in other regions prevented the rebellion from spreading further, and this limitation allowed royalists to find enough influential indigenous leaders who could raise indigenous troops to put down the rebellion.

After the victory at Sangarará, Tupac Amaru moved south to consolidate gains before turning back to attack *Cuzco* beginning on December 1780. Tupac Amaru failed to surround the city completely, but he attempted to negotiate the city's surrender, launching an assault on January 8, 1781, that he called off after only 2 days. As Spanish and *creole* reinforcements advanced from Lima, *Cuzco's* creoles and powerful *caciques* joined the royalist cause, limiting the rebels to guerrilla actions and eventually capturing Tupac Amaru and his family. After the execution of Tupac Amaru and Bastidas in *Cuzco* on April 6, 1781, surviving family members and rebel commanders led forces south, linked up with *Aymara* rebels, and continued the Great Rebellion there until defeated in late 1781 and subdued by 1783.

The documents to follow reveal how Tupac Amaru and the other leaders started and sustained a massive insurrection. Scholars describe the emergence of a new Andean political consciousness by the 1780s. Historian Charles Walker even characterized Tupac Amaru's revolt as "protonationalist," meaning that it emphasized the existence of a unique body of people (a nation) and attempted

---

[6]Colonial law obliged only indigenous peoples to pay *tribute* in two installments, to serve in rotating labor drafts called *mitas*, and to buy at fixed prices goods from outside their communities called the *reparto*. The Crown insisted that *cacique* aid in the collection of these revenues and laborers levied on an entire town, and Spanish officials held *caciques* responsible for any shortfalls.

[7]"[F]armers, scribes, urban tradesmen and artisans, muleteers, caciques, and . . . school teachers[.]" Kenneth J. Andrien, *Andean Worlds: Indigenous History, Culture, and Consciousness under Spanish Rule, 1532–1825* (Albuquerque: University of New Mexico Press, 2001), 215–216.

[8]Kenneth J. Andrien, *Andean Worlds*, 216.

to win political rights for this nation.[9] Calling Tupac Amaru's rebellion "nationalist" generates debate: Although the insurgents proposed a break with the colonial past based on claims to a natural and long-standing Andean identity via *Inca* heritage, no modern nation state yet existed, and the rebel leaders never specified exactly what form of government they fought for. Yet, the defeat of the movement did not mark the end of Andean *campesinos'* engagement with independence, as Marión's Chapter 28 in this section shows. *Creole* elites, however, structured their governments based on western ideals rather than Andean concepts in the nineteenth century, and they denied indigenous peoples full participation in their nation states. Even so, Andean alternative nationalisms did not simply fade away: Indigenous activists would reemerge in the late twentieth century to once again challenge what they saw as "bad government."

[9]Charles F. Walker, *Smoldering Ashes: Cuzco and the Creation of Republican Peru, 1780–1840* (Durham, NC: Duke University Press, 1999), 17, 51–52.

Questions to Consider:

1. What actions did the rebel leaders take, and how did they try to rally people of different ethnic groups to their cause?
2. What factors and events suggest that this was primarily a tax revolt, and what evidence suggests that the uprising sought fundamental changes and perhaps even the end of colonial rule? Which evidence do you find more compelling, and why?
3. Why was Micaela Bastidas critical of her husband's military actions? What does her letter to Tupac Amaru suggest about the role and importance of women in the uprising?
4. How do the ideas expressed by Tupac Amaru in this chapter compare and contrast with independence ideas espoused by Bolívar or Morelos in the next two chapters?

The Inca's Coronation, November 4, 1780[10]

Don José I by the grace of God, *Inca*, King of Peru, Bogotá, Quito, Chile, Buenos Aires and the Continent. . . .

As it is agreed by my Council in many public and secret meetings that the Kings of Spain have usurped my people's crown and domains for about three hundred years: robbing my vassals with their unbearable [taxes, *tributes,* and customs duties], *Viceroys, Royal Courts, Corregidores* and all the other Officials—all equal in their tyranny: selling Justice to the highest bidder with Notaries who help most whoever pays more: the Ecclesiastical personnel participate in this, with no fear of God: abusing the natives of this Kingdom like beasts: — taking only the lives of those who do not steal: —all deserving the severest punishment:—For that, and because the just clamor has reached Heaven:

In the name of God Almighty. I order:—that none of the taxes mentioned be paid, nor that any of the European Officials be obeyed, they are intruders and untrustworthy; only the Priesthood should be respected, paying them the Fees, Tithes and First Harvests, as they are given to God: and the Tribute and Royal Fifth to your King and Natural Lord [Tupac Amáru].[11] . . .

I order this Pledge made to my Royal Crown be read out and publicized in all of the Cities, Towns and Places in my Dominions: giving all vassals and loyal subjects the news soon, giving all those who will rebel the punishment they deserve. Decreed in this my Royal Seat of Tungasuca, Capital of these Kingdoms. —*Don José I*—By order of my lord the *Inca* King—*Francisco Cisneros*, secretary.

[10]*Source*: José Félix Blanco, ed., *Documentos para la historia de la vida pública del libertador de Colombia, Perú y Bolivia* (Caracas: Imprenta de "La Opinión Nacional," 1875), vol. 1, 158–159.

[11]Royal Fifth refers to the 20-percent tax given to the Crown on all precious metals and stones mined, loot taken in battle, and slaves sold.

Ultimatum Sent to the City of Cuzco, November 20, 1780

Don José Gabriel Tupac Amaru, Indian of the royal blood and principal Line:

Let it be known to all the *creole* compatriots, residing in the city of *Cuzco:* —that given the heavy yoke that squeezes them so hard, and the tyranny that they bear with this burden, without the Spaniards' sympathy for their plight, and exasperated with them and their lack of pity—I have decided to shake off this unbearable burden, and end the Spaniards' bad government that is responsible; for this reason the *Corregidor* of this province of Tinta died on the public scaffold, to whose defense came *Chapetones*[12] and *creoles* from Cuzco. They paid with their lives for their audacity. I regret only the death of our *creole* countrymen, whom it has never been my desire to harm. I want us to live together as brothers in one body politic; for this reason, I make it known to the *creole* countrymen—that if they accept this ultimatum, no harm will come to their persons or to their property; but if they ignore this my warning, and do the opposite, they will be ruined, transforming my clemency into cruelty and fury—reducing this city to ashes; and as I said I have the forces to do it; I have at my call sixty thousand Indians, and more from other provinces that have offered support and are under my command. Thus, do not take lightly this warning that is born of my love and clemency. —The Priests shall be respected according to their rank, and in the same fashion the Nuns and Monasteries; my only goal is to cut off the bad government of so many big thieves that have been picking our pockets. In short I will learn your intentions, and recognize the decision you choose, rewarding the faithful and punishing the rebels, you know your choice—so afterwards do not allege ignorance. This is what I can tell you. —Tungasuca. November, 20, 1780. —*Don José Gabriel Tupac Amaru, Inca.*

---

[12]Literally, the term *chapetones* meant "soft feet" and was an insulting reference to Spaniards that was used to distinguish Spaniards born in Spain from American-born individuals (*creoles*) who also enjoyed the rights and privileges of the "Spanish" legal category.

Letter to Tupac Amaru from Micaela Bastidas Puyucahua, December 6, 1780[13]

Dear Chepe, You are causing me grief and sorrow. While you saunter through the villages, even very carelessly delaying two days in Yauri, our soldiers grow tired and are leaving for their homes.

I do not have any patience left to endure all of this. I am capable of giving myself up to the enemy and letting them take my life, because I see how lightly you view this grave matter that threatens the lives of all. We are in the midst of enemies and we have no security. And for your sake all my sons are in danger, as well as all our people.

I have warned you sufficient times against dallying in those villages where there is nothing to be done. But you continue to saunter without considering that the soldiers lack food supplies even though they are given money; and their pay will run out soon. Then they will all depart, leaving us helpless, and we will pay with our lives because they (as you must have learned) only follow self-interest and want to get all they can out of us. Now the soldiers are already beginning to desert, as Vargas and Oré spread the rumor that the Spaniards of Lampa joined by those of other provinces and of Arequipa are going to surround you; the soldiers are terrified and seek to flee, fearing the punishment that might befall them. Thus we will lose all the people I have gathered and prepared for the descent on

---

[13]*Source:* June E. Hahner, ed., *Women in Latin American History: Their Lives and Their Views* (Los Angeles: UCLA Latin American Center Publications, 1984), 36–37.

Cuzco, and the Cuzco forces will unite with the troops from Lima who have already been on the march against us for many days.

I must caution you about all this, though it pains me. But if you wish to ruin us, you can just sleep. You were so careless that you walked alone through the streets of the town of Yauri, and even went to the extreme of climbing the church tower, when you should not commit such extreme action under present conditions. These actions only dishonor and defame you and do you little justice.

I believe that you were occupied day and night in arranging these affairs, instead of showing unconcern that robs me of my life. I am only a shadow of myself and beside myself with anxiety, and so I beg you to get on with this business.

You made me a promise, but from now on I shall not place any faith in your promises, for you do not keep your word.

I do not care about my own life, only about those of our poor family, who need all my help. Thus, if the enemy comes from Paruro, as I suggested in my last letter, I am prepared to march out to meet them with our forces, leaving Fernando in a designated place, for the Indians are not capable of moving by themselves in these perilous times.

I gave you plenty of warnings to march on Cuzco immediately, but you took them all lightly, allowing the enemy sufficient time to prepare, as they have done, placing cannon on Picchu mountain, plus other trickery so dangerous that you are no longer in a position to attack them. God keep you many years.

Tungasuca, December 6, 1780.

I must tell you that the Indians of Quispicanchi are worn out and weary from serving so long as guards. Well, God must want me to suffer for my sins. —Your wife.

After I finished writing this letter, a messenger arrived with the news that the enemy from Paruro are in Archos. I shall march out to meet them though it cost me my life.

The Inca's Letter to Cuzco's City Council, January 3, 1781[14]

Ever since I began to free the natives of this kingdom from the slavery of the Corregidores and the other people who, far from acting with charity, defended these extortions that violate God's law, it has been my desire to prevent deaths and warfare, on my side; but because Cuzco's defenders commit such horrors—hanging without confession various supporters of my cause and dragging others, causing me such pain—I am compelled to require this illustrious Cabildo [city council] to stop its residents from committing such excesses and allow me to enter the city. If this is not done, I cannot delay another instant my entrance into the city with blood and fire, sparing nobody.

For this reason the Reverend Father Friar Domingo, the Doctor D. Ildefonso Bejarano, and the Captain D. Bernardo de la Madrid are coming as emissaries. They can give me notice what this Cabildo resolves in this important matter. All arms must be surrendered, regardless of the station or special rights of the person who employs them; otherwise they will suffer the rigor of a just war of defense. . . .

I am the last remaining descendant of the Inca King's royal blood in this kingdom: this stimulated me to achieve by every means possible the cessation of the Corregidores' abusive impositions of inept people in every post, charge, and ministry: hurting the miserable

[14]Source: José Félix Blanco, Documentos para la historia de la vida pública del libertador de Colombia, Perú y Bolivia, 160–161.

Indians and other people and even the laws of the Kings of Spain; laws which I see from experience are suppressed or ignored. Since the conquest here, these vassals have not looked to advance the law, rather the laws have been applied to trick and rob the miserable population, without allowing them to breathe a complaint. This is so notorious, that no further proof is needed, besides the tears of these unfortunates that have filled their eyes for three centuries. This state has never allowed them to find the true God, except to give the *Corregidores* and Priests their sweat and labor; such that, having inquired throughout most of this Kingdom about the spiritual and civil government, I find that the number who make up the national population, do not have the Evangelic Light, due to the bad example they are given. The exemplary execution of the *Corregidor* of the province of Tinta, was motivated because he went against the Church; and in order to stop the other *Corregidores*, that act of justice was necessary. My desire is, that this kind of *Gebes* [insulting term for Spaniards] be suppressed forever: that they cease their *repartimientos* [forced purchase of goods by Indians]: that in each province there be an *Alcalde mayor* of the Indian nation, and other people of good conscience, giving them a moderate salary with other conditions and conditions that shall be established in their moment; among the most indispensable is that a Royal Court be established in this city, where its *Viceroy* will reside and serve as [the Court's] President, so that the Indians will have these resources closer. This is the whole idea of my enterprise, leaving to the King of Spain the dominion that they have had, without withdrawing the obedience owed him, and the general commerce, that is the principal nerve to preserve the whole Kingdom.— May God guard Your Lordships.— On the field of Ocororo. January 3, 1781.— I kiss Your Lordships' hands[,] your greatest servant.— Don José Tupac Amaru, Inca.

The Inca's Letter to Cuzco's Loyalist Citizenry, January 9, 1781[15]

Even though with the letter dated the third of the present month I expressed to Your Lordships my desire to avoid the deaths, destruction, and the burning of houses that cannot be avoided if my side must continue a war in self-defense; yesterday it happened that my troops advanced with their usual ardor, gaining some territory without doing any harm, until the troops of this city launched an offensive invasion.— I find myself obliged to present to Your Lordships the disastrous consequences that follow: my Indians insist that I give them permission to loot the city. If I allow this, the city will be left ruined and its citizens converted into peasants. This is their intention because they offer to turn the city over to me, and in return they plan to populate it themselves, allowing no other people to live there. Believe me Your Lordships, it is my deliberate desire to cause no harm to anyone, and that these *naturales*[16] and the city dwellers are made to understand the truth, mainly that I have never supported this idea. I fear that this attack may occur because of the city's unthinking offensive actions, and then neither God nor the King can blame me.

I am letting Your Lordships know of this so that by means of the intermediary *don* Francisco Bernales you communicate your deliberations to me and the best course of action can be taken. —I am well aware that you will have reflected critically upon advancing the

---

[15]*Source:* José Félix Blanco, *Documentos para la historia de la vida pública del libertador de Colombia, Perú y Bolivia*, 161.

[16]People indigenous to the land; indigenous people.

Royal Tax regime, particularly stopping the forced sale of goods at fixed prices. But I am also aware that the *mestizos* and Spanish will happily contribute according to their wealth, even more than that rendered by the taxes. Proof of this is the rising numbers of them found voluntarily under my command as I have informed the corresponding Tribunals.

May Our Lord preserve Your Lordships for many years. —On the Heights of Piccho,[17] January 9, 1781. —I kiss Your Lordships' hands, your trusty servant. —Don José Tupac Amaru, Inca

Suggested Sources:

Excellent collections of documents from the Great Rebllion are available in Ward Stavig and Ella Schmidt, eds., *The Tupac Amaru and Catarista Rebellions: An Anthology of Sources*, trans. Ward Stavig and Ella Schmidt (Cambridge, MA: Hackett, 2008); and Melchor de Paz, "What Is an Indian?" in *Latin American Revolutions*, ed. John Lynch (Norman: University of Oklahoma Press, 1994), 191–205. David Cahill examined a multiethnic alliance during Arequipa's 1780 tax revolt. See David Cahill, "Taxonomy of a Colonial 'Riot:' The Arequipa

Disturbances of 1780," in *Colonial Spanish America*, ed. Kenneth Mills and William Taylor (Wilmington, DE: Scholarly Resources, 1998) 298–315. Not all indigenous *kurakas* supported Tupac Amaru. See Ward Stavig, "Eugenio Sinanyuca: Militant, Nonrevolutionary Kuraka, and Community Defender," in *The Human Tradition in Colonial Latin America*, ed. Kenneth J. Andrien (Wilmington, DE: Scholarly Resources, 2002), 241–258. An abridged version of the orders to execute the rebels is José Antonio de Areche, "All Must Die!" in *The Peru Reader*, ed. Orin Starn, Carlos Iván Degregori, and Robin Kirk (Durham, NC: Duke University Press, 1995), 157–161.

Charles F. Walker places the Tupac Amaru rebellion within a longer trajectory of Andean politics in *Smoldering Ashes: Cuzco and the Creation of Republican Peru, 1780–1840* (Durham, NC: Duke University Press, 1999). Carolyn Dean documents visual images and public displays of Inca heritage in *Inka Bodies and the Body of Christ: Corpus Christi in Colonial Cuzco* (Durham: University of North Carolina Press, 1999). In Bolivia, the rebellion continued under the leadership of commoners. See Sinclair Thomson, *We Alone Will Rule: Native Andean Politics in the Age of Insurgency* (Madison: University of Wisconsin Press, 2002). The short film *Qamasan Warmi* (dir. José A. Miranda [New York: Latin American Video Archives, 1993]) dramatizes the efforts of Gregoria Apaza, another indigenous female revolutionary leader, to connect *Quechua-* and *Aymara*-speaking revolutionaries.

---

[17]Hill overlooking Cuzco where the rebels established a camp.

Chapter 26

Father José María Morelos and Visions of Mexican Independence

Erin E. O'Connor, Bridgewater State College

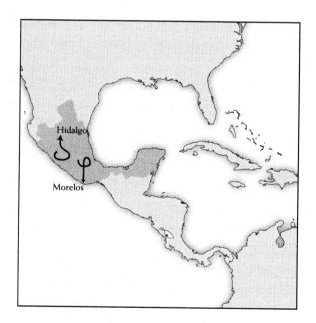

Parish priests leading a violent, multiethnic uprising to overthrow the Spanish colonial government might surprise many readers. Officially, the Catholic Church was supposed to support colonization and keep the populace loyal and obedient to the Crown and its colonial administrators. Fathers Miguel Hidalgo y Costilla and José María Morelos of New Spain (soon to become Mexico) did just the opposite, and their bid for independence earned them enduring fame as the first leaders to imagine and fight for a Mexican nation. Although the priests' actions may have been more extreme than those of other religious officials in the colonial era, there was a long history of priests in colonial Spanish America who were concerned with the plight of the poor and exploited. Still, Hidalgo and Morelos adhered to a more radical vision than other socially concerned priests, calling for an end to slavery and *tribute*, and for reforms that would establish an independent and representative government in Mexico. This chapter introduces readers to one of the most important surviving documents from this first struggle for Mexican independence: Morelos's 1813 "Sentiments of the Nation," in which he outlined his vision for the national government he hoped to establish.

The Hidalgo-Morelos movement resulted from a complex set of political, economic, and social factors in early nineteenth-century New Spain. Initially, *creole* responses to the 1808 Napoleonic takeover of the Spanish throne were mixed. Although some powerful Mexico City *creoles* remained loyal to the Crown, other *creole* elites plotted to rise up against the colonial government. One such plot was underway in the Bajío region north of Mexico City in 1810. When authorities discovered the plot, one of the main conspirators, Father Miguel Hidalgo y Costilla, made a preemptive call to arms in his now-famous *Grito de Dolores* (Cry of Dolores) on September 16, 1810. A well-educated *creole* parish priest in the town of Dolores, Hidalgo expected other *creoles* to join his protest when he made his call to arms. Instead, indigenous and *mestizo campesinos* answered his call, and his army quickly swelled to tens of thousands.

The agrarian poor in the Bajío consisted mainly of workers on large estates with some autonomous peasant communities mixed in. Racially, this was mostly a *mestizo* region, and even indigenous peoples living there were fairly Hispanicized in their language, customs, and dress. Although it had not been one of the more tumultuous regions during the colonial period, eighteenth- and early nineteenth-century changes made the Bajío potentially volatile. Eighteenth-century population growth put pressure on peasants and rural workers, who competed with

each other for limited land and jobs. These problems were compounded in the early nineteenth century when estate owners expelled some resident workers following a series of crop failures. Former estate workers resented both regional elites and the colonial system that failed to provide them with relief. Hidalgo's proposals offered a more tolerable government system that would provide tangible benefits for the poor, such as the abolition of slavery and *tribute*, and land reform. For *creole* elites, the Hidalgo insurrection brought to life their greatest fears: that the exploited majority might rise up against their so-called superiors. *Creole* and Spanish elites set aside their differences and banded together to defeat the insurgents. In March of 1811, loyalist forces captured and executed Hidalgo, but his army marched on.

Father José María Morelos took charge of the movement after Hidalgo's death until his own capture and execution in 1815. Morelos, sometimes referred to as a *mestizo* and at other times as an Afro-*mestizo*, was born to a poor family and worked as a muleteer before studying to become a priest. He joined Hidalgo's cause in 1811 and rose to prominence as an intelligent and able leader. Morelos tried, with some success, to bring greater order to the committed but largely undisciplined rebel forces. Less effectively, he also attempted to draw more middle- and upper-class *creoles* into the movement. *Creole* elites considered the insurrection an unruly "Indian" mob, despite Morelos's attempts to win them over with familiar political ideals. In December 1815, loyalist forces caught and executed Morelos, bringing an end to the first phase of Mexican independence. When independence finally came to the nation in 1822, under the military and political leadership of the Spanish officer Agustín Iturbide, it was a profoundly conservative movement that proposed to establish a monarchy and maintain the colonial social hierarchy.

The document "Sentiments of the Nation" allows readers to explore the political ideals through which Morelos attempted to broaden his support base. Although Morelos failed to win over moderates with "Sentiments," and royalist forces defeated the uprising, Hidalgo and Morelos strongly influenced the course of Mexican history. The central issue of land reform that drew so many poor *campesinos* into their armies remained unresolved throughout the nineteenth century, and land conflicts worsened over the long term. Nineteenth-century presidents and Mexico's congress focused on ideals of equality before the law and emulation of European models in politics and the economy while simultaneously pursuing policies that allowed large estates to expand at the expense of indigenous and *mestizo* peasants. Rising *campesino* frustrations with unresponsive governments resulted in a true social revolution in Mexico from 1910 to 1940. Though the 1910 Mexican Revolution fell far short of its promises to the rural poor, it produced land and labor laws that, at least initially, benefited the Mexican poor.

As Mexican politics and society changed from 1821 to 1940, the images of Hidalgo and Morelos also transformed. In order to claim Hidalgo and Morelos as rightful heroes of the independence period, yet without questioning the elitism of nineteenth-century nation state formation, nineteenth-century artists played down the more radical elements of the movements. They often portrayed Hidalgo and Morelos alone, rather than with the poor followers who made up the majority of the movement. They also presented the two leaders in poses similar to those in portraits of more conservative independence leaders in Latin America. Consider the first image of Hidalgo, an 1895 etching from the publication *Patria e independencia*. Hidalgo is standing at a desk, surrounded by books and papers to emphasize his scholarly background. In the second image, a "Mexican School" painting of the nineteenth century, Morelos was presented in a calm pose in full and formal attire. In contrast, the image of Hidalgo from Mexico's era of revolutionary state building emphasized the radical and insurgent nature of these movements and heralded the leaders as avenging. It was also painted by one of the most famous muralists in early twentieth-century Mexico, José Clemente Orozco. The mural in which the Hidalgo image appears is located in Guadalajara's Palacio de Gobierno (government palace). Hidalgo appears quite different in the twentieth-century image than in the nineteenth-century portrait, for it was precisely his role in leading Mexico's poor in a radical movement that made him an ideal hero during the process of revolutionary state building.

The document and images in this chapter capture the complexity of Mexican independence. In particular, they show that Mexico's rural poor were neither fully included in this radical independence movement nor were they summarily defeated at its conclusion. In Mexico, as elsewhere in Latin America, poor non-Europeans were aware of politics and engaged with the struggles and ideals of their times, but they would have to wait at least a century to see elements of their own versions of liberty and justice implemented.

Questions to Consider:

1. What kind of government did Morelos envision? How did he propose that citizenship, rights, and obligations be determined in the new nation?

2. Historians often comment on ways that Morelos infused this document with elements of colonial-style hierarchy. Where do you find such elements in the document? What do you make of the tension between equality and hierarchy in the document?

3. Morelos led a very different kind of movement than Bolívar. How similar or different were his political ideas? Did the two leaders' ideas correspond clearly to the kinds of movements they led? Why or why not?

4. Look carefully at the painting of Morelos. To what extent is Morelos's Afro-*mestizo* heritage apparent in this nineteenth-century portrait? Why?

5. Consider the radical messages of the revolutionary-era painting of Hidalgo. To what extent do you see this radicalism reflected in "Sentiments of the Nation"?

José María Morelos, "Sentiments of the Nation"[1]

1. That America is free and independent of Spain and of all other Nations, Governments, or Monarchies, and it should be so sanctioned, and the reasons explained to the world.

2. That the Catholic Religion is the only one, without tolerance of any other.

3. That all the ministers of the Church shall support themselves exclusively and entirely from tithes and first-fruits (*primicias*), and the people need make no offering other than their own devotions and oblations.

4. That Catholic dogma shall be sustained by the Church hierarchy, which consists of the Pope, the Bishops and the Priests, for we must destroy every plant not planted by God: *minis plantatis quam nom plantabir Pater meus Celestis Cradicabitur.* Mat. Chapt. XV.

5. That sovereignty springs directly from the People, who wish only to deposit it in their representatives, whose powers shall be divided into Legislative, Executive, and Judiciary branches, with each Province electing its representative. These representatives will elect all others, who must be wise and virtuous people . . .

6. [Article 6 is missing from all reproductions of this document.]

7. That representatives shall serve for four years, at which point the oldest ones will leave so that those newly elected may take their places.

8. The salaries of the representatives will be sufficient for sustenance and no more, and for now they shall not exceed 8,000 *pesos*.

9. Only Americans[2] shall hold public office.

10. Foreigners shall not be admitted, unless they are artisans capable of teaching [their crafts], and are free of all suspicion.

11. That the fatherland shall never belong to us nor be completely free so long as the government is not reformed. [We must] overthrow all tyranny, substituting liberalism, and remove from our soil the Spanish enemy that has so forcefully declared itself against the Nation.

12. That since good law is superior to all men, those laws dictated by our Congress must oblige constancy and patriotism, moderate opulence and indigence, and be of such nature that they raise the income of the poor, better their customs, and banish ignorance, rapine, and robbery.

13. That the general laws apply to everyone, without excepting privileged bodies, and that such bodies shall exist within accordance with the usefulness of their ministry.

14. That in order to dictate a law, Congress must debate it, and it must be decided by a plurality of votes.

15. That slavery is proscribed forever, as well as the distinctions of caste, so that all shall be equal; and that the only distinction between one American and another shall be that between vice and virtue.

16. That our ports shall be open to all friendly foreign nations, but no matter how friendly they may be, foreign ships shall not be based in the kingdom. There will be some ports specified for this purpose; in all others, disembarking shall be prohibited, and 10% or some other tax shall be levied upon their merchandise.

17. That each person's home shall be as a sacred asylum wherein to keep property and observances, and infractions shall be punished.

18. That the new legislation shall forbid torture.

19. That the Constitution shall establish that the 12th of December be celebrated in all the villages in honor of the patroness of our liberty, the Most Holy Mary of Guadalupe. All villages shall be required to pay her monthly devotion.

20. That foreign troops or those of another kingdom shall not tread upon our soil unless it be to aid us, and if this is the case, they shall not be part of the Supreme Junta.

[1]*Source:* Translated by Tim Henderson, "Sentiments of the Nation, or Points Outlined by Morelos for the Constitution," in *The Mexico Reader*, Gilbert M. Joseph and Timothy J. Henderson, Eds., pp. 189–191. Copyright 2002, Duke University Press. All rights reserved. Used by permission of the publisher. (Original text from Ernesto de la Torre Villar, Moises Gonzalez Navarro, and Stanley Ross, Eds., *Historia documental de Mexico*, Vol. 2. Mexico CIty: Universidad Nacional Autonoma de Mexico, 1964, pps. 11–112.)
[2]This article referred to the fact that Morelos did not want *peninsulares*, or men born in Spain, to hold public office in the new nation.

21. That there shall be no expeditions outside the limits of the kingdom, especially seagoing ones. Expeditions shall only be undertaken to propagate the faith to our brothers in remote parts of the country.

22. That the great abundance of highly oppressive *tributes*, taxes, and impositions should be ended, and each individual shall pay five percent of his earnings, or another equally light charge, which will be less oppressive than the *alcabala* [sales tax], the *estanco* [crown monopoly], the tribute, and others. This small contribution, and the wise administration of the goods confiscated from the enemy, shall be sufficient to pay the costs of the war and the salaries of public employees.

23. That the 16th of September shall be celebrated each year as the anniversary of the cry of independence and the day our sacred liberty began, for on that day the lips of the Nation parted and the people proclaimed their rights, and they grasped the sword so that they would be heard, remembering always the merits of the great hero, señor *don* Miguel Hidalgo y Costilla, and his *compañero, don* Ignacio Allende.

Chilpancingo, 14 September 1813

Father Miguel Hidalgo y Costilla.
Source: Picture Desk, Inc./Kobal Collection.

Father Miguel Hidalgo y Costilla mural by Jose Clemente.
Source: PhotoEdit Inc.

Father José María Morelos.

Source: Museo Nacional de Historia, Mexico City, Mexico/The Bridgeman Art Library International.

Suggested Sources:

There are few primary source documents available by either Hidalgo or Morelos beyond "Sentiments." A short (paragraph-long) series of reforms that Hidalgo decreed in 1810 is available in Benjamin Keen, Robert Buffington, and Lila Caimari, eds., *Latin American Civilization: History and Society, 1492 to the Present,* 8th ed. (Boulder, CO: Westview Press,

2004), 267. Other short documents can be found in Joseph M. Gilbert and Timothy J. Henderson, eds., *The Mexico Reader: History, Culture, Politics* (Durham, NC: Duke University Press, 2002) in the chapter on independence, including conservative views, such as Iturbide's "Plan of Iguala" and Lucas Alamán's description of the Hidalgo followers' siege of Guanajuato.

There are excellent scholarly studies of Mexican independence viewed from below. See John Tutino's pioneering study, *From Insurrection to Revolution in Mexico: Social Bases of Agrarian Violence, 1750–1940* (Princeton, NJ: Princeton University Press, 1989), in which he discusses how threats to *campesino* security led to their support for the Hidalgo-Morelos insurrection. For an update of some of Tutino's analysis that discusses the role of gender in the insurrection, see his article "The Revolution in Mexican Independence: Insurgency and the Negotiation of Property, Production, and Patriarchy in the Bajío, 1800–1855," *Hispanic American Historical Review* 78, no. 3 (1998): 367–418. For the foundations of agrarian protest in early nineteenth-century Mexico, see Eric Van Young's *The Other Rebellion: Popular Violence, Ideology, and the Mexican Struggle for Independence, 1810–1821* (Stanford, CA: Stanford University Press, 2001). Although independence benefited mainly *creole* elites, Mexican peasants were actively involved in the transition from colony to republic. For more information on peasants and politics in early nineteenth-century Mexico, readers should refer to the works of Peter Guardino, including *The Time of Liberty: Popular Political Culture in Oaxaca, 1750–1850* (Durham, NC: Duke University Press, 2005).

Chapter 27

The Many Views of Simón Bolívar

Erin E. O'Connor, Bridgewater State College

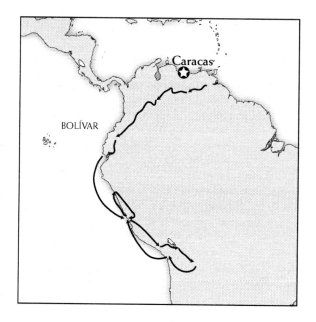

Simón Bolívar not only played a pivotal role in achieving independence for his Venezuelan homeland, but he also led armies to free Colombia, Ecuador, and Peru from Spanish rule. During and after the wars, Bolívar helped establish new governments, and scholars remember him partly for his broad and idealistic goals for the new nations. Despite the plethora of information about him, it is difficult to connect Bolívar to a clear set of political or social commitments. For example, similar to Thomas Jefferson in the United States, Bolívar initially advocated the abolition of slavery, but he backed away from the proposal when plantation owners resisted. Some of Bolívar's ideas or policies appear so deeply contradictory that it is difficult to feel certain of exactly what "The Liberator" (as many called him) sought to achieve with independence. This chapter allows readers to explore firsthand some of Bolívar's ideas and policies.

Bolívar hailed from Venezuela, a region that was not initially one of the most profitable colonial centers, but which had a strong economy by the eighteenth century due to its many cacao and sugar plantations. As with all Latin American plantation economies, Venezuelan planters' profits derived from the labor of African and African-descended slaves. By the independence era, race and class deeply divided Venezuelan society with a large slave population and an ever-growing (and frustrated) population of free blacks and *pardos* (dark-skinned peoples of mixed racial descent). Eighteenth-century *creole* elites were at once irritated by Crown policies and wary of upheaval from the so-called lower orders of society. Meanwhile, many free blacks and *pardos* were increasingly stymied by a racial system that set limits on the status and positions to which they could aspire.

Although not the first region in which *creoles* rose up against the colonial state, Venezuela's rebels were among the first to declare independence, in 1811. This declaration, however, marked the beginning rather than the end of the politico-military struggle in Venezuela. The Spanish military in Venezuela replenished its forces from the nearby garrison in Puerto Rico, and most conservative *creoles* remained loyal to the Spanish Crown. Moreover, many *pardos* initially supported Spain because the new constitutions failed to abolish slavery, and its property and literacy requirements left many *pardos* without a direct political voice. These divisions resulted from a colonial social hierarchy that left its mark on both the independence wars and on the new nation.

Bolívar himself was from a wealthy plantation-owning family in the Caracas region. As a boy, he received a liberal education, much of it in Europe. Well versed in Enlightenment ideas, Bolívar became one of the first *creoles* to join the struggle against the Crown when Napoleon's armies took over Spain. After initial defeats, he eventually began to win over many *pardos* and *llaneros* (cowboys from the interior, typically of mixed racial descent), which made victory possible against loyalist forces. His combined charisma, intelligence, and military ability explain why he successfully led independence armies throughout much of Spanish South America.

As South American nations achieved independence, Bolívar shifted his role from military leader to

Many paintings of Simón Bolívar portrayed him in military garb. How might Bolívar's pose, clothing, and facial features in this portrait have suggested that he embodied both military ability and the refinement that elites associated exclusively with European origins?
Source: Library of Congress.

statesman, and he helped forge several constitutions and national policies. Although his military campaigns and lofty ideas inspired many *creole* statesmen in the newly independent nations, Bolívar achieved few of his political goals. Originally he wanted a grand confederation of American nations, but in the end he only succeeded in establishing the republic of Gran Colombia in 1822, which later splintered into Venezuela, Colombia, and Ecuador due to regionalism, economic problems, and intraelite competition. The failures and limitations of his grand visions left Bolívar searching for ways to establish enduring political systems. As time passed, Bolívar's political ideas mixed radical Enlightenment ideals with conservative plans to continue many colonial practices. His "Message to the Congress of Bolivia," the first document excerpt in this chapter, captures one of Bolívar's attempts to adapt his political visions to meet what he viewed as the obstacles to establishing stable representative governments. Bolívar had just finished drafting a constitution for the new nation of Bolivia (named after him), and this speech recommended a government structure for Bolivia.

The legacy of colonial racial structures also haunted The Liberator. In addition to failing to abolish slavery, Bolívar was unable to terminate Indian *tribute*, the central feature of the colonial System of *Two Republics* in which adult indigenous men paid a head tax to the state. In order to establish equality before the law, Bolívar abolished the tax briefly in Gran Colombia, but the government's financial dependence on the *tribute*, combined with popular resistance to its elimination, left him with no option but to reinstate the tax in 1828 under the title "personal contribution of indigenes."

Although Bolívar made numerous references to racial matters, he never directly addressed gender issues in his public statements. In some ways, this was at odds with his private life: Simón Bolívar had a long-term and open affair with Manuela Saenz, a married woman from Quito. Saenz, considered a great beauty in her youth, had languished in an unhappy marriage from a young age. She and Bolívar became the great loves of each other's lives. Saenz also provided Bolívar with crucial political support: She spied on his opponents and even saved his life on two occasions, earning her the nickname *La Libertadora del Libertador* (The woman liberator of The Liberator). Despite his well-known affair with Saenz, Bolívar rarely made known his views on women's roles in politics and society. This chapter offers two statements that he made about women in his private letters. Although Bolívar rarely discussed gender matters in public, the excerpts suggest that elite ideologies of his time informed his ideas about citizenship.

Together, the documents in this chapter, like all of the documents in this section, reveal that the independence era was one of both profound changes and compelling continuities. Military and political officials of the independence period aspired to make a clean break with Spanish rule and to prove that they were capable of putting an end to the colonial inequalities that they identified as unjust, even tyrannical. Yet colonial legacies proved harder to

This painting of Manuela Saenz hung in Simón Bolívar's house in Caracas. Even though Saenz was both Bolívar's lover and confidant, she spent the last 25 years of her life despised and destitute, selling tobacco and living on Peru's northern coast. She died during a diphtheria epidemic in 1856, and her body was dumped into a mass grave. Her belongings—including most of Bolívar's love letters—were burned. A century and a half later, Saenz is regarded as one of South America's independence heroes.
Source: AP Wide World Photos.

transcend than men like Bolívar would have liked. In the realm of race, class, and gender relations, some of the most enduring and troublesome obstacles to the proclaimed goals of independence remained.

Questions to Consider:

1. How did Bolívar define "good government" in these documents? How did he justify his views? Can you find contradictions in these documents about what government should be like or what it should do?

2. What seemed to be Bolívar's greatest concerns when establishing social and political order?
3. How did Bolívar define citizenship, rights, and obligations within these documents? How did race and gender shape citizenship or citizens' rights and obligations? How different were the documents on citizens' rights and duties?
4. What proposed changes departed from the colonial political system? What continued from the colonial system?

Simón Bolívar's "Message to the Congress of Bolivia"[1]

Lima, May 25, 1826

. . . *Legislators!* Your duty calls you to resist the blows of two monstrous foes that do battle with each other reciprocally, both of which will attack you simultaneously: Tyranny and anarchy form a vast ocean of oppression surrounding a tiny island of freedom that is perpetually pounded by the violence of the waves and hurricanes that seek unremittingly to sink her. Behold the sea you hope to traverse in a fragile boat, its pilot utterly unskilled.

This draft of a constitution for Bolivia proposes four Political Powers, one having been added, without thereby complicating the classical division of all previous constitutions. The Electoral Power has been given powers not encompassed in other governments considered among the most liberal. These powers approach those commonly featured in a federal system. It has seemed to me to be not only convenient and practical but also easy to grant to the immediate representatives of the people the privileges most sought by the citizens of that particular department, province or canton. There is no higher priority for a citizen than the election of his legislators, magistrates, judges, and pastors. The electoral colleges of each province represent their specific needs and interests and serve to expose infractions of the laws and the abuses of magistrates. I dare say, with some conviction, that this system of representation features the rights enjoyed by local governments in confederations. In this way, government has acquired additional guarantees, renewed popular support, and new justifications for being regarded as preeminent among the most democratic governments.

Each ten citizens appoint an elector, so that the nation is represented by a tenth of its citizens. All that is required is ability, nor is it necessary to own property to exercise the august function of sovereign, but the electors must know how to write down their votes, sign their names, and read the laws. They must practice a trade or a craft that will guarantee an honest living. The only disqualifying factors are crime, idleness, and total ignorance. Knowledge and honesty, not money, are the requirements for exercising public authority.

The Legislative Body is constituted so as to guarantee harmony among its parts; it will not stand forever divided for lack of a judge to provide arbitration, as happens where there are only two chambers. Since there are three branches, conflict between two is resolved by the third, the question being argued by the two contesting sides, with an impartial third side deciding the issue. In this way, no useful law will be rejected, or at least it will have been tested once, twice, and a third time before this happens. In all negotiations between two adversaries, a third is appointed to settle disputes. Would it not be absurd, in matters so crucial to society, to dispense with this provision dictated by imperious necessity? The chambers will thus observe toward one another the mutual respect necessary to preserve the unity of the entire body, which must conduct its deliberations calmly, wisely, and with restrained passion. You will tell me that in modern times congresses have been composed of two houses. This is because in England, which has served as the model, the nobility and the common people had to be represented in two chambers. And if the same procedure was followed in North America, where there was no nobility, it is likely that their habit

[1]*Source:* David Bushnell, ed., *El Libertador: Writings of Simón Bolívar,* trans. Frederick H. Fornoff (New York: Oxford University Press, 2003), 54–64.

of being under English rule inspired that imitation. The fact is that two deliberating bodies will inevitably lead to perpetual conflict . . .

Under our constitution, the president of the republic is like the Sun, immovable at the center of the universe, radiating life. This supreme authority should be permanent, because in systems without hierarchies, a fixed point around which magistrates and citizens and men and events revolve is more necessary than in other systems. Give me a fixed point, said an ancient, and I will move the earth. For Bolivia, this point is a president for life. In him, all order originates, even though he lacks the power to act. He has been beheaded so that no one will fear his intensions, and his hands have been tied so that he can harm no one.

The president of Bolivia is endowed with powers similar to those of the American executive, but with restrictions beneficial to the people. His term of office is the same as that of the presidents of Haiti. I have chosen as the model for Bolivia the executive of the most democratic republic in the world . . .

The president of Bolivia will be even less a threat than the president of Haiti, since the mode of succession offers surer prospects for the health of the state. Moreover, the president of Bolivia is denied all influence: he does not appoint magistrates, judges, or ecclesiastical dignitaries at any level. This reduction in executive power has never been tried in any duly constituted government . . .

The constitutional restrictions on the president of Bolivia are the severest ever known: his meager powers only allow him to appoint the ministers of departments of the treasury, peace, and war, and to command the army. That is the extent of his power . . .

The president of the republic appoints the vice president to administer the state and be his successor. This provision avoids elections, which produce the scourge of republics, anarchy. Anarchy is the instrument of tyranny and the most immediate and terrible of dangers in popular governments. Compare the orderly succession of rulers occurring in legitimate monarchies with the terrible crises provoked by these events in a republic.

The vice president must be the purest of men. This is crucial, because if the president does not appoint a righteous citizen, he must fear him as an enemy incarnate and suspect even his most hidden ambitions.

This vice president must strive to win through his good services the credibility he needs to exercise the highest functions and to merit the greatest award given by the nation—supreme power. The legislative body and the people will demand high skills and abilities of this official, as well as blind obedience to the laws of freedom.

Heredity being the principle perpetuating monarchical regimes, and this is so throughout the world, how much more useful would the method I propose be for determining the succession of the vice president? What if hereditary princes were chosen by merit, and not randomly, and instead of squandering their lives in idleness and ignorance, they were placed at the head of the administration? They would without a doubt be more enlightened monarchs and bring prosperity to their people. Yes, Legislators, the monarchies that govern the earth have been validated by the principle of heredity that makes them stable and by the unity that makes them strong. Thus, even though a sovereign prince may have been spoiled as a child, cloistered in his palace, educated by flattery, and driven by every passion, this prince, whom I would make so bold as to call the travesty of man, has authority over human beings because he preserves the order of things and the subservience of his subjects through the uninterrupted exercise of power and consistent action. Then consider, Legislators, that these great advantages are embodied in the *president for life in the hereditary succession by the vice president.*

The Judicial Power that I propose enjoys absolute independence: nowhere else does it enjoy as much. The people present the candidates, and the legislature chooses the individuals who will make up the courts. If the Judicial Power does not come into being in this manner, it cannot possibly maintain its integrity, which is the safeguard of individual rights. These rights, Legislators, constitute the freedom, equality, and security that are guaranteed in the social contract. True liberal constitution rests in the civil and criminal codes, and the most terrible tyranny is that exercised by the courts through the all-powerful instrument of the law. . . .

It was to be expected, according to the sentiments of modern times, that we would prohibit the use of torture to attain confessions and that we would reduce the time allowed for motions in the intricate labyrinth of the appellate courts . . .

The responsibility of government officials is written into the Bolivian constitution in the most explicit language. Without responsibility, without some coercion, the state is chaos. I will be so bold as to ardently urge the legislators to enact strong, definitive laws concerning this important matter. Everyone speaks of responsibility, but it goes no further than the lips. There is no responsibility, Legislators. The magistrates, judges, and other officials abuse their powers because there is no rigorous procedure for controlling the agents of the administration. Meanwhile, it is the citizens who are the victims of this abuse. I would recommend a law prescribing a strict and formal annual accounting of the actions of each official.

The most perfect guarantees have been written into this draft: *Civil liberty* is the only true freedom; the others are nominal or of little importance insofar as they affect the citizens. The *security of the individual* has been guaranteed, this being the purpose of society and the source of all other guarantees. As for *property rights*, these will depend on the civil code that in your wisdom you will compose with all dispatch for the happiness of your fellow citizens. I have left intact the law of all laws—*equality*. Without this, all guarantees, all rights perish. To ensure equality, we must make every sacrifice, beginning with infamous slavery, which I have laid at her feet, covered in shame.

Legislators! Slavery is the violation of every law. The law that would seek to preserve it would be a sacrilege. What possible justification can there be for its perpetuation? From whatever perspective you consider this crime, I cannot persuade myself that any Bolivian could be depraved enough to want to legitimize this most abominable violation of human dignity. One man owned by another! A man regarded as property! One of God's images hitched to the yoke like a beast! Let someone tell us, where do these usurpers of men file their titles of ownership? They were not sent to us by Guinea, because Africa, devastated by fratricide, can only export crime . . .

Legislators! I will now make reference to the matter my conscience forbade me to include. In a political system there should be no preference for one religion over another, because according to the wisest doctrines, the fundamental laws are guarantees of political and civil rights. And since religion has no relevance to these rights, it is inherently indefinable in the social order, belonging rather to the moral and intellectual order. Religion governs man in his house, in his private space, and in his heart. Religion alone has the right to examine his conscience. The laws, on the other hand, observe the surface of things; they have jurisdiction only outside the citizen's home. Applying these considerations, is there any way the state can govern the conscience of subjects, enforce the observation of religious laws, and offer reward or punishment, when the courts are in Heaven, when God is judge? Only the *Inquisition* could stand for them in this world. Do we want to see a return of the *Inquisition*[?] . . .

. . . popular sovereignty [is] the sole legitimate authority of nations . . .

{T}he Sovereignty of the People [is] the sole legitimate authority of any nation.

Bolívar's Statements on Women, Independence Movements, and Politics[2]

Bolívar's description of female combatants in the wars for independence:

. . . even the fair sex, the delights of humankind, our amazons have fought against the tyrants of San Carlos with a valor divine, although without success. The monsters and tigers of Spain have shown the full extent of their cowardice of their nation. They have used their infamous arms against the innocent feminine breasts of our beauties; they have shed their blood. They have killed many of them and they loaded them with chains, because they conceived the sublime plan of liberating their beloved country!

[2]*Source:* From Evelyn Cherpak, "The Participation of Women in the Independence Movement of Gran Colombia, 1780–1830," in *Latin American Women: Historical Perspectives*, ed. Asuncion Lavrin (Westport, CT: Greenwood Press, 1978), 222, 229–230.

Bolívar's letter to his sister, María
Antonía, regarding women
and politics (1826):

I warn you not to mix in political business nor ad-
here to or oppose any party. Let opinion and things
go along although you believe them contrary to your
way of thinking. A woman ought to be neutral in
public business. Her family and her domestic duties
are her first obligations. A sister of mine ought to
observe perfect indifference in a country which is in
a state of dangerous crisis and in which I am viewed
as the point at which opinions meet.

Suggested Sources:

Readers generally interested in the independence
era could start by exploring John Lynch's classic
study of the period, *The Spanish American Revolution,
1808–1826*, 2nd ed. (New York: W.W. Norton,
1986); or Jaime E. Rodríguez O., *The Independence of
Spanish America* (New York: Cambridge University
Press, 1998). Both books offer overviews of important themes and issues.

For an English-language translation of major
sources by Bolívar that includes both public statements and private letters, see David Bushnell, ed.,
El Libertador: Writings of Simón Bolívar, trans.
Frederick H. Fornoff (New York: Oxford Univer-
sity Press, 2003). For a biography of The Liberator
that includes a discussion of developing historiog-
raphy around this pivotal figure who looms so
large over Spanish American Independence, see
John Lynch, *Simón Bolívar: A Life* (New Haven, CT:
Yale University Press, 2007). To consider South
American independence from female perspec-
tives, see Evelyn Cherpak, "The Participation of
Women in the Independence Movement of
Gran Colombia, 1780–1830," in *Latin American
Women: Historical Perspectives*, ed. Asuncion
Lavrin (Westport, CT: Greenwood Press, 1978),
219–234. Sarah Chambers provides a probing
analysis of Saenz's political views, focusing on the
years following Bolívar's death, in her article,
"Republican Friendship: Manuela Saenz Writes
Women into the Nation, 1835–1856," *Hispanic
American Historical Review* 81, no. 2 (May 2001):
225–258.

Chapter 28

Forging a Guerrilla Republic

Javier F. Marión, Emmanuel College, Boston

When still a teenager, the adventurous José Santos Vargas joined the anticolonial struggle as a guerrilla combatant and rebel scribe. He later wrote about those tumultuous years when he and other rural people from humble backgrounds helped establish a guerrilla republic and drive the Spanish out of the Andes. The Spanish American wars for independence were seminal moments in the history of the nations they created. Besides establishing political boundaries, the *revoluciones*, as they were called, served as a sort of crucible that legitimated the existence of the new nations and provided ideological parameters that informed their respective citizens of who they were as a people. The process of creating these nations has often been misconstrued as an exclusively *creole*[1]

---

[1]*Creoles* were American-born individuals normally of upper social rank.

affair, engineered by the urban, well-to-do classes with little impetus from popular groups. As with all things that characterize Latin America, however, the real story is much more complex and fraught with the contradictions of its colonial legacy.

The independence wars represented an unusual opportunity to bring about social change and reforms that resonated with concerns at local levels. As such, they attracted a multidimensional pool of participants who fought for different reasons as members of patriot and royalist armies or as affiliated guerrilla units. But their contributions were rarely acknowledged by historians and politicians, who either downplayed their significance or ignored them altogether. The first generation of national historians eulogized the war's military leaders, such as Simón Bolívar, José de San Martín, and Agustín de Iturbide, as responsible for Spain's defeat and, in varying degrees, as de facto, *creole* founding fathers. Subsequent generations of historians reinforced the relationship between the liberator classes and their respective nations in part because they relied on the personal letters and official correspondences and royalist and patriot officers' accounts of the war.[2] These writings mentioned Indians, *castas*, and displaced peasants as participants in the conflict, but they provided only superficial explanations on the origins, motivations, and guiding ideologies behind these groups' mobilization. It seemed that the popular masses served only as cannon fodder or as passive actors in a conflict they knew little about. Moreover they assumed that these groups lacked a meaningful sense of *patria* (nation), and, thus they were incapable of participating in representative forms of government. With few exceptions, this *creole* version remained the dominant independence narrative until the second half of the twentieth century when different sources were consulted.

In the following passages, readers can attempt to reach broader conclusions about the nature of popular politics by exploring rural sources from Bolivia's independence period (1809–1825). These include excerpts from the *diario* (journal) of José Santos Vargas, a combatant from the remote and mountainous districts of Ayopaya and Sicasica. José Santos Vargas was a rebel scribe, drummer, soldier, and guerrilla leader in the Sicasica and Ayopaya valleys between 1814 and 1825.

Vargas's account offers the unique perspective of a rural, *mestizo* combatant written in the period's common vernacular. Born to a family of modest means in 1797 and orphaned at age 8, the 14-year-old Vargas witnessed insurgent forces enter Oruro in 1811. He followed them through the countryside to Cochabamba and eventually found his way to the Indian community of Cavari (Sicasica district) where his brother Andrés Vargas served as a priest and became a wanted man because he was a rebel chaplain. After royalists captured Andrés in 1816, the young Vargas remained in the region as a member of the Cavari Indian community, eventually marrying an *Aymara* woman. Vargas joined the rebel forces in 1815 under the command of commander Eusebio Lira, who valued the boy's ability to write, appointing him scribe and drummer. Vargas enjoyed the arrangement. His proximity to Lira and his inner circle provided a special vantage point. It was Lira who gave him the sobriquet, "El Tambor Vargas" ("the drummer, Vargas").

Vargas recorded the actions and motivations of his compatriots in remarkable detail during the war years of 1814–1825. During this period, the insurgency was disconnected from urban independence movements in Buenos Aires, Cochabamba, La Paz, and Salta. The relative inaccessibility of the rugged regions of Sicasica, along with the adjacent district of Ayopaya, had attracted rebel groups seeking refuge during the anti-Spanish Katari rebellion (1780–1783),[3] and the districts again emerged as the epicenter in this new round of widespread resistance and guerrilla activity. By the end of the colonial period, Sicasica remained a predominantly "Indian" district where traditional corporate communities known as *ayllus* predominated and *Aymara* was the lingua franca. By contrast, *mestizaje*

[2]For example: Daniel Florencio Oleary, *Bolivar and the War of Independence* (Austin: University of Texas Press, 1970).

[3]The Katari rebellion was the Alto Peruvian (Bolivian) phase of the anticolonial movement known as the Tupac Amaru rebellion.

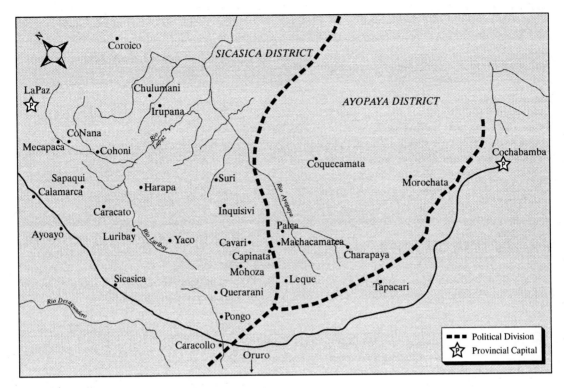

The Colonial Districts of Ayopaya and Sicasica.

in Ayopaya had been commonplace, and by the nineteenth century, *ayllus* had long disappeared, replaced by *haciendas* and Hispanic towns.

Independence fighters carved out an elongated rebel territory, oftentimes referred to as a *republiqueta* (mini republic) by contemporaries. Geography coupled with guerrilla tactics gave the republiqueta a distinct advantage in resisting colonial authority. When Bolivia achieved independence in 1825, the republiqueta was under the authority of José Miguel Lanza, a *creole* guerrilla leader. It was thus presumed that the Ayopaya-Sicasica republiqueta adhered to the same political precepts that guided Lanza and the *creoles* dominating the new Bolivian republic. However, according to Vargas's *diario*, Lanza did not emerge as leading rebel commander until 1821, and, even then, Lanza was met with stiff opposition from those who envisioned a very different notion of *patria*. The overarching

figure in Vargas's account was not Lanza. Instead, Eusebio Lira, a large, charismatic, and domineering individual of mixed descent from the Indian town of Mohoza, stands out. Lira presided as supreme commander over the republiqueta between 1815 and 1817, when he was murdered by members of another rebel faction. Vargas depicts Lira in almost messianic terms as a native son and indomitable guerrilla leader.

Vargas drafted two versions of his account of these events (in 1825 and 1852). He intended to have it published, but it only reached publication in 1982. The excerpts in this chapter were transcribed from the more complete 1852 manuscript. Vargas's diary reveals that the partisans articulated a highly localized concept of nation that privileged Andeanized notions of *honor*, kinship, and political legitimacy. The diary also suggests that war temporarily blurred social distinctions and created new forms of upward mobility for Indians and *mestizos* in the mid- to lower social ranges. They developed a highly flexible political culture indicative of Andean-Indian preoccupations with balance, reciprocity, and community. Vargas offered his version because "our political leaders here [in Bolivia] do not know of the events that occurred here, nor do the political leaders in Buenos Aires or in Salta. They do not know the names of those who fought, how they did it, in what time frame, and under whose leadership. They understood vaguely that troops dedicated to the *patria* existed in these parts but only as hearsay. They do not truly understand that the cause of American liberty was deeply rooted in every region."[4] Vargas directly contested the *creole* version of the war because he sensed that he and his compatriots were being excluded from the nation-building process. A variety of people imagined a life without Spanish overlords. They mobilized in large numbers and fought on many fronts to realize these alternatives to colonial rule. However, few of the commoner folk saw their visions turned into reality, and few left accounts of their efforts and their dreams. Vargas is one who did.

Questions to Consider:

1. What did Vargas and his compatriots mean when they used the word *patria*? Are they referring to the territorial boundaries of Bolivia, all of Spanish America, or the confines of their rebel republiqueta?

2. To what extent did the rebels practice and understand participatory forms of government, and whom did they consider their countrymen? How do these definitions of countrymen and forms of government compare to those proposed by Morelos and Bolívar in other chapters?

3. What was the relationship like between the rebel leaders and indigenous peasants? What does that relationship suggest about the extent to which the independence movement did (or did not) help to break down social barriers?

4. What motivated Vargas and his compatriots to participate as combatants? To what extent were these motivations uniform?

---

[4]*Source:* Archivo y Biblioteca Nacional de Bolivia (A/BNB), Directorio (DIR), 44B, fol. 5v.

Journal Entries by José Santos Vargas, Combatant in Bolivia's Independence War[5]

José Santos Vargas is Reunited with his Brother

1814 [exact date uncertain]. After three years I came in search of a brother I had. . . . *don* Andrés Vargas, a clergyman. I found him in Pocusco, near the town of Cavari. . . . He stretched out his arms to welcome me and he asked me in our conversations about everything I had seen during my travels. I first told him about my days as a school boy but later we talked about the war. He urged me to always embrace the cause of the *patria* and of the liberty of America: This is a just cause. The most just of all. It is the same cause being defended by the *porteños* (troops from Buenos Aires). God will always defend them because the king of Spain was not our legitimate sovereign. We need to defend the liberty of the *Patria* at all costs. We are obligated by God and by nature itself to defend our liberty from Spain's government because they only govern through the use of force and without the slightest interest to act on our behalf.

---

[5]*Source:* "Diario Historico de todos los sucesos ocurridos en las provincias de Sicasica y Ayopaya durante la Guerra de la independencia Americana, desde el año 1814 hasta el año 1825. Escrito por un comandante del partido de Mohoza, el ciudadano José Santos Vargas," Archivo y Biblioteca Nacional de Bolivia (A/BNB), Directorio (DIR), A/BNB, DIR, 44B, fols. 5, 165–168, 177v–185v, 209v, 288.

Eusebio Lira Pardons Marcelino Castro

November 20, 1817. Lira ordered his second lieutenant, Ignacio Borda, and others to Cajuata to arrest *don* Marcelino Castro. They arrested him in his home and he was brought to the town of Inquisivi. This Castro was once surprised by royalist troops who broke into his home and . . . the governor of La Paz, Juan Bautista Sánchez Lima had him conscripted into his army . . . he was brought to the city of La Paz and later . . . to the town of Sicasica where he was ordered to join the royalist commander, *don* José Castro Navajas. He followed Navajas everywhere. . . .

When he was brought before commander Lira, Castro explained that when he was first caught, the governor of La Paz, Juan Bautista Sánchez Lima, saw that he had large family and took pity on him. . . . He realized that Castro was poor and that his family could not survive without him. Lira's officers corroborated his story and urged Lira to pardon him. . . . To prove his own innocence, Castro reaches into his pocket pulls out a letter that describes his service to the *Patria*, particularly his role in helping a certain patriot named Juan Crisóstomo Gutierrez, a resident of Inquisivi. But he also [perhaps inadvertently] pulled out another document; a certificate of recommendation from the governor of La Paz, Juan Bautista Sánchez Lima that described the services he had provided to the royal crown . . . it was signed by Sánchez Lima himself.

At this point Lira read the documents and then handed them over to his secretary, *don* Juan Crisóstomo Osinaga. He sent me to muster the rest of the officers. They all arrived and the secretary read aloud the letter that Castro had presented of his own volition. The officers were left mute as was Castro who could not articulate a single word in his defense. Lira addressed the gathering:

Señores, distinguished officers, compatriots, and brothers in arms, I supported your judgment (concerning Castro's innocence) . . . but it now appears as though we've been deceived. We have an enemy to our cause in these territories and in our midst. I present to you this certificate of recommendation that was in his possession which retraces in detail his

whereabouts over a long period of time during which he served various enemy officers. If he were a true defender of the *Patria* he would have separated himself from the royalists at his first opportunity. . . . According to Sánchez Lima he never attempted to escape. This individual was with enemy troops on various occasions. He was with them at Curupaya on the 8th of January, acting as a guide; he was with Navajas at Lirimani and helped the enemy escape on March 8th. . . . Should we, *señores* and distinguished officers, considered these to be of service to the *Patria*?

Castro responded and claimed that he never served as a guide . . . other men served as guides but not him.

At this point the second lieutenant of the first company, *don* Manuel Patiño, requested permission to speak. He said that Marcelino Castro was a virtuous person and that he did not willingly communicate with the leaders serving the king. . . . He claimed that the certificate of recommendation written by Sánchez Lima should not be considered as sufficient evidence for him to be treated as a traitor. He continued saying that if Castro was a royalist he would have remained with the king's troops and not return to his home. He did not remain with them even though he was receiving a good salary to do so. Everyone knows that the king and his officers pay well. . . .

Lira again spoke:

If this man did not return to be with his royalist troops it is because he is acting as a spy among us. How do we know that he is not being paid? . . . This man will be jailed and watched by an armed guard.

On the 21st it was determined that he was to be executed and the number of guards increased to include twenty-five men. They called for the priest, doctor *don* Juan Gutiérrez to accompany him and to act as his confessor. Many of Inquisivi's residents called for Castro's release but to no avail. That night he received a visit from the sister of the priest, Juan Gutierrez; a woman named *doña* Petrona. She left Castro her *polleras*.[6] Other officers also visited and left him with women's accoutrements. Between two or

---

[6]Dress worn by some *mestizas*.

three in the morning Castro escaped from jail dressed as a woman and left his bed sheets bundled up to make it appear as though a person was sleeping there.

At four in the morning Lira learned of Castro's escape and this caused him to leap from his bed and act greatly disturbed. He summoned the Indians to pursue and capture him. . . . The Indians refused and told Lira that Castro should instead be pardoned. Lira was incensed. He threw the Indians from his home and ordered his men to scour the countryside in search of Castro.

By November 22nd, Lira's heart was calmed. That afternoon, after running some drills, he invited his officers to dinner at a local ranch. During dinner Lira proposed a toast wherein he expressed empathy for Castro's predicament. He feared that he may have unwittingly pushed Castro to the side of the enemy and against the *Patria*. He proclaimed that if Castro presented himself he would be exonerated in the name of the *Patria*.

Reaction to Eusebio Lira's Death

December 19, 1817. We broke camp at three in the afternoon. We monitored the countryside on the way to Palca. We discovered that the more than 3,000 Indians had gathered in highlands; their numbers covered the mountains as we approached the town. They were armed with lances, slings, and cudgels. We entered Palca at six in the afternoon. We learned that the Indians had at least eighteen firearms of all types. They had come from every town from both districts (Sicasica and Ayopaya), as far as Tapacari, Arque, and Paria and they had come to mourn the death of commander Lira. They threatened to destroy the division if it was indeed true that Lira was not alive. All night long they disturbed our sleep. They blew their horns and other war implements. Their noise making made for a very uncomfortable night.

On December 20th at eight in the morning we ascended the heights to meet with the Indians, directly above Palca to a place named Chuñavi. . . . We met with six *indios principales*[7] and they wanted us to

explain Lira's death. [Commander Santiago] Fajardo spoke with them and told them Lira was executed because he was a traitor. . . .

On December 24th . . . a large contingent of Indians descended to again speak with Fajardo; they wanted him to turn over the men responsible for Lira's death: sergeant major, *don* Pedro Marquina; the captain; the (insurgent) governor of Paria district, *don* Agustín Contreras; captain, *don* Eugenio Moreno; cavalry officer, *don* Santiago Morales; the ensign, *don* Pedro Granados; officer *don* Antonio Pacheco, sergeant *don* Manuel Miranda; and the soldier and Lira's personal escort, José María Torres. The Indians were convinced that these men were accomplices to Lira's murder. After a long dispute, Fajardo realized that he was completely surrounded by throngs of Indians. Realizing his danger . . . he promised to deliver three of the men in question once he returned to town. The Indians accepted. Commander Fajardo entered the town . . . upon being reunited with his men, however, he reneged on his promise. He instead ordered the Indians tend their fields and to their livestock and to mind their own affairs. He insisted that Lira's death was none of their concern and that the appropriate authorities in Buenos Aires and Salta would soon settle the matter. . . . Some of the Indians obeyed but others wanted to raze the town unless they saw Lira alive. . . . Fajardo announced:

Listen Indians, if my prudent reasoning does not persuade you to leave then I will have to disperse you forcibly.

Listening to this, the Indians responded in *Aymara*, "*Maya amparaqui Maya amparaqu*,"[8] Fajardo ordered his men to open fire. . . . The division fired into the air which caused many of the Indians to disperse. . . . Some sought asylum in the church where the town's women had already taken refuge. This caused quite a commotion. . . . The sight of these Indians entering the temple with lances and cudgels alarmed these women greatly.

On the 25th of December a large number of Indians arrived from Yungas with forty firearms. With them came captain *don* José Calderón, Rafael Copitas

---

[7] *Indios principales* exercised political and economic influence in their communities.

[8] "An eye for an eye." They were also willing to use force.

and the commander, *don* José Manuel Chinchilla. Gandarillas had not yet arrived but he was a short distance away. All of these arrived in the town of Machacamarca.

Having received this news, we left Palca for Machacamarca at six in the morning. At ten in the morning we were in the mountains overlooking Machacamarca below us. At eleven the Indians sent a certain Pedro Zuñiga a person of great patriot sentiment from the city of La Paz. The captain commander of Indians from the town of Mohoza, Mateo Quispe; captain commander of Indians from Ichoca, Benito Arguello; captain commander of Indians from Cavari, Mariano Lezcano; captain commander of Indians from Leque, Marcelo Calcina. These men told Fajardo who had arrived with armed escort that it was the people who should nominate the next leader who would govern them. They claimed to represent twenty different communities. They then demanded an election should take place or else they would not be held responsible for what would follow. Fajardo alone would be held responsible before God, before the *Patria*, and before the leadership in Buenos Aires. Fajardo agreed to proceed to Machacamarca and turn the division over to whomever the people choose. He wanted to retire to his house and rest. . . .

On December 26th . . . commander Fajardo joined the gathering and gave a brief speech:

Señores, distinguished officers, compatriots, and brothers in arms, you all know that I've been a patriot from the beginning, a soldier of liberty who never tainted his honor in regards to my convictions. I don't aspire to anything else, given my advanced age. . . . Those who represent the given towns should choose the leader of these territories. You can deliberate in any manner you wish but I don't wish to be included among the names that you will choose from. I don't aspire to that charge. I am a patriot and I will die for the *Patria* despite whatever course destiny brings because I have consecrated my life and blood to her cause.

After a while, *don* José Buenaventura Zárate spoke up:

. . . given that *don* Santiago Fajardo stepped down from his position we will need, on this occasion, to name a president and secretary to preside over this meeting. . . . Everyone unanimously agreed with this course of action. Fajardo nominated *don* José Buenaventura Zárate to act as president and captain *don* Ramón Rivero to act as secretary. When the votes cleared, Zárate emerged as president and Rivero as secretary . . . Zárate took his seat and said: *Señores*, are you willing to obey the leader that you yourselves will name? Will you blindly follow his orders?

He ensured that the *caciques*, mayors, and other officials who spoke in Indian dialects [*Quechua* and *Aymara*] understood what he was saying by speaking to them in their own languages. They all replied that they would respect and obey whatever orders came from their elected leader. Zárate insisted that everyone take an oath to that end and they all did so enthusiastically.

They then proceeded to the business of voting for the leader. The [insurgent] governor *don* José Manuel Arana voted for commander Fajardo, then sergeant major Marquina voted for Fajardo, followed by captain *don* José Calderón who also voted for Fajardo.

Fajardo responded:

We should not have held this meeting or these elections if we were to reach the same results.

President Zárate interrupted:

Silence, *señores*! You should all submit secret votes in writing. The Indians who cannot write should choose a trusted person to write and vote in your place.

Everyone agreed with this idea and did as they were told. At two in the afternoon the final tally was made and commander *don* Santiago Fajardo was chosen. Despite his words to the contrary it was of no use. He eventually accepted their decision and was sworn in. He then declared,

Señores, I already told you that I am an old man and this presents a problem. To complete the charge you've given me I will need a *compañero* [partner]; someone who will serve as my second in command. He would have the same responsibilities as myself but subject to my orders. . . .

Everyone approved of the idea. Fajardo then told everyone that his personal choice for the position was [insurgent] governor *don* José Manuel Arana. The president then instructed everyone to do another secret vote in writing. Everyone did as they were told and the vote went to José Manuel Chinchilla despite the presence of many who aspired to be second in command. . . .

Administrating Lira's Republiqueta

December, 1817 [exact date uncertain]. Lira did not pay the men in his division because he did not have the means to do so. On certain Sundays he distributed a small ration of two *reales* to those of all classes, without exception. On rare occasions he handed out two *pesos*. He did reserve productive agricultural lands for the troops where he arranged to have them fed and he ate alongside them. He provided clothes as best he could, mostly made with local textiles woven by the locals. He was able to purchase a variety of armaments. . . . Firearms were purchased from merchants in Oruro, Cochabamba, La Paz, Irupana, and Sicasica. Others were taken from the enemy in battle. He arranged for powder to be mined from local sources. Saltpeter from Mojsu-uma and the flats of Oruro was purchased clandestinely by his Indian allies. . . . Horses and mules were donated from Indian communities and local townsmen. His government lacked a tax base because he did not force the Indian communities to pay *tribute* [Indian head tax] nor did he collect the *alcabala* [sales tax]. The local priests regularly contributed with small loans and with whatever donations they could collect. Even some of the *haciendas* opposed to the *patria* contributed the costs of maintaining the troops. *Hacienda* owners as well as Indians from both districts provided the *Patria* with food, they never declined to help. Those who owned the least amount of grains were among the first to contribute. The towns and their inhabitants willingly took turns monthly in providing what the troops needed. . . . The townspeople served through their own energies, their own lives, and with their own interests in mind. . . . In this manner, the people supported commander Lira in his defense of the *Patria*, liberty, and American independence from Spain.

Arrangements were made to lease out lands in order to meet specific costs incurred by the division. In the district of Sicasica specifically, all of the lands and farms that belonged to the Marquee of Santiago, who was absent because he resided in Lima where he served the viceregal court; all of these lands were leased out to others.

In the district of Ayopaya Lira parceled out the *hacienda* of Punacache which had been abandoned by *don* Agapito Achá who was very opposed to the liberty of America. These lands were parceled out to 100 pairs of plowmen. . . .

These were the material goods claimed by the *Patria*. Some have falsely accused us of being robbers, thieves, and thugs. The fact that these things occurred cannot be denied and can be attributed to some of the Indians who joined the division as captains, commanders, or as commissioned agents; these were the same individuals that victimized travelers along roads and engaged in other unfortunate activities. But these things normally occurred along the fringes of the territory controlled by the cause of liberty and independence. At the same time, it should be mentioned that those who committed these crimes were pursued and punished.

News from the Outside

On the 24th of March, between Panduro and Aroma they encountered a party of 30 royalist infantrymen escorting the mail from La Paz to Oruro. . . . There we opened the mail and read it aloud. We discovered the state of affairs in Lima, Chile, and Colombia. It was the first time we had heard of Colombia and of general Bolívar and everything that had transpired. We learned everything then. Everything!

Suggested Sources:

For scholars writing peasants and *non-creoles* back into the history of the wars for independence in Latin America, see Peter F. Guardino, *Peasants, Politics, and the Formation of Mexico's National State, 1800–1857* (Stanford, CA: Stanford University Press, 1996); and Eric Van Young, *The Other Rebellion: Popular Violence, Ideology, and the Mexican Struggle for Independence, 1810–1821* (Stanford, CA: Stanford University Press, 2001). For the Andes, see Cecilia Mendez, *The Plebeian Republic: The Huanta Rebellion and the Making of the Peruvian State, 1820–1850* (Durham, NC: Duke University Press, 2005). A classic account of how liberal-republican ideas meshed with pre-Columbian expressions of political legitimacy after independence is in Tristan Platt, "Simón Bolívar, the Sun of Justice and the Amerindian Virgin: Andean Conceptions of the

Patria in Nineteenth-Century Potosí," *Journal of Latin American Studies* 25 (February 1993): 159–185. The Túpac Amaru Rebellion can be fruitfully compared with creole-dominated independence movements in the Peruvian highlands. See Charles Walker, *Smoldering Ashes: Cuzco and the Creation of Republican Peru, 1780–1840* (Durham, NC: Duke University Press, 1999). Rebecca Earle outlines the various Indian-oriented political programs described as "Indianesque" and employed by both royalists and insurgents in her essay, "*Creole* Patriotism and the Myth of the 'Loyal Indian,'" *Past and Present*, no. 172 (August 2001): 125–145. Lastly, a novelistic account of the independence wars can be found in Nathaniel Aguirre, *Juan de la Rosa: Memoirs of the Last Soldier of the Independence Movement* (New York: Oxford University Press, 1998).

Chapter 29

Slavery, Race, and Citizenship in the Empire of Brazil: Debates in the Constituent Assembly

Kirsten Schultz, Seton Hall University

In 1822, Portuguese-born Prince Regent *Dom Pedro I*, son of Portugal's king who had come to Brazil 14 years earlier to escape a Napoleonic army's invasion of Portugal, declared Brazil's independence from Portugal. The royal nature of the gesture notwithstanding, elite and popular support for the declaration had been forged the previous year within an emerging political culture of constitutionalism. In the wake of a successful rebellion in the city of Porto, Portugal, a provisional government

249

gathered to draft a written constitution. Supporters on both sides of the Atlantic claimed that a written constitution would guard against the tyranny of absolute monarchy and replace a corrupt old regime with virtuous national sovereignty. Initially constitutionalists also claimed that constitutional government would renew the ties between Portugal and its colonies strained by Napoleon's invasion and the transfer of the royal court to Rio de Janeiro in Brazil (1807). Accordingly, they included representatives from all of the territories of the Portuguese Crown.

By August 1821, however, with Brazilian delegates a minority (75 representatives out of 250), and before many of them had even arrived in Lisbon, the constitutionalists passed measures viewed in Brazil as contrary to Brazilian interests. Brazilian merchants' privileges were curtailed; the judicial courts established in Rio following the transfer of the court were abolished; and the heir to the throne *(Dom Pedro)* was ordered to return to Portugal, as his father (King Dom João) had been in 1821. The ideal of constitutionally sanctioned representation that had promised to preserve the unity of the Portuguese empire began, instead, to serve as the basis of rupture.

Following his declaration of independence in 1822, the prince *Dom Pedro* affirmed his support for *constitutionalism* and summoned to Rio de Janeiro representatives from Brazil's provinces to draft a constitution for the new Empire of Brazil. The elected representatives were well qualified for the task. Half had been educated at the University of Coimbra, Portugal, and many had subsequently served in imperial government and military service. They included lawyers, magistrates, clergymen, physicians, merchants, and landowners. Eighteen had been elected earlier to represent Brazil in Lisbon.

By April 1823 enough representatives were in Rio de Janeiro for formal proceedings to begin. As in other former European colonies in the Americas, one of the main tasks of the Assembly was to render a legal framework for the exercise of the popular or national sovereignty that had displaced the sovereignty of the king in the process of gaining independence. Thus, the representatives sought to define a balance of legislative, executive, and judicial powers as well as the scope of nationhood and citizenship. The first draft of this framework, the "Project of [a] Constitution for the Empire of Brazil," written

Titled *The Foundation of the Brazilian Nation* (September 7, 1822), this allegory of the Brazilian nation, made well after independence, represents the three races: the African slave, the native Indian, and the Portuguese. A São Paulo landowner and architect of independence, José Bonifácio Andrada e Silva, a Brazilian-born elite (1763–1838), sits with a banner draped over his knees, while the young Portuguese prince and first Emperor of Brazil, Dom Pedro I (1793–1834), who supported the declaration of independence, clutches a sword to his chest. Among Brazil's elites, Silva supported slave emancipation early on; he asked how a newly freed people could steal the freedom from others. How are the three races portrayed in this image? What does the allegory suggest about the author's view of the relations among these groups and their respective roles in an independent nation? How closely do these images of race and nation correspond to the ideas and problems debated in the Constituent Assembly?

Source: Private Collection/The Bridgeman Art Library International.

by a committee of representatives, was presented to the Assembly in September 1823.

What follows are excerpts from the Assembly's draft constitution and debates on the definition of citizenship in the Empire of Brazil contained in the draft. As many representatives agreed, "to attend to constituting ourselves, and giving the honorable title of Citizen" was a matter of forging an explicitly, and primarily, political identity. Yet the criteria for citizenship were various. Certain exclusions, such as those based on age, gender, and lack of wealth, did not generate discussion. Others were subjected to intense scrutiny and elicited the expression of passionate differences of opinion from members of the Assembly. These hotly debated criteria for citizenship included: legal status; perceptions of cultural, ethnic, and physical difference; and place of birth.

Of particular concern in these debates were articles of the draft constitution that recognized the existence and legacies of slavery. Slavery dominated early nineteenth-century Brazil's economy and society, and at least half of the population was of African descent (free, freed, and enslaved). In some regions of Brazil, patriots had encouraged slaves to enlist in the armed forces to fight for the cause of independence, promising freedom in return. Indeed, throughout the tumultuous 1810s and 1820s, slaves expressed hopes that challenges to the empire and the old regime would lead to an overthrow of the institution of slavery as well. In the wake of the transfer of the royal court to Rio in 1807–1808 and faced with internationalist abolitionist diplomacy, some Brazilian elites, including several representatives to the Assembly, expressed concerns about the moral, political, and economic consequences of slavery. However, preoccupied with the social and economic disorder that they imagined an immediate end to slavery would produce, these elites considered only the possibility of a gradual abolition at some point in the future. As a result, the drafters of the constitution had to reckon with the continuation of slavery in an independent Brazil. In Title II, Article 6, the draft constitution defined "Brazilians" as including "Slaves who obtain a letter of *manumission*." The law also recognized these former slaves, known as *libertos*, in articles of the draft constitution concerning voting rights.

In November 1823, confronted with the nativist (anti-Portuguese) speeches of some of its members and what he perceived to be the increasing disorder of the assembly's sessions, *Dom Pedro* ordered military units to disband the Assembly. The use of such unconstitutional measures (as defined by the draft constitution itself) to protect *constitutionalism* signaled *Dom Pedro's* willingness to forego liberal principles in order to maintain his power. Nevertheless, despite this move, the Assembly, its deliberations, and its draft constitution became the "principle source" of the 1824 Constitution, drafted by a council of statesmen appointed by the Emperor, including former members of the disbanded Assembly. Indeed, the Constitution of 1824 both bore the marks of the draft constitution and the earlier assembly discussions; it attested to efforts to clarify ambiguities and resolve conflicts that had surfaced in the past. In contrast to the draft constitution, however, the Constitution of 1824 did not recognize the institution of slavery, the existence of slaves, or the possibility of abolition. Perhaps these purposeful omissions reflected the counsel offered by one representative at the beginning of the citizenship debates that there were things "that were better repressed." This constitution formed the legal foundation for the Brazilian Empire until its overthrow in 1889.

Questions to Consider:

1. Why was the question of manumitted slaves so heatedly debated? What did their status mean to the nation?

2. How did the members of the Assembly define citizenship? What were the grounds for inclusion or exclusion from Brazilian citizenry and society? Was citizenship related to other forms of identity and allegiance? How does the scope of citizenship and voting rights defined in the draft constitution ("Project") compare with those of the Constitution of 1824?

3. To what kinds of principles and authorities did the representatives appeal in making their arguments?

4. What were the main points of disagreement among the members of the Assembly over the definition of "Brazilian"? Do these disagreements affirm or challenge historical understandings of the way elites viewed the poor and people of color in the nineteenth century?

Project of a Constitution for the Empire of Brazil[1]

Title II: Of the Empire of Brazil

Chapter I: Of the Members of the Society of the Empire of Brazil

Article 5: Brazilians are

I. All free male inhabitants of Brazil, and in Brazil born.

II. All Portuguese residents in Brazil before October 12, 1822 [the date of *Dom Pedro's* Acclamation to the throne].

III. Children of Brazilian parents born in foreign countries, who come to establish residence in the Empire.

IV. Children of Brazilian parents who were in a foreign country in service to the Nation, even though they do not establish residence in the Empire.

V. Illegitimate children of a Brazilian mother who, having been born in a foreign country, come to establish residence in the Empire.

VI. Slaves who obtain a letter of *manumission.*[2]

VII. Children of foreigners born in the Empire, as long as their parents are not in the service of their respective nations.

VIII. Naturalized foreigners, regardless of their religion. . . .

Title V: Of Elections

Article 122: Elections are indirect, the mass of active citizens electing electors, and the electors the Deputies [representatives], and equally, Senators in this first organization of the Senate.

Article 123. Those who are active citizens to vote in the Assembly primaries, or the parish:

I. All freeborn Brazilians, and *libertos* born in Brazil.

II. Naturalized foreigners . . .

Article 124: Exceptions:

I. Minors under the age of twenty-five years, not including those who are married, military officers who are twenty-one years old, recipients of higher degrees, and clergy of Holy Orders.

II. Sons of families who are under the power and in the company of their fathers, except if they serve in public office.

III. Servants, not including in this class foremen.

IV. Freedmen who are not born in Brazil, except those who have military commissions or [are in] Holy Orders.

V. The religious and whoever lives in a cloistered community, not including in this exception the religious of military orders or the secular clergy.

VI. Clerks, not including bookkeepers.

VII. Day laborers.

Article 127: *Libertos* born in any parts cannot be electors even if they have military commissions or [are in] Sacred Orders. . . .

[1]*Source:* Translated by Tim Henderson, "Sentiments of the Nation, or Points Outlined by Morelos for the Constitution," in *The Mexico Reader,* Gilbert M. Joseph and Timothy J. Henderson, Eds., pp. 189–191. Copyright 2002, Duke University Press. All rights reserved. Used by permission of the publisher. (Original text from Ernesto de la Torre Villar, Moises Gonzalez Navarro, and Stanley Ross, Eds., *Historia documental de Mexico,* Vol. 2. Mexico CIty: Universidad Nacional Autonoma de Mexico, 1964, pps. 11–112.)
[2]The term used here is *carta de alforria,* the legal document that established that a slave had been freed or manumitted.

Title XVIII: Of Public Instruction, Charitable Establishments, Correctional Houses, and Work

Article 254: There will be equal care to create establishments for the catechism, and civilization of the Indians, the slow emancipation of the Blacks (*Negros*), and their religious and vocational education.

Constitutional Assembly debates from September 27 and September 30[3]

... There began a discussion of article six ... "The slaves who obtain a Letter of *Manumission.*"

Mr. Costa Barros: I will never be able to accept that the title of Brazilian citizen is given indiscriminately to every slave who obtains a Letter of *Manumission.* Recently arrived blacks,[4] without a trade, without benefits, are not, in my understanding, deserving of this honorable prerogative; rather I see them as harmful members of society for which they are a burden [even] when they do not cause evil. I judge it is necessary to limit such a generality, conceiving this article in the following terms: "Slaves &c. who have employment or a trade."

It was supported.

Mr. França: This article six could pass if all of our slaves were born in Brazil because, having the right of territorial origin to be considered citizens as long as the civil impediment of the condition of their parents is removed, they would be restored *pleno jure* [with full authority] the benefit of this right, which was suspended by captivity; but since it is not the case, because a great number of our *libertos* are foreigners from different Nations of Africa ... it is clear that being coherent in our principles, that this article can pass regarding that which pertains to *libertos crioulos* [born in Brazil], but never to African *libertos* ... I offer an amendment so that we understand the article in the following terms: "The *libertos* who are native to Brazil."

It was supported. ...

Mr. Moniz Tavares: ... I judge that it is best that this article passes without discussion; [this] reminds me that some speeches of the celebrated orators of the Constituent Assembly of France produced the dreadful events of the Island of São Domingos, as some writers who have impartially written of the French Revolution affirm;[5] and perhaps among us some representatives, carried away with excessive zeal in favor of humanity, have expressed ideas (that are best repressed), with the intention of stirring up the Assembly's compassion for this poor race of men, so unfortunate only because nature created them tanned. I will say only that in the old system a slave had only to obtain a Letter of *Manumission,* and he could assume a military post in a corps, he had entrance to the sacred priestly ministry, without questions of whether he was or was not born in Brazil. ...

Mr. França: ... In the last session in which this subject was discussed I offered an amendment with the intention of limiting the privileges of the citizen to *libertos crioulos* only; and this was not due to less philanthropy than the authors of the Project [the draft constitution] appeared to have when they wanted to make [it] extend to *liberto* natives of Africa. I am philanthropic when it comes to providing the protection which they need, as the miserable persons that they generally are; but the force of my devotion does not lead me to a demented course [and] speech such that, without regard, the privileges of the citizen, which are denied to [those of] other parts of the world, are lavished on foreigners of Africa. ...

Sr. Alencar: I am of a contrary opinion to that of the illustrious deputy, and I say that the article is consistent with the principles of universal justice, and that the amendments seem to me to be unjust, contradictory and impolitic. I say that the article is consistent with the principles of universal justice because it still seems that we should make all inhabitants of the territory of Brazil Brazilian citizens, although we cannot rigorously follow this principle,

---

[3]*Source: Diario da Assemblea geral constituinte e legislativa do Imperio do Brasil* (Rio de Janeiro: Imprensa Nacional, 1824) 2, no. 10: 130, 133–140.

[4]The term used here is *Negros buçaes.* At the time, *boçal* referred to a recently arrived African and connoted an inability to speak Portuguese and unfamiliarity with Luso-Brazilian culture. The word also came to mean stupid and crude.

[5]Moniz Tavares refers to The Haitian Revolution (1791–1804) on the French colony of Saint Domingue. After the French Revolution began in 1789, and as the French National Assembly debated the status of the colonies and the institution of slavery, a massive slave insurrection began that culminated in the independence of Saint Domingue as Haiti in 1804.

without offending the supreme law of the salvation of the state. This is the law that prevents us from making slaves citizens, because besides being the property of others, and so we offend [this] right [of property] if we take away the patrimony of these individuals to whom they belong, we would diminish agriculture, one of the principle sources of the wealth of the nation, and we would open a hub of disorder in society, suddenly introducing into it a bunch of men who, having left the state of captivity, can hardly be guided by principles of well conceived liberty. . . . The illustrious authors of the amendments do not want those who only by virtue of being freedmen should be indistinctly Brazilian citizens; but what will they be, these who are excluded by the amendments? They are certainly not foreigners; because they do not belong to any society, nor do they have any *Pátria* (homeland)[6] that is not ours, nor do they have a religion that is not the one which we profess. . . . Furthermore, if by the principles of sound politics, we should curtail as much as we can the slave trade so that we may end it, it seems that we go more directly towards this end by granting to *libertos* the privileges of the Brazilian citizen, than by demanding that for this that certain conditions be verified. That a *liberto* has to have some trade or employment to acquire such a condition [citizenship] seems to me unjust; it is enough that he has worked all his life, without making him have to overcome one more obstacle. I see that the Indian who quickly enters our society, savage that he is, is a citizen; he does not know how to read nor write, he does not have a trade or a job, and nevertheless none of this impedes the recognition of him [as a citizen]; but it is understood that the slaves, who I judge to be in worse circumstances, should not be admitted even though in terms of customs they are much closer to our own, because they acquire them from their owners in the time of their captivity. . . .

Sr. Carneiro de Cunha: . . . I would add only that the slave who obtains his liberty has in his favor, generally speaking, the presumption of good

behavior and industriousness; . . . and because of this I think that such men well deserve the privileges of the citizen, without the obligation of having a trade or employment . . . Mr. França also excludes slaves from Africa: but I do not know why those born in our territory will be at an advantage over those [African-born] on this point, after being almost always enslaved, as the African has no one who protects him, from the time when he arrives he is always wretched, while the *crioulo* born into the bosom of a family enjoys some comforts, and has, generally, more respect. It does not seem just to me that the less fortunate are offered less assistance. . . .

Mr. Almeida e Albuquerque: . . . How is it possible that by the simple fact of obtaining a Letter of *Manumission* one acquires the right of citizenship? . . . Won't the fact that they [the African-born] are pagans or idolaters disqualify them? . . . How is it possible that a man without *pátria*, without virtue, without customs, torn, by way of an odious commerce, from his land, and brought to Brazil, may by way of a simple fact, by the will of his owner, suddenly acquire such important rights in our society? If Europeans, born in civilized countries, having customs, good education, and virtues, may not acquire the benefit of the rights of Brazilian citizen without obtaining a letter of naturalization, and this same naturalization requires that they profess the Christian religion, according to the Project [the draft], how can the African slave, devoid of all qualities, be of better condition? . . .

Sr. Costa Barros: . . . I know that there is no more wretched and horrific condition than that of the slaves, but not even for this [reason] should we understand that to indemnify them for the evils which they suffered should we receive them under circumstances that would be damaging for us. . . . Thus, I demand that they have a job or a trade. . . . Mr. Carneiro da Cunha says that the slave who acquires a Letter of *Manumission* shows with this proof of occupation and good conduct. . . . I am not persuaded of this; Letters of *Manumission* are almost always given because of love, and most slaves are poorly raised. . . .

José da Silva Lisboa: . . . When it is the *Liberal* Cause that is in question, it is not possible to remain silent, rather I should say with the classic Latin

---

[6]*Pátria* was a key word in political discourse at the time. Although in the 1810s it could refer to Portugal, in the process of independence it was invoked in reference to feelings of allegiance to Brazil or to more local regional identities.

[author] "I am a man; nothing pertaining to humanity should be strange to me."[7] It seems to me that it is right to make the article simple or broad, to get rid of any doubt, declaring to be a Brazilian citizen not only the slave who obtains from his owner a letter of liberty, but also he who acquires liberty by any legitimate entitlement. . . . I am opposed to the amendments. . . . I have as a guiding light the author of *The Spirit of the Laws*,[8] who advises legislators to maintain, when possible, simplicity in legislation. . . . Why will they make arbitrary distinctions among *libertos*, by place of birth, and service and trade? As soon as they [*libertos*] acquire the condition of *civil person*, they deserve the equal protection of the Law. . . . To be a Brazilian citizen is indeed to have an honorific title, but it is only civic rights and not political rights that are dealt with in the chapter under discussion . . . civic rights are limited to giving to the free man the *jus* [right] to say — I have a *pátria*; I belong to such a city or village; I am not subject to the will of anyone, but only to the empire of the Law. . . . When I link the article in question with articles 245 and 255 [sic],[9] it seems to me that they completely address the objections, in which some have insisted, by establishing a basis for the regulated benefits to slaves, proposing only their slow emancipation, and moral instruction. Africans themselves, notwithstanding the accusations of paganism and brutality, are susceptible to mental improvement, and for this reason can be called *tabulas rasas*.[10] Mr. President, in the era of liberalism, will the legislature be less equitable than in the time of despotism? . . . Enough, Gentleman, of the odious distinctions of castes, of differences of color. Now diversity[11] is an almost indestructible attribute of the population of Brazil. Politics cannot end such inequalities, [rather] it

should take advantage of all elements for our regeneration, but not add new inequalities. The class of slaves will henceforth look upon this august Assembly with the proper confidence in the hope that it will attend to their fate and the improvement of their condition, having insight the general good, as much as humanity inspires and politics may allow. . . . This consideration alone would be enough to sanction the controversial article, which to me seems to need only the following amendment . . . "The *libertos* who acquire their liberty by whatever legitimate entitlement."

It was supported.

Mr. Maciel da Costa: . . . Does a nation have an obligation to admit foreigners into the union of its society? No. Naturalization is a type of favor, and this favor is always regulated by motives of national interest. . . . If we agree that the admission of foreigners into the union of our society is a favor, if for this favor we demand conditions that political calculation induces us to impose; if upon the same individuals in whose veins runs Brazilian blood, and only because they were born in a foreign country, we impose the condition of residence, considering them half-foreigners; it frightens me to see that the African has only to obtain a letter of *manumission*, which is a deed that simply authorizes him to dispose of his time, and he enters *ipso facto* into the union of the Brazilian family, becomes our brother. . . . Not having doubt that the children of an African mother and father should be considered Brazilian because their birth in this country makes them ours, and they have this link to the country, the Africans, because they were born in a foreign country, because we cannot suppose that they have affection for the country in which they lived as slaves, should not be admitted to the union of our family without marrying a Brazilian woman and having a type of industry from which they live. . . .

Mr. Henriques de Resende: . . . As long as they were manumitted, *libertos* used to enlist in the appropriate corps and occupy military posts. . . . Why then in a system of liberal government are they to remain in a worse condition than they were in the era of despotic government? . . .

Mr. Maciel da Costa: . . . political security rather than philanthropy should be the basis of our decisions on this matter. Philanthropy laid the ground for the

---

[7]The Roman author, Terence (185 B.C.–159 B.C.).

[8]The French Charles de Secondat, Baron de Montesquieu (1669–1755), published the widely read *The Spirit of the Laws* in 1748.

[9]The article to which he refers is 254. See above excerpt.

[10]The concept *tabula rasa* (blank slate) suggested that people are not born with innate ideas.

[11]Silva Lisboa uses the Portuguese word *variegado,* which means "diverse" as well as, more specifically, "multicolored."

loss of the flourishing French Colonies. As soon as the declaration of the so-called rights of man[12] was heard there, spirits were enflamed and the Africans served as the instrument of the worst horrors that can be conceived.[13] . . . To diminish gradually the traffic in men and in the meantime treat those who are slaves humanely, this, Gentlemen, is all that we owe them.

Mr. Henriques de Resende: . . . The scorn with which owners or the whites treat the *libertos* will give rise to the aversion that both feel for each other. . . .

Mr. José da Silva Lisboa: . . . A more reasonable fear is that we perpetuate the vexation of the Africans, and of their offspring, showing scorn and hate, with a fixed system of never improving one's condition. . . . Let us leave behind, Gentlemen, the controversies over the color of peoples; they are physical phenomena that vary according to the degrees from the equator, the influx of the sun's rays and geological dispositions and other more profound causes that are not the subject of this discussion. The French were very white when they invaded Egypt and half-black when they left.[14] . . . Good institutions, with correct education, are what make men have the dignity of the species regardless of their color. . . .

---

[12]This is a reference to the French "Declaration of the Rights of Man," approved by the revolutionary National Assembly of France in August 1789. The first article reads "Men are born and remain free and equal in rights. Social distinctions may be founded only upon the general good." For the full text, see http://www.yale.edu/lawweb/avalon/rightsof.htm.
[13]Haitian Revolution.

[14]Napoleon Bonaparte led the French invasion of Egypt, then an Ottoman territory, in 1798.

Political Constitution of the Empire of Brazil, 1824[15]

Title II: Of Brazilian Citizens

Article 6. They are Brazilian citizens

   I. Those who have been born in Brazil, whether they are freeborn, or freed persons, even if their father is a foreigner, as long as he does not reside in Brazil in service to another nation. . . .

Chapter IV: On Elections

Article 90. The nominations of Deputies and Senators to the General Assembly, and of members of the General Provincial Councils, will be made by indirect elections, the mass of active citizens in Parochial Assemblies electing electors of the province, and these the representatives of the nation and province.

Article 91. [Those who] vote in primary elections

   I. Brazilian citizens who enjoy their political rights.

   II. Naturalized foreigners.

Article 92. [Those who] are excluded from voting in Parochial Assemblies

   I. Minors under the age of twenty five years, not including those who are married, military officers above twenty one years, recipients of higher degrees, and clergy of Holy Orders.

   II. Sons of families who are in the company of their fathers, except if they serve in public office.

   III. Servants, not including in this class bookkeepers, principal clerks of commercial houses, servants of the Imperial household [who do not wear a certain uniform], and administrators of rural estates and factories.

   IV. Clergy, and whoever lives in a cloistered community.

   V. Those who do not have an annual income of 100 *milreis*[16] from landed property, industry, commerce, or employment. . . .

---

[15]*Source:* "Political Constitution of the Empire of Brazil" (1824), from "Political Database of the Americas," at Georgetown University, http://pdba.georgetown.edu.

[16]*Milreis* was a unit of currency. The income requirements for voting were viewed by many as low. A wage laborer typically earned enough to satisfy the requirement in 100 days. See Graham, *Patronage and Politics* (pp. 103–104) in Suggested Sources.

Article 94. All those who can vote in parochial Assembly can be electors, and vote in the election of Deputies, Senators, and members of the Provincial Councils. The following are exceptions:

    I. Those who do not have an annual income of 200 *milreis* from landed property, industry, commerce, or employment.

    II. *Libertos* [freed persons].

    III. Criminals indicted in a judicial complaint or inquiry. . . .

Suggested Sources:

Roderick Barman provides an overview of Brazil's political independence in *Brazil: The Forging of a Nation: 1798–1852* (Stanford, CA: Stanford University Press, 1988). Emilia Viotti da Costa's *The Brazilian Empire: Myths and Histories* (Chapel Hill: University of North Carolina Press, 2000) offers analysis of social and cultural transformations and theories and practices of liberalism. On nineteenth-century political practice, see Richard Graham, *Patronage and Politics in Nineteenth-Century Brazil* (Stanford, CA: Stanford University Press, 1990). For emancipation in the United States and Brazil, see Celia M. Azevedo's *Abolitionism in the United States and Brazil: A Comparative Perspective* (New York: Garland, 1995). On defining citizenship, see Hilda Sabato, "On Political Citizenship in Nineteenth-Century Latin America," *The American Historical Review* 106, no. 4 (October 2001): 1290–1315; and Marcia Regina Berbel and Rafael de Bivar Marquese, "The Absence of Race: Slavery, Citizenship, and Pro-slavery Ideology in the Cortes of Lisbon and the Rio de Janeiro Constituent Assembly (1821–1824)," *Social History* 32, no. 4 (November 2007): 415–433.

Among the most extensive primary sources in English on nineteenth-century Brazil are those of the British merchant John Luccock, *Notes on Rio de Janeiro and the Southern Parts of Brazil; Taken during a Residence of Ten Years in That Country, from 1808–1818* (London: Samuel Leigh, 1820); and Maria Dundas Graham, *Journal of a Voyage to Brazil and Residence There during Part of the Years 1821, 1822, 1823* (1824) (New York: Praeger, 1969). Documents on Brazilian and Latin American slavery and its legacies can be found in Robert Edgar Conrad's *Children of God's Fire. A Documentary History of Black Slavery in Brazil* (University Park, PA: Penn State University Press, 1994); and Sue Peabody and Keila Grinberg, eds., *Slavery, Freedom, and the Law in the Atlantic World. A Brief History with Documents* (Boston/New York: Bedford/St. Martins, 2007).

A number of Internet sources also shed light on the problem of slavery. "Slave Movement during the Eighteenth and Nineteenth Centuries" can be found at the Data and Information Services Center of the University of Wisconsin *(http://www.disc.wisc.edu/slavedata/)*. "The Atlantic Slave Trade and Slave Life in the Americas: A Visual Record" (University of Virginia) (http://hitchcock.itc.virginia.edu/Slavery/index.php) offers images of enslaved Africans in nineteenth-century Brazil. The "Political Database of the Americas" at Georgetown University *(http://pdba.georgetown.edu)* provides links to online constitutions.

Chapter 30

Empire, Loyalty, and Race: Militiamen of Color in Nineteenth-Century Cuba

*Michele Reid Vazquez, Georgia State University**

In 1823, a group of twenty-four senior officers in Havana's militia of color defended themselves against slanderous comparisons to Haiti's black revolutionaries by proclaiming their loyalty to the Crown. Their response highlighted a paradox: Colonial elites tended to denigrate men of color, whereas at the same time, the Spanish Empire relied on them for military defense. The issue of arming men of

---

*Acknowledgments: My thanks to Leo Garofalo, Erin O'Connor, Christine Skwiot, and David Sartorius for their comments and suggestions on earlier versions of this chapter.

In this scene from the Haitian Revolution (1791–1804), independence leader Toussaint Louverture meets with European soldiers wearing a military uniform in his own army's encampment. For those opposed to slavery or trapped in bondage themselves, what might have been the impact of an image of a black military commander, a former slave and self-taught tactician, interacting as an equal with European officers, perhaps handing them an important decree or treaty (or even a safe conduct pass to defeated foes)? How would the same image have been regarded by Cuba's planter and merchant classes and the militiamen defending them?

Source: Library of Congress.

African descent became more complex in the late eighteenth and nineteenth centuries as political and social upheaval resonated across the Atlantic world, particularly in the Caribbean. During this age of rebellion and independence, the Haitian Revolution (1791–1804) took center stage. Its impact in the Americas as the first and only successful slave rebellion, the first black republic, the first country to abolish slavery, and the second independent nation

in the hemisphere (after the United States) reverberated throughout the region. Although the political shift exacerbated social tensions in colonial societies where racial hierarchies bolstered the slave system, the Spanish Empire expanded its recruitment of free men of African descent to strengthen its defenses against the tide of independence.

The conflicts over empire and race played a pivotal role in Cuba. Colonial expansion in the eighteenth and early nineteenth centuries and France's loss of its lucrative sugar colony, Saint-Domingue (present-day Haiti), enabled Cuba to begin its ascent as a major agricultural power. In addition, Spain increasingly used Cuba as a strategic point of defense to protect its territories from invasion. In order to augment Spanish troops in the Caribbean, authorities created militias comprised of free men of color. Whereas some officials highlighted the dangers of arming black men, others argued that their proven loyalty and military skills could not be ignored. The British occupation of Havana from 1762 to 1763 prompted officials to rapidly increase the number of battalions of color. In effect, the free *pardo* and *moreno* militias developed as an essential component of the Spanish Empire.[1] By the late eighteenth century, one in five free men of African descent participated in the militia, as compared to one in twelve men of full Spanish heritage.[2]

Military service emerged as an important source for claims of social status, honor, and masculinity in the free sector of color. Although most men served for nominal or no pay, their militia affiliation gave them and their families access to the institution's court system, pensions, and other privileges unavailable to civilians. Military participation also enabled them to appropriate some of the privileges of European *creoles*, which they used as an avenue for upward social mobility. For instance, militia families often intermarried to consolidate their real estate and slave properties and to reinforce their societal standing. Furthermore, involvement in local battalions gave

---

[1] *Pardos* are defined as individuals of mixed African and European ancestry with tan or brown skin; *morenos* are defined as individuals of primarily African descent with dark skin.

[2] Herbert S. Klein, "The Colored Militia of Cuba: 1568–1868," *Caribbean Studies* 6, no. 2 (June 1966): 20–21; Allan J. Kuethe, *Cuba, 1753–1815: Crown, Military and Society* (Knoxville: University of Tennessee Press, 1986), 8, 10.

pardos and *morenos* the opportunity to voice their concerns to colonial authorities. They could be particularly assertive regarding issues that could erode their group status or challenge their privileges as servicemen. Overall, membership in the militias bestowed *honor* and social validation upon a sector that experienced persistent racism and marginalization in Cuba's slave regime.

The geopolitical and social struggles of the era, especially the fears of "another Haiti," intensified race relations in the Americas. Cuba's increasing black population escalated these concerns. Moreover, authorities regarded free blacks' legal status, expanding numbers, and military service as dangerous examples for slaves in the colony.[3] Officials repressed at least six conspiracies, several involving militiamen, to eradicate slavery and colonialism. Because of their real and potential alliances with slaves and *creole* dissenters, militiamen of color were repeatedly forced to prove their fidelity to the Spanish Crown.

The following document, published under the title "The Exact Sentiments of Havana's Free *Pardo* and *Moreno* Spaniards" in 1823, is a group declaration supported and signed by two dozen prominent militiamen of color. It is a direct response to assertions in

the Spanish American newspaper *La Fraternidad* that accused free people of color of being dangerous and untrustworthy—as much of a threat as the slaves who revolted in Haiti.[4] The text serves as a window into the overlapping tensions and nuances of freedom, race, and slavery in Cuba during the breakdown of colonialism in the early nineteenth century.

Questions to Consider:

1. What examples did the militiamen of color offer as proof of their loyalty to Spain and their worthiness of respect as free men?
2. What did patriotism and *honor* mean to the militiamen, particularly given how they claimed the newspaper had described them?
3. What did the militiamen say about how they had been compared with Haitians? How did the militiamen characterize slavery in Cuba in comparison to slavery in Saint-Domingue?
4. How did the militiamen describe race relations in Cuba, particularly the relationship between people of African descent and those of Spanish descent?

[3]The census of 1817 listed 114,058 free people of color, 199,145 slaves, and 239,830 whites out of total population of 553,033. Kenneth F. Kiple. *Blacks in Colonial Cuba, 1774–1899* (Gainesville: University Press of Florida 1976), 86.

[4]The militiamen did not specify which South American country published the newspaper. However, several newspapers circulated in the early 1820s, including one in Colombia named *La Fraternidad*.

Declaration of Loyalty by Havana's *Pardo* and *Moreno* Militiamen, 1823[5]

If only the Spanish empire did not exclude Havana's free people of color, and instead admitted them into the society of human beings, opening its doors to the indistinguishable virtue of all who participate [in society]. If, with philosophical eyes, [the Spanish crown] considered Havana's free *pardos* and *morenos* as men endowed with reason, susceptible of all human knowledge, capable of possessing all the skills of learning and

teaching which we used to sustain the dignity, liberty, and defense of the fatherland. Although *pardos* and *morenos* are both denied and governed by the same laws that rule and govern the whites, we are all united without distinction with the bonds of religion. It is under these feelings of unity and allegiance to Spain that we, the free *pardos* and *morenos* of Havana, have read with horror and fear a shocking discussion by a Spanish American in the newspaper, *La Fraternidad*. Since peace and good harmony rule in this land [of Cuba], [the article] can be for no other reason than to induce malice and bad intentions.

[5]*Source:* Archivo Nacional de Cuba, Havana, Cuba, Comisión Militar, Legajo 60, No. 2, fols. 208–210.

We repeat, we have read and were scandalized by the newspaper article and we have been painfully influenced by that which would penetrate any human and sensible heart such as ours. This injury is so notorious because, while others have gained riches through our immense sacrifices, we have contributed our industry, our determination, and our efforts to honor the grand splendor of said land.

How is it possible that a [colonial] subject could have dictated such inflammatory ideas, in spite of the fact that we have repeatedly and unequivocally proven our loyalty and submission to the governing laws and the authorities that dispense them? Why insult us so, when there is not the smallest glimmer of suspicion, nor the most trivial motive of distrust to fear? Weren't we the ones that garrisoned this location [Havana] during times of war with foreign and powerful enemies? Weren't we the ones that cleaned and sustained the fortifications of Florida, Appalachia, and Pensacola, in the midst of misery and hunger, without complaining?[6] Finally, weren't we the first to rush boldly to garrison the castle of Saint John of Ulua?[7] We did all of this despite the abject condition in which we found ourselves, even after obediently and lawfully defending the Spanish monarchy. Who (we question the author of the thoughtless article) are the subjects that comprise and form the riches and abundance of this land? We dare the author of such a slanderous essay to make an accurate claim against the *pardos* and *morenos*, especially those who have farms and slaves, and who can be reasonably compared to the wealthy individuals of [Cuba]. We ask, would anyone of his class willingly want to lose their fortunes?

This is something so obvious and so clear to even the most clouded eyes of reason, yet, why does he induce distrust with the reckless publication of an article so inadequate to the ideas of the day such that it is irrelevant to the present circumstances?

By chance, would the author of the article be prepared to lose his properties in the upheaval that caused the spread of independence? Certainly not, we believe. How, then, does he intend to persuade the free *pardos* and *morenos*, who comprise this dependable class of people that we are, that we should lose our properties and endure the unfortunate effects of independence?[8] . . .

To expect that the free *pardos* and *morenos* of Havana are of the same condition as the independent *pardos* and *morenos* of the Island of Saint-Domingue, in the reckless majority, should be addressed. We are indeed free and do not have that yoke to break. The *mulatos* and blacks of Haiti were all slaves.[9] They were servants of tyrannous and cruel masters. We have not all been slaves, and perhaps the majority of us enjoyed the condition of free men; among our generation, many of us have never been slaves. Those who have been slaves had compassionate owners who treated them as sons. The French government did not allow its slaves their basic needs, much less their own goods. This was not so in Havana where the masters hired out their slaves, enabling them to save a proportion of their earnings to rescue themselves from slavery.[10] Perhaps this was the balance that kept our situation from being like Haiti.

Where did the author's fears originate to induce such distrust? Has he seen movements among Havana's free *mulatos* and blacks that made him suspicious? How can he be so reckless as to form such an unjust judgment of men who have not been involved in anything, although we have seen machinations of other Americans and Europeans? Who has seen us make but the slightest investigation of their

---

[6]This is a reference to free *moreno* and *pardo* involvement in Spain's conflict against England during the American Revolution.

[7]Spain controlled the fortress of Saint John of Ulua, situated in the port of Veracruz, Mexico, until the early nineteenth-century wars for independence.

[8]To avoid confusion with italicized Spanish words, underlined phrases denote material italicized for emphasis from the original text.

[9]In reality, not all blacks and *mulatos* in Haiti were slaves. Records from 1789 calculated the population of Saint-Domingue at approximately 28,000 free people of color, 31,000 whites, and 465,000 slaves. See Laurent Dubois, *Avengers of the New World: The Story of the Haitian Revolution* (Cambridge, MA: Harvard University Press, 2004), 30.

[10]This refers to the legal practice of *coartación*. In this process, typically requested by a slave and accompanied by an initial down payment, local authorities established a fixed price at which a slave could obtain freedom through self-purchase. Alejandro de la Fuente, "Slaves and the Creation of Legal Rights in Cuba: Coartación and Papel," *Hispanic American Historical Review* 87 (2007): 659–692.

disagreements? On the contrary, we have kept the most religious silence, calmly practicing [our military drills]. We have retired to our homes and avoided even the smallest gatherings so that no one could be persuaded that we had the slightest influence in the disagreements [between the creoles and the Europeans]. Our credo, according to the country's adage, is <u>Lazarus is the one who suffers.</u>[11] This is the irrefutable proof that we value our own interests and want to conserve our properties.

Returning to the article's comparison of us to the *pardos* and *morenos* of Saint-Domingue, we fearlessly say that, although the author is native-born [in South America], he has very little knowledge of his mother country. As such, he ignores the reasons that induced the *mulatos* and blacks of the old French colony to shake off the yoke of their dominators. The same circumstances did not occur here. We, the *pardos* and *morenos* of Havana, have been treated in such a way that there is almost no differentiation between us and the whites. The natives of this land can say that they are our brothers because we have been suckled from the same breasts. Our mothers wet-nursed and raised them with the same love as their own children. The [masters] freed them zealously. Indeed, most obtained their freedom after being treated with the highest gifts and esteem of their owners. We learned the first rudiments [of education] with them in the same schools, experienced childhood with them, blushed in the childish pastimes, and we have always been appreciated. We have received privileges and distinctions from these esteemed men. Commissions of high importance have been trusted to us, and we have fulfilled [our military duty] with precision, *honor*, and the appreciation and recommendation of the Leaders and the Magistrates.

We *pardos* and *morenos* are the ones who carried out the skilled arts in the highest degree of perfection with the admiration of teachers from other learned nations. We have properties necessary to provide for our families, to run our businesses, and to rent indiscriminately to those who need shelter. We have farms and slaves just like others [whites] who own such properties in Havana. And taking these things into consideration, how dare the author of the article announce [his opinions] in order to foster distrust and alarm the peaceful residents of this land?

Generally speaking, he neither qualifies his reckless comparison of Havana's free *pardos* and *morenos*, nor does he rigorously respect those of equal class from the island of Saint-Domingue. It is necessary to explain with which *mulatos* and blacks of that Island he is comparing us, and it is commonly known that the *pardos* and *morenos* from the French part suffered a shameful, cruel, and tyrannous yoke. But it did not happen this way with those from the Spanish territory [present-day Dominican Republic] where the majority were free and native-born in the interior and bordering towns where they lived, and where they possessed so much wealth that they were treated accordingly [with respect].[12] . . . The slaves who belonged to charitable masters, people who treated them with as much love and gentleness as they would towards their own family (witnesses of this assertion are innumerable among those of both sexes, regardless of color). [The author of the article, however,] offers no verification or motive why free blacks who belong to the Spanish empire would embrace the system of conspiracy then or in the future. Rather, we offer our commitment and indelible love of the mother country as the ultimate evidence of our loyalty. The slaves [in Santo Domingo] renounced freedom in order not to abandon their masters whom they looked upon as

---

[11]Lazarus became an important figure in Catholicism and in some Afro-Cuban religions, particularly in the Yoruba-derived faith known today as Santería. A Catholic saint linked to skin diseases and healing, the Afro-Cuban Lazarus is associated with the Yoruba deity Babalú Ayé, who is also connected to illness and curing. Christine Ayorinde, *Afro-Cuban Religiosity, Revolution, and National Identity* (Gainesville: University of Florida Press, 2004), 22; and Mercedes Cros Sandoval, *Worldview, the Orichas, and Santería: Africa to Cuba and Beyond* (Gainesville: University of Florida Press, 2006), 252–263.

[12]France and Spain both established colonies on the island of Hispaniola, Saint-Domingue (present-day Haiti), and Santo Domingo (present-day Dominican Republic). In 1790, the population of Santo Domingo comprised approximately 40,000 whites, 25,000 free people of color, and 60,000 slaves. Saint-Domingue contained roughly 30,000 whites, 27,000 free people of color, and 500,000 slaves. See "A Country Study: Dominican Republic," Library of Congress, http://lcweb2.loc.gov/frd/cs/dotoc.html.

parents. They constantly followed their masters wherever they emigrated, [remaining with them] up until the Spanish part of the island was taken over by Toussaint Louverture's troops.[13] They escaped and hid between the luggage and mattresses [onboard the ships that had] already embarked, in order to join their masters at sea. The author of the injurious article must have known of all this. No one can ignore such insurmountable evidence of pure loyalty and patriotism. There has never been such an example of resisting a government that offered freedom.

Nevertheless, our condition surpasses the highest level of the *pardos* and *morenos* of Saint-Domingue because each one's condition is at the grace of his beloved country. Dessalines, the cruel and tyrannous monster who aborted peace, set his sights on the capital [Santo Domingo] with twenty-seven thousand soldiers.[14] Only the *pardos* and *morenos* of that jurisdiction, in very small numbers, resisted the forces, sending them in shameful flight with the loss of eleven thousands of its combatants. Given the servitude in which the others [the Haitians] were born, they [the *pardos* and *morenos* of Santo Domingo] preferred their own state of hopelessness to the flattering offerings made by the bloodthirsty conquerors. It is impossible that they [the Haitian forces] would have attempted this with the *pardos* and *morenos* of Havana, so favored by the government and esteemed by the whites. We repeat, we oppose the excessive and highly offensive terms used to induce alarm in the city that has witnessed our fidelity and patriotism. [In other words,] our accusers are coconuts; those who observe silently and rejoice internally over other's disagreements, looking forward to the approaching day in which [the dissenters] might be exterminated. When or how has the antagonistic author been aware of a similar situation in which the *pardos* and *morenos* of Havana paused to observe the disagreements of whites in order to take advantage of the

moment in which we would exterminate them? If he has information, he should present it.

If we, the *pardos* and *morenos* of Havana, were not so satisfied with our loyalty, fidelity, patriotism, and adherence to the governing system, persuaded as we are by all the inhabitants that have placed their confidence in us and, according to the irrefutable evidence of our love and submission to the laws and the mother country, we would think, without recklessness, that this has been an invention to afflict, distress, and demolish us. Fortunately, we all know that this [article] has not been anything more than the ponderings of an emotional, uninformed mind.

How can the author say so decisively that we are of no better condition than the *pardos* and *morenos* of Haiti; that what happened there will happen here? Who would want to ring the bell to signal battle? It would be unprecedented recklessness. Only a man who sets out to offend us and who views us with so much horror could be capable of inventing such atrocious slander.

We, the *pardos* and *morenos* of Havana, leave our cause in the hands of all those who comprise this town. Do unto us the justice that is demanded, and if the judgment turns out to be that we have been reckless, the entire world knows that we will forever deny and dispute these vain suspicions. We swear on the coffers of the mother country that we belong to the same nation as the city of Havana, which we belong to and complement. And so, with these indissoluble connections, we constitute a family, and thus we all have the same desires and feelings. To persuade one otherwise is madness, a crazy presumption of whoever imagined it. We place our forces and bravery against any invasion that might rashly set foot on our ground with depraved visions of domination.

[Havana], despise the impertinent fears of cowards, those frauds void of truth and reason, put to rest any future neglect of your families because we remain in the shadow of good faith and love that you have always shown us. Be persuaded firmly of the fidelity in our hearts and our everlasting loyalty to the mother country.

The *Pardos* and *Morenos* of Havana
Havana, 1823
From the senior officials to his Majesty,

---

[13]In 1801, after conquering Saint-Domingue, Haitian revolutionary leader, Toussaint Louverture, invaded Santo Domingo and abolished and consolidated his authority over the entire island.

[14]After the death of Toussaint Louverture, Jean-Jacques Dessalines continued as the leader of the Haitian Revolution, became the new nation's first president, and eventually proclaimed himself emperor. To defeat the French and Spanish, he fought fiercely, blockaded cities, and burned towns.

Captain Monico de Flores
Lieutenant Francisco Abrahante
Lieutenant Marcelino Gamarra
Lieutenant Gabino Biera
Lieutenant Diego Analla
Lieutenant Joaquin Lopez
Second Lieutenant Damian de Soto
Second Lieutenant Pedro del Rey
Second Lieutenant Carlo de Flores
Second Lieutenant José de la Salud Martinez
Second Lieutenant Juan Enriquez
Second Lieutenant Lorenzo Pobea
Second Lieutenant Julian Patica
Second Lieutenant Matia Santa Cruz

Second Lieutenant Manuel Martinez
Second Lieutenant Elia Menendez
Second Lieutenant Juan Sedeño
Second Lieutenant Rafael Santa Cruz
Second Lieutenant Eusebio Marrero
Second Lieutenant Antonio Escobal
Second Lieutenant Santiago Bechomy
Second Lieutenant Simeon Pirmienta
Second Lieutenant Domingo Bandez
Second Lieutenant Claudio Brindis[15]

---

[15]They represented the highest militia rankings available for colonial Cuba's free *pardos* and *morenos*.

Suggested Sources:

Haiti's revolution changed the balance of power in the Caribbean and influenced economic trends and political movements throughout the hemisphere. See David Geggus, ed., *Impact of the Haitian Revolution in the Atlantic World* (Charleston: University of South Carolina Press, 2001). Matt D. Childs, *The 1812 Aponte Rebellion in Cuba and the Struggle against Atlantic Slavery* (Chapel Hill: University of North Carolina Press, 2006) addresses black militiamen's involvement in one of Cuba's major slave revolts. Several studies examine the creation and varied roles of militias and Afro-Latino militias in Spanish America: Peter Blanchard, *Under the Flags of Freedom: Slave Soldiers and the Wars of Independence in Spanish America* (Pittsburgh: University of Pittsburgh Press, 2008); Allan J. Kuethe, "The Development of the Cuban Military as a Sociopolitico Elite, 1763–83," *Hispanic American Historical Review* 6, no. 4 (November 1981): 695–704; Ben Vinson III and Stewart King, eds., "Introducing the 'New' African Diasporic Military History in Latin America," special issue, *Journal of Colonialism and Colonial History* 5, no. 2 (Fall 2004); and Peter M. Voelz, *Slave and Soldier: The Military Impact of Blacks in the Colonial Americas* (New York: Garland, 1993).

Related primary sources, novels, and films also illuminate the African experience in Cuba. Principal among these is Juan Francisco Manzano's account of his childhood in captivity, Juan Francisco Manzano, *Autobiography of a Slave*, trans. Evelyn Picon Garfield (Detroit: Wayne State Press, 1996). Travelers from Europe and the United States also detailed nineteenth-century Cuban slave society. For an array of descriptions, see Louis A. Pérez, Jr., ed., *Slaves, Sugar, and Colonial Society: Travel Accounts of Cuba, 1801–1899* (Wilmington, DE: Scholarly Resources, 1992). Karen Robert, ed., *New Year in Cuba: Mary Gardner Lowell's Travel Diary, 1831–1832* (Boston: Northeastern University Press, 2003) offers a rare glimpse of Cuba from a female perspective. Cirilo Villaverde's classic novel on nineteenth-century Cuba lends additional insights in *Cecilia Valdés or El Angel Hill*, trans. by Helen Lane (Oxford: Oxford University Press, 2005).

Cuban filmmakers excelled in examining historical themes on the screen. *La última cena* [The Last Supper], dir. Tomás Gutiérrez Alea (Cuba, 1976), is based on an actual revolt. Cuban filmmakers also presented the lives of free people of color in *Cecilia*, dir. Humberto Solas (New York: Latin American Video Archives, 1998); and *Placido: The Blood of the Poet*, dir. Sergio Giral (Cuba, 1986).

Glossary

Alcabala: The alcabala was the sales tax collected under the Spanish colonial state. Increases in this tax caused anger against late-colonial rulers. It was one of the taxes from which indigenous peoples were theoretically exempt (see Two Republics, System of).

Alcalde/alcalde mayor: A member of the cabildo town council who served as local judge and administrator (see Cabildo). The alcalde mayor was an appointed governor of a district similar to a corregidor (see Corregidor).

Altepetl: Nahuatl term from central Mexico for a city-state.

Angola: Refers both to the Portuguese colony in the western part of what is current day Angola, and an African "ethnicity," probably adopted by blacks from around that region, or who were shipped from the port of Luanda.

Arawak: Native person of the Greater Antilles or northern South America.

Audiencia: The highest Spanish American court hearing civil and criminal cases (called a relaçao in Brazil). Situated in ten major Spanish American cities (twelve in the 1700s) and composed of a president and judges, the audiencia (also real audiencia) also served as an administrative council issuing laws. In viceregal capitals such as Lima and Mexico City, audiencias assisted the viceroys. Bourbon-era reformers tried to limit creole influence in audiencias in the 1700s (see Bourbon Reforms, Creole, and Viceroy).

Auto de fé: Public events organized to carry out the punishments and executions ordered by the Inquisition. The ceremonies included processions through the streets and public shaming of the penitents and the condemned (see Inquisition).

Ayllu: Defined by sharing common ancestry, the allyu constituted the basic kin group and organizational unit among indigenous peoples in the Andes.

Aymara: Both a spoken language and a large ethnic group in the southern highlands of Peru and Bolivia (see Quechua).

Aztec: The name given to the Mexica people who expanded out of the Valley of Mexico to form the Aztec Empire. Their empire included both speakers of Nahuatl and many other ethnic groups (see Nahuatl).

Bahia: The captaincy of Bahia, Brazil, was a major slave importing region, especially for its sugar plantations that encircled the Bay of All Saints and the capital, Salvador.

Beata: Lay holy woman not in a convent. Living as a beata or with other beatas often served as an option for nonelite women and non-Spanish or non-Portuguese women with a spiritual calling but without the resources and connections to join a convent as a full member. Many women lived in convents as servants and slaves to the nuns or as lesser nuns who carried out the daily work to keep the convents functioning.

Bourbon Reforms: Eighteenth-century economic and administrative measures imposed by the Spanish and eventually the Portuguese Crowns to strengthen royal control over colonial tax collection, commerce, and colonial courts and officials. The tightening of royal control made the reforms unpopular.

Cabildo: Municipal council governing a city or town in Spanish America, usually composed of male colonists or their descendants. In towns and neighborhoods where they predominated, indigenous men or African descendants served on the cabildos. In the late-colonial period, some cabildos became focal points of opposition to European rule.

Cacique: Under Spanish rule, cacique became the general term for indigenous leader of all levels, often hereditary. Cacica referred to female ethnic chiefs (see Kuraka).

Calidad: Referred to the social status and reputational standing of a person, often based in part on the ethnic, religious, or noble identification of a person or family.

Campesinos: This term refers to members of the rural poor, typically either peasants who till their own land or workers on large estates. More commonly used toward the end of the colonial period and in present-day Latin America.

Cartagena: Cartagena de Indias is a large city seaport on the northern coast of Colombia. An entry point for many of the slaves in Spanish South America.

Casa de Contratación: Established in 1503 and abolished in 1790, the Spanish Crown's House of Trade in Seville (later Cádiz) regulated and taxed all travel and trade with the Americas and Africa and tried related cases.

Castas: The Spanish term castas identified a variety of people of mixed racial heritage (i.e., some combination of Spanish, indigenous, and African ancestry). Casta labels functioned as legal designations of ethno-racial status and sometimes determined official rights and obligations.

Cédula: The written authorization or royal decree with which Iberian monarchies determined so many of Latin America's affairs. Royal intervention and written laws added to the importance of courts and litigation, and people from many sectors of society availed themselves of the right to appeal to higher authority.

Chicha: Alcoholic drink made from fermented maize, quinoa, or sweet manioc in the Andes. Often the fermentation is initiated by chewing the maize or other starchy main ingredient. Used on social and ritual occasions from pre-Hispanic times to the present, the beverage became an important commercial item during the colonial period, often in the hands of female brewers and tavern operators, and often generating municipal tax revenues (see Pulque).

Chichimecas: From the Nahuatl, commonly translated as "Sons of Dogs," the term both denigrated the stateless, often hunting and gathering peoples to the north of the Mesoamerican states and honored their proud warrior traditions.

Confession: Also known as the Sacrament of Penance, confession involved cleansing one's soul of sins by relating them to a confessor. Confessing and then performing any penance the confessor imposed could return the soul to the state of grace considered necessary to receive the Sacrament of Communion.

Confessor: Priests who heard confessions and could grant absolution (see Confession).

Confraternity (irmandade/cofradía): Lay religious brotherhoods organized to celebrate religious festivals, provide for members' social welfare, and advance the social status of members (often from a particular occupation or ethnic group). If permitted by the confraternity's bylaws, any group in society, including women and slaves, could form or join confraternities.

Constitutionalism: The idea that constitutions should define the powers and actions of the state and rulers whether in monarchies or republics. Many political leaders in Latin America advocated constitutional government for their newly independent states.

Converso: Christian convert from Judaism. Often targeted by the Inquisition. In Spain, many Jews suffered forced conversion and became conversos (sometimes called New Christians).

Corregidor: A Crown official assigned to govern an indigenous district collecting taxes, administering justice, and distributing Indian laborers levied through the mita system (see Mita).

Cortes: A Medieval Iberian institution comprised of representatives of different parts of society (nobles, clergy, and the people) opponents of Napoleon's occupation of Spain (1808–1813) gathered as delegates to a parliament (cortés) from all over Spain and from Spanish America in the port city of Cádiz. Delegates debated which elements of liberalism could be adopted in a Spanish Empire, inspiring many in the Americas to consider an alternative to both monarchal rule and the subordinate role of the Americas. Spanish liberals refused to grant American populations meaningful autonomy, free trade, and equal representation. A similar group of delegates to a constitutional assembly gathered in Portugal and drafted a constitution.

Council of the Indies: Beginning in 1524, this Spanish council of state located in Seville administered affairs in the Americas and advised the monarch.

Council of Trent: This Roman Catholic Church council (1545–1563) held in response to Protestantism and Catholic calls for reform led to increased papal authority; improved seminary training; and a resurgence of prayer, mysticism, and Baroque art in Europe and the Americas.

Creole (criollo/crioulo): In Spanish, criollo identified nonnative, American people born in the Americas to European or African parents. In Mexico, for instance, criollo generally described an American-born person of Spanish parentage. In plantation-based societies, such as in the Caribbean for example, creole or criollo more often referred to American-born blacks. In Brazil, people used the Portuguese term crioulo in the same ways.

Cuzco: The ceremonial and administrative center of the Inca Empire of the fourteenth and fifteenth centuries. Cuzco remained a key Spanish colonial center for commerce, government, and the symbolism it held as the pre-Columbian capital.

Diaspora: The forced exodus and dispersal overseas of a large population such as the Jews expelled from Spain (Sephardim) and the Africans carried to Europe and the Americas as slaves.

Dominicans: This religious order of the Catholic Church joined the missionary effort in the Americas of converting the local populations to Christianity and establishing monasteries, convents, and Indian parishes in order to minister to both the colonized and the colonists. Bartolomé de Las Casas became one of the most famous Dominican missionaries because of his vocal opposition to the violence of the conquest and forced conversions.

Dom Pedro I (1798–1834): Portuguese-born son of Dom João VI, King of Portugal (1799–1826), went to Brazil as a child with the Portuguese royal family in 1807 as French armies occupied Portugal. When Dom João returned to Portugal in 1821, Pedro stayed behind in Rio de Janeiro as prince regent. One year later, rebuffing Portuguese demands that he, too, return to Portugal, he declared Brazil's independence from Portugal. He presided over Brazil's constitutional monarchy as emperor from 1822 until 1831, when he abdicated the throne to his son Pedro II (1831–1889).

Don/Doña: An honorific title in Spanish for men (don) and women (doña) of high social standing or commanding respect in a community. In the sixteenth century, only nobles used them, but over time their use expanded down the social hierarchy.

Encomendero: A Spanish colonizer, or indigenous ally, granted an encomienda by the Crown or by a conquistador authorized by the Crown (see Encomienda).

Encomienda: A population of indigenous people in the Americas entrusted to a colonizer by the Crown or Spanish conqueror. The encomendero could collect tribute in kind, cash, or labor from the encomienda Indians in return for Christianizing them and ensuring their loyalty to the Crown. The conquest and early colonial periods of the sixteenth century saw the largest number of encomenderos before the Crown's New Laws (1542) revoked the hereditary nature of the grant and increasingly employed officials named by the viceroy to distribute indigenous laborers (see New Laws).

Franciscans: Catholic religious order that carried out missionary work and established convents and monasteries throughout the hemisphere (arrived in 1524).

Gremios: Craft guilds that produced most of a city's everyday goods.

Hacienda (fazenda): Latin America's elite-owned large estates, with large workforces of poor rural workers, typically of indigenous, African, or mixed racial descent. Hacienda owners (hacendados) wielded both economic and social power over the men and women working on their estates.

Hidalgo: Literally "son of somebody" in Spanish, hidalgos constituted a lesser nobility in Spain. They originally received titles for military service during the Reconquest. They commanded respect but often little wealth (see Reconquest).

Honor: The good reputation and recognition given to a person (and his or her family) for an individual's moral qualities, virtue, heroic actions, or royal favor. Honor was gendered: Women's honor rested heavily on their modesty, submission to male authority, and sexual restraint. Honor was also racialized and associated with wealth: Authorities and elites often considered Indians, Africans, and castas incapable of being honorable, especially if they were poor. Dishonorable acts by individuals brought dishonor on their families (see Calidad and Castas).

Idolatry: Christians considered a rejection of Christianity or the worship of non-Christian deities idolatry. In the Americas, the Spanish and Portuguese labeled "idolatrous" pre-Columbian beliefs and practices and the survival of the practices under colonial rule. Campaigns to extirpate idolatry were frequently launched by local religious authorities in many places to expose and stamp out indigenous religious and ritual practices. Proponents of conversion by means of word and example clashed with those who condemned vestiges of indigenous religions as idolatry and employed coercion, judicial investigations, and corporal punishment to achieve adherence to Christianity.

Inca: The Inca ethnic group expanded from its stronghold in the valley of Cuzco during the fifteenth century to conquer various other ethnic groups up and down the Andes and along the Pacific. The Incas bound these peoples together into an empire (called Tahauntinsuyo in Quechua) with a central administrative and ritual center in the Inca capital city Cuzco. Inca also referred to the male ruler of this empire.

Indio (Indian): Spanish and Portuguese colonizers lumped people from many distinct indigenous ethnic groups and polities into one category called Indians and assigned them royal protections and exploitative obligations based on that classification. In both colonial and modern Latin America, the term "Indian" (indio) became a negative epithet.

Indio principal: Indigenous notables exercising political and economic influence in a community and often serving as a leader or boasting noble lineage. Early on in Mexico, the term designated the heirs of pre-Hispanic *pipiltin*, or nobility. Over time it came to identify those allowed to participate in the governance of Indigenous Republics, whether by ancestry or service (see Cacique and Kuraka).

Inquisition: The Pope granted Spanish and Portuguese monarchs the power to establish local tribunals to investigate and punish religious unorthodoxy. The Inquisition investigated a range of religious crimes ranging from serious cases of heresy and belief in Protestantism, Judaism, or Islam to lesser infractions (such as superstitious acts, blasphemous oaths, and priestly solicitation in the confessional). The tribunals subsisted on confiscated property.

Intendants: Royal officials in charge of economic development and implementing fiscal policy in new political districts instituted during eighteenth-century centralization and administrative reforms (see Bourbon Reforms).

Jesuits: A Catholic religious order founded in 1540. Arriving in Peru in 1568 and Mexico in 1570, the Jesuits both carried out missionary work among indigenous peoples in Spanish and Portuguese America and established numerous urban seminaries, schools, and ministries among African slaves. In the 1700s, both Portuguese and Spanish officials resented Jesuit independence and economic enterprises and expelled the order from their empires.

Kuraka: Native Andeans called their local ethnic lords kurakas, or they used the term cacique that the Spanish adopted in the Caribbean and Mexico (see Cacique).

Ladino: A general reference to a non-Indian, whether a person of European or mixed indigenous-European (mestizo) descent. Although used throughout many parts of Latin America, it is more common in Central rather than South America. When applied to indigenous people or Africans, ladino could also function as an adjective meaning Spanish- or Portuguese-speaking and Christianized.

Liberto: Liberto/a (freedman/freedwoman) referred to an African, Afro-Latin American, or mulato who was born to slavery but manumitted during his or her lifetime. Libertos' status and rights were often unclear, particularly their citizenship rights after independence.

Licenciado (licenciate): A lawyer or university-educated person.

Limpieza de sangre: Literally "purity of blood," the term referred to Iberian or Ibero-American lineages without Muslim or Jewish ancestors. Proving a man's limpieza de sangre (Old Christian status) was a prerequisite for holding high office or entering the priesthood. The concept effectively racialized or made hereditary and unalterable religious affiliation despite conversion: once a non-Christian always a non-Christian. It justified using lineage in the Americas to establish social status (see Calidad and Honor).

Manumission: The legal freeing of a person from slavery. Iberian slavery included mechanisms that enabled the enslaved to alter their status (changing masters, for example) or secure their freedom gradually or immediately (for example, purchase by a third party, or purchase their own freedom over time). Masters sometimes manumitted slaves who were too old or too sick to work.

Marco: A measurement of weight, roughly eight ounces.

Maroons: Runaway slaves who formed communities, called *quilombos* in Brazil and palenques in Spanish areas. The largest and most famous maroon refuge was Palmares in Brazil.

Maya: A large ethnic and linguistic group in Mesoamerica. Even though they were not socially or politically unified at the time of the Spanish invasion and colonialism, the various Maya groups shared many of the same cultural traditions.

Mercedarian: A Catholic religious order founded for the redemption of Christians captured during the Crusade wars.

Mestiza en habito de india: Label used to denote a person of Spanish and indigenous descent who used indigenous cultural practices, including, but not limited to, indigenous dress.

Mestizaje: Mestizaje refers to cultural as well as biological intermixing. In practice, cultural blending often gave greater value to European heritage.

Mestizo (mestiço): A mestizo (female: mestiza) is someone with both European and indigenous ancestry.

Mina: An African most commonly from the Bight of Benin, although the designation could refer to different places along the West African coast and inland at different times.

Mita: In the Andes, the Spanish expanded the Inca's *mit'a* labor system to levy laborers from local communities for work in state fields and public projects into a more onerous rotating, male, labor draft designed especially to provide cheap workers for private mining enterprises and building cities.

Montezuma: Aztec emperor at time of Spanish invasion (1519–1521). Died as a hostage of the Spanish force during fighting in the Aztec capital of Tenochtitlán.

Moreno: A Spanish word meaning "brown." Moreno referred to people of African descent and sometimes functioned to identify them as free of slavery or not African-born or lighter skinned.

Morisco: Christian convert from Islam. Spanish monarchs forced Iberian believers in Islam to convert to Christianity, and moriscos who rebelled could be enslaved and relocated to other parts of Spain. In 1619, the king expelled the remaining moriscos to northern Africa.

Mulato: A person of mixed European and African heritage.

Mysticism: Belief that direct communication or union with God is possible and can be achieved through prayer and devotional acts, rather than through the intellect.

Nahuatl: The language spoken by people in central Mexico and by the Aztec Empire builders (also called Nahua) (see Aztec).

Naturales: Residents, locals, or people born in that area. Due to the related concepts of native or indigenous, naturales is often automatically interpreted as Indian.

Negro: The Spanish word for "black"; referred to people of African descent in general.

New Laws: Responding in 1542 to complaints about colonizers' abuses of the indigenous populations, the Spanish Crown and royal advisers imposed royal authority and the power of viceroys and other laws in the Americas, thus reducing missionaries and conquistadors' supremacy in many regions and greatly undermining the power and longevity of the encomienda system. Spanish officials found it advisable to implement these changes gradually. In Mexico, gradual implementation met with more success than in Peru where Spanish colonizers revolted and killed the first viceroy (see Encomienda).

Notary: Notaries legalized transactions by keeping a written record of events. Official notaries purchased their positions.

Pardos: People with some African ancestry. In places such as Caracas, they made up the majority of the mixed-race populace. Free men of color (see Castas).

Patria: Meaning homeland or fatherland, patria is often invoked in Latin American nationalist rhetoric across a wide political spectrum.

Patria Potestad: Meaning "paternal power," the patria potestad was a legal term that gave the father of the family (the patriarch) legal rights and obligations regarding his children. While the children were minors, or if they were in some way unfit to govern themselves as adults, their father maintained control of their persons, assets, and actions. Historically, if a couple separated, the father would retain control over the children in his household (see Honor).

Patriarchy: A cultural system in which men control all positions of power and restrict women's opportunities.

Peninsulares: Persons born on the Iberian Peninsula, that is, in Portugal or Spain. They enjoyed considerable social and political prestige under colonial rule, especially with the Bourbon Reforms (see Bourbon Reforms).

Pernambuco: The captaincy of Pernambuco grew sugar and imported slaves.

Peso: An item of currency made of 8 reales.

Polleras: Traditional skirts worn by some women in the Andes.

Popular sovereignty: The political concept that the power to rule is legitimately derived from the populace rather than from royal or noble birth or divine favor bestowed on a monarch. In the late eighteenth and early nineteenth centuries, popular sovereignty was also defined as national: The members of a nation were called on to form a government and participate in the process of governance through elections.

Pulque: The juice from the maguey plant could be fermented to produce the alcoholic beverage called pulque in Mexico. Taverns proliferated in Mexico's cities and towns to sell the drink in the colonial era. As with all alcohol sales, local authorities both worried about drinking and profited from taxing it (see Chicha).

Quechua: The language of the Inca ethnic group, which they spread as they conquered a vast empire in South America in the mid- to late fifteenth century. Spanish colonizers and missionaries employed this "common language" to help establish their rule. They both promoted Quechua at the expense of other local languages and extended its use east into the Amazon region (see Aymara).

Real: A silver coin. Eight reales generally equaled a peso.

Reconquest (reconquista): The intermittent warfare and slow Catholic advance south across the Iberian Peninsula beginning in 718 and ending in 1492 when Ferdinand (of Aragon and Navarre) and Isabel (of Castile) defeated the last Islamic caliphate at Granada and then forced all their subjects to convert to Christianity from Judaism and Islam or suffer expulsion from the newly unified realm. The mounting intolerance and religious militancy that characterized the Reconquest is sometimes contrasted in literature and by scholars with a more tolerant period under medieval Islamic rulers of coexistence (*convivencia*) among believers in Islam, Christianity, and Judaism.

República: The idea that people belonged to separate groups each with distinct rights and privileges and obligations to the crown. In colonial society, this corporate structure gathered the Spanish born on both sides of the Atlantic, and eventually mixed race castas, into the *república de españoles* and the Crown's native vassals into the *república de indios*. This approach identified people primarily with one of these two corporate groups and limited social mobility (see Castas and Two Republics).

Rouen: A printed cotton fabric from Rouen, France.

Syncretism: The blending of elements of two or more cultural or religious traditions to create new and coherent sets of beliefs and practices. Folk Catholicism and the veneration of Mexico's Virgen de Guadalupe are sometimes given as examples of religious syncretism. A concept sometimes critiqued as describing what was essentially Christian domination of other belief systems.

Tianguíz: A weekly market in Mesoamerica that showcased agricultural goods, popular entertainment, and socializing. With Spanish rule, the term spread to South America.

Tenochtilán: The elaborate Aztec capital built on islands in a lake and canal system and connected by causeways to the mainland; 200,000 residents and impressive markets made Tenochtilán larger than any European city and equal to market centers such as Venice.

Tlaxcalans: An ethnic group in central Mexico opposed to Aztec expansion and quick to ally with the Spanish invaders and to help the Europeans expand their control into today's Central America. As a reward for their aid, Tlaxcalans enjoyed certain privileges under Spanish rule.

Tribute: A head tax paid exclusively by indigenous men between the ages of 18 and 60, tribute was the lynchpin of the colonial system of Two Republics (see later), and it continued to be collected in the independent Andean nations of Bolivia, Ecuador, and Peru until the 1850s. Tribute marked indigenous peoples as inferior to non-Indians, but it was also the means through which indigenous peoples claimed rights to communal land, local indigenous leadership, and exemption from other forms of taxation.

Trinitarian: A Catholic religious order founded for the redemption of Christians captured during the Crusade wars.

Two Republics (System of): Under Spanish colonial rule, subjects of the Crown were divided into two groups, or "republics." Members of the Republic of Indians held an inferior position: They paid a head tax (tribute) to the colonial state, and they provided rotating labor drafts. They were not allowed to own firearms or horses, and Spanish officials considered them appropriate laborers (rather than owners) for major mining and commercial endeavors. To help Indians meet tribute requirements, the colonial state allowed them access to land (both individual and communal) and exempted them from most other taxes and fees. Corporate organization granted to native communities under Spanish rule provided rights to elect governors and councils (with participation limited to local elites designated *principales*), and rights to lands that sustained local government and worship, and were distributed among families to sustain cultivation (see Indio Principal). Members of the Republic of Spaniards

enjoyed a privileged social and legal position, and they neither paid tribute to nor served in labor drafts. They did, however, have to pay other taxes, such as sales taxes, and provide military service should the state require it. Based on interethnic paternalism, the Two Republic system proved inherently contradictory, claiming to be protective of Indians while exploiting them (see República). The system's influence endured long after the end of the colonial rule.

Vecino: Property owner or citizen of a municipality.

Viceroy/Viceroyalty: The viceroy was the Spanish Crown's highest representative in the Americas, one in each colony, or viceroyalty. The viceroyalty of New Spain (Mexico) and the viceroyalty of Peru each had a Crown-appointed "vice king" with executive and judicial power. In the 1800s, Spain further divided the Americas, carving out the new viceroyalty of New Granada with a capital in Santa Fe de Bogotá and the viceroyalty of La Plata with a capital in Buenos Aires. In Brazil, Portuguese viceroys served as governors in the captaincies rather than over the entire colony.

Visita: An investigation carried out by secular or religious authorities. A *visita de idolatrías* investigated possibly idolatrous or anti-Christian practices and beliefs (see Idolatry). Regular investigations (visitas) were carried out after every viceroy's (or other high official's) term in office as a way to discourage malfeasance (see Viceroy).

Witchcraft (hechicería): Church and colonial authorities labeled as witchcraft magical attacks, many healing practices, divining, and rituals to influence other people's actions. People in the colonial Americas combined Iberian, indigenous, and African practices to create an ample body of ritual traditions and beliefs. Authorities condemned these and attacked practitioners but found them difficult to eliminate. The Church fought witchcraft with ecclesiastical investigations under bishops' authority or with the Inquisition in Crown-approved tribunals (see Inquisition). Many women and some men supported themselves as ritual specialists offering these services.